WHAT IS
REFORMATIONAL
PHILOSOPHY?

WHAT IS REFORMATIONAL PHILOSOPHY?

AN INTRODUCTION TO THE COSMONOMIC PHILOSOPHY OF HERMAN DOOYEWEERD

ANDREE TROOST

TRANSLATED BY ANTHONY RUNIA
EDITED BY HARRY VAN DYKE

PAIDEIA PRESS
2012

Translation of Andree Troost,
Antropocentrische Totaliteitswetenschap
Inleiding in de 'reformatorische wijsbegeerte' van H. Dooyeweerd
DAMON, Budel 2005

Translation by Anthony Runia

ISBN 978-0-88815-205-3

A publication of the
REFORMATIONAL PUBLISHING PROJECT
Kerry John Hollingsworth, Director
www.reformationalpublishingproject.com

In collaboration with
Daniel Francois Malherbe Strauss
University of the Free State, South Africa
and
Harry Van Dyke, Director,
Dooyeweerd Center for Christian Philosophy
Redeemer University College, Canada

Book design K. J. Hollingsworth
Text, Palatino 11/14
Cover Image NGC 3314 "Antithetical Galaxies"

TABLE OF CONTENTS

FOREWORD

The strong appeal by the late Professor Andree Troost (1916–2008) for a renewal of the Christian mind, and in particular for a brotherly cross-fertilization of Scripturally-directed philosophy and theology, comes at a time when the old rumors and complaints about the Amsterdam school of philosophy have virtually died down yet may still be lingering among theologians, both in its country of origin and in the English-speaking world. Troost whets his axe against his theological confreres who remain suspicious of philosophy and especially of "Christian" philosophy. At the same time he tries to coax a classroom of seminary students—the book is a worked out version of a lecture course—into accepting, or at least considering, that his philosophy in the Reformational tradition, as exemplified by thinkers like Herman Dooyeweerd, can be helpful in at least two ways: in averting many a pseudo-problem caused by old thought patterns of pagan origin, and in striking out for a renewal of theology based solely on God's revelation in His words and works.

Readers will find that Troost has written a pioneering work that pushes forward the frontier of biblically grounded philosophical reflection on such diverse topics as original sin, the sanctity of life, the distinction between church and kingdom, the relation between faith and apologetics, birth and death as mere moments in our full existence, and much more. His surprising, if not to say startling, exegesis of Col. 1 about the cosmic significance of Christ as the second Adam and the root of all of created reality leads, among other things, to a radical anthropology that sometimes takes one's breath away. As an accredited author on ethics, he has fresh, insightful things to say about abortion and euthanasia. Troost is an eloquent proponent of consulting general revelation and emphasizes its wholesome function in human life when it is read in the light of the central thrust of Scripture. His book wages a battle against the scientific worldview of the closed universe and opens a vista to a reality that is open to God and subject in all things and all its ways to His laws and ordinances.

Few introductions to Dooyeweerd's philosophy—and by now there are half a dozen—have treated it so consistently and intensively in interaction with the Christian faith and Christian theology. Earlier treatments of this kind, such as J. M. Spier's *An Introduction to Christian Philosophy* (1954) is updated and expanded by Troost in a profoundly original way. This book will inspire, stimulate and challenge both students of theology and theologically informed students of philosophy.

Spring 2011

Harry Van Dyke, Director
Dooyeweerd Centre for Christian Philosophy
Redeemer University College

AUTHOR'S PREFACE

The title of this book calls for an explanation. It harks back to a course of lectures that I gave in the years 1994–1998 to the students of the Reformed Seminary in the town of Amersfoort, the Netherlands, the theological school of the denomination known as the *Nederlands Gereformeerde Kerken*. The lectures were an introduction to the Reformational philosophy of Herman Dooyeweerd, sketching it in broad outline without repeating too much of what had been covered in various introductions by other authors. My purpose for writing this book has been to publish the lectures for interested readers. Its main feature is the focus on topics that are of particular interest to students of theology. I have therefore confined myself to cardinal themes in Dooyeweerd's philosophy, leaving aside the many personal variants that are in circulation today. Here and there I highlight themes that Dooyeweerd himself did not emphasize as strongly, but I believe I have worked these out in the spirit of his philosophy, for the sake of making it more accessible to theologians and offering new prospects for the necessary renewal of traditional, biblically faithful theology.

The main title of the original Dutch work, *Antropocentrische Totaliteitswetenschap* (Anthropocentric totality science), emphasized that the philosophy introduced in the book claims to be science, viz. a science about the totality of created reality, at least insofar as it is accessible to scientific investigation. That title at the same time signaled the place of man in the cosmos as being at its very center. Christians might have found a title like "Christocentric Philosophy" clearer, but that expression would have run the risk of creating more than one misunderstanding, such as that this philosophy is a kind of theology or that it seeks to be constructed on the basis of certain Bible texts, particularly those dealing with Christ. On the other hand, the term "Christocentric" could also have meant simply to emphasize the religious worldview that lies at the basis of this philosophy. But such a basis is not itself part of philosophy and so would have been somewhat out of place in the title, although it does indicate the most important of philosophy's non-scientific presuppositions.

Another, less serious misunderstanding might have arisen if I had used the word philosophy in the main (Dutch) title if that word were taken in its original and literal sense of "love of wisdom." In the interest of bringing some clarity in the often sloppy technical terminology used by philosophers I preferred the term totality science. Of course one is always free to continue to use the traditional terms, if only for convenience' sake, even though such terms may be fraught with the possibility of being misunderstood. This English translation has removed the term "totality science" from the title but of course retains it where the main text discusses the concept.

Few theologians realize that an orthodox or biblically faithful theology is in need of a philosophical foundation, and that in fact it always possesses and employs such a foundation. Some find the idea absolutely incomprehensible and perhaps for that reason reprehensible. Others even find it absurd or in any case "dangerous." The traditional standpoint, after all, is that a sound theology is exclusively based on Scripture and should not, and need not, build on any other foundation. This notion means for the core subjects of theology, viz. exegesis and dogmatics, that these subjects may have no other foundation than a faithful interpretation of God's Word. Sometimes the task of theology is formulated as reverently "repeating after Scripture."

In my own country, accordingly, it has been a tradition of more than a century and a half that Protestant seminaries and faculties of theology do offer courses in the history of philosophy, but only as an aid in detecting and combating the many "philosophical intrusions" into theology. As late as the 1940s, for example, systematic philosophy could not be taught in the Theological School in Kampen—much to the chagrin of Professor Klaas Schilder who openly expressed his disappointment about this in class. By contrast, at the Free University in Amsterdam by this time a course in Christian systematic philosophy was mandatory for all students, including students from the faculty of theology.

The orthodox tradition that relegates philosophy to the periphery is today regarded as untenable and outdated by virtually all great schools and currents of theology throughout the world (even among some American evangelicals). But what has not undergone a change in theological circles is the notion, stemming from the Western humanist tradition, that philosophy is just a neutral intellectual product of more or less sound logic and therefore an intellectual "tool," a formal conceptual apparatus, a mere "thought form," exchangeable at will for some other one. Presumably philosophy, in its successive schools and currents, can be utilized to make the content of one's own theology understandable to ever new generations and so replace the older tradition of "apologetics."

Theologians today will rarely reject the usefulness of this tool—still referred to as "formal" only—but they regard it as something that must be used with critical discernment. Philosophy in their view is an instrument that may, if desired, be adjusted to scientific trends generally, or be combined with or exchanged for a "new and improved" conceptual apparatus that is more in tune with the times. The background to this widespread but essentially unchristian idea will come up for discussion in more than one place in the book now before you.

In the meantime there has emerged since the 1930s a broadly developed Christian philosophy in the Reformed tradition. This is the philosophy that has been systematically elaborated largely (though not exclusively) by Herman Dooyeweerd (1894–1977). In many ways it was ahead of today's critique of the Enlightenment's rationalist ideal of a religiously neutral and socially impartial pursuit of academic learning, science and scholarship. However, "Reformational philosophy" (to use its familiar label) offers this critique in a new and distinctive way, a way that is closely related to its pre-scientific convictions rooted in the Christian faith and to its extensive theory of knowledge and philosophy of science informed by that faith.

Dooyeweerd's magnum opus, *A New Critique of Theoretical Thought*, was a prophetic call to our culture, and notably to the world of learning and scholarship, to turn back from its idolatrous infatuation with theoretical reason. Nor did it exempt theological science from this "new critique." For the pursuit of science in general, this school's discovery of the modal aspects in distinction from concrete entities has enabled philosophy and the various disciplines to go about their work with more adequate, albeit also more complicated, methods and results. As for theology in particular, its relation to philosophy has a certain structure which one might denote as the object of the philosophy of theology. I have attempted to provide a discipline-specific philosophy of that description in my larger work *Vakfilosofie van de geloofswetenschap* (Philosophy of the science of faith), which came out under the Damon imprint in 2004. The present book may be considered an introduction to that publication.

Andree Troost
Meerkerk, Holland
2004

CHAPTER ONE – WHAT IS PHILOSOPHY?

CHAPTER ONE
WHAT IS PHILOSOPHY?

1.1 INTRODUCTION

This chapter will not only provide an answer to the question posed in the title, but also to a question not often asked with enough critical sense: What is *not* philosophy?

I admit from the outset that I shall not try to give a so-called objective or neutral and generally accepted answer. Such an answer is impossible from a practical point of view. A historical dictionary of philosophy will usually cite a long selection of quotations by various philosophers stating what philosophy is, what it ought to be, what goal it pursues, and so on.[1] But every choice for one of these statements is subjective, also in the sense that such statements cannot be separated from someone's deepest, pre-philosophical, religiously determined convictions and views concerning life. So the obvious subjectivity of this choice need not land us in *relativism*. The subjectivity in question is inevitable and goes without saying, and as such is not normative (though it is subject to norms).

Even though well-considered definitions of what philosophy is or ought to be differ widely, there are some features that recur in almost all descriptions worthy of serious consideration. First, philosophy has to do with "thought" and, second, it deals with reality, and specifically reality as a whole.[2] Since my aim is not to provide an overview of many different definitions, I want to start on a positive note and share with you what Reformational philosophy regards as the nature and task of philosophy. For the benefit of theologians I shall briefly indicate from time to time what philosophy certainly is not. That will also serve the purpose of shedding light on contemporary philosophical debates.

---

1. The great *Historisches Wörterbuch der Philosophie*, vol. 7 (1989), devotes no fewer than 355 large columns to the entry "Philosophie." This article has also been published as a separate book.

2. Cf. also the beginning of the introduction in *Encyclopedie van de filosofie* edited by K. Kuypers et al. (Amsterdam: Elsevier, 1977).

1.2 A PROVISIONAL DEFINITION

The first and shortest definition that one can give of philosophy reads as follows: *Philosophy is theoretical thought directed to the totality of the temporal cosmos, from and to the origin.*[3]

Slightly more differentiated, the definition reads: *Philosophy is theoretical thought about the coherence and unity or totality of created reality that is accessible to thought, under the guiding perspective of the meaning that comes with reality's origin, mode of existence and destination.*

The same can be formulated slightly altered as follows: *Philosophy is the theoretical structural analysis of all temporal reality (to the extent that it is accessible to theoretical inquiry) in the perspective of its totality, that is to say, in accordance with the dynamics of all created reality in its divergence and disclosure from its Origin, its functioning under a correlate law, and its convergence and concentration in its destination.*

Later on in this chapter each element in these definitions will be clarified. The above is merely "provisional" and summarizing, and should also suffice to show in passing that I deliberately dissociate myself from current ("post-modern") disparaging talk about the "grand narratives" of "totalizing systems of thought." Reformational philosophy does in fact have a "grand narrative." It also offers a system that comprehends the totality of temporal reality as a guiding framework for theoretical thought. It already has this in one of its pre-philosophical principles of faith, that is, in the biblical belief in creation, a belief that is indeed *total* in the sense of all-encompassing. It is from this pre-scientific thought and knowledge that it derives its "grand narrative." It has not itself constructed this story scientifically, but it has chosen it on the basis of religious faith. For it is acquainted with a type of true knowledge other than just the theoretical-scientific type; it is also acquainted with "faith knowledge."

1.3 WHAT IS REFORMATIONAL PHILOSOPHY?

The Christian philosophy known by the name "Reformational Philosophy"[4] is defined as a distinct philosophical system by its starting-point

---

3. This formulation bears close resemblance to various related descriptions in Dooyeweerd, see e.g. *A New Critique of Theoretical Thought*, 1:4: "Philosophical thought in its proper character, never to be disregarded with impunity, is theoretical thought directed to the *totality of meaning* of our temporal cosmos." The question whether theoretical (i.e., *abstracting!*) thought, which philosophy also is, can truly attain to the *totality*, will be discussed below in sec. 1.8.6 in connection with epistemology.

4. Dutch: "Wijsbegeerte der Wetsidee" ("WdW") or also "Calvinistische Wijsbegeerte."

in the Christian faith and by the anthropocentric character of its philosophical outlook on reality. Although it seeks to be a Christian philosophy, it seems better not to call it theocentric or Christocentric, because what these modifiers refer to cannot be part of the actual philosophical system itself but belongs to its religious starting-point and its "prolegomena." The hope and aim of our philosophy are that its entire systematic view of reality will be governed by the Christian faith as a religious starting-point in the hearts of its practitioners and in their attitude to life (their ethos).

Reformational philosophy, in common with all truly scientific philosophy, has a systematic view of reality. The fact that in many respects Reformational philosophy differs both in content and in kind from most other philosophies is exclusively a consequence of its Christian starting-point, its view of life or "worldview," and its prolegomena. The differences do not stem from the problems philosophy deals with, but from the way the problems are formulated and answered.

1.4 THE BOUNDARY BETWEEN FAITH AND PHILOSOPHY, AND THEIR LINK

As a systematic investigation and account of the structures of created reality, philosophy is confronted in this reality itself with the limits of scientific investigation. These limits create certain "boundary questions" that scientific philosophy must, with logical necessity, address, yet which it cannot answer by means of further scientific investigation. These boundary questions pertain to the coherence, unity or totality, and origin of reality. They can be summed up as the theoretical question of the meaning of existing reality.[5]

1.4.1 BOUNDARY QUESTIONS

From its beginning, and with greater or lesser clarity throughout its history, philosophy has sought the answer to these questions of meaning. The wonderment and curiosity of people who had acquired a theorizing attitude of thought impelled them towards precisely these boundary questions. But even apart from the scientific domain of life, the question of the meaning of life urges itself upon all people as they live their lives.

---

5. Cf. my "De vraag naar de zin" [The question of meaning], *Philosophia Reformata* 50 (1985): 98–118 and 52 (1987): 41–65.

1.4.2 ULTIMATE AND DEEPEST CERTAINTY

Philosophers have always believed, however, that they could find the answers to the boundary questions through thought alone, or if not, that they could prove the answers, or at least render them plausible, by means of thought.

This was the mistake made in Western culture in the days when its intellectual life began to differentiate between non-theoretical and theoretical thought.[6] It showed its religious origin in a (pagan) secularized experience of reality and hence in a tendency to trust ultimately in human (theoretical) thought as an alternative source of deepest certainty, as against mythical and mythological faith and religious thought, or over against everyday opinions and "images" based on sensory experience.

This was a grave mistake, because these fundamental questions, which as such transcend temporality, cannot in principle be answered with scientific certainty alone. For this very reason we talk about boundary questions. We stand here at the limits or boundaries of man's ability to acquire certainty about the meaning of existence by means of his intellect alone.

1.4.3 TYPES OF CERTAINTY

There are various other kinds of certainty. Not all certainty is by definition logical-analytical. There is also, among other kinds, a certitude of faith. Indeed, certainty is at the heart of all kinds of real faith, as we will see later in various contexts.

The only way in which the basic or boundary questions mentioned above are finally or fundamentally answered with unfaltering certainty is by way of religion, either in a personal confession or in a confessionally stamped and qualified worldview held by an ecclesiastical community of faith or by an "intellectual-spiritual movement."

As I said, the certainty of these answers is a distinctive type of

---

6. It is by now an old-fashioned misconception that man in primitive cultures does not yet "think" but lives only with sensory "images." When W. Nestle describes the genesis of philosophy under the title *Vom Mythos zum Logos* (1940), he too uses "logos" mainly to refer to what would later be called "theoretical reason" or *critical* theoretical-scientific thought. He even describes at some length how myth-making man certainly does *think*, because the concept of causality functions in his primitive mode of thought so that it already contains a "function of the logos" (p. 17). Though this insight is correct, I cannot adopt Nestle's argumentation or explanation.

certainty, namely the certitude of faith. This is a type of certainty that is not scientific or theoretical but practical, that is to say, fully intertwined with and directed toward the practice of life itself, without the theoretical abstraction and detachment so characteristic of, for example, the scientific attitude of thought. So what we have here is a certainty of an entirely distinct order, one that cannot be characterized as a logical-intuitive certainty, nor as an emotional certainty, although these too are indeed types of certainty, alongside a number of other types.

Nor is the certitude of faith a mathematical certainty. Mathematical certainty relates to "earthly matters," whereas the certitude of faith is "an assurance of things . . . not seen" (Hebr. 11:1). To be sure, there is an analogy between the two types—both cases involve "certainty." But the certitude of faith is different in kind from logical certainty (be it scientific or not).

The certitude of faith is a certainty that bears the typical features proper to human faith, which in the heart's self-surrender is oriented to God and his revelation—or to what is held to be His revelation, however it is designated. The mathematical certainty that 2 times 2 makes 4 is no more fixed and certain than what God says in the reve-lation of his Word. That the opposite is often true in practice must be blamed on the weaknesses and lapses of our religious life and thus of the typical certitude of faith.

1.4.4 THE INFLUENCE OF FAITH ON SCIENCE

Whether or not they are given consciously and explicitly, the answers of faith to the boundary questions mentioned above influence the scientific view of the fundamental questions in the various *special sciences* or academic disciplines. We can think here of the fundamental question of linguistics: what is language? Or of legal science: what is justice? Or of historical science: what is history? Or of theology: what is religion and religious faith? And so on. Philosophy discusses these fundamental questions within the framework of its beliefs concerning the coherence and unity existing in reality. From here, via philosophy, these beliefs, this faith, influences the special sciences.

1.5 WHAT PHILOSOPHY IS NOT

Owing to its very nature, method and content, no science can focus on God as an object of inquiry. Genuine science therefore revolves around created reality ("man and world").[7] This also holds for (scientific) philosophy and even theology. Philosophy is not, and cannot be, a rational theory of God or a "conception of God" that has been constructed in a more or less rationally sound manner. God himself, as God, is not susceptible to human thought—not to philosophy, and not to theology either. Theology can only think scientifically about human religious conceptions regarding God.

In the light of Scripture it needs to be said that the Western sciences, and first of all philosophy, clearly suffered from a religious degeneration at their birth and early development. Partly as a result of this, scientific philosophy soon became an ideological and sometimes even theological ("metaphysical") basis for all its branches. This was a clear after-effect of the pre-philosophical pagan faith, including its pagan secularization, and philosophy was gradually even intended as a purely rational alternative to it.

In its initial period philosophy itself partly became a pagan theology and especially an ethics for intellectuals. In more or less secularized Christian circles it has remained so to this day for many people. After all kinds of psychological and psychiatric institutions presumed to have rendered pastoral counseling superfluous, recent years have witnessed the appearance of philosophers who run a "philosophical practice" in which they offer consultation for people with problems in their lives. In Germany such consultations cost about 50 to 70 euro an hour!

At some universities it is also possible to choose a subject called "philosophical practice," and for a few years now there has been a German journal entitled *Philosophische Praxis*. Such "philosophical practices" now also function in the Netherlands, partly as an alternative to spiritual care provided by pastors, psychologists or psychotherapists.[8] We see the same tendency in the popular "philosophy" courses for self-help as people search for "meaning" or

---

7. Professor Vollenhoven used to speak of "the *earthly* created," since non-earthly reality (heaven, angels, the deceased, hell) also forms part of created reality as a whole. In our philosophy, that part of reality falls under religious subjects which are not in fact accessible to scientific investigation and therefore remain outside our philosophical task. See also the end of this chapter.

8. Cf. the journal *Filosofie*, which in the issue of Aug./Sept. 1996 published an instructive interview with Dr. Gerd Achenbach, the first philosopher to start a "philosophical consultancy."

"personal identity"—often (understandably) combined with courses in "spirituality." This is the tragedy of the non-Christian life: lacking the biblical perspective it is nevertheless driven "by its very nature" to seek self-knowledge, meaning and stability in life.

Although this phenomenon to some extent goes back to Socratic views, it does not accord with the nature, task and possibilities of genuine (scientific) philosophy. Scientific philosophy by nature is not a worldview (though it remains structurally founded in a worldview and is even directed and stamped by it). Nor is it, as a whole, an "ethics" or "life theory," though a philosophical system worthy of the name will have a theory about procedures for action and normative structures for the way people live their lives.

1.6 NOT AN ALTERNATIVE FAITH FOR INTELLECTUALS

In the centuries that straddled the beginning of the Christian era no distinction was made between ethics and wisdom, and philosophy was not only to an important extent "ethics," but it was also said to be the search for wisdom (the word "philosophy" means love of wisdom). In those days philosophy was largely absorbed by "ethics," a situation that has returned in our own time, after the first half of the 20th century seemed to see philosophy being absorbed by epistemology.[9]

Philosophy cannot and should not be an alternative theology for intellectuals who are not yet prepared to make a radical break with faith in God yet who no longer trust the historic Christian faith or the established churches with their traditional or modernized theology or "ethics."

Nor can and should philosophy be "apologetics" in the way that it tried to function in Christian Antiquity, or later in Medieval Scholasticism, whether or not under the name "natural theology" or, as in our own time, under the label *Fundamentaltheologie."

Philosophy has a great and important but functionally limited task, which I briefly indicated in sec. 1.2 and which will have to be specified and explained further in this chapter and throughout the book. We will also have to look more closely at the difference

---

9. Despite modern scientific developments and modernity as a whole, all this is back on the table today. In 1996 Damon publishers, which also issues the journal *Filosofie*, came out with a book by Gerard Koek entitled *Verlangen naar wijsheid. Moderne filosofie en ouder worden* [Yearning after wisdom: modern philosophy and aging]. The aim of this book is to use philosophy to help older people in their (presumed) search for wisdom.

between "worldview" and "philosophy." Reformational philosophy recognizes a fundamental difference but also a close connection and intertwinement between the two, in which "worldview" is foundational.

In current usage the word philosophy (under the influence of the English language) may also mean a "well-considered system or approach" or an "overall policy." Thus a storekeeper may write in large letters on his store-window: *Our philosophy: Small profit, Large turnover,"* and a journalist may ask the coach of a soccer club: *"What was your philosophy going into this match?"*

More serious than these and similar usages is the frequent identification of philosophy with deeper reflection, or even with thought as such, regardless of the subject and the *attitude* of thought (more about the latter later). This is still commonly found in general parlance. Deeper reflection on, or thinking through, all kinds of practical problems or vital questions is often blandly called "philosophizing," or also "theorizing." This last word frequently carries negative or at least disparaging overtones.

Next, Christian usage mostly displays a tension between *philosophizing*, an activity that is regarded as authoritative and autonomous "thinking" (sometimes called "independent thought"), and *theologizing*, an activity that is only supposed to "believe" or "repeat" or "systematically order" the truth given in divine revelation. We will return to this at length in connection with a number of topics. In scientific usage we often find the inaccurate idea that the problem of the relation between faith and thought is the same as that between theology and science.

1.7 What Reformational philosophy is not

Various subjects from the previous section call for a specific application to Christian philosophy. The present section deserves particular attention because, from the outset, Reformational philosophy announced itself as being "grounded in God's Word" and yet it disappointed many sympathizers, in particular theologians, by its refusal to attempt, in the manner of traditional scholastic theology, to "infer" or "prove" all kinds of philosophical truths from Scripture.

1.7.1 IT IS NOT THEOLOGY

As they opposed the misconceptions which this reflects as to the nature of philosophy, truth, and faithfulness to Scripture, the first generation of its authors and supporters always maintained that Christian philosophy is not a kind of theology, as its opponents (including Kornelis Miskotte at the time) always claimed. This generation also maintained that there are no "overlaps" between philosophy and theology. At most the two sciences mesh in the specialized *philosophy of* theology. The latter, however, is not yet theology. Only a well-considered systematics and a well-tuned philosophy of science are able to keep the two sciences clearly separate and provide a correct description of the real connections that do exist.

In this introductory section we will have to confine ourselves to the proposition, to be clarified later, that philosophy is a total science and theology a specialized or aspectual science dealing with the typically religious life. In other words, theology is concerned with that domain in the practice of life that is characterized by the faith aspect, and primarily by the normative side of it.

1.7.2 IT IS NOT A SEARCH FOR WISDOM

Much of what has just been discussed under the question what philosophy is *not*, is also applicable to what Christian or Reformational philosophy is not. It is for instance not an alternative theological ethics. Nor should it presume, under the names "worldview," "philosophy of culture" or "philosophical ethics," that it can or should "guide" human life or "counsel" the Christian life. As we already said in another context, this was from the outset the presumption of non-Christian philosophy, and seldom as patently in modern times as in our own day. As in the case of those special sciences that are consulted for dealing with concrete problems, philosophy has only an ancillary task, which is moreover an indirect ancillary task since it can only become more concrete via the special sciences that are primarily called to serve that purpose. We will have to look more closely at this in discussing the relation between theory and practice.

Philosophy's presumption that it ought to guide human life goes back mainly to Socrates. This presumption sometimes links up with the etymology of the word philosophy, which means love of wisdom or, like the Dutch word "wijsbegeerte," a desire and quest for wisdom.

This was understandable in the early phase of the science. It was also linked to the secularization in ancient pagan culture. Faith in priests and their mythical stories suffered a serious decline in the 7th and 6th centuries BC. Pagan man wanted to take distance from the gods and rely more on himself. Pagan piety, the primitive mythical faith in gods, very gradually turned into folklore. In view of the immense significance of thought in human life, it was understandable (in retrospect) that people came to rely more and more on this thought, also in the everyday matters of private and public life.

Moreover, in this initial phase, as thought was crystallizing into (primarily) two different attitudes and activities of thought, this difference was by no means immediately apparent. Science and wisdom, theoretical and practical knowledge, were still appreciated in the same manner, without distinction.

The need for scientific knowledge and the desire to be wise were still designated by the same word in late Antiquity: *philo-sophia*. Worldview and philosophy were not yet fundamentally distinguished, just as an explicit distinction between faith and theology would not yet be drawn for a long time. This last distinction had long been implicitly and intuitively recognized in the church, but the two concepts would only be differentiated much later, in the late 1700s, by the German theologian and teacher of Schleiermacher, *Johann Salomo Semler*, who even tended towards a separation of the two.[10]

1.7.3 IT DOES NOT PRESUME TO BE A GUIDE FOR LIFE

Before the time of Socrates, philosophy, which initially was more obviously scientific, focused on the nature and the structure of natural phenomena. For a large part it was (in our modern eyes simplistic) cosmology in the physical and astrophysical sense of the word that still obtains today.

"For a large part," but not entirely. It also contained an element of alternative theology, for alongside or instead of traditional, mythological (i.e., religious) cosmogonic thought (Hesiod), there was also an attempt to find a more rational answer to questions of the Origin (the *Archè*) of all things.

But with Socrates, to paraphrase Cicero, philosophy was brought down from heaven to earth and into people's homes, to occupy itself

---

10. Oswald Bayer, *Theologie* (Gütersloh, 1994), pp. 391 and 392.

with everyday life. This time, however, philosophy presented itself, not on the religious basis of the mythological tradition, but rather on the cognitive basis of intellectual knowledge. This explains the great practical (especially political) pretensions of the philosophers, who tended to understand their secularized thought as philosophy or life wisdom. According to Plato, for instance, the (totalitarian) state ought to be governed by philosophers, though not by such superficial thinkers as the "Sophists" of the preceding generation.

The new status of philosophy also explains the rivalry between early philosophers and traditional priests. From time to time there were *"asabeia* trials," in which philosophers could be condemned to death for "impiety," "ungodliness" or "atheism," as in the case of Socrates. The rivalry centered on the true guidance of the masses towards a life that was genuine, happy, and pleasing to the gods. The Stoics in particular saw this endeavor as the search for wisdom, and called all science wisdom. Cicero called philosophy *dux vitae,* life's guide. This view is still endorsed by many humanist philosophers, who regard themselves as alternative shepherds of souls replacing church pastors. In the churches, however, many have assigned this role to theology as a science.

Of course, wisdom, in the sense of life wisdom, is extremely important—it is even more important than philosophy or any other science. As we said, it was understandable that theoretical thought and non-theoretical wisdom were often identified in the beginning of the history of science. A historical differentiation like the one at stake here does not crystallize in a short time. But in the centuries of the Modern Age the identification of science and wisdom is absolutely unjustified. Partly for this reason Reformational philosophy does not aspire to be a theory of wisdom, a theory of life (for instance under the name "ethics" or "philosophy of culture"), or a "Guide to a Blissful Life" (Fichte).

Reformational philosophy primarily wants to be scientific philosophy, based on and subservient to a worldview guided by the Christian faith. In its role as philosophy it is moreover the foundational science for the various branches of science. This will be discussed more specifically in connection with philosophy of science (chap. 15).

1.7.4 IT IS NOT A WORLDVIEW

Man's attitude to life—his "ethos," including his consciously religious worldview as well as wisdom—on principle and often also in practice precedes what is typically scientific activity, though it can also receive much support or confirmation from systematic philosophy. As we will see later in the chapter on "praxeology" (the philosophical theory of life practice), "ethos," as an offshoot of philosophical anthropology, can be taken to mean man's most fundamental stance, his total attitude to life in both the breadth and depth of human existence.

This ethos is always characterized by man's faith function, because the practical way of life in our temporal existence is structurally guided by the content of our faith. A worldview is the practical formulation of this total fundamental attitude, which lays the foundation for the entire practice of life. It manifests itself, for instance, in typical sayings, in a motto or device, in proverbs, personal habits—in short, in practical wisdom. For this reason Reformational philosophy does not want to function as a practical view of life or a worldview; these are of a religious nature and are therefore better guided by wise office-bearers in the church within the domain of their official duties or, if need, outside it.

The fundamental tone of scientific philosophy, virtually unbroken in our time, is the same as it was in the initial period of science: it strives to wield power over one's own life and the lives of others by means of thought—primarily by means of theoretical thought (plus any "applications" logically deduced from it). Its presumption is that, as philosophy, it is the true *dux vitae*, guiding life in a scientifically responsible manner. In early Christianity this presumption was often taken over by theology, which called itself—a source of status in those days—"true philosophy" (Augustine and others).

The rivalry between "philosophy" and "theology" that broke out in Christianity at that time—or, more precisely, the rivalry between the non-Christian and the Christian worldview—is still with us today and forms a temptation[11] for all Reformational thinkers engaged in these two sciences. So there is a great deal left to be thrashed out between Reformed theologians and philosophers, a dialogue that can only be fruitful if both parties are knowledgeable about each other's field of study. Otherwise

---

11. A "temptation" or trap into which philosophers and theologians easily fall, because scientists understandably like to "sell" their products to many students or large audiences. Hence they tend to pay too high a price for popularization, for "application" to practical or at least extra-scientific spheres of life; and they also tend to follow the vogue of speaking *critically* about the systematic and therefore abstract character of the strictly scientific.

we stay trapped inside the vicious circle of "unknown, unloved" and "unloved, unknown."

Failure to distinguish between philosophy and worldview also renders many internal philosophical discussions unfruitful. One of the particular merits of Reformational philosophy is that it learned to distinguish structurally and clearly between theoretical thought in scientific philosophy and (closely connected but not the same) practical thought in the religiously qualified worldview. Light can similarly be shed on the comparable and traditional problem of the relation between faith and theology.

1.8. WHAT THEN IS REFORMATIONAL PHILOSOPHY?

Let me now clarify the elements listed in sec. 2 in the provisional definitions of philosophy's task. This clarification, too, is brief and provisional. Its substance and thrust can only be fully recognized after we have spent ample time practicing and applying the entire system.

1.8.1 THEORETICAL STRUCTURAL ANALYSIS

There is a redundancy in the modifier "theoretical structural," since in a scientific context "structural analysis" is always "theoretical," though at a deeper level the pre-scientific ethos exerts a powerful influence on thought and knowledge. After all, theoretical philosophy is religiously determined via this ethos or "ground-motive." At the same time we must continually emphasize that philosophy is theoretical thought. The typical similarities and differences between non-theoretical and theoretical thought will be discussed in connection with epistemology (chap. 14).

My reason for briefly stressing this point now is that there is much so-called philosophy that no longer deserves to bear this name. From the outset philosophy was scientific, characterized by the theoretical. But nowadays public opinion often sees philosophy merely as a kind of vague meditation or pseudo-profound babble, and in any event—this is also said by many natural scientists in thrall to positivism—a purely subjective, unverifiable business that has nothing to do with real science.

Admittedly, philosophy itself has often been to blame for incurring this reproach and not being taken seriously as a science. It is frequently said to be mere "speculation," pseudo-profound fantasizing without a basis in hard facts. All too often, in fact, it tries to take over the much more important roles of worldview and pastoral care, and sometimes becomes fused with them such that it virtually ceases to be a science. It has thus reverted to the original position of rivaling the (then still pagan, mythological) religious faith and the worldview inspired by it. By contrast, Reformational philosophy stresses that philosophy aims to be a scientific (i.e., theoretical) analysis of the structures of temporal reality. In this respect it is related to the special sciences, but distinguishes itself from them by its totality character (cf. sec. 1.2).

1.8.2 A HUMAN ACTIVITY

Even if Reformational philosophy is self-consciously a theoretical, scientific, structural analysis, nevertheless it is and remains an entirely human activity. Much more is always at work in this human activity of thinking than thinking alone. The actual "thought acts" remain embedded in the whole way that humans function. Reformational philosophy has developed a theory of the principal features of human acts, including the thought act. This theory sees thought acts (including the theoretical ones) as successively founded in a deeper "layer" of "dispositions," while these dispositions (also called virtues or properties in other contexts) are in turn founded in the deepest layer of temporal human existence, in a person's "ethos."

In the anthropological theory of praxis (chap. 13) we will look more closely at these vertically layered dimensions in every human activity, in which all kinds of corporeal foundations will be discussed (psychic, organic, chemical, etc.). When scientific analysis, of whatever kind, fails to take into account these deep layers in human activity, it is working with abstractions that may put the unsuspecting scientist on the wrong theoretical track. This failure could lead to the human activity of thought becoming independent of the human I, and also of its socio-cultural and personal-corporeal conditionality. It could also lead to independence of the so-called "virtues," to an autonomous morality. Such a development would uproot (which is also to say: secularize) scientific thought, even in academic theology to the extent that it believes philosophy can be used as an exchangeable neutral "language game" or a formal "intellectual tool" (a telling term derived from "neutral" technology).

1.8.3 STRUCTURAL ANALYSIS

Typical philosophical language is by definition directed to the constant and the more or less variable structures of what exists in temporal reality and the temporal frameworks for human life expressions. Viewed from the Christian belief in creation, the constancy experienced in reality refers back ultimately, though not always directly, to constant structures or existential frameworks (often called "transcendental" conditions) given in God's work of creation. In the past this was sometimes expressed by the words: God created everything "after its kind." This expression, though rather too simplistic, contained the important element of truth that people believe in a divine order of creation, by which things are what they are, created "according to their nature" and mutually interconnected.

This nature of the various creatures and phenomena in the world displays all kinds of constant features, which make these entities recognizable, constituting their relatively fixed manifestations and properties, despite all the variability. Both philosophy and the special sciences investigate these constant structures, each in their own field, philosophy being guided by the integration of the knowledge acquired as it investigates the overall cosmic coherence and totality of temporal reality. In our case this coherence is analyzed more closely in the theory of the "law-spheres" or "modal aspects of experience" and in the theory of entities. These two theories form the core of the system of Reformational philosophy.

1.8.4 TEMPORAL REALITY

The modifier "temporal" that is often used in Reformational philosophy is of major importance. It expresses a concentration and fullness of everything temporal in a "supra-temporal unity or totality." We will examine this more closely in discussing the problem of time (chaps. 8 and 9) and in connection with anthropology (chaps. 10 and 11). So the expression "temporal reality" means the reality existing in time, though it is not yet total reality. "Temporal reality" has a "supra-temporal root dimension," its center and unity.

1.8.5 . . . INSOFAR AS ACCESSIBLE TO SCIENCE

All theoretical analysis of reality is exclusively related and bound to temporal structures in the sense of structures existing in time. All human acquisition of knowledge is bound to such structures. Though reality is not exhausted by its dimension of time, and scientific knowledge, too, is ultimately rooted in the supra-temporal unity of the human "I," yet the activity of the temporal cognitive process in the practice of science remains confined to what is accessible to theoretical analysis. The supra-temporal, for example, is not accessible to it. And certainly not God, as the word "theo-logy" would want to suggest.

The supra-temporal in created reality is open to human knowledge only as "idea-knowledge" (from Greek: eidein, to see), but not as a "conceptual knowledge" (from Latin: concipere, to grasp). In idea-knowledge we see, as it were, out and up through a window, and we get typically idea-knowledge of what we see there but cannot comprehend or "grasp" as conceptual knowledge. All religious knowledge which by its very nature relates to God and his revelation is, strictly speaking, more than conceptual knowledge, it is primarily idea-knowledge. The same applies to the most important part of human self-knowledge. Even Plato, who abhorred most traditional religious myths, ended up making new myths himself in order to obtain "idea-knowledge" which was conceptually beyond reach.

Obviously this also means that heaven, the realm of the dead, angels and demons fall outside the scope of scientific investigation. Likewise the future foretold in Scripture. Such religious subjects are not accessible to theoretical investigation (cf. the beginning of sec. 5 above). Only what we know about these subjects from Scripture is accessible to theoretical (exegetical and dogmatic) exploration as an element of human religious knowledge abstracted from full faith. This condition will have to be scrutinized further when we deal with "theological" epistemology.[12]

1.8.6 THE PERSPECTIVE OF TOTALITY

From the outset philosophy was "directed to the totality," as is often (positively or negatively) emphasized in the relevant literature. We already saw that philosophy thus moves in the borderland between what is and what is not accessible to theoretical inquiry. In this perspective it involves a tendency towards—an orientation to—the unity and totality of all earthly creation. More strongly than in the special sciences,

---

12. Cf. my *Vakfilosofie van de geloofswetenschap* [Philosophy of the science of faith] (Budel: Damon, 2004), chap. 12, sec. 6, and chap. 15.

philosophy's structural analyses thus manifest its religious, transcendent quality. For in the Christian faith we confess that the totality of all creation was created by God "in Christ" and that the entire "fullness" of creation is not only "through Him" but "in Him," and is also directed to Him, and saved, redeemed and renewed "in Him."

So instead of "philosophy" we could also say science of totality. But after two and a half millennia the term philosophy is hard to remove from academic usage. Nor is this necessary of course: it has come to form part of general parlance. But the term does have a multitude of meanings and is therefore often vague and confusing if not waffling or close to meaningless. In any theoretical context today the term philosophy needs to be clearly defined.

We can also note in this context that the totality of reality can be surmised by theoretically thinking man, but never demonstrated or proved. Man cannot form a concept of it. For this totality eludes perception. It also eludes logical analysis. It is presupposed in both; analysis cannot dissociate itself from it and cannot adopt an "objective" attitude toward it.

So there is no way of rightly "concluding" that this totality is a substance, a point, or in any case "some-thing." Only in an "idea," in which moreover a "pistical anticipation" is operative, can philosophic thought point beyond itself to what is indefinable, and what can only in a manner of speaking be intuitively "seen," known or surmised, and solely denoted by metaphors. So the fact that philosophy is a science of totality means no more than that its analyses are directed to—have a tendency in the direction of—the totality.

1.8.7 CHRISTOCENTRIC AND ANTHROPOCENTRIC VIEWS

Reformational philosophy has put much emphasis on a feature particularly characteristic of philosophy from the outset: namely, that it was, is, and remains, consciously or unconsciously, directed to the "totality" of what Christians call "created reality." Reactions to this emphasis revealed that this "totality" is often separated in our time from its initial identity with "unity" and from its enduringly active "origin" (the Archè). Instead of the expression "Christian philosophy," which has little meaning nowadays, it therefore makes sense at times to use a more objective and intrinsic name, such as "Anthropocentric Science of Totality."

Instead of "anthropocentric" we could also say "Christocentric," especially since Christ is also a man. If we want to emphasize the Christian character, the term "Christocentric," with its reference to the "grand narrative" of its religious source, is meaningful. But if we want to emphasize the scientific and philosophical character the term "anthropo-centric" is better. In my Preface I already pointed to the risk of misunderstandings entailed in the use of the term Christocentric.

At the same time biblical faith does not hesitate to talk about a totality of all created reality, because God's scriptural revelation not only makes several statements about "all things" (*ta panta*), but also designates this totality with reference to Christ as "the fullness" "in whom" all things have been created, in Him as "alpha," as "firstborn" creature (Col. 1:15)—in Him who is not only the alpha but also the omega, thus comprehending the entire alphabet of creation and history.

The real totality is therefore not a sum of the multiplicity in the diversity, but a unity and fullness in which multiplicity and diversity participate. It is not an arithmetical totality, nor a logical totality, nor yet a totality of physical, social or any other aspectual quality. It is a theoretical boundary idea, a point of orientation of and for philosophy, which for that reason is the science of totality. So this has nothing to do with the positivist caricature of a philosophy that supposedly ought to collect and order the main results of the special sciences.

Because, as we just noted, all things were created "in Christ," who was also a man, even the first man, the alpha, therefore Adam too was created in Christ and in and with Adam the entire human race. Christ was and is the "fullness" and the unity of all creation.

1.8.8 Divergence, disclosure

In present-day thought it has become customary to talk about the dynamics of reality or about its process character.[13] This emphasis betrays a fully justified reaction to a fossilized, so-called "realistic" mode of thought in terms of so-called unchanging "essential structures." In the first decades of its gestation Reformational philosophy

---

13. Think of the "process theology" of Alfred North Whitehead, developed in his book *Process and Reality: An Essay in Cosmology* (1929), a theology which is currently enjoying a revival.

was often interpreted by outsiders in this spirit, yet wrongly so. The constancy of the divine order of creation has very little to do with the Greek idea of unchanging "essential structures." In Greek thought they are no more than a distorting description of the reality of the constant factors in this order of creation.

In its orientation to the Origin, Reformational thought is ultimately guided toward the creation and redemption of all things by God "in Christ." Christ (who is both God and man!) is the root unity or "fullness" of all creation, and therein the "totality" as well. All things "hold together in Him" (Col. 1:15–18), who is also the "firstborn" (!) of all creation. Already in the creation of all temporal reality everything was taken "from Him." He is the "fullness" that goes beyond our temporal power of understanding, that can only be "seen" in a religious idea and therefore can only be known in a religious idea by means of metaphors.

Biblical images of the root or source of life provide in-"sight" here, because "from Him" the "fullness" and the "unity" diverged into the coherent multiplicity and diversity. Inversely, in the very convergence or concentration of reality a disclosure of reality takes place in the direction "toward God" and a manifestation that it is created "unto God."

This biblical insight prevents Christian philosophy in its theoretical outlook on reality from arriving at an uprooted, "undeified" view of the structures of reality which are then made autonomous, independent, self-directing—clearly divorced from faith, a secular view. This insight also creates an opportunity for "christianizing" a scientific, dynamic view of reality, also in the special sciences.

1.8.9 THE REALITY IN CHRIST

The biblical revelation regarding Christ (God and man) as the Origin or root unity containing all creation also reminds philosophic thought that nothing from the entire richness of creation should be abstracted from this distinctive religious depth-dimension. This dimension is not a supernatural, external addition to "creation proper," something that humans attribute to it. This rootedness "in Christ" is in fact the most important feature of the creature itself. To put it in old-fashioned (highly disputable) terms: it belongs to "the essence" of creation itself, to those things in creation that are not perceptible by the senses, which cannot be intellectually thought out either, but can only be known through faith.

Cultural development is primarily a process of disclosure, an organic image that says that what comes out of it is what was already in it, that is, "in Christ," in whom everything has been created. That this process and its results have been disrupted by sin does not detract from this reality of creation. "Disruption" even presupposes it. Abstraction from this is fundamentally nothing less than a form of secularization, real and imaginary, and a spiritual uprooting of reality. As we will discuss later, such theoretical abstraction also works to dehumanize the view of the non-human in creation. It is also in part for this reason that I call Reformational philosophy anthropocentric, an anthropocentric view of reality.

Regrettably, faith in Christ as the "firstborn" of creation has rarely if ever flourished in theology, and has never been able to flourish, because theological thought has been bound to a traditional immanentism[14] of time.[15]

1.8.10 CONVERGENCE AND CONCENTRATION

Entirely apart from philosophy and its terminology, the philosophical idea of the concentration of our life and of all creation is also well-known in a Christian's practical experience of faith. In faith (and in no other way!) we confess our participation in Adam's fall and in the life, death and resurrection of Christ, "with whom" we have been placed in heaven, "hidden in God" (Col. 3:3). The ongoing revelation in Scripture has taught us to understand our being created "unto God" in the sense that we are gathered and brought back in Christ, as under one head, to fellowship with God.[16]

Yet, as we said, we prefer not to talk about a Christocentric or theocentric philosophy. For philosophy as such does not—and qua science cannot—know anything about this, let alone verify it. Philosophy is not religious thought; it is a science. However, as a fundamental and boundary science it does stand at the boundaries of science, beyond which only faith and faith knowledge can and must

---

14. (*Ed.*) Immanentism: philosophy that discounts anything transcendent and looks for the ground and unity of all things within created reality itself.

15. Cf. chap. 3 below, and also my article "Geschapen in Christus. De wijsgerige concentratie-idee in bijbels light" [*Created in Christ: The philosophical idea of concentration in the light of Scripture*], *Radix* 20 (1994): 260–83. The idea is developed more fully in my philosophical treatise mentioned in note 12.

16. Perhaps this is also meant in 2 Peter 1:4, where it is said that we may become "partakers of the divine nature."

look. As part of its religious and then philosophical prolegomena, Reformational philosophy knows this orientation to the Origin and Destination to be precisely the root unity of all things in Christ. These principles of faith echo the well-known words of Scripture that all things are from, through and unto God. This knowledge, however, belongs to its non-scientific, though necessary, presuppositions.

Chapter Two – Prolegomena

CHAPTER TWO
PROLEGOMENA

2.1 WHAT ARE PROLEGOMENA?

The answer to the question, What are prolegomena? can refer to the literal meaning of the technical term prolegomena: those things which need to be said beforehand. Two connotations of the prefix "pro" play a role here: first, and before all else. Not only do the things in question, from inner scientific necessity, need to be said first because everything that follows presupposes what is said first. But in this case the necessity is so fundamental and strong that what follows is already to some extent implied in what is said first. What comes first is a beginning, a principle.

Early Greek philosophers called this the "archè," which is more than a casual preamble or merely the first line on a page. The archè is a principle that is present in everything that follows (from) it and remains valid in the here and now. The principle of state omnipotence, for instance, entails "in principle" many abuses in various domains of life, whereas the principle of "sphere-sovereignty" offers various ways of correcting social abuses, obviously likewise "in principle."

2.2 WHAT ARE A PHILOSOPHY'S PROLEGOMENA ALL ABOUT?

As we briefly indicated in sec. 1.2, every philosophy is theoretical thought that is directed to the totality of all creation. In philosophy this orientation leads thought—from inner necessity, as we shall see later—to the fact that we all experience the interconnectedness or coherence of very many different facts and things which present themselves to us in everyday life. On further reflection, this experience of coherence-in-diversity tends towards a notion of totality that can also be called unity, and vice versa.

Thus we experience in a plant, for instance, a plurality of component parts: root, stem, lateral stems, flowers. But at the same time we are aware of the unity of the whole: it is a plant. Another example: in all kinds of ways we experience a clear coherence in the plurality of our personal body parts, organs and internal processes, but we also experience more than just coherence. We also experience this diversity as a unity, the unity of our body, which in its turn displays coherence and unity with our total humanity. I have a body, but "I" am not simply identical with my body; in due course I can abandon it as an "earthly tent" (2 Cor. 5:1) and live on without this body. Summing up, we can say that philosophical prolegomena, whether or not they state it explicitly and consciously, are essentially about that which can be indicated in four words: diversity, coherence, totality and unity.

This orientation toward unity and coherence-in-diversity inevitably raises the question of what was first and what came later. For also between these there is a connection, a kind of coherence, namely a "temporal coherence." In any case, the human mind, in its view of life and the world, refuses to be confined to admiring the rich diversity in reality or the coherence-in-diversity that it manifests. It goes further and inquires into the "absolute" first, the "first beginning," the Archè, the origin, and into the final goal, the destination.

At least this was the thought process in the initial phase of philosophy. But what led people to think about these things? This too is a question which at bottom cannot be answered philosophically, but it can be answered in terms of a worldview as a foundation for philosophy. However, this difference between worldview and philosophy probably eluded the first philosophers and to this day there is confusion in common usage as to whether philosophy and worldview are two words for the same thing, or whether one is scientific and the other is not, or whether we are dealing with things that are scientific "to a greater or lesser degree." We will return to this at length in a systematic context, particularly in connection with philosophy of science. The last section of the present chapter, however, will offer a few provisional comments on the subject.

2.3 FAITH PRECEDES PHILOSOPHY

The subjective need to reflect on the coherence in the everyday diversity within us and around us—on its totality and unity, on the beginning or the origin of our life and of everything else—was by no means always there, at least not in the way that philosophy would gradually come to reflect on these matters, namely, in a questioning mode. Before the sciences emerged, people knew these things, knew them from the start, a priori, and also knew them with certainty; and this knowledge was passed down naturally from generation to generation in the form of myths. For myths gave, and still give, answers to these questions.

Now myths are typically religious phenomena. They "reveal" what people "believe" a priori in faith (whether that faith is the Christian faith or not). But just as all pagan religions, as well as Christianity, are familiar with the phenomenon of apostasy and secularization, so this also took place in ancient Greece during the "Golden Age" of Pericles (5th century BC). It is sad, but this man, who was responsible for the great flowering of ingenious architecture and the building of many famous temples for the gods, had himself become largely secularized (as a pagan) and no longer believed in his gods. He was also friends with Democritus, one of the first philosophers who held that everything, including the unity and totality of all existing reality, was based in matter. For these men, matter sufficed to explain the nature and structure of all things. There, they held, lay the beginning, the Archè. That is what they believed.

This case merely serves to illustrate the proposition that faith, no matter what faith, precedes and is active in the process of answering the ultimate and deepest questions that a human being can ask: questions about the origin, the Archè of all things; questions, too, about the meaning of existence as a whole and about its future destiny. In the mythical belief of the pagans these "questions" (assuming they were asked so explicitly), with everything they implied, were answered in an (always slightly varying) story of origin, which often was also a real "story of creation." Religious rituals re-presented this story, kept belief in it alive, and so passed it down to future generations. Even if these questions and the answers were not expressed in so many words, people did live with the self-evidence of an undoubted faith in a reality thus understood and experienced, in which "the divine" played a real and omnipresent role.

2.4 MYTHOLOGY AND WORLDVIEW

What was received in this way was a religious tradition. Like everywhere else, for various reasons the Greek religious traditions as early as the eighth and seventh centuries BC started to be disputed and undermined by unbelief. The ensuing struggle to preserve religion, along with forces from the cultural process of differentiation, led to the birth of mythology. This term refers to the products, chiefly made by poets, of remodeling and rhetorically reinterpreting the original, orally transmitted stories of religious faith. In these stories as now retold the myths were criticized to some extent, but also expanded into a full-fledged worldview. The process was inaugurated by Homer (c. 750 BC) and particularly Hesiod (c. 700 BC). Their poetic works represented a fundamental attitude to life and the world, put into words. As such it was a view of life that formed a transitional phase to philosophy, which emerged relatively soon after. Philosophical thinkers started to meditate and reflect—explicitly, critically, and with detachment—on the spontaneously arisen, religious worldview.

This period of pagan secularization also saw the breakthrough of various cultural developments. In addition to the aesthetic art of poetry, human life specialized in all kinds of expert knowledge and types of thought. This had already been the case thousands of years before, particularly in the East and South, but it gained momentum in sixth-century Greece, as elsewhere in the same period. Karl Jaspers called this the "Achsenzeit" (Axial Age). Crucially to Western culture, a new way of thinking developed at this time: theoretical thought, with its creation of abstract theory. So this was not the development of "thought," as one often reads, but of a certain differentiated type of thought, linking up with the religious overall conception contained in the worldview.

In the name of logical thought (without further differentiation) religious certitude regarding the great questions of life was gradually replaced by intellectual certainty, in which questions were asked and answered that an average person would not tend to ask—highly abstract questions about what ordinary people long knew already, from generation to generation. For instance: questions about the origin and meaning of all things; questions which, assuming they were explicitly asked, were not real "questions" or agonizing problems, because people already knew the answer, thanks to traditional religion. But in the process of secularization the tone of these questions became increasingly critical and people no longer wanted to answer them religiously with reference to the traditional myths. In former times these myths had been the end of all possible questions, the final and satisfactory answer.

Unfortunately, the scientifically thinking pioneers of a new era marked by a new intellectual culture (including for instance the theology of Xenophanes) now saw their answers as better alternatives to the traditional priest-taught religious answers of public opinion. Religious truth (doxa) was turned into intellectual truth (epistèmè). In other words, scientific answers to the deeper questions of life were propagated and in their turn believed (!), this time as "rational alternatives" to the mythical answers of faith that had been passed down via the stories of poets and priests and established rituals.

2.5 FAITH AND REVELATION

Only now are we able to arrive at an answer to the question posed at the end of sec. 2.2: what brings a human being to inquire into the Origin, the Archè, of all things and thus of himself? Why do I want to know how all things are structured, what the connection between them is, what their unity and its origin is? Clearly, these questions also imply man's inquiry into himself.

The questions can only be answered by faith, and faith bases itself not on human inquiry or reflection but on revelation, and thus on an authority who reveals.

Having arrived at this final point, the Christian faith is the only faith that puts an end to all that searching and questioning and at the same time provides an explanation, to the extent that this lies within man's capacity to understand.

As a first step in providing answers, the Christian faith begins by entrusting itself to God's revelation and confessing that God, the God of the Scriptures, is the creator of all things. The divine work of creation is the true Archè, the principle. This answer of faith basically puts an end to all earnest searching and existential questioning, also to the anxiety that this may involve. As Augustine so famously confessed: "My heart is restless until it rests in Thee." Every other answer can only give temporary and illusory rest.

A second step in this answer of faith is the recognition that God not only created all things, but that he created them "unto Him." This explains why a human being, after (ir)religiously losing God, always resumes his searching and questioning, and again finds or fails to find God (or "a god" who is mistaken for God). Man can't help himself. He has been created this way. In popular parlance: that's what makes him tick. He cannot not believe. His faith may be misdirected, so that its content is wrong; but it is a structural anthropological given that man has been created "unto God." This, expressed in a theoretical context, is a philosophical and also theological translation of God's revelation that all things are created "from him, through Him and unto Him."

In this connection medieval scholastic theology talked about a *desiderium naturale*, a natural desire for God, a yearning after Him. Quite apart from its many interpretations in Catholicism, this notion has always been rejected by Protestant theology. Rightly so, insofar as most theological interpretations failed to do justice to the confession of man's radical depravity and apostasy from God as a result of sin, the breach with God. But we should not forget the element of truth in it. A "desire for God" is a "given of creation"; it concerns the (normative) structure of being human.

2.6 Pagan myths and Christian faith

The above answers to man's fundamental questions to some degree resemble the answers given in many pagan myths. But precisely the light of true revelation by the only Creator of all existing reality makes it clear that all other mythical answers and all answers produced later by deified thought bear a resemblance to the truth revealed by God. They resemble it more or less in the way a caricature resembles what it is meant to represent. It is not pure nonsense but distorted sense, skewed original truth, perverted reality. It is the defective and more or less powerful deviation from the norm for all human faith: the revelation of God. That is why the non-Christian religions of ancient or modern pagans always contain one or more elements of the wisdom and truth that are also present in the Christian religion. Belief and unbelief are not wholly alien to each other: they are structurally related as the two main types of subjective human faith: well-directed or ill-directed, biblical or unbiblical faith. Unfortunately, in life the two are usually mixed.

2.7 Two kinds of prolegomena

Above we encountered several "prolegomenal" ideas and terms which in the end, to be systematic, must be divided into two groups, practical and theoretical prolegomena, or in other words: existential and scientific prolegomena, primary and secondary prolegomena if you will.

We started our discussion with some profound and all-encompassing questions, which included so-called "life questions." These, after all, impinge on our own existence. They are questions of origin and destination and, between these two points, of the duration and manner in which created things exist. From out of the origin these created things are directed toward their destination.

The answers to these fundamental questions are of the nature of faith. Consciously or unconsciously, they are a response to what God has revealed about these matters. That is what we understand by the practical or primary prolegomena. Scientific philosophy or theology is not yet in the picture here. These are religious issues which are more or less familiar to all nations and peoples, issues with which many struggle in search for answers when the answers have grown dim or gone lost through a lapse or crisis of faith. For a healthy and mature Christian faith whose content is centered in Christ this searching and groping, this struggling and striving is in principle a thing of the past. Lapses and crises are usually overcome through the power of Christ. That is what the life of faith experiences in practice.

But above we also encountered views and terms that are more abstractly and systematically involved in the same issues. Thus we talked about coherence-in-diversity, about unity and/or totality. But here we can only say that the questions are legitimately posed and were in fact addressed by philosophy from the outset. In the light of Scripture, however, we know that the answers to these questions can only be given religiously. But the Greek philosophers, partly as a result of (pagan) secularization, wanted to leave the myths and their gods out of it, and they believed they could answer these questions with detachment, through wide-ranging observations and rational reflections.

Nevertheless, the inquiry into and search for the origin, mode of existence and destination of existing reality, in short: for its meaning, was legitimate and understandable. The more so when we realize that God created all things, including people, "unto" Him, launching them in a direction towards Him.

Here, then, we find ourselves in the borderland of faith on the one hand and knowledge and science on the other.

Here we have arrived at sound questions (asked in a scientific attitude of thought), with religious answers. If it is true—which we will examine later—that religious knowledge and science cannot be separated, then we are here in the borderland common to both. Here is a limit that theoretical reflection cannot cross, and every attempt to do so will result in untruth. That can happen in two directions.

Sliding from faith in the direction of science (e.g., theology), we transgress this limit when we begin to inquire into the origin and destination of all things and our own life even while our interest is no longer primarily and existentially directed "unto" God, to God Himself in an attitude of listening and believing, but instead is more intent on, say, nailing down a perfect, or the only possible, formulation of the religious truth in question. In such a case faith has become theology. However, God's own revelation in Scripture gives us its answers in many different expressions and narratives, not in fixed concepts or logical propositions.

Conversely, scientific thought can overstep the boundary of religious truth when it presumes to answer with confidence the ultimate and deepest questions which science itself cannot answer with any scientific certainty. Internally, however, science cannot ignore these questions or leave them unanswered. It must answer, it cannot not answer, but this answer is by definition a religious answer, which cannot be "verified" in the manner of science.

As we shall see in connection with epistemology, not all truth is scientific truth, as little as all truth is religious truth. The same can be said about "certainty," which is mostly used in an unqualified sense. Not all certainty is typical certainty of faith. That is why we have distinguished in this section between two kinds of issues that belong to the presuppositions of systematic philosophy: pre-scientific and theoretical issues, questions of faith and typically philosophical questions.

2.8 CHRISTIAN ANSWERS TO THE PRELIMINARY PHILOSOPHICAL QUESTIONS

The starting-point for developing a Christian philosophical system therefore lies in the Christian confession of faith, to the extent that it answers the life questions which are also the preliminary philosophical questions. This Christian confession of faith relates primarily to what Scripture reveals about the creation of all things by God, man's fall with its consequences, and the redemption and renewal of creation by God's grace through the work of Christ and his Spirit.

Thus our confession is captured in three words: "creation, fall and redemption." This is not theology, but pre-scientific practical faith, the first principles of a Christian's life and thought—even if one were to go and interpret this content of faith less correctly or if it functioned less than adequately in one's life as a whole.

How does Reformational philosophy answer the philosophical question of the coherence in this immense richness of creational diversity which all people can experience every day? It answers that this coherence is given in a divine order of creation. For philosophy this is a religious answer which can be systematically elaborated by philosophical inquiry, though not by the method of logical deduction but by a "transcendental-empirical" method.

This method will be examined more closely in connection with epistemology. Other subjects to be discussed there will include entity structures, anticipations and retrocipations as linking elements between the various aspects, and in particular the structure of time. Especially this last problem takes us back to the borderland between science and faith. This explains why in the writings of Dooyeweerd he almost always talks about the "temporal" coherence-in-diversity in reference to the diversity that exists "in time," as distinct from the so-called "supra-temporal," the (temporally) transcendent, the "full temporal" that possesses all aspects of time concentrated in itself ("concentration point"). This coherence is embedded in and guaranteed by time. As a consequence, it is itself of the nature of time, as distinct from its "supra-temporal" or "temporally transcendent" root of existence "in Christ" by virtue of the creation.

How does Reformational philosophy answer the question of the possible unity of all things? Again, this question is characteristic of most great philosophical systems. It asks about a unity that includes all coherent, interconnected diversity, so that unity and totality can sometimes be used synonymously. Reformational philosophy answers that this unity is the supra-temporal fullness given "in Christ." For in accordance with the word of Scripture all things have been created "in Him" (Col. 1:16). He is their "root." "In Christ" as well, the post-fall creation is being preserved and redeemed from evil.

As for the question of the origin and destination of all things, we have already pointed to the Christian confession of God as Creator and Redeemer. God gave all creation a fundamental orientation to

Himself, to his Kingdom, for his own "honor and glory."

Because the three fundamental philosophical questions—of the origin, unity in coherence, and destination of all things—cannot really be separated from each other, the answers can be said to comprise a threefold basic idea of philosophy, of all philosophy in fact.

Philosophy's actual work of systematic inquiry will therefore always have to tackle its questions at the middle element of this one single basic problem, namely at the question of unity-in-coherence. After all, it is to the structures of creation that scientific thought has access, and that is where it finds its field of work. Though it can pose the scientific question of the origin and destination of all things, it cannot answer this question philosophically. Philosophy relies on inquiry into the structures of the cosmos as such, into the "distinctive nature" of all diversities, into their mode of existence and their coherence or interconnectedness; and only in this way and from there can it inquire into their origin and destination.

2.9 FAITH, WORLDVIEW AND PHILOSOPHY

At the same time we should not forget that in the sixth century BC and following, only a very few people adopted this new attitude of thought in which life and world are viewed from a theoretical-philosophical perspective. That has been true throughout the centuries since. Even in our time, when it comes to scientific philosophy only a very small minority among educated people follow this path. The vast majority, including academics, do without philosophy. They have a worldview and outlook on life that is intuitive, geared to practical knowledge and based on experience. For all that, however, their basic views are no less guided, from beginning to end, by religious convictions, be they Christian or not. But usually this is not theoretically accounted for or consciously worked out in any philosophical system.

All people, including professional philosophers, possess a worldview. Often they falsely present their philosophy as a learned discussion of so-called life questions or societal problems, but in fact they are treading on all kinds of specialist domains, such as economics, political science, sociology, psychology, and so on. Often, too, they enter the domain of what are really reflections and reasonings that belong to a worldview, under the pretext that philosophy too should be "practical," or should be able to reach a wide audience. But basically this amounts to a self-negation of philosophy, or at least an abandoning, to a greater or lesser degree, of its scientific character.

Many humanists will often draw a distinction between philosophy and science on the basis of the otherwise correct insight that philosophy cannot theoretically "prove" its ultimate presuppositions. But a philosophy that confines itself to formulating its religious starting-points with a view to serving praxis by applying them in an "ethics" has in fact abandoned its scientific character and negated itself as a theoretical philosophy in the usual sense of the word.

To the extent, meanwhile, that philosophers, under the guise of anthropology, philosophical sociology or epistemology, give answers to concrete practical problems, they are in fact very often inspired by a deeper, pre-scientific worldview and by practical wisdom. In a pseudo-scientific or non-specialist way, they will cheerfully enter the domains of all kinds of special sciences.

Every worldview is by definition characterized by faith (cf. sec. 1.6.3). Questions about the origin, unity and destination of life and the world and everything in them are questions that are always answered by a conscious or unconscious, Christian or non-Christian faith. Viewed anthropologically (hence philosophically), these questions and the answers given to them in the practice of life are based on a deep layer in the human mode of existence which we call ethos. In this ethos the concrete practice of life in all its diversity is integrated into what we can also call a mentality or an attitude to life. A conscious worldview is an articulation of this. More about this in the chapter on anthropology.

Ethos forms the starting-point that is part of the structure of all human life. Ethos is active as an inspiring and direction-giving motive force, and it influences the entire practice of life, including the pursuit of science. Hence ethos can also be called "religious ground-motive" (Dooyeweerd). Anthropologically speaking: ethos is active prior to all practice of life, including therefore philosophical thought, where it is also, in essential matters, decisively active.

To conclude this chapter I refer to Figure 12 in the Appendix as a possible summary of it.

CHAPTER THREE –
TIME AND TEMPORAL TRANSCENDENCE

CHAPTER THREE
TIME AND TEMPORAL
TRANSCENDENCE

3.1 An anthropocentric transition

The pre-theoretical principles of faith, designated in the previous chapter as the *primary* prolegomena of philosophy, were briefly summarized in the confession of creation, fall and redemption. In the Christian pre-theoretical and religiously qualified outlook on life and the world, the view of all things in reality is fundamentally stamped by the Christian faith, both according to its law-side and its subject-side: to its law-side, by the revelation of God (the "law of faith"); to its factual subject-side, either positively governed by divine revelation or negatively at odds with it.[17]

In the theoretical, and therefore *secondary*, prolegomena of philosophy, we started from philosophy and arrived at certain philosophical answers to the questions of coherence-in-diversity, unity and totality, and origin and destination. These philosophical questions could not be answered by philosophy in its own strength, but the answers to be given were inspired, guided, governed by one's faith or worldview.

Proceeding from the heart of philosophical problems, that is, from the problems regarding *the structures of existing reality*, Reformational philosophy primarily sees the answer to the question of coherence in all diversity, and even that of the unity and totality of all diversity, in the divine order of creation, and thus ultimately finds it in man, who occupies the central position in that order of creation.[18]

---

17. The distinction between the law-side and the subject-side of reality will be explicitly dealt with in the next chapter (sec. 4.9).

18. The relation between Christ as man (Col. 1:15-20) and Adam will discussed at various points in what follows.

Up to a point, our philosophy recognizes and acknowledges this answer as a moment of truth in many systems of pre-Christian, non-Christian, or typically humanist currents in philosophy. However, there it is no more than a "moment of truth" within the framework and context of religious and scientific untruth. Humanism, for instance, continues to struggle with the great problem of the tension, indeed the irreconcilable conflict, between the typically human and the typically non-human. In modern philosophical thought this problem is usually referred to as the tension between freedom and nature, two terms which may be replaced by several variants, such as autonomy and unfreedom, or freedom and determinism, creativity and fate, and the like. The mild and usually evasive word "tension" is therefore often and more openly and honestly replaced by "gap" or "contradiction." This raises the pseudo-problem of how this gap can be truly bridged. Ultimately this problem is already inherent in the ancient dualisms of mortal and immortal, matter and spirit, body and soul.

Just now we referred to this anthropocentrism in humanist thought as "no more than a moment of truth." For as soon as another word is said here, a different view of man emerges, stamped by a different world-view. At bottom a worldview is also itself religiously determined and is therefore fundamentally a faith-based view.

Thus the existential, practical prolegomenon of Reformational philosophy is contained in the Christian view of man and the Christian outlook on life, which through the eye of faith see man in connection with Christ—not only as regards his redemption by Christ from the consequences of sin and from God's judgment on sin, but already "before" the creation, or rather: from "the beginning," from the "primordial age." Man, like all other creatures, was "created in Christ" (Col. 1:15 ff.). The Christian and, subsequently, the theological view of man should therefore be Christocentric. This will also have to be the religious principle of a Christian philosophical anthropology.

3.2 MAN AND THE NON-HUMAN

If the philosophical question is now raised as to the coherence in the immense diversity within the created order, the Christian faith inspires an analysis of this coherence as a law-like coherence, correlated with a certain order, which can be understood in the light of Scripture as the world order or the divine order of creation. That single creative will of the only true God is the origin and focal point from which all created diversity is "dispersed" and into which it again "comes together" by way of this order of creation. All things are "from God and unto God." By virtue of being created "unto God" *a dynamics has been put into creation*—has been inserted into the order of creation as the law of life for reality.

Pre-Christian Greek thinkers called this a cosmic order, and specifically an order of nature governing human and non-human reality. They surmised and believed that this coherence-in-diversity, this normative order, was the work of the gods, as is evident from the countless creation myths among the Greeks (as it is among virtually all peoples and races). However, in the course of time this religious conjecture was eliminated by a pagan secularization process that effected a demythologizing and horizontalizing view of nature and reality. This process of religious apostasy saw the birth of the sciences, in which philosophy led the way; and from the time of Xenophanes and especially Aristotle, a kind of ("metaphysical") theology went along with a secularized view of reality.

Man's creaturely bond with (the human "nature" of) Christ brought man, too, in the central position of Christ. "In Christ" man participated in Christ's unitary and root position, of which the revelation of Col. 1:15-17 says that Christ is the first creature and that all things have been created "in Him" and also exist "in Him."

Through the centuries the above Scripture passage was hardly able to play a role in theology, obstructed by the Western outlook on reality, which in terms of religious content was co-determined by the demythologizing and horizontalizing tendency of Greek philosophy. At the time of the creation of all things the creaturely supra-temporality of Christ as man manifested itself in the person of Adam, in whom "all things," including all people, were "comprehended." "We," you and I and everybody, have therefore "sinned in Adam" (Rom. 5:12); "we too were in paradise" (as Professor Klaas Schilder once put it in class).

The Christian tradition therefore rightly speaks of man's "royal position" with respect to creation. This fine image, though incomplete like all metaphors, can be deepened and supplemented by the philosophical idea that numerous subject-object relations in human life intimately interweave man as subject with—weave him into—the so-called "outside world," the "objects." In the chapters on epistemology we will return to this in connection with "subject-object relations." Here we merely announce this as an example of how man is intricately intertwined with the non-human cosmos as well.

3.3 Coherence is not yet unity

The close and inner coherence of things should not be confused with unity. It remains a condition of interconnectedness among the great diversity of all things, and also within these things. Man's temporal mode of existence shares fully in it, is as it were woven into this interconnectedness, and through this coherence is interwoven with all that is non-human.

But unity is different from coherence. How? Philosophical lexicons often call unity "in an absolute sense" indefinable, and rightly so. They sometimes add, wrongly, that such a total or absolute unity therefore does not exist and must be branded an "unreal philosophical speculation." However, a Christian philosophy must judge differently. Reformational philosophy has a solution to the supposedly insoluble problem of the definition of "unity." This philosophy talks about a very real, but *transcendent* unity—that is to say, a unity which "in principle" contains all the multiplicity and diversity existing in time and at the same time transcends them. That is why it is indefinable. For to define is to reduce something to something else, thus staying within the multiplicity and diversity.

So the word "transcendent" here has an altogether philosophical meaning and not a direct theological one. It means "going beyond time," hence *temporally transcendent*; and therefore the unity in question here can be called, by approximation,[19] a "supra-temporal unity." This supra-temporality should therefore not be confused with God's eternity. It remains a creaturely, or somewhat more accurately: a supra-aspectual, supra-functional, and also a *typically human* supra-temporality. About the world of good and evil spirits philosophy as such cannot say anything.

3.4 Transcendence and immanence

Christian usage, especially in theology, sometimes describes the difference between God and creature as that between transcendence

---

19. We might also say by "idea-knowledge," as distinct from conceptually; cf. chaps. 14 and 15 below on theories of knowledge and science.

and immanence. The idea here is that God is exalted above all creatures. In a Latin term, God is said to be the Transcendent One, or in a horrid philosophical abstraction "the transcendent" or simply "transcendence." Extreme schools of thought sever the bond of the Transcendent One with the creaturely, with the so-called (cosmically) immanent, as in "deism," or else they erase it, as in "pantheism" or in radical materialism and idealism. By contrast, the Christian position is often sketched as a view in which God is both transcendent and immanent with respect to creation. He is elevated above the creature, but also somehow present in it.

My own intellectual tradition explicitly addressed the crucial and primary issue of the relation between God and creation. It found that this relation cannot be properly characterized by means of the dilemma of transcendence and immanence. For these terms still admit of various incorrect philosophical interpretations. I will have to return to this in discussing "the law" for and in the creation order, since Vollenhoven spoke consistently, and Dooyeweerd on a few occasions, about "the law as the boundary between God and cosmos." The two founding fathers of Reformational philosophy said the same thing but did not exactly agree on what it meant.

Here I confine myself to the remark already made above that Reformational philosophy (in Dooyeweerd's version) primarily relates transcendence and immanence to *time*. In other words, "transcendence" in its language is always temporal transcendence, supra-temporality—but not "eternity." So when Dooyeweerd (after *c.* 1930) often uses the term "temporal reality" almost as a routine technical term, the modifier "temporal" is well-considered and usually indispensable. It is intended to say less than the expression "total" reality, restricting it to what exists in time.

On the basis of Scripture the Christian faith has always been aware of this restriction as a self-evident truth. "Temporal life" is by no means a full description of our existence.

Consequently, immanence here is always temporal immanence, that which exists and functions in time. So both words, transcendence and immanence, do not relate directly to God, as they do in theology. Philosophy as such does not talk about God; it deals with the creature, though in the form of inquiry it is familiar with the boundary question of the origin and destination of reality. But as a scientific discipline philosophy cannot *philosophically* answer these questions. Within this reality, however, in the structure of the creaturely, it can distinguish between the temporal mode of existence and its supra-temporal or transcendent dimension.

In the temporal mode of existence, the structural multiplicity and diversity of existence, as well as the coherence between them, is typical of the temporally immanent, while unity and totality are its *temporally transcendent concentration.* This is not to say that there is no diversity in the temporally transcendent, but, as far as we know, it is limited to a dichotomy that is not structural but centrally religious. The Bible and the Christian worldview talk about the kingdom of light and the kingdom of darkness, about the antithesis between them, about the kingdom of God and the dominion of God's adversary Satan, about angels and demons. Next, the Bible talks about the central battle in man's heart between "the old" and "the new" man, a species of warfare that is not just individual but that defines the human community: the "old man in Adam" and the "new man in Christ."

3.5 MULTIPLICITY AND FULLNESS

The supra-temporal can also be suitably called, with a reminiscence of the biblical expression "fullness of time," the *full temporal.* This term (mainly introduced by Willem Ouweneel) has the advantage of repudiating the incorrect suggestion, often heard, that the supra-temporal has been dualistically added "separately above" time, as something extra, or as something "supernatural."

"Full temporal" says that time is not absent, on the contrary, but that it incorporates, comprehends or concentrates "all time," all that is temporal, within itself, just as a sun-glass brings together many rays of light. In this full temporal unity, time as succession, as past, present and future, is transcended and concentrated, as in a "focal point."[20] In the full temporal, past, present and future are always together, without an internally split dualism between time and "supra-temporality," between time and fullness of time.[21]

---

20. Cf. my article "Geschapen in Christus" cited in chap. 1, note 14.

21. The fact that past, present and future are often run together also in Scripture, with all the exegetical problems this poses, has prompted many studies of what is called "the biblical concept of time," a concept that is clearly different from how we usually speak about past, present and future. Many theological problems, both dogmatic and exegetical, could be solved if we could break with the horizontalist

The problem that many people have with this distinction between *temporality* and *full temporality* may also have to do with the traditional separation between time and eternity, that is, between creaturely temporality and divine eternity. As if there is no third possibility! Another factor of continuing influence here is probably the Platonic tradition of the *chorismos*, the separation between idea and reality, specifically in the context of a secularized view of reality in which the divine and the creaturely exist parallel to each other, in total separation. The concentrated supra-temporal unity and fullness of the creaturely has no place in this view of reality; or it is deified. The human spirit or the soul is then considered more akin to God than the body.

3.6 THE TRANSCENDENT UNITY OF THE HUMAN HEART

The Bible assigns great and central importance to the human heart. A well-known instance is the exhortation of Proverbs 4:23: "Keep your heart with all vigilance; for from it flow the springs of life." A good concordance will give you many instances of the mystery, depth, inner quality, central significance and temporal transcendence of the heart in human life. It is a metaphorical or "idea-knowledge" designation of what exceeds our understanding and grasp.

Of course this does not mean that the Bible provides a philosophy of the human heart, or of supra-temporality or transcendence. We are free to criticize the philosophical theory of supra-temporality, provided we have good arguments for doing so, based on a correct understanding of what we are criticizing. But unlike a practical outlook on life, the philosophical attitude of thought is foreign to the Bible, as is the reporting of "scientific truths" (that is to say, of modally articulated truths, like archaeological facts). When the Bible talks about "knowledge" the word does not denote anything like "science" but means simply knowing or having wisdom. In the days of the Old Testament writers there was virtually no cultural differentiation in knowledge between the two main types we distinguish today: concrete everyday knowledge or truth, and abstract theoretical knowledge or truth existing next to it and for the sake of it.

By contrast, as we have noted before, philosophy has focused from the outset on searching for the coherence and unity of all things. Reformational philosophy, captive to what Scripture says about the

---

view of reality that dominates our Western cultural tradition.

human heart, is not indulging in a "speculative fantasy" when it recognizes this unity of human life as a *transcendent root unity*. As regards the individual human being, it can then be said that his entire existence is incorporated or comprehended in that unity of his heart. His heart concentrates the fullness of his temporal existence, and thus also transcends his "temporal diversity." A person's temporal existence does not exhaust the reality of his life or the inner structural coherence of its diversity. He lives on, even after his corporeal death,[22] and also then remains nonetheless the same total person, possibly with a distinct or new name as recorded in the "book of life" (Rev. 2:17; 20:12).

3.7 IDENTITY

It follows that a person's "identity" does not simply reside in his corporeality or in his personality or in a certain social and/or psychological situation, but primarily in his heart. That is why human identity is primarily religious; that is to say, it is determined by his positive or negative relationship with God in and from the center of his existence, whether or not it has remained in the old Adam or has been placed back "in Christ."

So as soon as we talk about the *individual* human heart, we must remain aware that very often this too is still a kind of abstraction. To begin with, by virtue of the divine law-order man is woven into the totality of the temporal world of his fellow man through all kinds of social relationships—ties and bonds without which no human being exists or is even conceivable. But besides this, and even primarily, there is the so-called "spiritual" or at least supra-corporeal, supra-temporal and supra-local bond of man with his fellow human beings in a supra-individual and supra-temporal religious unity, in a humanity within which the individual human heart participates in Adam and in Christ, "in whom" man has been created. As an image of God and an image of Christ, God also created the man Adam as "head," as a *root unity* that goes beyond and remains beyond temporality—as the unity of all the human beings that would issue from him over time. "In him" God made his covenant with all people. "In him" we all broke this covenant when this Adam sinned (Rom. 5:12), and we all fell out of our original unity "in Christ." Thus when we describe

---

22. Corporeal ("physical") death is often meaningfully called "temporal death," as distinct from "eternal death."

Reformational philosophy as *anthropocentric* this has nothing to do with an egocentric, subjectivistic or individualistic emphasis.

The concrete temporal communities of people here on earth have therefore a supra-terrestrial and supra-temporal, transcendent dimension, namely their "root unity." Not to see or recognize this entails a horizontalist perspective on human reality, and of cosmic reality in general, a perspective that has been stripped of its religious root or depth dimension. For now, therefore, we conclude this anthropocentric introduction to cosmology, to return to the more complex problem of time and history at a later time.

3.8 HOLISM?

Through a great variety of New Age movements, our age once again opposes the traditional dualistic outlook with a so-called holistic one. It is important, however, not to identify holism with the Reformational view of the unity of man and of human life.[23] The element of truth in holism is that all life is a whole that is more than the combination or sum of its parts. Understandably, therefore, holism first emerged in biology, as a reaction against physical, mechanistic explanations. Explanations from an exclusive starting-point in the "parts" of a whole (in this case the physically qualified substructure) cannot do justice to the distinct nature of many (organically qualified) wholes. However, holism differs from the Reformational view in that the biotic or organic viewpoint, which certainly has a place within the totality of temporal reality, cannot penetrate to the true, if you will "absolute," unity of everything that belongs to created reality. It leaves out of consideration the entire transcendent, supra-temporal, spiritual center, the deep root dimension of this reality.

3.9 UNITY AND TOTALITY

Earlier on I sometimes used the words *unity* and *totality* alongside each other. This suggests that they refer to two different things. But Reformational philosophy also uses these words interchangeably. The reason for this is that *totality* is a term that can be defined: it relates to

---

23. It is unfortunate that Gordon Spykman uses the term "holism" for his views, views which have been clearly influenced by Reformational philosophy; see his *Reformational Theology: A New Paradigm for Doing Dogmatics* (Grand Rapids: Eerdmans, 1992), pp. 243 f.

a multiplicity in time. Thus one can say, to use a word from Scripture, that "all things" have been created by God. The expression "all things" (*ta panta*) is therefore a sum of these, and in this sense a totality.

But the same totality of "all things" can also be described differently, by referring to a unity in which this entire totality is included, comprehended or concentrated. In that case we talk about the (temporally) transcendent "fullness" or "unity," which strictly speaking is something different from the non-transcendent totality in time in the sense of the sum total of all that exists in time, past, present and future. Thus "creation" (or "created reality") is that kind of comprehensive and all-encompassing term that expresses the commonality or unity of all that exists.

As we have observed in another context, this "transcendent fullness" can be called a philosophical translation of the biblical revelation (Col. 1:15–20) that all things have been created "in" (not just "by") Christ and have their "existence" or "continuance" in Him—we can also say: their unity, or "root unity."

This scripture is also closely connected with the revelation that all things have been created from, by and again unto God. This latter condition expresses that "all things" have been created with a direction, a tendency, a dynamic orientation to the Creator, from whom they have issued and unto whom they have also been created. In the light of Scripture, therefore, the philosophical idea of the unity and totality of reality and its orientation to or tendency toward its destination is not pure speculation lacking a basis in reality, but rather a serious philosophical translation of, and response to, what Scripture in its own way reveals in the name of God.

3.10 Pyramidal concentration tendency in human nature

For a Christian, therefore, it is not strange that the question of the origin and totality of all things is characteristic of philosophical thought. After all, we know, as we said, that all things are created *unto* God, that is to say, oriented to Him, turned towards Him. This is in man's nature. Man was created this way. "All things" possess this pyramid-like concentration tendency. In this connection Calvin talked about the *sensus divinitatis*, awareness of the divine.

Roman Catholic philosophy, particularly in Aquinas, calls this the *desiderium naturale*, a natural desire for God. Various interpretations of this expression have been given, some good, some unacceptable. Taken literally, it could mean a denial of the biblical truth that sinful man is by nature turned away from God. But this meaning is not absolutely necessary. The expression can also mean what Scripture calls man's being created *unto* God. That is to say, man's nature has been created in such a way that he, as an image of God, is in fact by nature (that is, according to his typical human nature) oriented to God, and ought to orient himself to God. It is man's normative nature or structure to do so consciously.

This factual normativity is not annulled by sin, but negatively realized in sin. God's law of creation remains valid, even if there were no one who subjected himself to it. God is then replaced by an idol, which functions "as God," that is to say, as man's ultimate and deepest point of reference, regardless of what specific form this idol takes. For this idol can be all kinds of things. It is always, however, something that is taken from the creation order and then elevated to some form of the absolute. In opened-up cultures this is usually some aspect of man himself.

3.11 THEOLOGICAL RELEVANCE

In this chapter we have taken a preliminary, anthropological step in the direction of a philosophical cosmology or view of reality, which I believe is of clear and direct theological relevance. This is easily surmised if we consider that (usually unconscious) theories of man occupy an important place in all of theology, and not just in dogmatics. We can think here of practical theology, but also of exegesis.

As a few examples from dogmatics I mention five problem areas in this subdiscipline: the presence of Christ in the sacraments (according to the "order of Melchizedek"); the doctrine of "original sin"; the meaning of "the one holy catholic church" ("which except a man believe faithfully, he cannot be saved"); the role of Christ as Mediator of creation; the Christological theory of the "two natures."

All these theological doctrines or *loci* are affected by the philosophical view of reality and in particular by the view of its transcendent dimension, namely, Christ as transcendent, supra-temporal "firstborn," in whom all temporal reality was created as in a unity and fullness (Col. 1:15–20) and in whom man participates religiously in the supra-temporal heart of his existence (cf. metaphors like those of the vine and its branches and the body and its members). The doctrine of Scripture (*locus de sacra scriptura*) is also strongly co-determined by our general theoretical view of reality—which is better able to strengthen and deepen our Christian faith regarding the Bible as God's word than traditional theories about Scripture, whether critical theories or orthodox, "biblically faithful" versions. Many of the latter, no less than Higher Criticism, are stamped by rationalist philosophy, particularly in the modern form of positivist scientism. That is why the switch from orthodoxy to liberalism is not a rare phenomenon; there is more unintended affinity between the two than people care to know.

Compared with traditional views that are conditioned by non-Christian philosophy, our philosophical thought as a theoretical analysis of reality "from and to the Origin" can bring about a radical Christocentric turn in our academic theology. As a science, after all, theology is occupied with an important part of reality, namely, with the domain of human faith as well as with all the non-human on earth as objects of faith. The scientific view of this domain or province of the total kingdom of God is decisively determined by the philosophical view of the totality, in particular also the view of this totality's relation to God.

Is there a way to reconcile this philosophical view with postmodernism?

CHAPTER FOUR – COSMOLOGY:
CENTER AND LAW-ORDER IN THE COSMOS

CHAPTER FOUR
COSMOLOGY: CENTER AND
LAW-ORDER IN THE COSMOS

Prior terminological remark: By "cosmos" Reformational philosophy means the whole of creation, but in a philosophical context we must obviously qualify: the cosmos "insofar as accessible to scientific inquiry." Thus "cosmos" here does not include that part of creation which we can know only by faith, such as angels, demons, "the throne of God," heaven and hell.

4.1 ANTHROPOCENTRIC COSMOLOGY AND COSMOLOGICAL ANTHROPOLOGY

Cultural anthropology in the last three or four decades has greatly emphasized that man is intimately intertwined with what is not strictly human in our world. Landscape and climate, flora and fauna, cities and villages, highways, canals and railways, agricultural and pastoral areas, all of this has been almost entirely or partly shaped by human activities. This also applies to human customs in the sphere of eating and drinking, social intercourse, religious ritual, the use of media, sexuality, commerce and art. Again, both in form and content human life appears intimately interwoven with many types of social structures such as states, churches, organizations, marriages, families, social and economic classes, village or tribal communities, urban neighborhoods, and so forth. The reverse is also true: man and his environment influence each other reciprocally. Still other important factors are the phase of history one lives in, and the living traditions one stands in.

All this helps to explain why scientific analysis and systematization of the relations between man and world endeavor to do justice to this intricate interlacement and to give an overview of it with the use of diagrams. Given philosophy's current possibilities to explore our world, we can no longer simply say that reality consists of matter and spirit, or nature plus culture. We do greater justice to these two by speaking of *the one, integral reality of man and world* and then going on to distinguish (not separate) between a natural *side* and a cultural *side* of the same concrete reality. These two "sides" (more on this term later) are then to be taken as summing up a great diversity comprised by each of the two sides.

From the outset Reformational philosophy has focused strongly not just on the great variety but also on the *texture* of all that diversity in reality. This is illustrated most impressively in its theory regarding the human practice of life.[24] We are going to examine this theory more closely on the basis of a distinct cosmology and anthropology, both of which therefore need to be discussed first.

For the time being we shall express this particular insight and this orientation by speaking of a *cosmological anthropology* and an *anthropocentric cosmology*. This means, among other things, that no correct philosophical totality view of cosmic reality can be had without starting from man's *central position* in the cosmos and *man and mankind's fundamental orientation* to this cosmos. There is a reciprocal participation in each other, and thus implicitly an orientation to the center or existential "root" of both in the one Christ, in whom all things have been created. In Him the human and the non-human are one. As the alpha and the omega, Christ encompasses "all things."

4.2 THE TRANSCENDENT DIMENSION OF THE COSMOS IS CENTERED IN MAN

The expression we used just now, "man's central position," indicates more than reciprocal interwovenness. It highlights something about the relation between man and world that goes beyond "interconnectedness" or "interwovenness." Man is *central* in the cosmos in a very *unique* way, in a way that goes beyond what can be grasped in a spatial metaphor like "center." The centrality of man's position in the cosmos is, philosophically speaking, anchored in the supra-temporal *fullness* of his existence, in the "heart" of his total being.

This is a statement about a reality that defies sense perception or logical verification. Fundamentally it goes back to the religious prolegomena of philosophy, so in this case it harks back to the Christian confession of faith according to texts like Col. 1:15–20 that all things were created "in" Christ, that they exist "in Him," that man participates in Christ in the heart of his

---

24. See below, chap. 13: Praxeology.

existence (thus entirely!), and that man is "part" of that "spiritual body" of which Christ is the head and we are the members.

This confession of faith thus refers via Christ to the central position of man in the cosmos. "Man" is not seen here by himself, or as an "individual," but as the *total man*, who does not exist by himself, so not apart from *mankind*, nor detached from what is *non-human*. It is man in his *connectedness* to the environment, to fellow human beings, to fellow believers, to the entire creation and to his transcendent root in Christ as the "first" creature, the "alpha."

We called this last connection the "transcendent" dimension of man, the "supra-temporal" or "full temporal" dimension. Let me point out once more that these expressions serve to indicate, among other things, that man is more than his temporal existence and that he is not absorbed or exhausted by this existence, as every believing Christian knows. What is more, the expression "transcendent dimension" also implies that man's many-sided temporal existence is fully incorporated and *concentrated* in this "supra-temporal center," concerning which no science is possible, but only *faith*.

As an example I merely mention man's continued existence after his physical death. His so-called "immortality" or "imperishability" can never be real in the natural-scientific sense of the word; nor can it be *proved* in that sense; it cannot even be rendered *plausible* without reference to prior convictions grounded in some religion (of whatever kind). As hard as Christian "apologetics" may try, its efforts in this regard, too, are doomed to fail.[25]

Our so-called "supra-temporal" or transcendent existence which *includes* our *temporal* existence—and so is totally different from what is meant by the Greek dualistic concept of soul—is concretely what Scripture calls our "being in Christ," our being members of his "spiritual" body. This is a *reality* that can only be recognized and known through faith. We are not "drawing inferences," we are not constructing a theological "theory," but we *believe*, in accordance with the Scriptures, that we died and were buried with Christ and were raised from the dead and ascended to heaven with Him.[26]

---

25. In my view, traditional apologetics is based on a concession to outsiders who prefer to look for the deep and existential certainty that all people crave in logical and scientific certainty rather than in the distinctive certainty of faith.

26. Just as we believe that we sinned "in Adam." But this is a different subject, if a

4.3 A HORIZONTALIST COSMOLOGY AND SCIENTIFIC ABSTRACTION

Failure to take into account this position of man in the cosmos leads to an uprooted and thus undeified view of the cosmos itself, as if God did not exist and Christ did not exist, or as if they are not "relevant" to cosmic reality or the sciences dealing with this reality. That is what today we might call a purely "horizontalist" cosmology or view of reality.

In philosophy, therefore, and in the practice of any scientific discipline, we will embark on a wrong course if we ignore this pre-scientific dimension of reality known only by *religious faith*, or if we consider it irrelevant to science, or mentally place it above and beyond "our concrete reality." Formulated in a *philosophical* context, Christ himself and our human participation "in Him" are therefore that famous "Archimedean point" which particularly in the initial period of philosophy played such a central role and which in humanist thought is identified with "Reason." We will deal at greater length with this subject in chapter 8 (philosophy of time), and also in connection with philosophy of science in chapter 15.

It is quite another matter that we can consciously and temporarily abstract from this temporally transcendent dimension, even as we remain aware that we are then no longer dealing with full reality but with an abstraction. Such a reduction is proper to scientific abstraction (cf. the remark that prefaces this chapter). This makes it possible for Christian and non-Christian scientists to communicate with one another, which is almost always necessary. What science is capable of is confined to investigating and analyzing temporal reality that can be experienced empirically. The religious view of this reality, we have argued, always influences the investigation and the analysis, sometimes clearly, sometimes less so. But as a religious (or anti-religious) view it should still be distinguished from theoretical insights and theoretical truths which at best are always partial truths.

With regard to the relation between man and cosmos, therefore, we can for the moment consciously forget about man's central position and focus our attention on that which has engaged scientific thought from the beginning: the interconnectedness and interwovenness of all diversity within the cosmos in a certain *"order."*

---

related one, because here too the "supra-temporal" is at issue.

4.4 CREATION'S ORDERLINESS AND "TRANSCENDENTAL" STRUCTURES

All special sciences, including the science of history, study their fields of inquiry with a view to gaining knowledge about something universal. Rather than the individual case as such, the incidental, they ultimately search for the more generally valid, the more universally real, the common features of specific phenomena and their interrelationships. The economist is usually not interested in a single family budget, but the study of a thousand family budgets provides him with certain data for his theory about consumer behavior in a certain area. The same goes for some of the life sciences: these disciplines research the specific features proper to, say, a large number of individual horses, fishes or sunflowers.

The patterns in both natural events and human activities are indicative of the existence of laws, standards, values, rules, norms, customs, structures, or whatever one may wish to call them. Starting from our worldview, we confess that all this regularity or orderliness somehow displays the active presence of God's constant will, God's rules, God's ordinances (whether or not intended only for a certain period).

This insight also plays a role in the word "law-idea." A Christian who investigates what is found in *nature* knows that he is investigating what was created by God or what was shaped by man using this created reality. In the structures of *human* life and society this is probably even more complicated than in non-human nature, as we will examine later. But *all* creation was created by God as God wanted it to be. God's will as the Creator is primarily the *law* for existence, the law of life for man, animals, plants and things, each "after its kind." Hence we can observe law-conformity, regularity, orderliness in all of this. The same even applies to the disorderly, the chaotic, the anti-normative, for we could not even name this negativity without presupposing the possibility of positive orderliness or normativity.

It is crucial, however, not to *identify* every status quo as being exactly in accordance with God's law. Rather, we have to recognize God's law primarily in the *principles* of the *foundational structures* of concrete reality. In philosophy these foundational structures are often called "transcendental structures" (in the sense of "the conditions for the possibility of" the concrete). Reformational philosophy is happy to adopt the term transcen*dental* structures, in part because it refers consciously to the transcen*dent* origin, source or root unity of these structures. In philosophy, these transcendental or foundational structures may not, on principle, be theoretically separated from the concrete structures, even though this does not always come to the fore in a concrete problem.

Accordingly, our philosophical prolegomena, bordering as it does on both faith and science, can summarize this point as follows:

> *The divine command to exist, the law of creation, is the principle of the transcendental structure of created reality, creating the conditions for the possibility of concrete existence.*

4.5 THE WORLD-ORDER AND ITS WIDESPREAD ACKNOWLEDGMENT

As we saw in the previous section, Christian philosophy has an additional argument, over and above what is generally believed, for specifying the close relationship between man and the rest of reality. On the basis of its religious prolegomena it links up with the idea of a world-order in the sense of a cosmic order of reality, which it prefers to call *order of creation* or *creation order*. The term "creation order" expresses the Christian worldview that articulates the belief that God is the creator of "all things," of our entire reality and of everything that takes place in it in law-like fashion. In the Bible this totality is often summed up in expressions like "heaven and earth" or "all things" or "the visible and the invisible," and its orderliness is referred to by terms like "ordinances" and "precepts." (Obviously these biblical expressions are no scientific concepts, nor are they intended to be.)

From ancient times almost all great religions and many philosophical systems took note of this world-order and in some way or other reckoned with it. There are in fact many names for it. The ancient Indian religion called the world-order *rta*. In the Vedic period *rta* was replaced by the narrower concept of *satya*, which is more confined to the "moral" order. Buddhism had *dharma*, China *tao*. In Egypt the world-order was called *ma'at*. The Sumerians spoke of *me*, the Russians of *pravda*. Stoic philosophy referred to the universal *Logos* and identified it with the deity (who, given the religious indifference of those days, could be called Zeus or Christ or any "higher power"). The Stoics also identified the *Logos* with divine providence as well as with human reason, the *"logos"* that participated in the divine.

4.6 THE CREATION ORDER AS COSMIC LAW-ORDER
AND COHERENCE

Of course, these views differ considerably among themselves in the way they *interpret* the revealed and actually perceived orderliness in the world and in human existence. The Christian idea of the creation order expresses a worldview that is inspired by the fact of God's self-revelation as the Creator and therefore also as the Lawgiver. With a commanding word he called all things into existence—more specifically to existence *thus* or *so*, each "according to its nature," "after its kind."

Accordingly, the order we all experience is a divine law-order, an order which qua law *holds* for creatures, which are *subject* to it. To the extent that these creatures belong to the human sphere, we can say that they "answer" to the law as well as being "subject" to it. Human life *responds* to, and partly also *answers* to, God's (creative and redemptive) Word, and to live is first of all to be "answerable" or "accountable." Always and ever, our existence takes place *de facto* —in whatever way, positively or negatively—in relation to God's law.

Thus *in our philosophy* the primary meaning of the term "subjectivity" is always: subjection to the law. In fact, Vollenhoven liked to pronounce the Dutch word *"subject"* with the emphasis on the second syllable: *"het subjècte,"* because this tacitly alludes also to the law to which subjects are subject.

In a non-scientific context and in ordinary language there is often an opposition between subjective and objective, in the sense of personal or arbitrary over against generally accepted, universally valid and verifiable. However, as we shall see in chapter 6, both subject and object belong to subjectivity in the sense defined above.

Now it is this creation order, as the one all-encompassing law-order, which also *internally* connects and entwines everything that has been created. It is the intricate law of life for everything and as such drives and directs to its destination the dynamic process of being and unfolding that is so characteristic of created things.

> *In other words, by virtue of and in subjection to this single, many-sided, intricate law-order, no creature exists of and by itself as an independent, self-standing entity, detached from the law of creation that holds for it. Everything exists in the correlation law–subjectivity, more precisely: in the correlation of the* law-side *and the* subject-side *of this concrete existent. Nor does any creature exist independently* opposite other creatures. *The cosmic law-order also interweaves everything in a mutual coherence.*

The standard separation (and not just distinction) between "norms and facts" is therefore philosophically incorrect and demonstrably has a non-Christian origin in secularized paganism, a mode of thought that tried mentally to eliminate the divine from the non-divine. This existence of all creatures in the *correlation of law and subject*, this two-sidedness of all things, is one of the fundamental ideas of Reformational philosophy (in Dooyeweerd's version). The correlation is also referred to as the *meaning* of existence. We should bear in mind, however, that the "meaning" of things involves more than just this correlation, as we shall see later.

4.7 The idea of substance

What we have just discussed is a fundamental notion that pits the Christian view of reality particularly against the idea of "substance." This idea sees reality as a complex of "substances" and starts from a separation between God and the creature and then accords the creature independence vis-à-vis God.

This is another reason why we prefer to speak, not of "ontology" (the doctrine of independent "being," from Greek *to on*), but of philosophical cosmology ("philosophical" as distinct from astrophysical cosmology). For the cosmos exists only in the correlative bond with the law of God. This can also be religiously expressed in words like these: every created thing exists only in the religious connection with God and with his ever present and active creative and redemptive word. Theologically speaking, this is implicit in the idea of God's providential rule "by which he upholds and governs all things."[27] Sadly, this is not always realized, often resulting in a

---

27. *Heidelberg Catechism*, Lord's Day 10.

deterministic interpretation of God's providential order that has led to contradictions between human freedom and divine providence— as in Stoic philosophy, from which Christian theology borrowed the term "providence."

In traditional philosophy "being" (*to on*) did not have a relation to God. There, "substance" was separated from God instead of being only distinguished from him, and it was also deemed capable of being "independent." This prepared for what would later be called "deism" and which we might call horizontalist secularism in the view of reality. Once we discover this we stand amazed at how such a view of reality, even if implicitly and unconsciously, came to be used in orthodox and every other brand of theology. But this is uncovered only over time as Reformational philosophy studies the basic principles of traditional philosophical ways of thinking.

4.8 THE LAW-ORDER AS COHERENCE AND UNITY

Further analysis of the structures of the great diversity among created realities (chapters 5 to 7) will show to what extent and in what way these laws of existence for the various creatures are internally connected. So it is understandable, even if improper, that there are all kinds of "isms" in which the initiators and their followers are fascinated by the universal phenomenon of, say, "life." Then "life" comes to be seen as the foundation of all reality (as in vitalism). Similar "isms" arise with the physical, the economic, morality, politics, the church, art and beauty, power, or (as among many contemporary thinkers, often including theologians): language or hermeneutics. This absolutization of something that does actually exist is the main source of many "isms" in science.

The tremendous interwoven coherence of all laws for and in existing reality occasions not just the regrettable derailment of "isms" but also the correct awareness of a coherence that actually encompasses everything in subjective reality, a coherence which according to its law-side is called by Reformational philosophy the "cosmic law-order." The term "creation order" can be taken to sum up both the law-side and the subject-side.

But here too (cf. sec. 3.3) coherence is not yet the same as unity. Many interconnections are empirically demonstrable; unity is not. Unity cannot be experienced purely by the senses. It transcends the entire experiential coherence in which human thought, too, functions. It "precedes" the coherence in the sense that it (i.e., the unity of God's creative will in Christ) is presupposed in the coherence and makes this coherence possible, including the multiplicity and diversity present in it. Recall the image of the "root."

4.9 UNITY AND COHERENCE ACCORDING TO LAW- AND SUBJECT-SIDE

This transcendent unity, *viewed in terms of the law-side*, is the unity of the divine Creator's will—of God's creative word that calls into being *this* or *that, thus* or *so*, onto paths of unfolding and developing. All things have come into being from and through this Word, also in time. *Viewed in terms of the subject-side*, this unity is the temporally transcendent fullness or root unity of all creation, that is to say, it is the pre-existing and transcendent *Christ,* who is God *and* man. Thus the *unity* of reality, which all major philosophers have sought from the beginning right up to our own day, has a law-side and a subject-side, a divine and a creaturely side.

This unity is not an imagined unity but a revealed unity, a unity that can only be known and acknowledged in faith. It is a unity that reminds us that in all the diversity and all the coherence within that diversity that we experience in our temporal life, we are constantly dealing with—as our worldview would express it—the one will of the Creator God, the creative will which he *actualized* first of all in Christ, the "first-born of all creation," the "alpha" (Rev. 3:14). It is there that we find the one source or root of all creaturely diversity as unity: in the will and law of God, revealed in Christ. There is found, *also in terms of the subject-side*, the unity of all created reality, which qua unity is likewise summed up and realized in Christ.

Scripture points in the same direction when it says about the law-side: "For whoever keeps the whole law but fails in one point has become guilty of all of it. For he who said, Do not commit adultery, also said, Do not kill" (James 2:10–12). The commandments are all united in God's will. And as regards the subject-side, Scripture says that all things (*ta panta*) "consist" in Christ, are "held together" in Him (Col. 1:17), are "joined together" under Him as under one head (Eph. 1:22; 4:15–16).

When this (root) unity in creation, and particularly the unity on the law-side of creation, is not recognized, we can rightly speak of an *undeified and uprooted* outlook on reality, or of a *horizontalist* view of reality. Such a view negates both God's immanence and reality's enduring bond with the Word through which and in which it has been created.

So we should not go along with the present-day aversion to so-called "metaphysical speculations" when dealing with the full and true reality that is accessible only to the eye of faith and faith knowledge. There are more things in man's temporal sensory modes of experience than can be accounted for in traditional philosophy. This is not a fantasized "other" reality, some *super*-natural or *meta*-physical reality, but our *own everyday* reality, that is to say (philosophically speaking), *insofar as* its supra-temporal fullness or root unity is concerned, according to its law-side and its subject-side—its "transcendent depth dimension," its participation in Christ who is its "alpha" or "root" (Rev. 3:14; 5:5; 22:13,16).

4.10 THEOLOGICAL RELEVANCE

The above view of reality is very important for theology, for instance in the doctrine of creation, which to my knowledge has not yet found an acceptable solution to the exegetical problem of all things being "created in Christ"[28]—not even in the "Christomonism" of Karl Barth.[29] As a result, the prevailing theological doctrine of creation has remained considerably poorer than is warranted by Scripture. So far, the New Testament enrichment of the Old Testament creation account has been conspicuous by its absence from systematic theology, despite many exegetical discourses on "the cosmological significance of Christ" in connection with Col. 1:15–20.

This lack also renders theological ethics virtually ineffective in its contact with the other sciences, since it presents its own "theological ethics" in a super-naturalist vein as the normative link between faith

---

28. Cf. my article "Geschapen in Christus" cited in chap. 1, n. 14.

29. Nor in the recent extensive studies by Christian Link, *Schöpfungstheologie angesichts der Herausforderungen des 20. Jahrhunderts* [Creation theology in the face of the challenges of the twentieth century], 2 vols. (Gütersloh, 1991); and Abraham van de Beek, *Schepping. De wereld als voorspel voor de eeuwigheid* [Creation: The world as prelude to eternity] (Baarn, 1996).

and reality, between theology and the (other) sciences.[30] Rome does this in "moral theology" which, based on Scripture, is regarded as the supernatural completion of "natural philosophical ethics" (which may or may not be Christian). It does so, of course, on the basis of its ground-motive of "nature and grace."

Our philosophical law-idea also has theological significance for the doctrine of providence, in that it enables us to fend off the present-day unorthodox repudiation of this doctrine more radically than is possible from a substantialist and horizontalist view of reality (usually imbued with moralism). God sustains his creatures with the power of his normative word of creation, which can be resisted and transgressed in man's freedom of choice.

The theological doctrine of original sin also needs to be mentioned here. In my view, this doctrine has not yet found an acceptable solution to the exegetical problem occasioned by the scriptural given that *we* have sinned *"in Adam."*[31] Systematic theology's theory of a "juridical imputation," sometimes moderated and supplemented with the idea of "corporate thinking," is *in its standard traditional form* incompatible with the letter of the relevant texts and also incompatible with God's justice.

To these examples we could add the doctrine of the church and the doctrine of the Lord's Supper. But elaboration of these and possibly more examples belongs to the field of dogmatics, and in principle is only possible if that discipline can detach itself from its modern view of reality colored by pagan philosophy.

4.11 The correlation of law and subjective reality as the correlation of law-side and subject-side

It should by now be clear that one of the main features that distinguishes Reformational philosophy from prevailing currents is its strong emphasis on the *relation, the reciprocal connection* between law and that which is subject to the law, namely all of created reality. We called this relation a *correlation.* That means, as we noted earlier, that

---

30. Cf. my extended review article of the *Handbuch der christlichen Ethik*, ed. Anselm Hertz, 3 vols. (Freiburg im Breisgau, 1978–82), in *Philosophia Reformata* 46 (1981): 68–90; 47 (1982): 69–77; 49 (1984): 150–63; 50 (1985): 66–84.

31. "Not me!" a student shot back in one of my catechism classes; "I wasn't around yet for a long time!" But see below, Appendix, Figure 2.

we cannot separate norms and facts, as if they are distinct matters that can be dealt with in isolation of each other as the scientist develops his theories. Indeed, as we argued above, norms and facts are two sides of *the same thing, the law-side and the subject-side of concrete reality,* of every creature.

This correlation is a central moment in "the meaning" of reality. With this concept we confess, right within the domain of science, the religious relation of all creatures to God and to his immanent presence and activity.

To speak of *sides* (law-side and subject-side) is at the same time to warn against some Platonic *absolutization* of the law (as "idea," or, as in Augustine, law as "divine thought") in relation to what is subject to it. This fallacy is found, for instance, in the philosophical idealism (still influential today) of nineteenth-century German philosophy. Such an absolutization manifests itself in our own time as well in the notion of "value," as in the "philosophy of values" practiced, among others, by Nicolai Hartmann.

The uncritical adoption of present-day talk about "norms and values" in society, and even the definition of ethics as "the science of norms and values," follows the same line. For this is an incorrect *substantialization of the law* (akin to Platonism), which fails to do justice to God's active, self-revealing *immanence* in his creation. There are not two separate realms: a world of facts and another world of "norms and values." Vollenhoven once characterized "values" as "realized norms," thus clearly as something on the subject-side. "Values" are not themselves norms, but at most concrete ideals or examples.

On the other hand, acknowledging the correlation is also a warning against a possible derailment of a Christian tradition that *onto*-logically separates God's law from God himself and as a result becomes incapable of doing full justice to *God's self-revelation in reality.* All too often in theology, Article 2 of the Belgic Confession is a dead letter when it comes to God's revelation in nature.[32] "General revelation"

---

32. Belgic Confession, art. 2: "We know Him by two means: First, by the creation, preservation, and government of the universe; which is before our eyes as a most elegant book, wherein all creatures, great and small, are as so many characters leading us to see clearly the invisible things of God, even his everlasting power and divinity . . ." Ignoring this confession is often covered up by invoking "*sola Scriptura.*" But in its historical context this slogan of the Protestant Reformation was partly a protest against the Roman Catholic theological tradition which needed a

is not likely to be denied, but many theologians are unable to do anything with it in practice because they think scriptural revelation is so much clearer about creation.

4.12 RENEWED INTEREST IN "REVELATION AND EXPERIENCE"

4.12.1 OBJECTIVISM AND SUBJECTIVISM

Traditionally, theology often talks about objectivism and subjectivism, depending on whether the discussion of personal faith puts "too much" emphasis on, respectively, revelation or experience. Faith is sometimes equated with "head knowledge," with affirming the truth of revelation; or it is viewed in a *combination* of such affirmation with indispensable "heart knowledge," with deeper or more "emotional" affects, like love and trust, growth and enrichment, feeling touched or stirred in one's innermost being, and the like. The contrast, besides containing a number of good intentions, also entails a *philosophically colored view of the nature of human faith*. At this juncture, let me illustrate some of the problems this poses, problems that traditional theology is unable to solve.

4.12.2 THE CORRELATION OF FAITH AND REVELATION

First of all, neither divine revelation nor human faith should be identified with theology, that is to say, with a *human theoretical interpretation* of revelation and faith. Revelation is a word from God in which God himself is and remains actively present. God's revelation remains an intentional activity of God, aimed at man. It cannot begin to "lead a life of its own" apart from man, or as something "objective" that exists by itself "over there" and is conceptually appropriated (or spurned) by us "over here." So it is not an "objective truth" apart and separate from God, nor from its addressee: man(kind). That would involve a *deistic* separation between God and creature and a substantialization of the creature. *God's revelation is God revealing himself in creatures.*

This, then, is an example of the above-mentioned *correlation*, in which God's revelation is the norm, the normative content for our

---

"natural theology" and a "natural ethics" as a preliminary step leading up to the supernatural throne of *Regina Theologia*.

believing, our faith, and which lies on the "law-side" of the life of faith. And since faith is something creaturely it can become the object of a variety of scientific disciplines, one of them being theology.

To have faith is to believe, which is a *subjective human* activity; and faith is the product, the result of believing. By virtue of the creation, man is endowed with the function of believing, the capacity for faith, as one of his modes of experience. Thus faith, in a constitutive sense, is "proper" to being human. God's revelation is the structural *possibility and content* of this faith. Without revelation there is no faith. And conversely, all faith is oriented to this divine revelation. Faith is "the conviction of things not seen" (Hebr. 11:1) which one nevertheless *believes*, and *ought* to believe, and ought to believe *well*, that is, in accordance with revelation as the norm for believing.

4.12.3 Objective revelation and subjective experience?

Theology has traditionally debated the relation between *revelation and experience* in utter disregard of the correlation between them.

Up till now it has been common not to question the word "experience" by simply asking: *what kind of experience* do you mean? An emotional experience? A cognitive experience? A love experience? A religious experience? A theologically stimulating experience? A devotional experience? It is also common to relate the word "revelation" to something that takes place above and outside man, something supernatural or extra-creaturely, something that comes to man from outside as an "objective truth," like a lightning bolt "straight down from Above" (Karl Barth). Hence the usual reproaches, back and forth, of objectivism and subjectivism. The awareness that something is out of joint here leads to the reaction of those who allow the difference between revelation and experience to become blurred or even to disappear altogether and who no longer recognize a valid norm for their subjective religious experiences.

Objectivism as it is most often used would then mean that faith and proclamation talk about *the truth* as an "objective given" existing outside and apart from man, as "doctrine." Belief in this is therefore no more than intellectual knowledge, a *cognitive* experience, even if people often realize that this is not yet true faith. Terms often used here are "historical faith," "miracle faith," "provisional faith" or "intellectual faith," all with slightly different connotations. Hence people believe (at least in orthodox circles) that such "faith" needs a complement, needs to have "experience" added to it.

But added to what exactly? To faith, or to "head knowledge"—or are these seen as the same? And what is this addition—what does it consist of? Of a heartfelt love of God? Of appropriate emotions? And where can one get such an addition? Does faith really consist of (only?) two *components*: an intellectual component plus an emotional component, which together make for true faith only in combination? Which theory from anthropology or psychology of religion is being applied here to the question what faith "is composed of"? What other "functional possibilities" might a person possess from which one could derive "elements" for making statements about the *nature* of faith? Or does a human soul consist only of reason and feeling? Can such a theoretical approach be inferred from Scripture? Can correct answers to these questions be "proved" from Scripture? The history of dogmatics is full of such attempts—and full of disagreement on the matter.

4.12.4 LORD'S DAY 7 OF THE HEIDELBERG CATECHISM

Theology in the Reformed tradition does indeed suggest such a theory, as is echoed in the formulation of the answer given by the Heidelberg Catechism to the question, "What is true faith?" The answer given is: "True faith is not only a sure knowledge . . . but also a firm confidence . . ." As a *church dogma*, however, this answer should not be read as if it proposes to be a theological-dogmatic or a philosophical-anthropological theory. The literal words of a church dogma are not normative for theology.

Yet, almost inevitably, in order to render the biblical content of faith, a church dogma makes use of the standard (philosophically influenced) language of the day. Nevertheless, not its possible theological formulation should be ecclesiastically normative, but the *biblical* content it refers to. Otherwise the interminable polemics among theologians about what the confession "really" says simply continues, often with schism as a result. The difference is then felt to be a *difference in belief,* so crucial a difference that communion of the saints is no longer believed possible.

All the same, the view we reject—about faith as a compound of intellectual knowledge and emotional, loving trust—is not without an *element* of truth that should be honored. Philosophy of faith and philosophy of religion will have to render account of this in the scientific discipline of theology; but such an account will have to be based on what is discussed in the next chapter, the theory of modal aspects.

4.12.5 TO HAVE FAITH IS TO HAVE EXPERIENCE OF FAITH

If we refuse to split faith up into "affirming" objective truth plus subjectively "experiencing" it (whatever this "it" might be), the problem assumes a very different theological complexion than we find in our tradition. We then come to consider Christian *faith as such* a typically *distinct* "mode of experience," one of the many possible human modes of experience. We then no longer distinguish between "faith" and "experience of faith," but instead see faith or believing as simply one mode of experience alongside other kinds of life experience—for instance, the experience of beauty, of love, of justice, of health and vitality, of eloquence, of logical distinctions, of technical skills, of economic savings, and so on.

If you never ride a bicycle you will never acquire cycling experience. If you never buy and sell you will never acquire business experience. If you never get involved in politics you will never acquire political experience. If you don't ply a trade or practice a profession you will never acquire any work experience. If you don't drive enough you will never be an experienced driver. The same goes for faith. Faith is born of practicing faith. Believing grows by doing it, by believing, just as a toddler learns to walk not via stories or theoretical lessons but by doing it, by trial and error. Faith, "by definition," is experience of faith.

We can therefore say: without faith no experience of faith. The experience of faith cannot be added to an existing faith-without-experience but is something proper to faith itself. Without faith no experience of faith; and without experience of faith no faith.

However, a structural analysis of faith that a student of theology would require can only be given after we have set out the theory of modalities and the theory of entities as well as the theory of the so-called "enkaptic structural interlacements" of the substructures within entities.

4.12.6 Mysticism as a complement? "Spirituality"

Today's desire for "experiencing God," also called "spirituality," is reaching out for something that is more than just believing deeply in God, loving him, listening to him and serving him as we daily walk with him in all the ordinary things of life. The desire also intends more than just to rise above the ordinary fallible human ebb and flow in the intensity or depth of nearly all our life experiences— more than just to overcome the ups and downs that the emotional experience of faith also shares in. The trend in question goes further and is typical of the *mysticism* of all ages and all peoples in virtually all religions.

Mysticism in religious life is always fed by the desire for more than just ordinary faith, a desire that is the direct result of interpreting faith *theologically* (with varying influence on non-theologians) as a cognitive function. Thomas Aquinas, the "Christian Aristotle," once gave this definition of faith: *fides est aliquid rationis*, faith is an intellectual matter; while in other places, following Augustine, he added: "perfected by love." The trend we are talking about is known in specialist literature as the combination of "scholasticism and mysticism" as they complement each other. In Protestant circles it is also known as "theology and experiential pietism," "the objective and the subjective," or even as "Reformation and Second Reformation."

Hence, in the heyday of Protestant scholasticism (c. 1550–1700) many "Fathers of Dordt" freely drew much of their theology from medieval theologians and mystics. Next to Thomas Aquinas they often used his rival and contemporary Bonaventure (both died rather young in 1274). The "Second Reformation" in the Protestant world, which was a partial, mixed reaction to the rationalism of Protestant scholasticism, followed more the line of Bonaventure and the German mystics, with which all forms of pietism more or less linked up. The fathers of the Second Reformation did not fully fathom the *mistake* of the mystical *way of thinking*, nor the mistake of an otherwise understandable reaction to rationalism. The mystical way of thinking cultivated all kinds of criteria for authenticating "true piety," in which the degree or measure of a person's sense of guilt and need for redemption played an important role.

4.12.7 THE SWING OF THE PENDULUM AND HOW TO OVERCOME IT

Throughout history, from the second century until today, the two "emphases" have alternated in reaction to each other. Now that the current trend (in reaction to rationalism and intellectualism both inside and outside the church) seeks to re-emphasize "spirituality"—seeks to embrace mysticism, the esoteric, a sense of God and transcendence, subjective experience, and the like—we are already beginning to hear some theological circles voicing their concern: "Enough of that already!" Sometimes we even hear the call for a return to "scholasticism" (of course again in combination with a "healthy mysticism"). This change of climate can also be detected from time in time in the publications by what is known as the Utrecht School.[33]

After three to four decades in which "Reason" has been quite generally criticized, it is seeking to regain its self-confidence. Even dogmatics is quietly being propagated again after being displaced for decades by exegesis and "practical theology." The current dearth of interest among elders and pastors in systematic theology may well make way fairly soon for a renewed interest in it. In the light of the history of theology this would seem virtually inevitable.

The *dilemma*, however, with its rival poles or emphases, can in principle be overcome, at least in part, by developing a new philosophical-anthropological view of human faith, human life and reality in general. It will be a view that differs fundamentally from the popular "wisdom" of trying to strike a balance between two *errors*, both of which are felt to be ("half") *truths*. But both are more than just one-sided positions. They are two fallacies which think they need each other in order to remain "in balance." To borrow an image from A. Janse in the thirties: a lame leg is not healthy, but someone suffering from this disability will not heal and become any more balanced if his second leg becomes lame too.[34] What is needed is a different

---

33. (*Ed.*) A trend of thought in the theology department of the University of Utrecht during the 1990s, initiated by philosopher of religion Vincent Brümmer and practiced by his students. It held that theological statements should first be tested for logical consistency before their truth content is considered.

34. (*Ed.*) For A. Janse, see the life-sketch by Bennie J. van der Walt, "Antheunis Janse van Biggekerke (1890–1960): Morning Star of a Reformational Worldview," in idem, *The Eye Is the Lamp of the Body: Worldview and Their Impact* (Potchefstroom, 2008), pp. 189–229.

philosophical hermeneutics and a different theoretical-philosophical view of reality and human life.

Chapter Five – Cosmology:
The series of modal aspects

CHAPTER FIVE
COSMOLOGY: THE SERIES OF MODAL ASPECTS

5.1 ORIENTATION SCHEMES

Every philosophy uses orientation schemes that stake out the main paths in the landscape of reality. Familiar ancient orientation schemes include: natural and supernatural, material and spiritual, good and evil, human and non-human, temporal and eternal. As regards man, a well-known scheme is that of body and soul, or the tripartite scheme of body, soul and spirit. Another example of such a primary orientation is the doctrine of faculties with its classification of intellect, feeling and will. Other schemes relating to man (or to things in general) are inner and outer, higher and lower, subject and object, freedom and constraint, visible and invisible, and so on and so forth.

Thus many philosophies talk about "categories" or "fundamental concepts" that are to orient us to the basic facts of our reality. But this easily carries with it the Kantian suggestion that these fundamental human concepts actually make our experiential reality *possible*. One example of this line of thinking would be that we experience the objects around us as spatial *because* we have the concept of space *a priori* in our mind; whether there is spatiality *outside the concept* of space, an objective space *in and of itself*, cannot be determined with logical certainty.

Reformational philosophy is not first of all concerned with our concepts or classifications, but with a finely nuanced recognition of the distinct differences in *reality itself*, and then, in the second place, with a correct concept or idea of this reality. Classifications should try to formulate the creaturely differentiation in reality itself. It is not a matter of having a subjective or invented *"perspective,"* as people like to say nowadays, or of playing "schema-games" (Hans Lenk) or "language games" (Wittgenstein). The main concern, particularly in

against post- modernism

71

the present chapter, is to recognize, name and analyze as accurately as possible the sides or aspects of concrete reality. None should be forgotten here (or wrongly classified under another), and none should be mentioned superfluously when it is already implied in another. We call these sides or aspects of reality "modal aspects," a term which refers to the *modi*, the modes of existence or ways of being.

The theory of the modal aspects of reality and experience, dealt with in this and the next chapter, forms the starting-point for the special sciences. Each of the sciences has its fundamental idea and central concepts, and all of these are oriented to the basic phenomenon governing their entire field of research. Language, law, sociality, logical analysis, beauty, faith, love, space, number, energy, and so on, are all examples that function as a kind of "last word" in the theoretical understanding of the various sectors of reality. They form the respective ground-ideas of the relevant special sciences and are at the same time the criteria for demarcating each special science from the others. Thus the faith aspect is the basic notion of "theology," which I therefore prefer to call the science of faith, this being (at least in the last three centuries) a more adequate name than (scientific) "theo-logy."[35]

5.2 Modal aspects are not entities

Reformational philosophy has made an original contribution to the development of philosophic thought particularly through its theory of modal aspects. This theory linked up with the earlier and well-known distinction between various "modes" of existence and its practical application in, for instance, the division of universities into faculties. The distinction of sectors or modes of existence in reality has been theoretically refined and deepened by our philosophy in a scheme of some fifteen aspects. Inasmuch as it is a subjective interpretation of reality, the scheme should be treated as "tentative" and "open to revision": further reflection may lead to a change, for example, in the number of aspects.

Before discussing these aspects in more detail, we should point out that modal aspects are not in the first place concerned with *concrete* phenomena such as things, plants, people, acts, events, common structures, and the like, nor with any groups of these. Modal aspects

---

35. I discuss this at length in my book *Vakfilosofie van de geloofswetenschap* [Philosophy of the science of faith] (2004).

are *modi, modes of* existence, *ways or manners of* being, not concretely existing "beings," "things" or "entities" (from *"ens,"* existing thing, a "being"). Modal aspects denote the how, the "thus-or-so" quality of things, not the concrete "this" or "that" itself (thing, event, act, word, etc.).

Failure to take this difference seriously or a tendency to overlook or ignore it (a topic to which Dooyeweerd even devoted two separate volumes of his three-volume principal work) is one of the reasons why Reformational philosophy is beset by persistent and superficial misunderstandings in Christian circles. One of the clearest examples of this is objecting to a faith aspect because "Scripture does not speak about it in this way." True enough, Scripture does not teach philosophy and does not have modal aspects, nor does it teach what the faith aspect as such is. But it does speak concretely about faith as something different from moral virtues, or justice, or health. It speaks about the concrete faith of pagans or Jews or Christians, about little or great faith, about real lack of faith, and so on. In all this, however, it speaks very practically, without philosophical intentions and without providing "data" (*sic*) for the formation of theoretical paradigms. More on this later, in chapter 7, which deals with concrete things or "entities."

5.3 LAW-SPHERES, MEANING-SIDES, MODALITIES, MODAL ASPECTS, MODES OF BEING, MODES OF EXISTENCE

The above are six different terms which have succeeded each other over the years without essentially differing in meaning. Reformational philosophy is inevitably engaged in a continual struggle with the language of our traditions, in order to keep misunderstandings to a minimum. Language too is not just a tool, not some technical instrument reflecting a neutral view of life. The patterns of thought underlying language have been mainly stamped in our Western culture by the language and life experience of the cultural dominants in our intellectual-spiritual heritage—by pre-Christian *paganism*, and then by *humanism*, and of course partly by *Christianity*. Thus each of the six terms mentioned in the heading of this section has its pros and cons as regards clarity or its potential for misunderstanding. Each term is liable to misunderstanding because it can be interpreted in the light of prevailing thought.

The earliest of these terms in Reformational thought is the word *"law-sphere."* This contains a reminiscence of the nineteenth-century expression "sphere-sovereignty" that was still common in the first half of the twentieth century in a large part of the Christian community in the Netherlands. It refers to specific and circumscribed areas of life. The laws, norms or regularities obtaining in a certain area are different from those in force in another zone of life. Apparently there are *groups* or kinds of laws: economic laws, laws for organic growth, principles of justice, logical principles, laws of motion, linguistic laws, and so forth.

However, an objection to the term "law-sphere" (*wetskring*), together with the name "philosophy of the law-idea" (Dutch: *wijsbegeerte der wetsidee*), is that it may wrongly suggest that this philosophy is solely concerned with laws, or only with the "law-side" of reality. The false impression may also arise that Reformational philosophy focuses exclusively on the more concrete dimension of *things* ("entities"), and not on that of the modal *aspects*.

Modalities, modal aspects and *modes of being* (or *modes of existence*) have become the most common and most useful expressions. But again it is important here to distinguish the meaning Reformational philosophy attaches to these terms from their meaning in generally accepted usage. This applies especially to the term "aspects." In common parlance this term usually means *groups* or particularly *parts* of *concrete* phenomena or events, thus a certain *selection* of these. The inside or outside of an object, the cause and consequences of an event, are also called "aspects" in general usage.

Reformational philosophy instead links up more with the grammatical meaning of the term: "point of view." Aspect comes from *"ad spicere,"* to look at something from a certain vantage point. In that case you do not see everything, but you do see a certain "side" of the concrete object. This "side," *taken by itself and separately* (and that is what we do in a theoretical approach), is therefore an abs-traction, sub-tracted from the concrete whole.

5.4 MEANING AND ITS MEANING-SIDES

Then there is the term *"meaning-sides."* This term is the most profound one. The element "meaning" refers to reality as meaningful. The view of what "meaning" is and what it stands for is a *religious view*, a view that expresses what we believe regarding the (1) origin and (2) final purpose or destination of all things, as well as (3) their mode of being before God, in his covenant and under his law, his promises and rule.[36] This existence has meaning. In view of what we just said about the import of "meaning," we could also say: existence, reality, *is* meaning; or: to exist is *to be meaning*.

As regards created reality, Christian *philosophy* can build on this "being meaning" by further specifying our *temporal mode of existence* as a "subjective" (subjected) existence in correlation with God's laws of creation. Only this mode of existence, this *middle part of reality* as it exists *in time* between its divine origin and its ultimate destination, is open to theoretical analysis and the resulting systematic, scientific interpretation of it. Accordingly, even in scientific philosophy the term "meaning-sides" of the cosmos continues to reflect the religious starting-point, since the notion of "meaning" contains a reference to origin and destination, both of which can only be grasped in faith. The term "meaning" contains a reference to the law-side of reality, the norms and laws with which reality must comply; in short, "meaning" refers to the *mode of existence* of reality in a correlation of law and the subjectivity subject to it. But to ask about the laws (for existence) is to ask implicitly about the Law-giver.

Accordingly we like to say in our *philosophy*, which makes *theoretical* statements about reality and its law-structures, not just that reality *has* meaning, but above all that it *is* meaning. Reality does not *exist* in any other way than in this correlation with (God's) laws, stretched between Origin and Destination. Thus, on principle, reality is not susceptible to being mentally separated from this correlation (unless it be in theoretical abstractions).

The believer who is versed in Scripture will be reminded rather quickly that Christ, too, is called "the alpha and omega," the beginning and the end of all things. This provides a religious defence against the historicizing secularism that proposes to look at ("natural"!) reality apart from Christ, a reality that is supposedly "neutral" or of unknown origin (the Big Bang theory for instance). At this point, by way of supplement, scholasticism, whose main characteristic is that it wants to combine "neutral-scientific" views with biblical faith, adds "Christ" as the "supernatural" perfecting gift of grace for that "natural reality."

---

36. More about this in my article "De vraag naar de zin" [The question of meaning], *Philosophia Reformata* 50 (1985): 98–118; 52 (1987): 41–65.

5.5 (QUALIFIED) FUNCTIONS

Finally, a few remarks about the term "function." Initially this term was used in the same sense as law-sphere or aspect, and sometimes it is still used that way in careless writing. But this usage is apt to lead to the above-mentioned misunderstanding of mistaking an abstracted aspect for something concrete, of confusing *thus-or-so* with *this-or-that*. We usually take a *function* to mean an activity, a concrete functioning of concrete realities, so a concrete phenomenon. That is altogether different from an abstract mode, way of being, mode of existence or aspect of reality.

Let me illustrate this with an example. Our digestive process is a concrete function, an event that is sometimes also called one of our "aspects" in ordinary usage. There is no objection to this in everyday language, but in our theoretically honed *scientific* language "aspect" is an abstract point of view, which either qualifies or does not qualify the concrete phenomenon under investigation. Thus the digestive process is a concrete biotic *event* which from an *aspectual* point of view is biotically qualified rather than, say, physically, or spatially, or quantitatively, or logically, and so on. All these aspects can certainly be distinguished in it, but they do not *qualify* the concrete phenomenon known as "digestion."

Thus, to mention another example, jurisprudence (in the sense of decisions of the courts) denotes a concrete function within the juridical modality or mode of being and is qualified by it. Besides jurisprudence there are other concrete functions or activities that are juridically qualified, such as signing a contract, enacting a law, bringing a case before the courts, testifying before a judge, and the like.

Philosophy of theology in particular is a discipline that suffers from a disregard for the difference between aspects and entities, above all in relation to the subject "faith." Concrete faith is not an aspect, modality or *mode* of existence, and conversely: the faith aspect is not concrete faith but an abstract "side" or *mode of being* of it. The faith aspect remains a theoretical product of philosophic thought, albeit one of fine quality, in my view, and indispensable in the sciences. On the other hand, the concrete activity of faith, of believing, is *realizing* a concrete *given* of creation, *realizing a function created into* the whole of human nature.

5.6 ENUMERATION AND ORDER OF THE ASPECTS

Here follows a provisional list of the modal aspects and their meaning-nuclei.

15. **the pistical aspect**

meaning-nucleus: (religious) faith, certitude, surrender

14. **the ethical aspect**

meaning-nucleus: love (in ethical relationships)

13. **the juridical aspect**

meaning-nucleus: lawfulness, retribution, justice

12. **the aesthetic aspect**

meaning-nucleus: beauty, harmony

11. **the economic aspect**

meaning-nucleus: frugality, moderation

10. **the social aspect**

meaning-nucleus: sociality, social intercourse

9. **the lingual aspect**

meaning-nucleus: symbolic signification, language

8. **the historical or formative aspect** ✗ how is this an

meaning-nucleus: formative power, culture aspect? aren't all aspects shaped by this? ✗

7. **the logical-analytical aspect**

meaning-nucleus: distinguishing, identifying difference

6. **the sensitive aspect**

meaning-nucleus: feeling, emotionality, affect

5. **the biotic aspect**

meaning-nucleus: organic life, vitality

4. **the physical aspect**

meaning-nucleus: energy, force, change, dynamics

3. **the kinematic aspect**

meaning-nucleus: mobility, mechanical motion

2. **the spatial aspect**

meaning-nucleus: continuous extension

1. **the numerical aspect**

meaning-nucleus: number, discrete quantity

✗ aren't there some missing? ✗

5.7 FOUNDATIONAL AND TRANSCENDENT DIRECTIONS

The order of the aspects followed in the list, from 1 to 15, is not a random sequence. Each aspect presupposes the previous one in a fixed direction. Space presupposes quantities and allows spatial figures to be measured and counted. Organic life is not the same as mechanical motion but it does presuppose the phenomenon of motion. Logical-analytical distinguishing presupposes the presence of organs like the brain and the senses. Human social intercourse presupposes language, and the economic aspect presupposes human society. Faith is more than moral respect and love of neighbor, but it does presuppose respect and love for our fellows and is not "true faith" without them—something that also applies to intellectual distinguishing: faith is more than and different from intellectual labor but it does presuppose the making of rational distinctions.

Accordingly, it is possible to distinguish two directions in the list: a foundational direction, from top to bottom, and a transcendent direction, from bottom to top. In the transcendent direction this is also an order of increasing complexity in the entire structure of the aspects. Each successive aspect presupposes another new, earlier aspect. In the opposite direction each previous aspect does contain more anticipatory moments yet these are not always concretely "opened up," although they do contain a converging tendency towards the totality and unity. But this will be dealt with more broadly in a later context.[37]

5.8 Meaning-nuclei of the modal aspects

As was mentioned already, the theory of modalities or law-spheres refers to fundamental differences in the modes of existence of all created reality. The theory is intended as a scientific recognition of what Christians like to call, in biblical language, the differences of creatures *"each after its kind"* (cf. Gen. 1).

Life experience tells us that there is a difference between the life of plants, animals and human beings, and the non-life of stones and stars, of metals and mechanical motions. Numbers and triangles do not possess organic

---

37. For a discussion of meaning-nuclei, see sec. 5.8 below. For differences of opinion about the list of aspects and possible amendments, proposed by authors like Jan Dengerink, Calvin Seerveld, Dick Stafleu, Willem Ouweneel, and others, see René van Woudenberg, *Gelovend denken; inleiding tot een christelijke filosofie* (Amsterdam and Kampen, 1992), pp. 75–113. Useful comments on various aspects in L[eendert] Kalsbeek, *Contours of a Christian Philosophy* (Toronto, 1975), pp. 95–118. The theory of aspects was originally developed in H. Dooyeweerd, *De Wijsbegeerte der Wetsidee* (1935-36), 2:3–356, amended and expanded in the 2nd edition: *A New Critique of Theoretical Thought* (1953-58), 2:3–426.

life either. But what *is* this "life" that is typical of some creatures but not of others? The same question can be applied to the other modes of being: what exactly is law, what is language, what is logical distinguishing, what is beauty, what is love, what is faith, and so on?

Before answering this question I must again warn against a common misunderstanding mentioned earlier. When talking about some concrete love relationships, for example between spouses and between parents and children, we are not yet talking about the common element in these three different types of love: marital love, parental love and filial love. That common element is much more abstract, and this abstract element, which is implicitly present in different "types" of concrete loving—this *universal* element in the concrete and particular—this is what we have in mind when our theory of modalities deals with the distinctive nature of the *aspect* or *modality* of love. This distinctive nature is found somewhere in the common *nuclear moment* of love.

Every aspect, every modality is built up of three moments. The first of these is the so-called *nucleus*.[38] That is the subject of this section. The two other moments (the so-called anticipations and retrocipations) will be discussed in sec. 5.10.

Thus the nucleus of the life aspect is life, of the love aspect love, of the juridical aspect justice, and so on. The list displays these nuclei for every modality. A nucleus guarantees the distinctive character of a modality, which is not reducible to anything else. The nucleus also qualifies or characterizes the non-nuclear moments, the "analogies," which we will discuss, again, in sec. 5.10.

Irreducibility means, strictly speaking, that a nucleus cannot be defined, because to define is to describe by means of other concepts or to reduce to something else. Something that has its own unique nature cannot be described by concepts derived from something else, because we then lose insight into that unique nature. It is therefore difficult to find an accurate designation for the various meaning-nuclei. Hence we often use more than one or even more than two different words in the list of sec. 5.6. Our insight, our in-tuition, plays an important role here.

The meaning-nuclei mentioned by Kalsbeek are mostly nouns, which may wrongly suggest that the concrete things or activities

---

38. (*Ed.*) Dutch: *kern*; sometimes translated as "kernel."

thus named *in their concreteness* are seen as meaning-nuclei of the meaning-sides. Kalsbeek himself points to the danger of this misunderstanding.[39] Often I therefore prefer words indicating a neutral abstraction, like lawfulness, frugality, the vital, the social, the moral, the harmonious, the economic. But this part of the theory of modalities—the correct designation of nuclei—will always remain a subject of debate. The problem is also connected to possible new developments in the relevant special sciences.

Every term we derive from our living spoken language refers to something concrete. But the meaning-nucleus is the qualifying *moment* in a meaning-side, and as such is very real and essential but not anything concrete; instead it is very abstract. The term by which we refer to a meaning-nucleus appeals to our theoretical intuition. Such a term is "evocative," that is, it evokes an *intuitive understanding* of something that cannot be put precisely into words. In other words, a meaning-nucleus is essentially indefinable. Epistemologically speaking, every definition is either a *tautology* (repeating the same thing) or a *petitio principii* (begging the question), or else reduces something to something else, thus cancelling the very particularity to be defined.

By means of concepts one can only point to what is intended, in the expectation of being intuitively understood. In such cases we therefore speak, not of a concept, but of an *idea*—the idea of "love" for instance, or the idea of justice, the idea of beauty, the idea of faith. An "idea" is sometimes also called a "boundary concept."

Since meaning-nuclei are "original," that is *irreducible to each other,* the term that designates a meaning-nucleus must also be a "final" word, an irreplaceable word; but such a word is hard to find. In the nature of the case, of course, it will always be possible to correct the hypothetical designation of a meaning-nucleus and replace it with a better one.

5.9 Distinctiveness of the modalities

Initially Dooyeweerd called the irreducible nature proper to the various modes of being the cosmological principle of "sphere-sovereignty." However, this worldview term, derived from Groen van Prinsterer (1801–1876) and Kuyper (1837–1920), is less suitable for scientific philosophy, because in the past it was used only for the distinctive nature

---

39. See Kalsbeek, *Contours of a Christian Philosophy*, pp. 97, 100.

and interrelation of concrete social structures such as state, church, family, school, and so on. *Philosophically speaking*, however, the basis for "sphere-sovereignty" was the practical, worldviewish recognition that everything created has a nature of its own. This recognition remains the basis for the philosophical elaboration of "sphere-sovereignty" that resulted in the theory of the elementary, foundational "elements" in reality, namely the theory of the modalities.

Accordingly, the distinctive nature of created things also implies the concept of *cosmological* sovereignty, that is, the *irreducibility* of all aspects that can be discovered in the cosmos. It is impossible without internal contradiction to reduce all liquids to different forms of water or to reduce all living creatures to a higher or lower species of animals. Nor is it possible to reduce faith to justice, to rationality or morality, or to see language as a form of thought, or vice versa: to see thought as a form of language. Beauty cannot be reduced to economy, nor to justice, and so on.

To disregard this cosmological principle of the irreducible distinctive nature of the aspects is inevitably, as regards science, to lapse into some or other "ism." Materialism proposes to reduce everything to matter, vitalism reduces everything to something organic, psychologism reduces everything to a feeling, logicism takes everything to be logically determined, moralism wants to reduce justice and faith to love, etc.

In this way Reformational philosophy can detect an *element of truth* in the various "isms" and schools of thought in science, but also their shortcoming: namely, that they fail to do justice to the irreducible distinctive nature of the other aspects and so come to *absolutize* what they regard as primary. They make something relative into something absolute, mistaking something aspectual for unity or fullness. Instead of distinguishing between qualifying and non-qualifying aspects, they reduce all aspects to variants of the one aspect or of the few aspects which they consider most important. This is the inexhaustible source of all "isms" in science.

The "element of truth" referred to above will now be explained in sections 10 and 11.

5.10 TWO KINDS OF ANALOGIES

As indicated, an aspect does not just consist of a nucleus. Each aspect can be said to be structurally connected with all the other aspects by so-called *analogical moments.* That is to say, each aspect contains not only the nucleus but also moments or elements that force us to think of the other aspects. We call these the analogical moments or analogical structural elements. "Analogical" means to say: for all the dissimilarity there is something similar as well.

"Growth movement," for instance, denotes not only an organic phenomenon (growth), but at the same time suggests the kinematic phenomenon of motion. If we talk about the great "distance" between a prime minister and his chauffeur, we are not referring to something spatial, because the distance between a minister and his chauffeur is sometimes very small indeed; rather, we are talking about a "social distance" which obtains even then. If we talk about "concept formation," we are referring to our activity of logical thought (in conceptualizing), but this also involves a form-giving element which is not logical but technical or formative in nature; in concept formation we *form or shape* various conceptual elements into a conceptual unity. Again, if we talk about the "emotional language" of a passionate speaker, and observe the marked difference compared with the dry-as-dust language of a legal document, we are not only talking about different kinds of *language* but also about sensitivity, which the term "emotional language" harks back to, as well as about the juridical element present in the typical legal texts of, say, a deed of sale.

All these examples involve a phenomenon that clearly goes with a certain aspect yet at the same time contains a reference to an earlier or later moment, that is to say, to something that brings to mind one of the previous or following aspects. In the case of analogies that point back to an earlier aspect we call them retrocipatory analogies or "retrocipations"; in the case of analogies that point forward to a later aspect we call them anticipatory analogies or "anticipations."

Some other examples of retrocipations are "jurisdiction" (in the sense of governing domain: the right to exercise authority within the limits of a specific spatial area so that certain laws apply only there), or also "aesthetic experience" (the enjoyment of hearing a beautiful piece of music). A jurisdiction is a juridically qualified entity that points back to the spatial modality; an aesthetic experience is an aesthetically qualified event that refers back to the sensitive modality.

Some examples of anticipation are these: when we talk about a feeling for language, a taste for beauty, a sense of justice, we are actually talking about *feelings*, that is to say, phenomena which belong to the sensitive ("psychical") aspect. But these are not just feelings without further qualification. Rather, they anticipate later aspects by pointing forward to, respectively, the aspects of language, the aesthetic aspect, and the aspect of justice. Thus they are anticipatory moments *within* the actual modality of the sensitive.

5.11 THE UNIVERSALITY OF EACH MODALITY

We have now looked at some examples of the phenomenon that every modality contains structural elements which refer to other aspects by means of analogies. In this way each and every modality reflects all reality according to all its aspects. We call this the *universality of each modality*.

Naturally the first aspect, that of number, does not have retrocipations, and the last aspect, that of faith, does not have anticipations. These are the two exceptions to the rule that all aspects are interwoven by means of anticipations and retrocipations. But it is true of every aspect, without exception, that it can be detected somewhere within all the other aspects in a non-original but *analogical* form, so that we can speak of the universality of every aspect throughout cosmic reality.

The phenomenon of the universality of every modal aspect explains the origin of many absolutizations in theory as well as practice. For all such absolutizations work with something that is actually true. They observe something real and get so deeply affected by it that they are barely capable of seeing anything else. Much is no longer seen in its irreducible nature but is reduced to that one truth. The result is socialism, capitalism, psychologism, logicism and rationalism, legalism, materialism, spiritualism, and so on. Thus in our own time there is a movement that may well be called "linguicism," an "ism" in which all kinds of diverse human functions are viewed as linguistic phenomena and all kinds of schools of thought as players in various "language games."

And yet, these absolutizations are virtually inevitable if people are unaware of the only correct remedy for all these "isms," namely, to see the *supra-modal* basis of unity of all the different functions. That basis lies in the human heart, which is transcendent and therefore overarches all diversity (including our intellectual labor, and all our other activities bound to time and place)—in the heart, that is, as the *fullness and unity* of all aspectual and functional diversity.

5.12 THE PROCESS OF DISCLOSURE IN HISTORY

The "universality" of every aspect, meanwhile, is more than the presence of all aspects in every other one. It is not a static quantity. There is a *dynamics* at work here, that is to say, movement—movement in a certain direction. At bottom we are referring here to the dynamics in all reality that is directed to God. It is implied in the biblical notion that "all things" are created *"unto God."*

But there is more to be said. This directedness to God also constitutes the religious quality of life in the sense that what it contains according to God's creative intention can also to a greater or lesser degree emerge from it. Sometimes we speak of a deepening or "enrichment" of our life. We can also use the more theoretical term "disclosure" here. There is always a *process of disclosure* going on in reality, a process which, in the *perverted form* of a dynamic directed-ness to idolatry, will manifest its very opposite as a *process of closure.*

In the practical language of everyday life we often also talk about progress or stagnation, about healthy growth or a downward slump. In short, the universality in which all aspects of life are connected with each other is a *process* that operates "dynamically" in life.

5.13 GOD'S LAW-ORDER AND MAN'S THEORY ABOUT IT

Universality shows that created reality exhibits an orderly sequence of intimate modal interwovenness. As Christian believers we can speak here of the divine *law-order.* Not, of course, that this divine law-order is identical to any theory about it in our philosophy. No, God's will and law have been clearly revealed, but not in such a way that we have them "ready to hand," that we can completely grasp them with our understanding.

The divine mystery of God's active presence has been revealed in his handiwork (in theology we talk about God's immanence, and also about "general revelation" or "creational revelation"). Nevertheless, our philosophical *theory about* this divine law-order is no more than a human attempt at approximation, a hypothesis and therefore a fallible human work, fundamentally open to correction. No more, but no less either.

I mean this: it is not a human fantasy that makes no sense at all. The divine law-order exists and God rules his creation through it. But our theoretical knowledge of it is undoubtedly inadequate and open to debate. However, in faith we know that we are not talking about human fantasies but about inadequate human theories regarding *fundamental realities* which in philosophy we also call the created *structures* of the cosmos.

5.14 ORDER AND DURATION

In sec. 5.11 we saw that the analogies within every modal aspect interweave all aspects with each other. But the theoretical analysis of this phenomenon is and remains an abstract activity. The analysis consists of *abstracting* the elements of concrete reality (the aspects with their nucleus and their analogical retrocipations and anticipations) *from* the real inner continuity of their actual modes of existence in concrete entities.

Hence this provisional theory of the interwovenness of the aspects by means of analogies can be said to display a shortcoming. For however closely it approximates the coherence of aspects by pointing to the clearly structured "mesh" of anticipatory and retrocipatory analogies and by pointing to their internal dynamics, yet this does not fathom the mystery of concrete reality itself. For concrete reality also displays, amid and among all its separate components and entities, an *integral continuity*. All those many aspectual elements cannot just be concretely seen and pointed out in reality.

The abstract theory about it is therefore, like all theory, basically directed to *the structural side* of reality, in other words: to the *law-side*, not to things themselves in subjective concrete reality. That is why we talked about the *coherence* of modalities in the divine *law*-order, *which is an order of interconnected and affiliated diversity of laws and norms within the whole of concrete reality.*

By definition, this recognized diversity of elements cannot be theoretically bridged, not even by the idea of a single law-order. Nor can this idea completely explain their internal coherence, interrelationship and dynamics. Our theory of the law-order, like every theory, remains necessarily confined within the logical (and all other) *diversity* which it presupposes. But deeper than this orderliness and coherence lies its inner *continuity*.

We saw earlier that the law does not exist without the subjectivity subject to it. And vice versa. Now then, the said *continuity*, which cannot be conceptually analyzed by means of even the most subtle distinctions, *is the concrete subjectivity which is correlate with the law-order.* This subjectivity—this quality of being subject to—can be interpreted via the *idea* (not "concept") of *universal time,* which as a continuous dynamics pervades all reality in all its dimensions and aspects and keeps it *internally* together. This universal time gives reality its *integral* coherence, which lies deeper than the "connection" of everything that we can theoretically (thus by abstraction) distinguish in it as elements.

Thus the law-order itself can also be understood as a temporal order, not only in the physical sense of clock time, but in the universal sense of the *cosmic* order of *time* in all aspects.

Temporal order and temporal duration are each other's correlate: they are, respectively, the law-side and the subject-side of "cosmic time" in all aspects of "temporal reality."

Chapter Six – Cosmology: Subjects and objects

CHAPTER SIX
COSMOLOGY: SUBJECTS
AND OBJECTS

6.1 DEFINING THE PROBLEM

In everyday language we distinguish between subjects and objects. Traditionally this language was influenced by theoretical-scientific thought. The influence was also reciprocal, the more so as science failed to distinguish between the law-side and the subject-side of reality. Partly as a result, scientific language displays considerable vagueness and confusion about the states of affairs referred to by the words subject and object.[40]

I believe that, given the philosophical view of reality that received its initial elaboration in the theory of modal aspects, we can gain a clearer insight into the problems that occur here. We approach the topic of subjects and objects from our understanding of the *meaning* of all creaturely existence in time. The conclusion we reached earlier was that we need to understand reality's mode of existence (*in time*, thus between origin and destination) as *a correlation between law and that which is subject to the law*. This means in the first place that objects, however further defined, are also subjects, in the sense that they belong to creaturely reality and are subject to the law(s) that hold for them.

Vollenhoven accordingly, when pronouncing the Dutch words, used to differentiate between "*sùb*jecten" and "subj*è*cten"; but this distinction was perhaps too subtle to be widely followed. The insight they express, however, remains fundamentally important for a Christian philosophical view of reality. Objects, too, are *subject* to the law-aspects that hold for them, just as the *relation* between subject and object is

---

40. Early Protestant scholasticism called "subject" what we today are mostly accustomed to call "object." Cf. Friedrich Mildenberger, *Grundwissen der Dogmatik*, 4th ed. (Stuttgart, 1995), p. 61.

subject to the law-aspects. So being an object does not detract from being subject(ed), but it is a *certain way* of being subject(ed), a way that is characterized by *being in relation to* an (acting) subject.

All this also has rather far-reaching consequences for philosophy of theology and for theology itself, as we will discuss at greater length later. For now we will just present the concept without elaborating on it. The problem of the subject-object relation is of concern to theology especially in hermeneutics, which must deal with the relation between truth and reality, in particular in the relation between myth, history and "story." This is also relevant to the question whether and *how far* one can agree with Rev. Nico ter Linden's notorious statement about the biblical "stories": "They are true but did not really happen."[41]

The subject-object problem is also important for dogmatics, which has to deal, among other things, with knowledge of God. It is a traditional theological issue whether God himself can be an "object" of theology, while probably many people in the West still wonder whether a human being can know God, and if so, how and with what certainty. We will consider this more closely in discussing the problem of truth and looking at the phenomenon of "interpretation."

The problem also presents itself when we ask whether and, if so, to what extent Scripture can be called an "object" of faith and/or theology. And the problem also plays an important role in traditional theology when it distinguishes between "subjectivism" and "objectivism," usually for unconscious reasons stemming from one philosophy or another.

The debate about all the problems just mentioned should be based in part on what we are discussing in this chapter and which must be applied later in epistemology and then in philosophy of theology. Once again this will reveal the error of assuming (as many orthodox theologians also do) that epistemology is a neutral, purely scientific technical instrument which does not affect the formulation and evaluation of the topics discussed. It is equally erroneous to see epistemology as a *theological* instrument the moment the discussion relates to statements or topics from the Bible.

---

41. (*Ed.*) Nico ter Linden: a popular preacher (b. 1936) in the national church, known for his appearances on TV and at national events, and for his modern retelling of the Bible stories under the title *Het verhaal gaat . . .* [The story goes . . .], 6 vols. (1996–2003).

6.2 SUBJECT-OBJECT SPLIT OR SUBJECT-OBJECT RELATION

The first thing to be said when theoretically analyzing the nature of subjects and objects is that we have to overcome the well-known and notorious subject-object "split." This is a wish that is found among many philosophers, including those of other persuasions than ours. Sometimes they rightly seek a unity, even a "higher unity." But this cannot succeed if subjects and objects remain *independent* entities opposite each other and if the only way out is to search for some *external* bridge or link, some overarching structure or balance between these two *independencies*. This tendency, by the way, is not uncommon in traditional dualistic views.

The habit of thinking marked by immanentism[42] and underlying this dualism does not recognize a *concentration* of temporal reality in a *temporally transcendent totality and unity*. Later we will discover once again how it is there, in that totality and unity, that the *internal coherence* of all diversity in reality is *anchored*.

The subject-object split can be overcome by means of the religiously determined *theoretical boundary insight* that the internal coherence in all empirical reality is given with the intra-temporal *world order* and the resulting interwovenness of "everything with everything," including subjects with other subjects and with objects. They do not stand alongside or opposite each other in an external relation of phenomena existing by themselves; rather, they are mutually dependent, not only in their concrete functioning but *in their very existence as such*. Starting from pre-theoretical experience, we can best illustrate this, to begin with, via the theory of modal aspects, though we will not always be able to avoid anticipating the subject-object relation in the theory of "entities" or "individuality structures" that we will deal with in the next chapter.

6.3 EVERYDAY EXPERIENCE AND THEORETICAL THOUGHT

In everyday life we often experience subjects and objects as two separate things. I am sitting here, my table is there and a chair is over there. But if we express our experience in a statement, schoolchildren already learn that such a statement or "sentence" can be divided

---

42. (*Ed.*) Immanentism: a brand of thought that does not reckon with a transcendent Creator and perforce has to seek the ground and integration of reality *within* the created order.

up into a subject, predicate and direct object. Subject and object are interconnected by the predicate, by an action word, a verb. Now then, *this holds not only for the linguistic representation of the experience, but also for the experienced reality about which the statement is made.*

Kant denies this actual interconnectedness because he makes human thought (at least in his philosophical work) so absolute that it is fundamentally *separated* from all non-thought. Nevertheless, he does realize that he has reached the limit of his intellectual powers. His thesis therefore is that the thing in itself, as it is in itself, is unknowable. In his view, *"das Ding an sich,"* the actual thing, is therefore located in another world, whereas the concrete thing that I can see standing in front of me is only a "phenomenon." This view derives originally from Plato.

This, then, is the theoretical subject-object split, the gap that many philosophers through the centuries have sought to bridge, challenged by the simple everyday experience of reality. Their attempts failed because they persisted in starting with the split, with a dualism, namely the *"Gegen-ständ-lichkeit"* of all objects standing opposite "thought." That thought had also been substantialized, abstracted from the concrete thinking human being in the fullness of his life, and from his rootedness in religion and culture.

Sometimes Kant interprets the *thinking "I"* in somewhat the same way as our philosophy talks about the human *heart.* As a consequence, he absolutizes thinking in relation to all other human functions, as if man's entire humanity is concentrated in his intellect. Originally this view was mainly inspired by Aristotle. Aristotle saw the human intellect as the highest and defining part of man. This led to the classical philosophical tradition in which *man himself* was seen as an *"animal rationale,"* a creature *defined by reason.*

That "opposite" stance (*Gegen-stand*) is a certain kind of "relation" all right, but it is an artificial one—*at least in one* (historically evolved) *type of thought,* namely theoretical thought. When we come to discuss epistemology we will look at the difference between, on the one hand, pre-scientific thought, which is woven into the nature of all human functioning in all normative aspects, and on the other hand, scientific or theoretical thought.

In relation to scientific thought there is actually a certain element of truth in the theory of the so-called "subject-object split." Traditional philosophic thought usually realizes this but expresses it in a distorted way. Scientific thought does indeed contain a specific, albeit artificial, "Gegenstand relation," a relation of opposition that is not present in the practical thought of our everyday experience, not even as we relate to something that we experience as "strange." For even as we relate to something as "strange" we are giving a certain subjective, concrete qualification of this relation as we encounter and experience it. The subject-object relation is a *reciprocal relation*. Moreover, we should distinguish here between potential and real, between latent and disclosed. The following example may clarify this further.

6.4 EXAMPLE: THE VISIBILITY OF A CHAIR

Take the visibility of concrete objects, for instance of a chair. We could call this visibility a "quality" or property of the chair. In our everyday life we experience this visibility as something of the chair itself, and not as something that we have (mentally) added to the chair. In our everyday experience a chair *itself* is visible. That is to say, the chair is visible on a fundamental level, or in principle. Obviously the chair can be made actually invisible by changing the circumstances (a hidden place or lack of light). But this does not detract from the *possibility* of seeing the chair, thus from its visibility. Hence objects are often latent (hidden), while they can be made patent (laid open, dis-closed). This, too, belongs to the existence of the chair, to its "essence" as it used to be said. In Reformational philosophy this laying open is therefore called "dis-closure." In principle the visibility is implicit in the chair itself, in the chair as such. It needs only to be disclosed. This process of dis-closure pervades our entire life.

The above argument assumes that the chair is an object *in relation to* subjects, and specifically in a *sensitive* relation. Potentially there are human or animal subjects that stand in a sensitive or sensory relation to *this* chair. Whereas humans, animals and also chairs are without exception subjects—subject (subjected), that is to say, to a whole series, large or small, of distinctive laws—chairs are always objects in (a *possible*) relation to sensitive subject functions of humans or animals. The relation between subjects and objects is therefore reciprocal, though not always actual (in the sense of concretely present). This reciprocal relation is always there potentially, but it becomes actual only when the subject-object relation is "realized" or "actualized"; so in our example: the relation is realized in the actual *seeing* by a human being and the *being seen* of the chair within the full concreteness of this human being and this chair in their reciprocal relation to each other.

6.5 Object functions, formerly "primary and secondary qualities"

At an early stage already, philosophy began to pay attention to the difference between the various "properties" of things. An apple's size and hardness, its juiciness or ripeness are different qualities compared to, say, taste or smell. The former qualities are called "primary," the latter "secondary." But why? Is it enough to say that the "primary" qualities are in the apple itself, whereas the "secondary" are only subjective human experiences? And why might an apple not have still other qualities which can be classified under other kinds, for example visibility, knowability, cheapness or dearness, cultivatability, being owned by, being beautiful or ugly, being an object of faith, and so on?

Applying now our philosophical orientation scheme of the theory of aspects, we can define the traditional "primary" qualities more exactly as spatial and physical "qualities," and the "secondary" qualities as, for instance, psychical (sensitive) "qualities." But we can go further and observe that all those other qualities mentioned above have their own real existence too. These are often denoted by a word in which the suffix "able" or "ability" occurs. But in every case we see that all these so-called "qualities" exist only in a relation, namely in the subject-object relation. We therefore prefer to call these "qualities" *object functions*, while at the same time terms like being countable, measurable, edible, visible, beautiful, nameable, marketable, and so on, express the relation to people who exercise their various *subject functions* in the subject-object relations referred to.

Thus a Communion cup is not simply a cup, but an object of faith that does not just derive its "nature," its *distinctiveness*, from the cup form, nor from the tin or silver material, but from its function in the faith life of the congregation. To mention another example: the Bible, even scientifically speaking, is not just an ordinary book, not just a literary-historical object, but a book evoking people's belief (or unbelief) by virtue of its content. This relation, too, latent or actualized, belongs to the full reality of the book.

6.6. THINGS CAN EXIST IN MANY WAYS

All the subjective functions of entities in all aspects have their opposite in objects, which are object functions of the same or of other entities. The subjective spatial function of the measurable extension of a thing stands opposite to the objective measurable extension of another thing, so that they reciprocally delimit or even exclude each other: where this stone lies, no other stone can lie at the same time. A human person's *subjective* sensitive function has its opposite in the stone's *objective* functions of sensitively perceived (experienced) heat, cold, roughness, smoothness, visibility, nameability, beauty, and so on. This sensitive objectivity *on the one hand* is potentially *proper* to things like stones; *on the other hand* it can only really function as such in an actual connection with the *subjective sensitive functions of a human being or an animal*.

In the actualization of what is already there potentially, that is to say, in the experience (perception) of these object functions, these functions are fundamentally *dis-closed* as "qualities" that are latently present. Thus it is possible to see the entire concrete experience of reality as being involved in a cosmic process of disclosure which for a large part is historically founded. For instance, it was apparently not until the eleventh and twelfth centuries that people developed an "open eye" for the *beauty* of a mountain landscape like the Alps.

In the logical aspect we speak of a stone's knowability, in the economic aspect of its price or valuation, in the aesthetic aspect of its beauty or ugliness. In the juridical aspect the stone can be owned by someone; in the faith aspect the stone can be seen as one of God's creatures. Another example: in the faith aspect the Bible as a book can be the Word of God or (in the case of inadequate faith or lack of faith) no more than a collection of ancient literature; and so on. A stone or a Bible or a wedding ring or anything at all can function as an *object* in every aspect, but always *in relation to* a subject function, such as analyzing, fashioning, naming, owning, appreciating as beautiful, cherishing, believing that the object is part of creation, estimating, determining or paying its economic value, and so on.

All this is schematically represented in Figure 1 of the Appendix.

6.7 Object functions can also be qualifying functions in entities

Reality is unthinkable without the subject-object relation between human and non-human creatures (things, plants, animals). In the case of non-human realities these subject-object relations are usually more important than things "in themselves," that is: things theoretically separated (abs-tracted) from their real connection with people. Thus tools, vehicles, houses, statues, a traffic sign, a piece of music, a Bible are in reality much more than just compounds of molecules, vibrations, light waves, materials, and so on. Their reality is much richer. The things just listed are in fact examples of identity structures that have their guiding or qualifying aspect (their "destination function") not in their own highest *subject* function but in one of their many object functions with which they are interwoven into human life and by means of which, conversely, the human mode of existence is interwoven *into* the "outside world," the world "surrounding" it.

(The latter terms, by the way, should be taken with a grain of salt: what we call the "outside world" is so *integrally interwoven* with our human subjectivity that the so-called *"subject-object split"* can be little more than a faulty mental construction, an erroneous fantasy that is reinforced by terms like "surroundings" and "outside world." The terms in quotation marks, when not used in a practical but in a theoretical context, may betray the influence of an absolutization of sensitive perceptibility, as if these sensitive object functions were the most important.)

Accordingly, we call a statue an (aesthetic) *art* object, a Communion cup or a pulpit or a pew Bible *religious* objects, an axe with which a murder has been committed a *juridical* object (a *"corpus delicti"*), a manufacturing plant an *economic* object, a wedding ring an *ethical* object, and so on.

6.8 An illustration by way of summary

As an entity structure a valuable painting does not have its guiding or qualifying function in the physical-chemical aspect, in which it surely has its highest *subject* function, but rather in its aesthetic *object* function, so in the aesthetic aspect where human aesthetic contemplation and art appreciation typically belong. But this object function remains "latent" or "closed" (hidden) if it is not actualized and thus "disclosed." This is the case when the painting is stored in a safe as an investment on account of its high market value (i.e., its economic object function). But no sooner is it hung in a living room or a museum, than its qualifying aesthetic object function is *disclosed* and the painting achieves its destination. The formulation sometimes used for this is that the *"destination function"* lies in the guiding or qualifying modality. But this destination does not come into its own in the "closed" situation, though it does form a "latent" part of the painting's full reality.

In this way all non-human "nature" is disclosed in human "culture" when the *potential* cultural functions of the non-human are *actualized*. Thus this potential definitely belongs to the reality of the objects involved. Next, the *latent* object functions, which are typical of, for example, semi-manufactures, tools, bricks, paint varieties, musical instruments, and so on, also need to be *disclosed in the actualization* (i.e., realization) of these object functions in relations to the many subject functions of human beings. This happens for instance when we assemble a bookcase out of pre-cut wood, paint a room, build a house, play the piano, administer baptism, and so on and so forth.

CHAPTER SEVEN –
COSMOLOGY: ENTITIES

CHAPTER SEVEN
COSMOLOGY: ENTITIES

7.1 TWO COSMIC DIMENSIONS

7.1.1 RECALLING FIGURE 1

In describing the object functions we anticipated the subject of "entities." These we will discuss now. We classified the concrete things of reality into a number of realms or kingdoms, including the kingdom of animals and the kingdom of plants. We then distinguished: numbers, space, motions, things, plants, animals and human beings. Though only provisional, this was the principal classification of concrete creatures, an orientation scheme that connects firmly with our primary experience of reality. With regard to these realities our concepts are still often "impressions," firmly tied to sensory images in our concrete and full experience of reality.

7.1.2 PRIORITY OF THE THEORY OF ASPECTS

It was intentional that we discussed the theory of modal aspects or *modes* of being first, and then distinguished it sharply from a second dimension, that of the more concrete entities. We had to do this because the *scientific* analysis of reality, by whatever discipline, does not give us a theoretical perspective on our "object of inquiry" except *via the gateway* of fundamental aspectual concepts. These fundamental concepts, you will recall, relate to the *several aspects* of full reality, to their nuclei and their analogical elements (anticipations and retrocipations). These are those key concepts ("categories") like the spatial, the physical, the vital, the lingual, the juridical, and so on.

In every scientific discipline, theories are always formulated in concepts which, without exception, approach the object of inquiry from the perspective of some or other *aspectual mode of being*. An example: if we use the expression "depth psychology" we approach our object of inquiry via the gateways of both the sensitive aspect ("psycho-")

and the spatial aspect (in the metaphor "depth"). A second example: a farmer will differ from an artist when looking at a given landscape, and a land developer will look at it differently from a lawyer. Everybody, including the non-scientist, but certainly the scientist, can look at a certain part of reality from a different viewpoint than others do.

Let us take another example, this time from theology. Someone who uses theological arguments in theological discourse does more than just apply logic (in the case of dogmatics) or literary and textual theory (in the case of exegesis). The subject of the discourse each time is implicitly approached as a *topic for faith*, involving the use of some or other *faith concept*. After all, theology is the science of people's faith-life. When theologians talk about "heaven," for example, they are not posing a question of cosmography as to the location of heaven in the universe. Nor are they asking whether heaven is "a place or a condition." Both questions are uninteresting to theology; or rather, they are inadmissible. The Bible is a religious, not a scientific book; its truths are religious, not scientific. Heaven is a faith object that may only be treated by theology in the manner of faith. Only faith questions are appropriate, not theoretical questions of science. Not even theology should try to get "beyond" this.

That is also the reason why speculation about the (creaturely) duration of a day of creation leads to putting an inadmissible question to the Bible. The days of creation were God's days, of which Scripture teaches that they cannot be counted and measured by our measurement of time, even though human language is employed to talk about them ("evening and morning," "the fourth day"). For God, a day is like a thousand years and a thousand years like a day: immeasurable, incalculable for us. When Genesis 1 talks about creatures being created on a certain day we are not dealing with a *physical* question about the duration of that day but only with the religious question of the Origin, the "beginning," the *Archè* of these creatures. Following in the footsteps of Paul we may even extend this question to that of the destination: Why created? And to what end? The answer: they were created *"unto* God."

7.1.3 DEFINING THE PROBLEM

For the sake of brevity we are talking in the present context about the cosmic dimension of the modal aspects or modes of being, *and* about the cosmic dimension of the various concrete structures. In other words: the dimensions of *modalities* and *entities*.

How, now, are these two dimensions connected? To raise this question is to ask: what is the relation between *concrete "things"* (things in the broad sense of the word, so "entities," concrete "somethings") and their cosmic *aspects*? To answer this question, we will be looking in sec. 7.2 for the "bridge" between the theory of the modal aspects of "things" and the theory of concrete "things."

7.1.4 TERMINOLOGY

We need to start with a few terminological remarks. The term "things" is unsatisfactory. By a thing we mean a concrete object, usually a so-called "lifeless" thing. But as we shall see later, the building pattern, the architecture of a "thing" is very similar to the "structure" of all kinds of other concrete "phenomena" in reality. Some or other *"thing-structure"* is also typical of concrete actions, social relations, action situations, events, organs, plants, animals, works of art, business firms, elements of all of the above, and so on and so forth. In short, a "thing-structure" is typical of everything that is a concretely existing and functioning *something*.

The ancient philosophers would say: it is typical of a *being* (in Greek: *to on*, hence the name ontology or (general) theory of being; in Latin: an *ens*, in English: an *entity*). Dooyeweerd's starting-point here is *an individual something*, in distinction from a species, and he therefore talks about an individuality, the building plan of which he calls an *individuality structure*. Henk van Riessen and others prefer to speak of an *entity* with an *identity structure*.

It is inadvisable to use terms like "being" or "ontology" in our own philosophical discourse. Naturally everybody is allowed to be lazy every now and then, or adapt to the language of his discussion partner or adopt ordinary speech; but these words are definitely unsuitable in our own systematics. They carry pagan connotations which cannot be "transformed" into a Christian context. These philosophical terms rely entirely on the idea of an existence by itself, apart from God. There is an unbridgeable gap between the Greek philosophical concept of being (*to on*) and the Christian view of reality.

The term "phenomenon," which is firmly established in general usage, also bears a heavy burden from the history of classical metaphysics. Metaphysics distinguished between, on the one hand a constant and invisible *essence* of things, knowable only to the in-sight of theoretical reason, and on the other hand the variable sensory *phenomenon* (from Greek: "to appear"), which is not *true* reality and knowable only by the senses (Plato and Aristotle). In current non-scientific usage the term phenomenon is usually innocuous, that is to say, it no longer carries its original, literal meaning.

7.2 THE BRIDGE BETWEEN THE MODAL DIMENSION AND ENTITIES

(a) Our theoretical analysis of concrete empirical data presented us not only with a survey of the "kingdoms" of concrete entities, but also with a large number of *modal aspects* or *modes* of existing and functioning (the theory of modalities). The latter constitute the theoretical "angles" or points of view from which we can scientifically approach concrete entities. But these "angles" have enabled us to identify only the distinctive approach used in a given discipline. We have not yet advanced beyond distinguishing and further analyzing *aspects* and their interweaving retrocipations and anticipations along with the fundamental concepts and metaphors based on them. This still does not mean that we are able to account for the *internal unity, continuity and totality* of the phenomenon under investigation. On the contrary, the unity, continuity and totality of this bit of reality, precisely because it is reality, are *presupposed* as we distinguish modal aspects in that phenomenon or, as the case may be, in its parts.

Our *"naive experience"* of things in their concreteness, as well as the act of logical distinguishing inherent in this "naive experience" in the ordinary practical use of "common sense," *are foundational to theoretical concepts*. Practical empirical knowledge—so-called "naive" knowledge —precedes any theoretical distinguishing and *continues to form the basis* of scientific, aspectual conceptualization. This practical use of the mind relates to the *concrete* dimension of reality that we now turn to.

Scientific conceptualization always presupposes this practical, pre-scientific or non-scientific conceptualization. All its theoretical concepts relate to certain modal (aspectual) figures. The less this is the case, the poorer the *scientific* quality. In our time much is presented as "science" that is little more than a passing on of somewhat ordered practical experience in a limited field by a man or woman "on the ground." This can be very useful and necessary, but it is hardly *science*, not even if a university chair is established for it.

The present fashionable aversion to "abstract" science whose practical usefulness or "social relevance" is not immediately evident, is not beneficial for the quality of science. By its very nature science is primarily called to search for *abstract scientific truth*, regardless of its practical value, even if that is a legitimate issue. We should also remember that scientific truth is never "the full truth." This also applies to theological truths.

(b) Meanwhile, thanks to theoretical analysis of the aspects in which the concretely given functions, these very modal aspects provide us with an indication for acquiring insight into the *totality structure* of concrete entities. Take for instance the *juridical aspect*. *All entities function in this aspect*. When we consider a state, a church and a private association (say, a bowling club) from the perspective of the juridical aspect (in which justice is therefore the qualifying nucleus) we discover within this aspect of these three instances that a *different kind of individuality* is typical of constitutional law, church law and association law. We speak in this case of "types of law." That is to say that these three social structures function in three different ways within the same juridical aspect. In these different spheres of life justice demands a distinct type and character of law, in close connection with the nature or goal of the social structure in question. Not all law is the same law.

"Church law," for example, is different from criminal law or civil law. It is therefore right that the subject "church law" is not taught in law schools but in theological seminaries or in departments of theology. In a theology curriculum a course in church law has in common with other courses that it discusses issues related to something that is modally qualified by the faith aspect, namely the church (cf. sec. 7.3.2 below).

The "atmosphere" and manner in which justice is applied is different in each case. The subjective experience of law likewise differs in the internal spheres of state life, church life and an association. Someone who, in the daily operation of a church or an association, applies the relevant legal or customary rules (church law, association by-laws) as if they were public state laws or the legal terms drawn up by a notary public is soon liable to be known as a "formalist."

Whenever church law is used "purely formally" in a church or a denomination, for instance with the principled argument that "church law is law" or "that is what the Church Order says," it may indicate that brotherly love or the awareness of a common bond of faith in the one Body of Christ is weak or has even disappeared among the church members as the result of some secondary cause. Usually it is also a symptom of absolutizing (deifying) what is historically relative, namely church law, or one particular theological interpretation of Scripture.

Apparently juridical functioning *differentiates* or *specifies* itself into these three (and many other) *typical modes* within the juridical aspect. Church law is an entirely different type of law compared with the constitution of a sports club, or commercial law, criminal law, marriage law, martial law, and so on. (Incidentally, in our philosophy the use of the adjective "typical" always relates to types, in the sense of "kinds" of entities; see also the next two paragraphs.)

(c) Thus, to mention another example, human love specifies itself into the *typically* different ways in which love functions between spouses (marital love), between parents and children (familial love), and between friends (affection). The general heading "love of neighbor" does not allow love to be expressed everywhere in the same form. I must love my "neighbors," the lady next door or my secretary, just as I must love my wife, but each time in an entirely different, typical way!

Another example: the organic function of reproduction specifies itself into various (modal) *types* in plants, animals and man, and within these types into many *subtypes,* such as seed plants, spore-bearing plants, insects, birds, mammals, etc. Thus (to mention one more example) within the modal economic aspect there is a difference between the modes of economic functioning in, say, political economy, business economy, regional economy, home economy, church economy. The members of these communities or working associations do not always have the same "rights and duties" financially speaking (think of a family with small growing children); they do not always need to "cut their coat according to their cloth" but sometimes must be prepared to budget for deficits or debts. In certain situations people may say: first we will determine how much we need to spend and then we will organize the revenues (this is not infrequent in the context of a faith community). In a family it is usually the other way round.

(d) Accordingly, it is *within* the general modalities in which concrete entities function that we already discover the *individuality* of these entities *expressed on a modal level,* in *types* of modal functioning. The general structure of modal aspects admits of a diversity of more concrete *specifications in the functioning* within this modal structure. This means that within concrete entities, which function in all aspects, this functioning is woven into a certain aspect in a way that is related to the distinctive type of these entities. As soon as we refer to these *types* of entities, we speak in this sense of "typical." Thus in the lingual aspect of a statement we can distinguish between technical language, typical poetic language, children's language, biblical language, and so on.

The modal aspects in which entities function are therefore present in these entities in a *modal-typical* way. We can generalize this and say: *the modal dimension of the aspects of reality is woven into the dimension of entities in a modal-typical way.*

Thus marital love is different from friendship, sculpture different from poetry, home economics from political economy, interaction with neighbors from interaction with fellow passengers in a streetcar, church law from criminal law or property law. And theological language, if it is properly theological, is different from pulpit language.

But apart from this it remains true that all things function in all aspects.

The *modal types* of the aspectual functions are therefore the bridge between "things" and their "aspects," or more precisely: between thing-*structures* and the *structures* of the other aspects.

7.3 THE TOTALITY STRUCTURE OF ENTITIES

7.3.1 THE IDEA OF A THING AS UNITY AND TOTALITY

The term "totality structure" in the heading of this section refers to something of which, at least scientifically, we do not have a *concept* in the strict sense of the word. We do have an *idea* of it. The "idea" of a totality structure refers to the structure or architecture of "things" in our concrete empirical reality and is *approached* from the perspective of the modal concepts relating to the spatial aspect. "Structure" is, after all, a term which literally points to layers stacked on top of each other, while "totality" points to a whole in which parts can be distinguished.

These *modal, aspectual* (in this case spatial) terms *point to* something that must signify much more than just the spatial aspect of things. This "image," this metaphor *points to* the *idea* of the thing-totality, which embraces an *inner, integral unity* of its distinguishable moments or components, and embraces that unity *continuously*, for as long as the "thing" exists.

7.3.2 FOUNDING AND QUALIFYING ASPECTS

In order to be able to distinguish *this* concrete thing here from *that* thing there—to designate the two *different* things properly—we need criteria and orientation. Pre-theoretical, "naive" experience easily and promptly distinguishes between a cow and a tree, between a company and a family, without using any theoretical criterion. But in a theoretical approach, in which we come at a given reality from aspectual points of view using concepts of modal function, we must, in order to grasp the thing-totality, link up with those modal aspects that play a very special role in the whole. For all entities we find two such aspects, which we call the *founding* and the *qualifying* aspects.

As an example we mention a "thing" (a concrete activity) like eating bread. This can be an ordinary daily activity with the family which we call for instance "having breakfast"; but it can also be a typical religious activity, namely when we are partaking of the Lord's Supper. What matters is which aspect *qualifies* the activity as a whole.

7.3.3 RADICAL FUNCTIONS ("NUCLEAR ASPECTS")

We can say of a marriage, as of all entities, that it functions in all aspects; but in this case we can also say that the moral love aspect, containing the modal-typical marital love, is the *qualifying* aspect. That is why marriage can be called a community of love. Marital love, however, also has a typically organic foundation, the biotically qualified, modal-typical figure of gender difference and sexual intercourse. Thus the biotic sexual function and the moral love function are the two dominant functions that are most *characteristic* of the entire construction of the entity type "marriage." Reformational philosophy also refers to them as the two *radical functions*. The biotic aspect contains the *founding* function of marriage, the love aspect the *internal destination* function. I will clarify the latter term after the following subsection.

7.3.4 EXAMPLES

I first want to give some more *examples,* without going into detail. A company is *qualified* by the economic aspect and *founded* in the historical aspect (in the formative power of capital in the organizational substructure).

A state is *qualified* by the juridical aspect as a community of law, and within that by the *public-legal* way it functions. Thus it is does not function in terms of church law, as "theocrats" would like to see, nor in terms of commercial law. But the state is *founded* in the historical aspect, in its monopoly of armed force ("the power of the sword") over a circumscribed territory.

A church is an organized community of faith, *qualified* by the faith aspect, and *founded* in the organized administration of church functions, principally and usually by "office-bearers." In terms of content the latter "give form" to the life and thought of the members in this church community—so again typically something in the historical aspect.

A plant is *qualified* by the biotic mode of being (the organic functions) but *founded* in a substructure which is qualified by its functions in the physical-chemical aspect or, colloquially speaking, in "matter."

7.3.5 THE INTERNAL DESTINATION FUNCTION IS A GUIDING FUNCTION

(a) The *internal destination function* mentioned above (sec. 7.3.3) was referred to earlier (in sec. 7.3.2) as the *qualifying* aspect. We can also speak here of the *guiding* aspect or the guiding function. In the theory of aspects and/or functions, after all, we are not dealing with *static* entities but with *actual functioning* (that is, *active* functioning) in certain *ways,* in "modi," in "modal" ways of existing and functioning.

(b) The whole of each entity is engaged in an enormous amount of activity. Reality is "dynamic." The "thing" *functions* in all aspects, not just in those aspects in which the entities have *subject functions.* But *the way in which* a given entity functions in a certain aspect cannot be explained on the basis of that aspect alone. The physical-chemical processes in a plant are *different* from comparable processes in the soil in which it grows, because the former are *encapsulated* in living organisms. The organic aspect of life *guides* what takes place in the physical-chemical functioning of a plant.

Another example: when a husband and wife respect each other's *rights* in a healthy marriage, this doing *justice* to each other is not a purely juridical, formal "correctness," which is also possible in the relation between a well-bred unmarried gentleman and his house-keeper, or between a supervisor and his female staff member. Justice should be done in all relationships, but in a marriage this juridical functioning is *guided* by—colored, stamped, one can also say *qualified* by—the moral love function. To put it somewhat poetically: the entire experience of marriage, including the "rights and duties" in it, is overlaid by "the glow of love," also the element of doing *right* by each other. The structure of marriage therefore has its internal *destination* function not in juridical impeccability but in marital *love*, the love that also allows internal and external marriage *law* to blossom.

A final illustration: one of the functions of our faith is a logically qualified activity. A believer distinguishes and reflects. But faith is much more than this. Faith is first of all to believe in God's Word, affirming it *a priori* in submission, trust, obedience and love. I say "*a priori*," so not *on the basis* of theological inquiry or apologetic arguments. The reflecting or logical distinguishing that is necessarily interwoven with faith is not its *qualifying* function. If it is, that is to say, if believing is identified with thinking—people with different beliefs are often said to be people with different "ideas"—then it is rightly called intellectualism, an over-rationalization or over-theorization of faith. This sort of faith need not just be *complemented* with emotionality, pietism, "spirituality," and so on, but it needs to *change* into real and heart-felt *believing*.

(c) The addition "internal" (to "destination function" in our penultimate illustration) is necessary, because we are not dealing here with some or other *external* objective. Spouses can make a concrete marital relationship subservient to many objectives which have nothing to do with the *internal* nature of a marriage. A married couple can make itself available, for example, for mission work, for a charitable cause, for scientific research (think of Pierre and Marie Curie), for increasing the population of a country or the membership of a particular church or community of faith, etc. etc. But these are all external options. In the entire complexity of its functioning in all aspects, the *internal normative structure* of marriage (and of every other entity) always has one aspect in which its functioning *guides* the functioning in all the other aspects. This is therefore what we call the *internal destination function* that all other functioning within this entity is (or should be) *attuned to*.

Another example: as a community of faith the church has as its *internal* destination function to nurture and build the common Christian *faith*. At the same time all kinds of circumstances or emergency situations may mean that the church pursues external objectives which do not, strictly speaking, belong to its proper task, such as supporting or condemning a certain public policy, caring for the poor, organizing theological training for ministers, and so on. If we make one of these external objectives the main or primary duty, we obstruct a correct view of the true nature of the church organization and confuse main issues and side-issues, necessity and desirability, defining tasks and incidental tasks.

7.3.6 IDENTITY STRUCTURE

(a) Above, in sec. 7.1.4, we encountered the term *"entity structure,"* a term for which I (in company with Henk van Riessen) have a slight preference over Dooyeweerd's "individuality structure." Be that as it may, the entire building plan, the "architecture" of a "thing," is called the *"structure."* And it is thanks to this structure that the "thing" is a separate entity, a (human or non-human) *individuality*.

This is also how we *experience* the things around us. In *"naive" experience* we are not conscious of the many separate functions in the various aspects of things. Instead we see, use and experience things *in their totality and unity*, and in this way we experience their *identity*. Even without theoretical analysis we know what we are dealing with.

In his laboratory a biochemist is perhaps able to draw up a whole list of all the organic and inorganic substances present in a glass of wine. But at a banquet he will drink and enjoy the wine in the same way as his table companions who know nothing about biochemistry. I know nothing about engines, but I hope I use my car as efficiently as a car mechanic does his.

(b) So it is not the case that philosophy invents this unity and totality after the fact, as a logical construction. Rather, this *unity and totality* of things is "transcendental," that is to say: it is *a priori*. This means that it is the reality of this unity and totality itself which makes our "naive" experience possible to begin with, and this experience in turn is the basis for any *theoretical* distinguishing and abstracting of the various *functions and aspects of* this unity.

7.3.7 KANT'S DING AN SICH

The philosopher Immanuel Kant, and many following him, turned this fact around. In Kant's view, we experience only *aspects* of things, which he called their "secondary properties," for instance their sensory perceptibility. The actual "Ding an sich" ("the *being*" in ancient philosophy) lies behind and beneath these properties, and that, he says, we cannot know. The actual thing in its unity and totality, according to Kant, is but a *hypothesis*, albeit a necessary one.

In this line of thinking, however, our practical experience of life is over-theorized. Not separate functions or aspects are *given* to us, while concrete things are mere hypotheses, but it is the other way round: we experience the concrete unity, identity and totality of things *in* and *despite* the multiplicity of aspects and functions that we can distinguish *in* them after adopting a detached, theoretical, abstract point of view. That is why the *identity* of things is *given* in their unity and totality. That is why we *experience* that hammer, that tree, this coat, that child as *always the same*, despite and throughout the changes that take place *in* them in the course of time and in the changing of the seasons, as they are worked over and wear down or grow and expand. Hence the term *"identity structure."*

7.3.8 THE IDENTITY STRUCTURE IS AN INTERNAL
STRUCTURAL LAW OR STRUCTURAL PRINCIPLE

The identity structure of concrete "things" has the character of a law. It is the *internal structural law for entities,* forming part of the entire *law-side* of reality. This guarantees the coherence between the diversities within things, as it also guarantees their unity, totality and identity. When dealing with entities of which the qualifying aspect is one of the *normative aspects* (as distinct from the law aspects: see Figure 1, numbers 7 through 15), we do not speak of an internal structural *law* but of an internal structural *principle*. Those normative aspects appeal to man's freedom *to give form to* the structural *principles* of human actions, situations and relationships. Below, in praxeology, we will discuss the process of "norming" and positivizing, and address the question of what "principles" are.

7.3.9 THE DIVISION OF ENTITIES INTO TYPES

(a) The first and provisional orientation in "kingdoms," which we gave in sec. 7.1.1, can now be enlarged upon. All animals have their internal destination function in the instinctive-sensitive, the "psychical" aspect. As entities they are *qualified* by this aspect *as* animals, in contradistinction to all other entities. In this aspect they have their last ("highest") *subject* function. Thus plants have their last subject function in the organic aspect and on that basis they are classified as belonging to the plant kingdom. Material entities that lack the *subjective* organic function form the kingdom of minerals, alongside the plant and animal kingdoms. A group of entities that differs from another group through the number and make-up of its subject functions is called a *radical type*.

(b) But the radical type of "animal kingdom," qualified therefore by the psychical aspect, not only includes the animals themselves, but also their objective *"formations,"* such as a nest, a snail's shell, *"symbiotic communities"* such as a colony of ants or a parasitic relationship. Likewise the same psychically qualified (here as well *objectively* psychically qualified) radical type includes the biosphere, on which the various types of animals depend as their necessary condition for life: the leaf as the living environment of aphids, the sea as the environment for plankton, fungi in relationship with certain wild orchids, and so on. The so-called "biosphere" is therefore not qualified by its last (biotic) *subject* function, but by its biotic or psychical *object* function in relation to the subject functions of plants or animals.

(c) *Within the radical types*, which therefore cannot be reduced to one another, as evolutionism claims, there are other subtypes which cannot be reduced to each other either. Within the animal type, for example, are found the subtypes insects, fishes, amphibians, mammals, birds. We call these subtypes *genotypes*, with various sub-subtypes like families, species and so on.

(d) When there are types that differentiate themselves into various subtypes owing to external environmental influences, we talk about *variability types*. These include many cultivars in the plant kingdom and breeds in the animal kingdom.

(e) Finally there are the "borderline cases." Microscopically small entities include some specimens of which it is impossible to say with certainty whether they belong to the plant or the animal kingdom. But such borderline cases would not exist if there were no borderlines.

7.3.10 Between realism and nominalism

(a) Thus we can see that the *identity, unity* and relative *durability* or *continuity* of things or entities is guaranteed by their law of existence, which in this chapter we have called the *internal structural law* (or structural principle) or also *identity structure*. With this theory we occupy an intermediate position between the two philosophical traditions that dominate the problem of classification in the various special sciences. The earliest tradition is that of *realistic metaphysics*.

This tradition wanted to account for the relatively continuous identity of things despite our experience of their changing forms and properties. It sought this identity in something which apparently was not perceptible by the senses and presumably accessible only to reason. Thus Greek philosophy introduced the idea of an enduring *"essence"* above, behind or within the variable and transient phenomena. Our rational knowledge of things was supposed to focus on this "essence," for knowledge of the changing phenomena was always outdated; it turned false as soon as the phenomenon changed. We only knew the enduring thing itself when we knew its *essence*, which apparently was inaccessible to our *senses*.

(b) This idea, chiefly elaborated by Plato and Aristotle, is not as absurd as was later claimed by nominalism. Realism had hit upon something which guarantees the actual durability, the relevant constancy and identity of things. These "essential features" do not in fact lie only in objective, sensory qualities. Instead, according to the alternative of Christian philosophy, they lie in the *structural type*, the internal law of existence for things. This is very different from the supernatural, static "essence" that Plato considered *above* and Aristotle *in* things, as an "ideal form" knowable only to theoretical reason and separate from the *material content* that we perceive only through our senses.

The insoluble problem of realism is therefore the question how "form" ("idea") and "matter" can together be a *"substantial unity,"* an *"essential unity,"* since they are fundamentally alien to each other. Of course there are many attempts to overcome this dualism, for instance in the idea of the copy theory (Plato), of inherent purpose or teleology ("form" in "matter": Aristotle), the idea of participation (Thomas Aquinas).

(c) *Nominalism* rejected this platonizing *idea-lism* and said: only what we experience empirically is real. We know this horse and that horse, but not *the* horse. *The* horse is just a *name* (Latin: *nomen*, plural: *nomina*, hence "nominalism"). General concepts, "covering concepts" are mere names to which no reality corresponds. *Meta*-physical ideas or "essences" are fantasies. ("Meta" is a Greek prefix meaning after, above or beyond.)

But nominalism cannot account for the incontrovertible fact of our everyday experience that we use *concepts* by which we designate the true reality of the *likeness*, the *commonality* which is shared by different horses and which differs again from what all concrete buttercups have in common.

Nominalism does not see that this undeniable experience of commonality or regularity demonstrates that there is a *common rule* to which individual entities conform. But this regularity, this law-conformity, this orderliness *points* unmistakably to the rule, the law, the measure, the order which really exists and which communally *holds for* all individuals of a certain type and from which each derives its *own* (mutually corresponding) *nature*.

This is not a rigid metaphysical "essence," true enough. But neither is it an unreal fantasy. It is the *structure,* which on the law-side of entities determines their *nature,* their *modes of existence* and *functioning,* just as a measure, law or norm *determines* how the subjectivity subject to it will exist and function. Only *on the basis* of this subjective *law-conformity* and (in cases where the law is a norm or a rule) on the basis of this *normativity* or *regularity* are entities knowable and recognizable.

(d) A painting *as such*, in and of itself, so *qua* aesthetic work of art, is not perceptible to the senses. Only by applying (usually unconsciously) an aesthetic norm do we distinguish a work of art from a random piece of linen with some paint on it. In the same way a marriage *as such* is not empirically perceptible either. Only after (intuitively) applying a norm (standard) can we perceive a *"norm-*al" marriage and distinguish it from a cohabiting couple or from a relationship of mutual care-giving. Again, only by applying linguistic norms do we distinguish human speech from animal sounds.

And so we could adduce countless examples to illustrate that facts, realities—in particular typically human realities—are not simply perceived "purely empirically" but rather "transcendental-empirically," that is to say, taking into account their supra-individual *law of existence*, which is their *possibility of existence*, their inner law of life, their structural principle. That is the same as applying standards or norms, already in our perceiving of them!

7.3.11 THE INTERNAL PROCESS OF DISCLOSURE IN ENTITIES

In sec. 6.4 we talked about the internal process of disclosure in the dimension of modal aspects. Every fundamental mode of being (modality) can be deepened and disclosed in its functioning. This happens when the "anticipations" (the anticipatory meaning-moments) are developed or activated. Let us look at some examples again.

Justice is deepened or disclosed into *fairness* by the anticipation of morality. *Love* as mutual sympathy is deepened and disclosed into mutual *trust, admiration and tender care* by anticipation of the pistical aspect of religious trust. By anticipations of the economic aspect *language* is disclosed into *"fitting" discourse* that employs neither too few nor too many words to say something concisely and cogently, thus effectively. *Juridical anticipation* in the lingual aspect renders the meaning of words *"unambiguous,"* so that vague and equivocal terms are avoided as much as possible. This disclosure is particularly indis-pensable in scientific language, though that language often excludes those people who are unfamiliar with the subject.

Now then, this internal process of disclosure in the *modal aspects* underlies the process that takes place in *entities*, that is, in concrete, real things, social structures, actions, events. Reality as a whole displays an enormous dynamics of internal processes. Physicists teach us how much goes on in the atomic and molecular structure of matter. Things are even more complicated in the organic processes of a biotic nature. And mapping out the psychical is next to impossible, given the many theories about drives, feelings, perceptions and instincts. Human life is exceedingly complicated in activities such as thinking, acting, socially relating, each with its own complex totality structure. In thought, in action, in society, man functions not only in the law-aspects of his "nature" but also in all norm-aspects of reality, *actualizing* a vast series of *possibilities* intrinsic to all those aspects.

Later, in praxeology, we will discuss how in the practice of human life this entire process of disclosure actually takes place (consciously or unconsciously) under the *central* direction of a concrete (conscious or unconscious) *faith*, because this faith is the primary manifestation of the *religious orientation of the heart*. But it depends on the *content* of the faith whether this process of disclosure takes a *progressive* or a *reactionary* direction in human culture and in one's personal life—in other words, whether a true *dis*closure takes place or instead a *closure* through a central orientation "downwards," to retrocipatory meaning-moments, to the "substrate." This perverts "being unto God" into being unto oneself, or turning toward idols.

Again, our *faith* is *disclosed* in the reading or hearing of a Bible story when it is primarily focused on what God says in it, perhaps directly to us personally. But our faith is suppressed, obstructed or possibly even lost and denatured into "unbelief" when its direction is primarily *retrocipatory* towards the "substrate," for instance towards the historical question (and perhaps the scholarly answer) how exactly the events of the story occurred in detail. That is also the fundamental mistake made in the traditional *Lives of Jesus*, but also in the so-called harmonization of the Gospels, which even John Calvin still attempted to do. That is more theology than enrichment of faith. Fundamentalism is steeped in it.

7.3.12 ENKAPTIC INTERLACEMENTS

(a) The entities, as we saw, combine the analogically interwoven modalities into an *internal structural whole*, into a *totality* with its own identity. But the entities themselves, too, are not unconnected. They in turn are interwoven with each other in various ways. We will notice this time and again in the chapters to follow: in anthropology, in sociology, in praxeology, and later in epistemology. In the context of the present chapter we will therefore make a few introductory comments.

(b) For their existence and survival plants depend entirely on sunlight and minerals; people and animals depend on plants and minerals. Public universities depend on state power; business companies and political governments depend on each other; works of art depend in part on the material from which they are made; and so on. There is an extraordinary interlacement between entities of the most diverse types, hence the traditional temptation to approach all these strong interlacements and mutual dependencies theoretically by means of *the scheme of the whole and its parts*. Yet this often makes for misrepresentations, because some relations can be characterized in terms of this scheme while others simply cannot.

(c) In this chapter we will confine our analysis of this interlacement to sketching *the difference* between a *whole with parts* and a whole that consists of an *"enkaptic interlacement"* of relatively independent entities which are "encapsulated" or "bound" in each other.

(d) Against the background of the general structure of entities, as set out in this chapter thus far, the *part-whole* relation appears as a relation *within a single entity*. The relatively independent component parts do not have *their own independent internal destination function*. Examples are the roots, branches and leaves of a tree, the organs or "parts" in a human or animal body, the local branches of a national organization, and municipalities and provinces within a state. All these examples certainly display a *relative independence* or *limited autonomy* of the parts. The parts do have their own function, but that function is entirely qualified by the internal destination function of the whole. A stomach, a lung, a foot, a leaf, a modern city, a bicycle wheel, these are not complete identities but parts of an identity, because they cannot develop their own *internal* destination function apart from the whole. They do have this function, but it is a partial function of the destination function of the whole. If these parts are introduced into a different kind of entity, they become *"part"* of the destination function of something other than the entity of which they used to "form a part," for example, a bicycle wheel in a work of art, a rhyme word or a metaphor in a love song, in an occasional poem, or in a church hymn. We will look at this in more detail later, particularly in connection with philosophical sociology.

(e) An entirely different situation is represented by minerals that are incorporated and "bound" as nutrients in organic structures. The atoms and molecules of these substances have their *own* identity structure which can be woven into all kinds of combinations and then perform their own function there. Their own internal destination function (in the physical aspect) remains independent, and with its own mode of operation it is incorporated—*encapsulated*—in a structure that has its destination function in *a different modality*. These cases no longer involve the same type of connection as in the part-whole relation. Reformational philosophy calls this type of interlacement *enkapsis*. Thus a block of rough marble has an entirely different identity from the aesthetic sculpture made from it. Marble as a natural product is then enkaptically interlaced—encapsulated—into the work of art, which is qualified in an entirely different way. The same is true of wood in a chair, or a one-man business in a family, or a church building in a local congregation.

The above can be summed up in two tables:

PART – WHOLE
the same qualifying functions
examples:
organs or parts in a body
plasma and nucleus in a cell
provinces and municipalities in a state
hands and numbers of a clock

ENKAPSIS
not the same qualifying functions
examples:
medicines in a body
atoms and molecules in a cell
objects: a snail's shell; a spider's web
the linen in a painting

7.3.13 DIFFERENT TYPES OF ENKAPSIS
Different types of enkapsis can be distinguished:

• *Foundational enkapsis*, e.g., molecules in an organism, a financial department in a firm, the drives in a person's life, the work of a head of a family.

• *Symbiotic enkapsis*, e.g., bacteria on skin, mosses on tree-bark.

• *Territorial enkapsis*: a state and its territory.

• *Correlative enkapsis*: plants and animals in their habitat, which so conditions them that they cannot live outside of it; but also vice versa: they *make* this bio-environment, this biotope.

• *Subject-object enkapsis*: a snail and its shell, a spider and its web.

7.3.14 SUMMARY OF THE CHARACTERISTICS OF AN ENTITY
(1) An entity is an individual whole (more simply: a matter, a thing, an event, a situation), which is therefore also called an *individuality*.

(2) Like everything in reality, an entity has a law- or norm-side and a subject- or factual side. We call the law-side the entity's *structure*.

(3) The *identity* of an entity is contained in its *type*, that is to say, in the way in which all aspects of the universal law-order are attuned to each other and work together in this particular entity. That is why we call the structure of an entity its *identity structure*. On the basis of its own type, it gives to the concrete functioning in all aspects of the structure its own "typical" character, the identity of its kind, and its individual identity.

(4) Because an entity in principle functions in all aspects, we talk about the *universality* or *totality* of every entity. This expresses that, in those aspects in which an entity does not function as subject (e.g., an animal in the economic aspect), it still functions there as potential ("latent") object (for example, as merchandise). That is why we can say that all concretely existing reality functions in all cosmic aspects, and is even composed, constituted, constructed by those aspects.

(5) The principal feature of the *entity type* mentioned under (3) is that in all structural types two aspects play a special role, one as a *qualifying* and the other as a *founding* aspect. The first, the guiding and qualifying aspect, orients the internal functioning of the entity in all other aspects to the internal destination of the entity. Hence this aspect also contains the entity's *internal destination function*. The second is the founding aspect, in which the entire mode of existence of this particular entity type is *founded*. The functions in these two salient aspects of the identity structure are called the two *radical functions*.

(6) The identity structure guarantees not only the identity but also the *continuity* of the entity throughout all developmental phases and temporal changes that take place in the processes of genesis, existence and demise.

(7) Distinguishing various types of entities should first of all be oriented to the qualifying modality of the entities. All the principal types obtained are called *radical types*. Within the radical types there are *genotypes and sub-genotypes*. Within the class of genotypes we can distinguish *variability types*.

(8) Like modalities, entities are interconnected by the cosmic temporal order of earlier and later. Accordingly, by analogy with anticipations and retrocipations, there are not only modal nuclei of aspects but also encapsulations of relatively independent entities in what are called *enkaptic interlacements*. This type of interconnection is fundamentally

different from that of the whole and its parts. In enkapsis, entities retain their own internal and distinct character, whereas in the part-whole relation the functions of the parts are qualified and guided by the typical function of the whole. It is possible to identify a wide variety of types of encapsulation.

Chapter Eight – Philosophy of time: Temporal reality and primordial time

CHAPTER EIGHT
PHILOSOPHY OF TIME: TEMPORAL REALITY AND PRIMORDIAL TIME

8.1 TIME IN EVERYDAY EXPERIENCE AND IN PHILOSOPHY

8.1.1 ONE'S CONCEPTION OF TIME IS EMBEDDED IN INSIGHTS DERIVING FROM FAITH AND WORLDVIEW

Almost from the very beginning of Western science, philosophers have had a philosophy of time. Yet again there is little consensus about this topic. Almost all philosophers acknowledge the problem. Their views on time, however, are strongly linked to their religious pre-scientific worldviews. In addition, these views depend in part on the philosophical conceptions regarding *total cosmic reality* itself. This suggests a close relationship between *time and reality* and a direct link to the views of both, as will become apparent in this chapter.

We wish to show in particular that *the fundamental philosophical view of time is* *directly* linked (and not just indirectly, as in most other sciences) to *insights deriving from one's faith and one's worldview.* One's view of time is located in the borderland of scientific philosophy where philosophy's basic ideas are intertwined with one's pre-philosophical worldview and religious outlook on life.[43]

In what follows we shall see that a philosophy of time can never be meaningfully conceived as a separate subject, detached from a (concealed or professed) *cosmological whole.* A philosophy of time cannot haphazardly be thought up, no more than, say, a philosophy of science.

---

43. Recall that the two are so interwoven that philosophy inevitably asks theoretical *questions* about cosmic diversity, coherence and unity or origin yet cannot itself *answer* these questions because such answers can only be given by faith.

8.1.2 Augustine. Philosophy of time and worldview

Ever since Augustine (354-430) grappled with the problem of time, there has hardly been a philosopher whose philosophy of time does not somewhere recall Augustine's famous words: "What is time? If nobody asks me I know; but if I want to explain it to somebody who asks, I do not know."[44]

In the course of this chapter we hope to explain how Augustine arrived at this statement, and why this statement is quoted so often, also in the philosophies of time in our own day. Apparently people are always aware that there is a pre-scientific intuitive knowledge and certainty which is distinct from theoretical philosophy.

Only, reflection on this difference in *epistemological* theories often leaves much to be desired. A clear theoretical distinction between *worldview* as a practical outlook on life and all reality, and *philosophy* as an overall theoretical analysis, is often lacking or forgotten. This is sometimes excused by the fallacious epistemological thesis that there are two kinds of philosophy, a scientific philosophy and a philosophy-as-worldview. But this is incorrect because—:

(a) a philosophy is by definition an overall scientific analysis whereas a worldview is a practical outlook on life, so that the concept of "worldviewish philosophy" is just as contradictory as the expression "practical science";

(b) scientific philosophy never exists by itself without being founded in a worldview and in this sense is always determined by a worldview, without being a worldview itself. Conversely, a worldview, as held by almost all people, can easily exist without philosophy.

8.1.3 Pre-theoretical experience of past, present and future.

It is indeed true that as long as we do not make a theoretical "problem" out of it, we understand perfectly well what time is. We *experience* the passing of hours, of days and years, and of the countless changes that take place in them. We *remember* "past" time and what happened in it, and what we ourselves experienced in it. Also, we are *focused on* future time with our plans, expectations, uncertainties and questions. In all this we sometimes lament the general transience of life and everything that occurs in it, since past, present and future can also be experienced as rising, shining and

---

44. Augustine, *Confessions* 11.14.

sinking, or more neutrally: as birth and demise—even as we human beings experience most intensely the "present" and often want to "hold on" to it when we think that time "goes too fast" for us.

Moreover, as Christians we know by faith that there is also a reality (namely, the person and work of Christ) that involves both the beginning and the end of time. Our Christian worldview therefore "views" the transience of all things differently from a worldview ruled by another faith. This will turn out to be crucial for the scientific philosophy of time.

8.1.4 Does time actually exist?

very good question

In our practical worldview we therefore do not abstract time from what happens in it. If we do, we are soon in trouble. Think of what we call "the present." We experience the present and are perfectly capable of distinguishing "today" from yesterday and tomorrow. But as soon as we theoretically detach these terms (past, present, future) from *what happens in them*, and begin to ask, for example, what *is* the present, what *is* the "present time," or even more abstractly: what *is* time actually?, we see the significant present vanish theoretically into nothingness. For every moment, as soon as I am aware of it as "present" and want to grasp it, has become past again and escapes my grasp. "Soon" can be in the past only a second later.

In fact, theoretically, at least in *this* abstraction, there is no room for a present between past and future. In this theoretical approach the present is comparable to a mathematical point without extension, an imaginary point that moves continuously towards the future, but remains always, at least in theory, suspended between past and future. In the moment of the "now" the past perpetually moves up towards the future, which becomes the past in almost the same moment. In this theory, the "now" has in effect become a shadowy nothing, a pure idea and no longer a reality.

Accordingly, throughout the history of the philosophy of time all kinds of philosophers have claimed that the present does not exist, and some have even argued that past and future do not exist either, that time therefore is actually nothing, that it simply does not exist. Time is a succession of point-like nothings. And a thousand times nothing is still nothing. Only things and events exist—the argument continues— which *we* squeeze into periods of time for the sake of convenience. But this is a purely subjective *addition* to reality. The added time is not anything real; it is but a product of our own thought.

8.1.5 THE BASIC ERROR OF TRYING TO MEASURE TIME

This conundrum is an indication that we are on the wrong track. *We are trying to measure the present*, and find it impossible. So there is no present then?

We refuse to have our experience of past, present and future taken away from us through some fancy theory or silly denial. Past, present and future are, and always have been, vibrant and conscious experiences of every human being (once past a very early age). They refer to something real: to our own concrete reality. The line of reasoning set out above breaks down on the undeniable reality of this experience; that is, it breaks down on the reality of time itself. So what is the theoretical error?

The basic error of these lines of reasoning, I think, is that we are divorcing time from reality in a process of abstraction. Next, we attempt to understand what this isolated "time" is *in and of itself*. In this way we can come to the logically correct conclusion that time as such, in and of itself, does not exist. In other words, time *"an sich"* is indeed a human product of abstract thought. This is not necessarily false, for abstraction may be correct as well as incorrect. But in the present problem Augustine was again right when he wrote in a less well-known passage: "There can be no time without a creature."[45]

So whoever characterizes time as change or transience (which is not entirely correct in my view), at least does not divorce these notions of time from reality—which changes or passes away.

The same can be said about "everyday" reality. This reality does not exist without time either. Not a single atom of reality exists apart from time, and literally everything in our concrete experience of reality has a specific *duration*, is involved in the all-pervasive and all-encompassing "flow" of time, in short: *exists in time. Reality* itself is "charged" with time or temporality, like a live electric wire. Almost everything in our "temporal life" is unmistakably subject to the process of generation, existence and demise.

"Almost"—because "full reality" does not exist in time *only*. More on this in our next chapter. But first we need to add another comment about the expression "temporal reality."

---

45. "Nullum tempus esse posse sine creatura." Augustine, *Confessions* 11.30.40.

8.1.6 DOOYEWEERD ON "TEMPORAL REALITY"

To my knowledge, Dooyeweerd is the philosopher who most fully addressed this subject. So much so, that one of his most frequently used expressions is "temporal reality." This is a standard expression in his vocabulary. Reality has a *temporal character,* and that is why it can be philosophically referred to as "temporal reality." Conversely, time fully has the character of reality, as we all know for certain in our pre-theoretical awareness of time. In our everyday lives we are intensely heedful of "time" as an unassailable reality.

In all kinds of contexts, accordingly, the words reality and time can sometimes be used interchangeably in one and the same sentence. Time is reality, reality is time. However, we cannot always say that in quite this way, as we will see in what follows.

8.1.7 TIME AND CONTINUITY

In certain contexts, Dooyeweerd sometimes speaks of time as a continuous "bottom-layer" in reality.[46] This might suggest a difference between this bottom layer and the reality above or outside it; yet that is not the tenor of what he is saying—just as the electric current "in" a wire does not have a separately locatable place somewhere inside the wire yet does make the wire itself into a functioning electricity wire, without a wire being by definition a charged wire.

The *"continuity"* of time and reality does not mean that the structural differences between "thus or so" (the difference between modal aspects) and between "this or that" (the difference between entities) are thereby cancelled. The continuity is a characterization that says that *all articulations* in time and reality are not actually as sharply defined and separated as our *concepts* of them. Compare the inner continuity between trunk and branches, even though we are clearly dealing here with two different (sub)entities. *"Continuity"* is the term that refers to and accentuates this *"integral coherence"* in and of concrete reality itself, primarily *as opposed to* the scientifically necessary abstraction or isolation (of whatever part or aspect) *from* the integral continuity of reality and time.[47]

---

46. Cf. *A New Critique of Theoretical Thought*, 3:65.

47. It is therefore wrong, in my view, to see time as a modal aspect in the cosmic law-order, as is being proposed by Jan Dengerink in his book *De zin van de werke-lijkheid: een wijsgerige benadering* [*The meaning of reality: A philosophical approach*]

8.1.8 TIME AND SUPRA-TEMPORALITY WITHIN CREATED REALITY

We should not forget either that Christian thought always takes "reality" in this context to mean *creaturely* reality. Whenever this concept would come up in philosophy or in some other science, Vollenhoven preferred to differentiate between "earthly subjects" and "heavenly subjects" (heaven, and spirits, angels, messengers).[48] The non-earthly creatures cannot be investigated by any science, not by philosophy and not even by theology. Theology, too, depends here on the biblical testimonies, which do not provide information for science but only for faith.

When we come to discuss time we will learn that in regard to time Dooyeweerd differs from Vollenhoven in defining "earthly subjects." Dooyeweerd distinguishes between the temporal and the supra-temporal *within creaturely* reality. In this way he extricates himself from the theoretical dilemma of time or eternity, creaturely time or divine eternity. *Tertium datur in Christo*—in Christ there is a third way, as we will develop further on in relation to this subject.

Meanwhile we can provisionally note that time cannot exist without something that is not time. More on this later in sec. 8.2.6.

8.1.9 THE DURATION OF TIME

The integral continuity between time and reality does not therefore cancel out the diversity that exists within it—no more than that the continuity is *exhausted by* a *modal-analogical coherence* within this diversity, in other words by the universality of every aspect. As well, we *experience* the duration of time very differently depending on our culture or the phase of our culture, on our personality, our moods, our preoccupations, etc.

Our awareness of differences in the way we experience time is very real. Thus *"duration"* is a subjective given, a relative concept,

---

(Amsterdam, 1986), pp. 244–45. If this were correct, it would be impossible to see time as *cosmic continuity* on account of its own modal and therefore limited character, and cosmic continuity would then be entirely *absent* as a subjective correlate of *the cosmic order*. As a result, the deepest dimension of the total intramodal *cosmic coherence* would be gone and this coherence would be equal to little more than a mesh of *discontinuous* anticipations and retrocipations between the similarly discontinuous order of meaning-nuclei. Consequently, the necessary *theoretical* discontinuity could then not be relativized and overcome in an idea of continuous coherence.

48. Dirk H. T. Vollenhoven, *Isagôgè Philosophiae: Introduction to Philosophy*, ed. and trans. by John H. Kok and Anthony Tol (Sioux Center, IA, 2005), pp. 19–21.

depending on and related to the concrete situational *"enduring" reality* and our subjective experience of this. For instance, the duration of time in our dreams often diverges strongly from clock time by which the "length" (or rather, the physical and/or organic duration) of the dream can be measured. Apparently the *psychical duration of experiencing and sensing* is different from the revolution of the clock's hands. Only this last duration usually serves as an objective measurement of time.

An *historical* experience of cultural eras from the past can sometimes be had when getting to know the life of elderly villagers, Bedouins, Australian aborigines who, like some tribes in New Guinea, are in part or in certain respects still living in the Stone Age. Yet all of them, measured by the yardstick of our calendar, are *our* "contemporaries" in *our* lifetime and *our* cultural era, in which elements of a remote past nevertheless still exert a certain influence.

8.1.10 TIME AND HISTORY

The element of earlier and later in the history of civilization is a question of creation's progressive unfolding, or also of its degeneration and decadence. God's work of creation was itself not "bound" to his creature *time*, did not take "place" "in time," for instance "at the beginning" or "in the middle" of time. It was not an *"historical act."* God himself stands above his law of creation, above the order of time and above history. He *"created"* all this in his own divine time, in which "a thousand years are like a day, and a day like a thousand years." Translated into philosophical terms, this means that God's time (insofar as we can talk meaningfully about it) cannot be "defined" by creaturely concepts of time, nor is it "measurable" by creaturely standards like moments of time and periods of time. God's time is his "eternity."

Scripture does give "dates" for God's work of creation, but "in a manner of speaking," thus *metaphorically*, with images necessarily drawn from created reality. This is *no less truth* than historical truth, or than *the physical truth* that 1000 years are not one day but 365,000 days. That is why the traditional problem of how long the six days of creation lasted is fundamentally insoluble, because wrongly put. They are not creaturely calendar days but God's *divine days*. The revelation concerning them does not occur in an ordinary narrative of human history but rather in a *revelation* about *God's* works, works that cannot be measured by creaturely, human measurements of time, works that are not subject to God's temporal order for reality. The truth of this revelation is not an *historical* truth that historical research can discover or "establish." To repeat: for God one day is like a thousand years and a thousand years like one day. God is not circumscribed by or subject to his own creative framework. (*Deus legibus solutus est,* people said in the Reformation: God stands above the law for the creature.) The truth of the "six-day creation story" is not a truth of scientific history but *truth of a different and unique type.*

In point of fact, the truth of Gen. 1 (and following chapters) is *religious* truth, characterized and qualified not by human thought, nor by creaturely history or other verifiable "data," but by *divine revelation* of a divine work, a work which in the absence of this revelation would be completely unknowable, but which thanks to this revelation has become knowable *in the sense of faith knowledge.* The Genesis account is not traditional lore reflecting human fears. It is not a projection of human dreams or wishes. Nor does it provide historiographical knowledge, or theological knowledge, or literary-aesthetic knowledge, or linguistic knowledge. Rather, it provides knowledge of a totally *different, distinctive* type,[49] namely *faith knowledge.* Its truth is not scientific truth, nor "empirical truth" in the usual sense of that expression,[50] nor yet artistic truth. It is *religious truth.* It is knowledge about "the invisible things of God," evidence of "things not seen." Yet it is truly human, entirely anthropomorphic knowledge about that which is no longer human or creaturely, namely, the work of God.

To "establish" theologically that in terms of literary type Gen. 1 is ordinary history, a rendering of *historical* events, is to ignore the uniqueness of divine revelation and the *divine nature* of creating, as if those things could be "defined" by creaturely concepts about time and history, or by concepts about a "something" or a "nothing." My line of reasoning is not a plea for embracing well-known "negative theology," but only for recognizing the distinctive character of faith life, as distinct from forms of life which "by their nature" are differently qualified (such as, for instance, theology).

---

49. We will discuss the various types of truth and knowledge in chap. 14.

50. "Empirical knowledge or empirical truth" usually presupposes a secularized idea of what empirical (experiential) reality is. This concept ignores the faith aspect of reality.

8.1.11 "IN THE BEGINNING" IS NOT A TYPICAL DATE IN HISTORY

Scripture refers to the "date" of the creation as "in the beginning." This is an expression that is often found in myths as well, but to avoid any association with myths we can also say in theological exegesis: "in primordial time," which is a date that cannot be scientifically plotted on our earthly calendar, nor defined, but which we *believe*. "Somewhere" in "primordial time" lies the *origin*, the "Ur-Sprung," the *Archè*. Not *in* history, not in time, but *so to speak* "prior" to it, which is impossible literally, because time did not "yet" exist. For primordial time contained the origin of all time, in God.

That is why at the beginning of this section we put the word "date" between quotation marks. For it is not Scripture's intention in Gen. 1:1 to indicate a *typically historical* date—which would always presuppose a created historical time, and so would not be applicable to the creation itself of time. Scripture's intention is to reveal the *divine origin* of reality. Hence the creation is not an "historical event" and the account of it is not a typically "historical narrative" or an "historical description." It is a *testimony*, a faith testimony of the biblical writer about what God *revealed* to him "in word and deed," thus a *revelatory testimony*.[51]

The scientific battle against the *belief* in evolutionism is therefore by definition unfruitful and doomed to fail. It will not convince those who *believe* in evolutionism. Fundamentalists who insist on regarding Gen. 1 as an inspired and therefore (?) accurate representation of *history* make the *same rationalist (scientistic) error* as the scientists who cannot vouch for the evolutionist hypothesis as a scientifically established theory yet who nevertheless *believe* in it as an indubitable truth. Theirs is a belief, however, that is grounded in science and so needs to be "adjusted" from time to time, just as is the case for all science, including theology.

In the same way the orthodox theological tradition that rejects the evolutionist hypothesis *because it is at odds with the Bible* is in need of adjustment. The belief in evolutionism, insofar as it must be combated, must be combated by *natural scientists* with scientific arguments, not with ill-matched arguments that can supposedly be taken from the Bible as though they were theoretical "truths" about all kinds of historical data in the history of reality.

---

51. Cf. my article "Nieuw zicht op de mythen" [A new perspective on myths], *Philosophia Reformata* 65 (2000): 18–52.

8.1.12 CREATION AND GENESIS

The biblical phrase "in the beginning" is not the same as the "Big Bang" of evolutionist theory. It stands for the divine act of creation itself, which theologically needs to be sharply distinguished from the "genesis" of the world and the individual creatures. This *genesis* took place and takes place *in time*—possibly including a certain degree of evolution, which may be implied, or at least is not excluded, in all those expressions at the beginning of Genesis that talk about the role played in "bringing forth" other creatures by those creatures that had already been called forth (Gen. 1: 11, 12, 17, 24; 2: 9, 19, 21). God's *act of creation* was and remains an act of the eternal God (Gen. 1:1)—also where this divine act of creation is manifest in the creation of the human nature of Christ (the Alpha, the first creature) and in *the genesis of the world*, as further indicated in Genesis 1 and 2.

Accordingly, *primordial time* is *more* than what we can denote in our temporal categories by the word "beginning." After all, "beginning" in our world of experience is always the beginning-of-something, which therefore already presupposes this "something" and belongs to that something, is part of it. Here theology, traditionally and to a certain extent rightly, makes reference to God's eternal counsel, which is not however something of the creature itself, nor its historical beginning, but its divine origin.

To interpret "in the beginning" in light of the Hebrew *bereshit* as *"primordial time"* or *origin* is sound in terms of literary history and seems very plausible in my view. In almost all religions the reference to a primordial time is the religious answer to questions that worldviews and philosophies raise about the origin of all things. The *beginning* of the world in the sense of its *"commencement* in time" is therefore not the *origin*, the actual "supra-temporal" creation, but belongs to the *"genesis"*-in-time of all that had already been created ("already": that is to say, "in the beginning").

Theologians have often recognized and discussed this difference between *beginning* and *primordial time*, particularly in the problems surrounding mythology. Unfortunately it has led many to talk about an "eternal creation," a *creatio continua*, because it is the work of the eternal God. However, the mere term "continua" already *presupposes* (created) time, and is also at odds with a "creation-from-nothing." The idea of a continuous creation reflects a mistaken philosophy of the relation between God and creature, between God's eternity and created time. We will return to this later. The main point to make here is that theological thought believed from the outset that it could put everything down to the simple dilemma of (divine) eternity and (creaturely) time. As a result, both religious understanding and theological exegesis of the expression "in the beginning" were basically frustrated. Also, it left no room for understanding the New Testament where it supplements Genesis 1 with the revelation that God created all things "in *Christ*," in Christ who is God *and* man, *the "Alpha"*(!), "the firstborn of all creation" (Col. 1:15) in his supra-temporal fullness and totality.

8.2 TIME AND REALITY

8.2.1 TIME AND REALITY ARE BOTH MORE THAN PHYSICAL
The above introduction already touched on all the essential points of the Reformational philosophy of time. We will now look at some of these points in more detail. We have become familiar with various kinds of time experience. It would be unrealistic to reduce this practical life experience largely to subjective fantasy and consider the time we experience as "clock time" to be the only "real" time. Reality is much broader and richer than physical reality, and real full time is much more than just clock time, or calendar time, or emotional time, or time in our dreams, or the cultural time of "historical eras."

8.2.2 RIGHT AND WRONG ABSTRACTIONS
We can make much more progress if we do not try to make a theoretical separation between *full* reality and time—or rather: if we are *aware* that this theoretical separation is a provisional and artificial product of our thought, an "artefact." This artificial product can only perform its useful service provided (a) it is a correct abstraction, and (b) we do not confuse this product (of our thought) with concrete reality itself, just as we cannot identify concrete history with its abstracted and subjectively described historical aspect.

We found that a sound theoretical view of time is impossible if time and reality are separated. As a result of such a separation, after all, reality would no longer be reality and time would become a surreal chimera, which brings us back to Augustine's quandary (see sec. 8.1.2).

Newton took such an abstract theoretical view of time when he devised the concept of "absolute" time (from Latin *ab-solutus*, separated), a time that surrounds all things. As if time were an all-encompassing "void" after all! Reality in itself would then be timeless, and time itself would be *empty*, a large empty *space* as it were.[52] Even Einstein claimed that for this reason our practical division of time into past, present and future is an *illusion*.[53] Indeed, the main trend in present-day philosophy of time still holds that time is a *subjective human framework of organization*, added by "us" to a reality which in itself is timeless.[54]

8.2.3 TIME HAS THE SAME ARTICULATIONS AS REALITY
There is an alternative to the faulty abstraction that detaches time and reality so as to philosophize separately about the two. In time we can follow the same articulations that we also found in reality in the theory of modal aspects. Many seemingly insoluble problems caused by the theoretical separation of time and reality turn out to be pseudo-problems when we start from a better definition of the problem.

We do this by applying the distinction of modal aspects to time as well, and therefore by also speaking about temporal aspects as reality aspects that are different by nature and cannot be reduced to each other. And of course we claim that these aspects are connected to each other, even in a *continuous* coherence, so not only via *discontinuous* antici-pations or retrocipations.

The theoretical discontinuity of the mutually irreducible aspects with their analogies remains valid, provided that its secondary, artificial nature is not forgotten, or the discontinuity which we noted is not regarded as the only true reality. As we said earlier, the concrete continuous coherence cannot be sufficiently explained by the complicated interwovenness of all modalities through their

---

52. In the spirit of German idealism and later phenomenology, R. Laut takes up this approach in his book *Die Konstitution der Zeit* (Hamburg,1981).

53. Cf. H. Genz, *Wie der Zeit in die Welt kam. Die Entstehung einer Illusion aus Ordnung und Chaos* [How time came into the world: The birth of an illusion out of order and chaos] (Munich, 1996). Genz states that Einstein was right in thinking that "the separation between past, present and future amounted to a mere, albeit stubborn, illusion."

54. Cf. Kurt Weis, ed., *Was ist Zeit? Zeit und Verantwortung in Wissenschaft, Technik und Religion* [*What is time? Time and its explanation in science, technology and religion*] (Frankfurt am Main, 1993).

anticipations and retrocipations, for to do so would be to stay within the non-continuous *interwoven* coherence between the still discontinuous analogies.

8.2.4 "TEMPORAL REALITY"

When we said in sec. 8.1.6 that time and reality are in a certain sense identical, we intended to emphasize what has been argued so far. We can now adopt a more lapidary expression: *Our entire experiential reality with all its aspects is time by nature, is "temporal."*

This wording seems to say that reality's nature is transitory, transient, fleeting, perishable, corruptible, passing away. To a certain extent that is true; yet that is not what we mean in the first place. We have something quite different in mind: our experiential and actually experienced *reality* is so pervaded by time that nowhere is it time-less and everywhere it is *intrinsically temporal.*

In relation to our concrete everyday reality, Dooyeweerd therefore prefers to talk in his philosophy about "temporal reality," with a view to differentiating it from the *"supra-temporal" concentration point* or the *unity* of that reality. This difference will be discussed in the next chapter. (I put the word "supra-temporal" between quotation marks, not only because it is a frequently used technical term in Dooyeweerd's philosophy, but also because the term is not precise, being rather a provisional metaphorical aid. This will also be discussed later.)

8.2.5 PAST, PRESENT AND FUTURE. TRANSIENCE

But what does the temporal nature of reality consist in, or what are its characteristics? It is impossible to determine the nature of time (by itself, that is, apart from reality). But starting from the concrete experience of reality, we can say that everything that happens in reality and that we experience in temporal reality can be approached by means of the fundamental category of *generation-existence-demise*, or of *past, present and future*. That is to say: everything that exists in reality, every *state* of affairs, is involved in a *"course"* of events or a *"course"* of action, in a process, and everything in reality has a certain *duration*.

We tend to sum this up in the term "transience." We experience the world, with everything in it, including ourselves, as *transient*. This element too (so alongside that of temporality) is implied in the expression *"temporal reality,"* as discussed above. It applies to things, to plants, animals and human beings, to societal relationships, to situations, activities and events. It is the transience of all earthly life in "temporal reality."

8.2.6 Temporality contrasts with non-temporality

For the Christian understanding of reality, this also means that "temporal reality" is not yet *full or complete* reality.

If everything (in earthly creation) were time, in the sense of temporality, time could no longer be distinguished from non-time. It only makes sense to speak of temporality if a distinction can be made between temporality and non-temporality. Thus, in our usage, "time" always contrasts with what is non-time, with "eternity" or with "supra-temporality." In the same way the *full* reality of creation is *more* than *temporal* reality, more than transience or finiteness. It stands in a distinct relation to the "fullness," the "unity" or the "concentration point" *of* this temporal reality. More on this in the next chapter.

Chapter Nine – Philosophy of time: Full temporality and modes of time

CHAPTER NINE

PHILOSOPHY OF TIME: FULL TEMPORALITY AND MODES OF TIME

9.1 TIME AND TOTALITY

9.1.1 THE PROBLEM OF TIME REQUIRES A PHILOSOPHICAL TOTALITY VIEW

As we saw in sec. 8.2, we are one-sided if we try to characterize time from the perspective of just one or a few aspects of reality. Even if such attempts contain an element that is real, they inevitably lead to a generalization, if not an absolutization, of that particular *aspect* of time. Yet, by its very nature, scientific thought (which includes the task of defining, ultimately with the aid of the most basic categories) is tied to an *aspectual* approach to concrete reality. How then do we catch sight of the *totality* of time in its full reality?

It seems to me that we can achieve this in the same way that we gained insight into the totality of each of the entities themselves: from an *idea* of totality, in this case an idea of *cosmic* totality—the cosmic totality, that is, as distinct from the "thing"-totality of the various entities. Such an idea can be drawn directly from our practical *experience* of reality. Our experience of reality-in-time is one of the *continuous, enduring interconnectedness* of all the phases, parts or aspects that we can distinguish within the totality. "Everything is connected to everything else," as the saying goes.

"Interconnectedness," however, or "coherence" is not yet "totality" in the sense of a unity. Totality is a *unity* in which all diversity, undifferentiated, is implicit, hence fully present. The idea of a total coherence in which everything is implicitly present does *tend towards* a unity, but the actual existence of any unity still cannot be logically proved. *It cannot be proved* on the basis of "temporal reality." Yet many important schools of philosophy have always looked for such a proof. A famous example is "thinking the One" by Plotinus (204–270), the ancient philosopher who exerted a powerful influence on Christian thought via Augustine, Dionysius the Areopagite (c. 500) and the many varieties of mysticism.

9.1.2. THE UNITY AND TOTALITY OF THE COSMOS IS SEEN THROUGH FAITH

Dooyeweerd's Reformational philosophy *qua* philosophy is likewise focused on "the one," the totality or unity of all diversity existing in coherence. Thinking in the special sciences (including theology) never *starts* with the idea of unity, yet always arrives there from within, via the need to distinguish its own fundamental concepts from—and see them in connection with—those of other sciences. A theological definition of faith, for instance, will always have to distinguish faith from other human activities in its own philosophical terms and answer the question whether faith is composed of other human faculties or is a unique and distinctive human function. The answer to this problem cannot, of course, be derived or logically "deduced" from Scripture, nor "repeated after" Scripture, but is *by its very nature* a philosophical problem.

At the same time, this distinctive diversity in scientific approaches continues to call for a conception of the coherence and the totality or unity. That is why a religiously neutral science, in whatever field, is impossible. Consciously or unconsciously, the single threefold presupposition of all science—that of the *coherence, unity and origin* of the enormous diversity in reality—functions in every science.

Here therefore lies the real inner point of contact between faith and science. It's not we who have to make this point; it already *exists* a priori. It can be detected in the philosophical depth-layer of every science, and particularly in the *prolegomena* of philosophy where all sciences necessarily end with basic questions they cannot answer, questions that can in fact only be answered on the basis of some or other *religious faith*.

That is why we deliberately spoke just now of the *"inner"* point of contact between faith and science. This idea of Christian science is therefore fundamentally different from the scholastic idea which, starting from the nature/grace scheme, applies as a criterion for

Christian science the discovery of scientific truth through "deducing from," "comparing with," or even "repeating after" Scripture, also in regard to internal scientific problems.[55] Almost automatically this leads to "transcendent" criticism or external criticism "from above,"[56] which will always fail to impress scientific thinkers, including most Christian scientists, because it compares results of scientific research with biblical statements (literal or theologically refashioned by ourselves) which were never intended to answer any theoretical questions, from whatever science.

9.1.3 FAITH, TOO, IS PART OF LIFE'S REALITY

In pointing to the tendency to search for a unity of reality, as witnessed in the philosophical tradition of centuries, we have only said something about the *structure*, not yet about the subjective *direction* of philosophical thought. That direction of thought towards a totality is always a *religious* direction. It is a direction that is taken *from out of* the human heart, under the *guidance* of concrete human faith. It is a tendency that is typical of the nature with which man (in his connection with all that is non-human) has been created: namely, *"unto God."* After the fall, this (normative and dynamic) structure of creation can only function more or less properly on the correlative subjective side under the gracious guidance of God's Spirit.

Undeniably, the concrete experiences that all human beings have of reality include (consciously or unconsciously) the experience of faith, or in other words: to have (a) faith is no less part and parcel of being human. This faith is structurally (i.e., normatively) oriented to God, to His revelation, or else to what takes its place in a subjective idolatrous orientation. An example of such idolatrous devotion is

---

55. This is the current trend in theology, which finds the link between faith and science notably in theological ethics. A case in point is the *Handbuch der christlichen Ethik*, cited in sec. 4.10 above, a three-volume manual that is self-consciously based on this idea. Unfortunately, this trend continues to be followed also by Reformed theology, owing to its uncritical adoption of classical and humanist ("demythologized") views of reality and science and owing to the important role of science in practical life. As a result, even if it is no longer formulated so openly, we can almost always detect in theology the early medieval and post-Reformational idea that theology, as "the true philosophy," particularly in its ethics, is the *"dux vitae"* (life's guide) and later the *"regina scientiarum,"* the queen of the sciences.

56. I recently read a statement by a well-known Dutch theologian from a Reformed church who said: "Theology comes from above, philosophy from below"!

the pagan belief in creation myths or in other myths about spiritual beings and their relations with the human world. In Western culture this idolatrous mythological faith was replaced by faith in (scientific) Reason.

The truth of faith relates, among other things, to *full* reality, also to the full reality of time and the full truth about time and reality. That is the (normative) *structure* of faith—though sadly, not always its concrete subjective *reality*.

This approach to the totality of time from our aspectual experiences of time, *including* the experience of faith, makes it philosophically possible for us to approach the totality of time also from the opposite direction, namely from that totality or unity itself, thus concretely from the *content* of faith as regards the deepest reality, whatever faith it may be.

9.1.4 THE CHRISTIAN CONTENT OF FAITH REGARDING THE SUPRA-TEMPORAL

In *biblical* faith we know of Christ, of Him who in the last Bible book is repeatedly called the first and the last, the beginning and the end, the alpha and the omega (Rev. 1:8, 17; 21:6; 22:13). Why is He referred to in this manner? At least one answer to this question is given to us in Col. 1:16, which says that all things were created *"in Him,"* in Him who was himself the first creature—"the firstborn of all creation" (Col. 1:15), "the beginning of God's creation" (Rev. 3:14), the "alpha"! However, this was not in the *temporal* order of reality but in its supra-temporal order, which Scripture sometimes calls (of course not philosophically but *religiously*) "the order of Melchizedek, without father, without mother, without descent, having neither beginning of days nor end of life . . . a priest continually" (Heb. 7:3), "a high priest forever" (Heb. 6:20). Our earthly definitions of time do not apply here. In faith we must and can look beyond them to a "supra-temporal" reality.

Christ himself was very conscious of this, witness the fact that He, "not yet fifty years old," said: "before Abraham was, I am" (John 8:57–58). In my view, it is unbiblical and squarely against the Reformed standards to separate here, as exegetes commonly do, the divine nature of Christ from His human nature and to take this "I" of *Jesus* Christ as being spoken about His divine nature only. This is a (rather poor) scientific, theoretical treatment (if not to say, maltreatment) of a truth about God that has been revealed to us in *myth-like form*. Jesus, God *and* man, as He spoke there with the Jews, was in fact "before" Abraham. He said so himself![57]

That said, Heb. 5:11 warns us that this is a subject about which much can be said but which is difficult to explain. It is "solid food"; not everybody in the church can understand it immediately (Heb. 5:12–14). On the other hand, one need not be a Biblical scholar to notice how the Bible often talks about past, present and future in a very different way from what we are used to.[58] It does so also, or particularly, where our salvation is concerned.[59] Theology, with its traditional time/eternity dilemma, is encumbered in this regard by the legacy of secularized paganism which, in the period when first poetry and then science arose, started to dissociate itself from the myths as if they were pure nonsense.

In this respect original paganism with its *mythology*—that is to say, with its openly confessed pagan faith that governed all of life—was wiser than the culture of science emerging at the time. At least it had some religious awareness of supra-temporal, sometimes "miraculous" events and situations that could not be approached with standards deriving from our everyday experience of time and space or from theoretical thought.[60]

Emergent science in the sixth century BC *wanted to place mythological faith outside "thought"* (epistèmè) *as mere "opinion"* (doxa). *Thus it gave birth*

---

57. It is better not to call this the "pre-existence" of Christ, because this term mistakenly suggests that it was an existence *before and outside of time*, purely in "eternity," and *therefore* exclusive of Christ's *human* nature. This ignores the creaturely character of supra-temporality (better: "full temporality"), forcing commentators to introduce a theoretical separation between the two natures of Christ and to relate these words of Scripture to the *"logos asarkos."*

58. Besides the text quoted, compare also the *perfectum propheticum* or the *praesens propheticum*: when Isaac was born, Abraham saw the day of Christ in this. Think also of the "eschatological" passages in Scripture. And so on. All these have been reasons for developing a so-called "theological concept of time," which many theologians have taken great pains to elucidate, including Karl Barth, Oscar Cullmann, Rudolf Bultmann and Hendrikus Berkhof.

59. On this, see my three articles in *Opbouw* 40 (1996), nos. 11–13 (pp. 206-07, 224-25, 248-49), entitled "In Christus geheiligd" [Sanctified in Christ], "Theologische probleemstellingen" [The framing of theological questions], and "Ons leven *in* en *uit* Christus" [Living *in* Christ and *out of* Christ].

60. Cf. my article "Nieuw zicht op de mythen" [A new perspective on myths], *Philosophia Reformata* 65 (2000): 18-52.

to the (incorrect) theoretical separation of faith and science. It wished to have thought, like reality itself, demythologized. This internal pagan secularization of the experience and conception of reality contains the source of what would later become in Christianity (which adopted this intellectual attitude[61]) the two-realm theory of nature and the supernatural, nature and grace, thinking and believing, faith and science, church and world, theology and philosophy, and so on, and so forth.

9.1.5 PHILOSOPHICAL TRANSLATION OF RELIGIOUS CONTENT

At first blush, many people are puzzled by the fact that Reformational philosophy would take religious awareness of the supernatural and interpret it in terms of supra-temporality or full temporality as the concentrated unity and totality of all reality. One reason for this puzzlement is that we have been living and thinking for two and half millennia in a culture in which the *concept of reality* (and so also the idea of time), based as it is on pagan secularized thought and the parallel development of a theoretical conception of reality, has been *demythologized, undeified, horizontalized, reduced and externalized.*

Later on in this chapter we will consider this subject further from the perspective of *the philosophical foundation* of Dooyeweerdian philosophy, a prolegomenon that is often forgotten when the fine points of this philosophy are being discussed, causing such topics to be almost automatically misunderstood. This is nowhere more clearly demonstrated than in the way its philosophy of time has been criticized. Yet if we assent to this philosophy we will discover that the *totality* of time is also its *concentrated unity and fullness.* As we just saw, this is signified by the *content* of the *Christian* faith which, following Paul, refers us to Christ and the creation of all things "in Christ," to *our* (own!) fall in paradise (Rom. 5:12), to our being crucified, died, buried and resurrected *with Christ,* and to the reconciliation and renewal of "all things" given in Christ (Col. 1: 19, 20).

The resulting philosophical idea of totality and unity naturally functions at a different level from the concepts of totality relating to intra-temporal totalities, like that of a modality or that of the thing-structure in the various kingdoms and their interlacements. However, these ideas of totality relating to entities in time *converge* in the central cosmic

---

61. Bultmann rightly pointed this out, albeit with an entirely different appreciation from ours, and also with an entirely different alternative.

unity and totality of what is repeatedly referred to in the Bible as "all things" (*ta panta*). That is not "another world," not a separate heavenly kingdom, not some "supernatural order." It is the *supra-temporal* order or depth-dimension, the "order of Melchizedek," in which all temporal historical events in Christ's work of salvation *have brought to a focus* in a single point, as it were, their more-than-historical actuality—their "eternal," supra-temporal (in the sense of full temporal) operation.[62]

This also explains why Paul and even more John (and the Old Testament prophets, for that matter) often talk about past, present and future in a totally non-chronological way, as if the events of salvation history can be placed with complete randomness and even simultaneity in the past, the present or the future. This occurs even in combinations of past and future, as when the Bible speaks of the need *to be* sanctified in Christ (in temporality) and at the same time of the reality of *having been* sanctified in Christ (in full temporality).

This supra-temporal "order" of Melchizedek can only be known by faith, and can thereafter be interpreted in worldview, philosophy and science (including theology) as the concentrated unity and totality *comprehending all* time or times.

Even without philosophy, in the language of biblical faith and the Christian worldview, we can indicate this unity by pointing to Christ, "in whom all things (in past, present and future) *exist*" (Col. 1:17)—and always have existed, because He is the Alpha, the first creature, the supra-temporal "fullness" (e.g., Eph. 4:13), and because He is the Omega and so encompasses the entire ABC of reality, from origin to consummation.

It is to be hoped that this revelation and this faith will one day gain a hold over our Christian life and thought, and be integrated into it. But so far this lies outside the purview of theology, shackled as it is to a view of reality based on notions from secular philosophy.

9.1.6 SUPRA-TEMPORALITY: NEITHER TIMELESS NOR EXTRA-TEMPORAL

It is *simplistic* to say that Reformational philosophy regards the whole of *created* reality as temporal in the sense of "being in time." But it is

---

62. Cf. my article "Geschapen 'in Christus.' De wijsgerige concentratie-idee in bijbels licht" ["*Created in Christ*": *The philosophical idea of concentration in the light of Scripture*], *Radix* 20 (Oct. 1994): 260–83.

downright *false* to say that it harbors a dualism, or even just a duality, between temporality and the supra-temporal. "Supra-temporality" does not mean extra-temporal, apart from time or timeless, but the opposite. The idea of supra-temporality refers to the ordinary earthly time of our ordinary pre-theoretical experience, but then seen in *its unity, fullness or totality*. An entire age in our heart! (Eccl. 3:11).

Nevertheless, supra-temporality remains a creature, creaturely; it is a *created fullness* of time, not a "created eternity," as Thomas Aquinas put it (at the price of an internal contradiction). This question will have to be discussed in more detail further on in this chapter, since philosophy, as we argued in the first chapter, is theoretical thought focused on the unity or totality of cosmic (in the sense of earthly created) reality.

Here, in the notion of unity or totality, inseparable from both the temporal diversity in reality and the *"Archè"* or origin of everything (namely Christ), lies the *point of contact between philosophy and human faith*, regardless of the religion in which this faith concretely functions. The philosophical problem of time cannot be (properly) discussed as a separate subject without starting from the *fundamental tendency of all genuine philosophy: namely, its overt or covert orientation to the totality, the unity and the origin of concrete reality, including time.*

In the Christian faith we confess this tendency towards the origin as being created into reality. All things were created *"unto* God," according to Scripture. We confess this unity and totality of "all things" to lie "in Christ," in whom all things were *created*, not only redeemed and re-created.

Regrettably, Christian teachings as proclaimed in the churches have usually been confined to the doctrine of sin and salvation but without the backdrop of both in *creation*. And yet the reality of creation includes the *meaning* of creation's existence: its origin, mode of existence and destination, as well as the meaningfulness of our daily activities.

Rather than holding to the biblical view of creation in Christ, we abridge the belief in creation to an intellectual notion regarding a *fait accompli*, a bygone event from the past. The result is that our confessional view of reality is rationalistically degraded, reduced and warped, with all the attendant consequences for theology—primarily for ethics, but also for exegesis and dogmatics. In this way, present-day exegesis cannot help but be further wedded to *scientistic positivism* with its view of reality and history that has been reduced to temporality.

9.1.7 ORDER AND DURATION: THE LAW-SIDE AND SUBJECT-SIDE OF TIME

Like all creaturely reality, time has a "law-side" and a "subject-side." So as not to enter into too many details, we will limit ourselves here to a few remarks, following on what we already said in chapter 4, particularly in sec. 4.7.

The law-side or norm-side of time can be called *temporal order*, whereas the subjective, factual or experiential side of time can be referred to as *temporal duration*. Temporal duration is made possible by the temporal order and in principle is governed and guided by it.

The temporal order manifests itself in, among other things, the *irreversibility* of the order of the modal aspects. Each aspect "pre"-supposes the previous one, that is, the "earlier" one in cosmic time, which is not a logical or chronological "earlier" but a fully cosmic structural given. All anticipatory moments in every aspect anticipate a following aspect, one that comes "later." Hence we also talk about *earlier and later* aspects in the cosmic law-order or divine order of creation.

9.1.8 THE DYNAMIC OF TIME

The dynamic nature of this temporal order comes out in the "restlessness" of all subjective existence, most directly, clearly and consciously in human life of course. Human life contains an *urge to open up culturally*, a prompting that is aroused and made possible by the temporal order and that will not leave us alone. "Our heart is restless until it finds rest in God," Augustine already wrote.

The "last" aspect, the "boundary aspect" where functions the life of faith, gives this dynamic the religious "direction" towards the place where rest can in fact be found. In every human faith this refuge is found in God or in what people of non-Christian faith substitute as an alternative deity, their idol.

Thus we understand so much the better that creation's restless mode of existence and its restless dynamics express the biblical revelation that we have been created *"unto God."* The reality which some philosophers refer to as *"das metaphyische Bedürfnis"* (the metaphysical need) and which Calvin called the *"sensus divinitatis"* (the awareness or possibility of experiencing a deity) can be theologically expressed as man's innate and therefore ineradicable (non-believers sometimes speak of "incurable") need for religion or religiosity. Both in and outside of Christianity, periods of secularism are regularly followed by a period (a "new age") of revived religiosity, mysticism, "spirituality," or whatever it is called. We are experiencing this phenomenon in our own day. But it cannot always be characterized by the biblical expression "return to God." Far from it; religiosity as such is not always true religion. Godless Israel was at the same time full of gods and very religious with "the provocation of their offering" (Ezek. 20:28)!

9.1.9 THE TOTALITY (OR "FULLNESS") OF TIME
In the foregoing we emphasized the *unity* of time, in which all moments of time or time periods are concentrated into a supra-temporality or full temporality. This applies both to the law-side of time (temporal order) and to the subject-side of time (temporal duration). Both sides also enter the picture when we emphasize the *totality* of time.

We saw that all created reality has its unity and totality in Christ. This is primarily a *supra-temporal totality*, which is not un-temporal, not timelessness, not extra-temporality, but which may be called *the fullness of time*. This expression also occurs in the Bible (Gal. 4:4), where it is not, of course, a philosophical statement about the structures of time, yet does point to something that seems strange to us and does not occur in everyday usage. Hence we often read the expression as meaning "the ripeness of the time for..." or "the right time for," expressions that refer to favorable circumstances.

However, this biblical expression cannot be understood outside of faith. It refers to something that transcends our temporal reality and in no way depends on favorable circumstances. It concerns the coming of God's Son in the flesh, the coming of what is also called *"the fullness of Christ"* (Eph. 4:13, probably an explicative genitive: the fullness which Christ is).

This coming of Christ was more than just an incidental historical event, more than a mere date on a calendar, though it was that too.

It was this "more" that Rev. Ter Linden must have had in mind when he made the (incorrect) statement about biblical stories that they are "true, but did not really happen." With this provocative statement he may have meant to say, among other things, that much more and something far more important can be said than merely, or mainly, that it really happened *historically*. The certainty of this historical truth can, at most, be a theoretical certainty, starting from a scriptural reading based on a certain theory of inspiration. But the content of *faith* includes the *depth-dimension* of all historicity in its supra-temporal root or unity, and thus entails also a distinctive solidity and certitude oriented to the "fullness" of God's revelation in Christ. This typical *certitude of faith* should therefore not be (positivistically) identified with the kind of certainty that historical science provides. Faith cannot be "proved" correct, as if scientific certainty—including the certainty of theological science—is more certain than the certitude of faith. An intellectual "defense of the faith" can never offer the certitude proper to faith itself, let alone "confirm" or guarantee this certitude of faith. *Fides* non *quaerit seu quadrat intellectum*! Faith does not seek understanding but consummates it.

The Incarnation was the *fullness* of all calendar dates together, and therefore was in some form or other *always real and actual*. It has sometimes been spoken of as "eternity here and now." But the term "eternity" should then not just be understood as God's eternity, but as the supra-temporal concentration of all creaturely temporality, as the "fullness" of it.

This means that the historical event in Bethlehem is *more* than a purely historical fact. More, too, than what existentialist theology calls a *"historisches"* fact (based on the distinction between the historians' *Historie* and the existentialists' *Geschichte*). It was what Bultmann called "eternity here and now," though his particular interpretation of this otherwise acceptable expression is unacceptable to us.

In theology, I believe, it is best to hold on to the biblical expression and speak of "the fullness of the time" (Gal. 4:4) or "the fullness of the times" (Eph. 1:10). This already involved everything else that had happened before Christ's birth or that would happen after the exact calendar date of his birth. In short, our whole salvation was involved—not yet *revealed or expressed* in time, mind you, yet already truly existing. Consider also the "transposing" of Christ's death on the cross on Golgotha around the year A.D. 33 to the temporally transcendent in Rev. 13:8, which speaks of "the Lamb that was slain from the foundation of the world." This involved the *full temporal* (or "supra-temporal") reality, the religious *totality and identity* of time and reality. This also involved, to mention just one example, our personal sanctification "in Christ."

Via Heidegger, Gadamer and others, philosophers of history in the second half of the previous century well understood some of this and expressed it in, for instance, the distinction between "Historie" and "Geschichte," in seeing past and future *in each other*, and in de-ideologizing the human selfhood. In doing so, however, they failed to rise above the *immanence* of all events within temporality. Dooyeweerd would say: they remained wedded to "immanence philosophy."

9.1.10 SUMMARIZING CONCLUSION

The foregoing means that with regard to time, as with our concrete experience of reality itself, we need to distinguish between (a temporal) totality and its many *aspects*. This temporal totality of time (not to be confused with its supra-temporal unity and fullness) is called universal or cosmic time. This cosmic universality of time can be comprehended in an *idea* of time. It is the idea (not a concept) of the universal inner coherence in reality itself, both according to its law-side and its subjective factual side. But it is, more precisely, a *continuous* coherence between modal modes of being, between modalities and entities, between entities among each other, between subjects and objects, and between all phases and periods within the fundamental category of genesis, existence and demise. This *continuity is the continuity of cosmic time,* which does not cancel the *theoretical* distinction of the articulations just mentioned, but does enable us to realize that a theoretical distinction is still no more than a *logical* approach to reality.

This comprehensive, rich content of reality, including the temporal aspects, is religiously confessed as an expression in *diversity and coherence* of a unity and fullness that is a (temporally) *transcendent* totality, in which all this diversity in time and reality is *concentrated.*

Against this backdrop we will now look in greater detail at the modal or aspectual diversity in the reality of time, thus at the temporal diversity in concrete "temporal reality."

9.2 TIME AND MODALITY

9.2.0 INTRODUCTION
9.2.0.1 ZENO OF ELEA
Before giving a more detailed exposition on the philosophical problem of time, we will first briefly compare this problem with an entirely different problem which is nevertheless connected with it at a deep level. *Zeno of Elea* (490–430 BC) claimed that the champion runner "fleet-footed Achilles" can never overtake a tortoise if the latter is given a head start. Suppose the tortoise has an advantage of 100 feet, then Achilles must first make up these 100 feet. That takes time, however little. In this short time the tortoise has also advanced some distance, which is new ground for Achilles to make up. While he does so, the tortoise advances again and Achilles again has to make up more ground before he can overtake the tortoise. And so on. Though the gap between the two gets smaller and smaller, it is never bridged. The initial situation returns every time, if on a smaller scale. Hence Achilles can never overtake the tortoise.—So, what is the error in this logical argument?[63]

Starting from the doctrine of mutually irreducible aspects, each with its own nature, we can answer that the error lies in the identification of motion and space. *Motion* cannot be reduced to *spatiality*. Motion cannot be adequately defined in terms of space, as if motion were no more than a displacement in space that takes time. Both modalities are distinctive, mutually irreducible, original modes of being of reality. Anyone who attempts to reduce movements to a configuration of spatial distances, like Zeno, must fail. The theory clashes with how we practically experience the reality of the facts: Achilles can effortlessly overtake the tortoise.

9.2.0.2 TIME HAS MODAL ASPECTS
In the same way it is never quite possible to "measure" time. Sometimes we can, sometimes we cannot. It depends on which *aspect* of time, and of reality, we have in mind. Using a clock we can indeed measure time and express the exact measurement in centuries, years,

---

63. Philosophers are still debating the correct solution to this problem, nowadays often using mathematical irrationality theories; cf. J. Mittelstrass, *Enzyklopädie Philosophie und Wissenschaftstheorie*, vol. 2 (1984), *s.v.* inkommensurabel.

days, hours, seconds, and thus accurately define these segments of time. But is this "time"? Is this the only time, the real time? Or are we merely dealing here with an *aspect* of real time?

Clearly, we can only answer in the affirmative once we compare it with another experiential aspect of time, for instance emotional or felt time. "To me that short moment felt like an eternity," somebody can say after experiencing a horrible situation. In the same way we also experience the opposite: "pleasant hours pass quickly," "time flew by." These experiences are real experiences. They are experiences of time that are of a different kind when compared with so-called clock time, which is time in its physical aspect, where time has a mode of being that can be measured by standards deriving from the hands on a clock face and ultimately from the earth's rotation around its axis or its revolution around the sun.

Those other experiences of time are not just random, purely sub-jective inventions or illusions. They are experiences of concrete modes of truly existing (indeed subjective, but also objective) temporal duration, of temporal phenomena which as such are subject to cor-responding laws, so that they are also to a certain extent predictable. We know that in certain situations we are liable to forget clock time, and so we set an alarm or some other timer.

On account of reality's temporal character and on account of time's reality, time too has its "aspects," that is to say it has various modes of existence and ways of being experienced. Probably in all the modalities of reality that we distinguished in the theory of aspects, time expresses itself each time in a distinctive way characteristic of that aspect. I will not develop this too broadly in this introduction, nor enter into current discussions about some of the details of this philosophical theory. Let me merely indicate some examples.

Note again that the history of philosophy has produced various "definitions" of time, which were actually definitions of some or other aspect of time that was then taken to be time itself.

9.2.1 NUMERICAL TIME

"Natural numbers" have their own unchanging sequential order, which is irreversible. Our subjective counting does not automatically agree with this order. We can skip numbers or count back even into negative numbers, but in doing so we remain bound to the natural positive order, which we can ignore or reverse only in counting subjectively. Apparently this is something proper to numbers themselves, the familiar "earlier" and "later" in the *series* of "natural" numbers. This "sequential" order can be seen as a typically numerical expression of the "progression" of all time (sometimes referred to today as time's "arrow").

In their natural order these numbers go "successively" from small to large. This "magnitude" of numbers is an anticipatory moment in the direction of space. Primarily, however, the magnitude of a number remains a quantity. It does not become spatial; it remains numerical. So in this case the word "magnitude" is a metaphor. But this "anticipation" (the term is likewise a metaphor!) manifests again, in a numerical way and so in a limited sense, an aspect of the full *dynamics* of time in the continuity of cosmic time.

9.2.2 SPATIAL TIME

In the theory of aspects we saw that the nucleus of the spatial is continuous extension. Time occurs in this as a simultaneous presence of the concrete space of reality and its constituent parts, so of points, lines, planes and volumes. But this *simultaneity* is not the same as timelessness. On the contrary, it expresses that where there is space, this space within its limits is everywhere at the same time. Strictly speaking, the expression "simultaneous presence" can therefore be seen as a pleonasm, which could be replaced by the single word *simultaneity*—just as, strictly speaking, "continuous extension" as an indication of the meaning-nucleus of the spatial aspect is likewise a pleonasm, since extension as such is already continuous.

But this simultaneity is not a feature of the spatial aspect as such. It is simultaneity, being "at one and the same time," because it relates to the spatial aspect of *concrete things*, which are always things-in-time. So we can formulate it like this: the spatiality of a concrete thing expresses itself *in time* as simultaneity because within its spatiality this thing is everywhere at the same moment. Thus time manifests itself here as a limited simultaneous (omni)presence.

9.2.3 KINEMATIC TIME

Since the third aspect does not yet involve physical movements but "kinematic" motions, as studied in the science of kinematics in which the causes of the moving forces can still be disregarded, we are dealing in this order of motion with a fundamental *reversibility*. For in kinematics all processes are reversible. Also, in kinematics all motions *qua* movement are fluent, continuous. Here time manifests itself in its modal feature of *universal continuous flow* or *interactive dynamics of coherence*, noticeably so in organisms and the human mode of existence founded therein.

9.2.4 PHYSICAL TIME

According to the experts, time in the physical aspect manifests itself as *non-reversibility in succession*. This is shown by the sequential order of cause and effect. In everyday life physical time is primarily objectified in clock time and also in calendar dates—in "day and hour."

9.2.5 ORGANIC TIME

In this aspect, (universal or total) time is expressed in the progression of the life process.

(a) The organic process is characterized by *development and decline*, in the progression of germination, growth, maturation, ageing and dying. Physical irreversibility is here enhanced by finality, that is, goal-orientation, purpose.

(b) The *phases* in organic processes, as in historical processes (see below), cannot be demarcated from each other mathematically (that is, quantitatively) by means of clock-time units such as years. Our internal biological clock is not synchronous with our watch.

Thus it is impossible to indicate the exact moment when a person or animal comes into being in the process of generation, or when death has set in. This requires biological and psychological criteria; but even these can only mark certain *aspects* of corporeal death or corporeal life. In the case of human beings, moreover, clerks at the Records Office will apply a juridical criterion when they ask for a doctor's certificate.

Man, as we will see in the next chapter, is not exhausted by his temporal mode of existence. That is also the reason why the (wrongly formulated) problem of the exact time of human generation and death finds its answer outside the area accessible to scientific analysis.

This fact is not important in the first place for the *juridical* problem of abortion and euthanasia (in the end-of-life phase), or for the *medical* problem of the criterion for terminating life (for the purpose, say, of organ transplants), but it is especially important for the moral and religious questions that arise here.

(c) *Full humanity comprises more than a person's lifetime, that is to say, more than its beginning and its end in time* (cf. Appendix, Figure 2.) Therefore it cannot be delimited or measured by any aspectual criterion. We have long known this in faith, indeed we find it quite normal: we have no problem confessing that "temporal or physical death" is not the end of our existence.

Theology's crutch here was always the pagan doctrine of an "immortal soul." In practice this tool for use in apologetics usually leads to a *materialistic view* of the beginning and end of our temporal human existence. Both are then pinned down to an *organic* moment in time (the fusion of egg cell and sperm cell at conception, implantation in the uterine wall, to an exact moment for establishing cardiac arrest or brain death). In turn this often causes people to wrongly introduce the term "murder." In the end, the way people think and talk about these issues is governed by how they view man's heart, life's transience, and the relation between them.

Here, too, "ethics" is based on a theoretical view of reality (and in this context: on an anthropology) which is philosophical in character. The question at which point in time an organically qualified fetus has become or will become a human being cannot be answered scientifically. Any answer one might give depends on a subjective *religious interpretation of the observable facts in a concrete case.* But the *grounds* for this belief, erroneous or not, can never be found in theoretical hypotheses about organic facts, the more so when these facts can only be established scientifically and with sophisticated medical technology. Every real belief (or "unbelief") is based on man's reception and interpretation of *divine revelation.*

9.2.6 PSYCHICAL TIME

The characteristic feature of emotional time (seen from the subject-side) is its striking discrepancy with physical time.

(a) Depending on whether we are emotionally tense or bored, clock time in this psychically qualified mode of experience can run fast or slow. Think of expressions like "we waited forever," "time just flew by," and so on (cf. sec. 9.2.0.2).

(b) Psychical time as continuity manifests itself in *mood, temper, atmosphere.* This is a residue, a disposition that arises as a deeper layer in our act-life when specific feelings persist for a time.

9.2.7 LOGICAL-ANALYTICAL TIME

In this aspect, time is expressed in the functioning of presuppositions, and of premises in a syllogism. The conclusion is always "logically" later than the arguments, and these in turn are "later" than the "starting-points" or "pre"-suppositions. The line of thinking which must be followed from those starting-points to the conclusions is completed subjectively in a shorter time by one person than another, so that he or she understands more quickly.

Those starting-points comprise all kinds of initial, not typically logical, conditions (health, intelligence, social class, economic position, moral inclination, religious environment, group bias, etc.). But in addition the very structure of scientific thought contains "ground-ideas" or basic premises regarding a general view of reality, and these will form the foundation of every special science. Such basic premises (e.g., "everything is matter," "every human is a reincarnation," "everything was created by God," etc.) sometimes dominate the way the special sciences frame their problems.

When it comes to science, these transcendental ideas and basic categories are logically prior to concept formation in the special sciences. They are part of the *cosmological* "a priori." From an anthropological perspective, they reside in the *cosmic* a priori of the depth layers of ethos and of dispositions in the logical acts. This will be clarified in chapters 10 and 11 on anthropology.

Primary in all of life—and logical thinking is no exception—is the a priori, religious-ethical content of one's *attitude to life,* one's *ethos.* Within the logical aspect, ethos is, in turn, logically prior to the basic concepts and lines of reasoning. Ethos is a structural *a priori,* a necessary ("transcendental") fundamental or starting condition, while ultimately the *religious* position of the human heart in the transcendent spiritual community with Christ and his followers has the deepest and last (or first) word.

9.2.8 HISTORICAL TIME

In the aspect of formative power, cosmic time manifests itself among other things in historical eras and cultural periods.

(a) The experience of historical time, again, is distinctive in its incongruence with clock time. We already pointed to some of our contemporaries in the 21st century who are still living in (the cultural period of) the 19th century, or even in some respects in the Stone Age, like the tree-dwelling Korowai tribes of Irian Jaya. Among these people "time" seems to have "stood still," which is in fact partly the case, if only from the viewpoint of the historical aspect. It is also in the sense of historical time that we understand the cultural figures of progress, conservatism and reaction. The phenomena of tradition, evolution and revolution display features of deceleration, average progress or acceleration in historical time.

(b) The problem historians have of dividing history into periods clearly shows that historical time (time periods or eras) cannot be precisely demarcated by means of calendar time. The times "flow into each other," as people say. Thus professional historians often disagree on when the Middle Ages started and ended. The same goes for the Renaissance and the Enlightenment; in addition, these were cultural phenomena that did not take place in every country at exactly the same time. It is clear in any case that such periods cannot be precisely defined in terms of calendar dates. This last method of dating is useful only as a first overall approach, which becomes significant only when based on a view of the character of such a period in terms of cultural history.

Another point of general agreement is that all cosmic time shows a dynamic progression of past, present and future. But we already saw in sec. 8.1.4 that in our concrete experience of life and time we do not primarily experience the "present" in the physical aspect of clock time, but in the *biotic* aspect of the length of time we live, or in the *historical* aspect of the cultural time we live in. In other words, by "the present" we mean first of all "our present time." Particularly from an historical point of view, that time may display cultural progress in one area and stagnation or even reaction in another.

9.2.9 SYMBOLIC TIME

Language is one of the elements functioning in the aspect of "symbolic signification." We can distinguish here between tenses: past, present and future, each of which can be further divided into, for example, simple past, past perfect, and so on. These distinctions in tense refer to very real modes of experiencing duration, which in this way are objectified into linguistic judgments. Punctuation marks like periods and commas, and musical symbols also have an objective-symbolic duration; that is to say, they refer approximately to a tempo or pause to be observed, to a rest, to a retardation or an acceleration.

9.2.10 SOCIAL TIME

In the social aspect with its social norms and subjective social customs, the "before" and "after" of time has a separate *social meaning*: "Ladies first" is an (outdated?) normative custom. On many occasions (at least in our culture) we are supposed to be present exactly "on time," that is, at the agreed upon time; in a variety of circumstances we are to wait for "the proper moment"; and so on. Social rank and social importance, but also entire cultures have a lot to say about the duration and the *before* and *after* of such social obligations as greeting, calling on someone, letting someone go first, having people wait, breaking off a conversation or a visit, never arriving "on time," and the list goes on.

9.2.11 ECONOMIC TIME

Time also plays its distinctive role in our economic valuations.

(a) This is evident, for example, when we attach greater value to the present than to the future by agreeing to pay interest on loans. Today the borrowed sum may have greater economic value for us than the much larger sum that we will have to give back in 10 years' time (as principal plus interest). The opposite holds for lending, investing, or paying pension contributions. It is our economic situation and what we desire in that situation that create such a big difference in valuation between present and future. This is also shown by the business of trading in the futures market or by the difference between hourly wages and piecework.

(b) "Periodic increments" in wages or salary are intended to express the rising economic value of labor as a result of increasing work experience. The "periods" with which the "periodic increments" are connected are therefore not just calendar periods, but genuine *economic periods of time* based on calendar periods. They are time periods of an intrinsically and typically economic character, based on calendar time, to be sure, yet as a specific kind of time not *qualified* by calendar time.

(c) The typically economic aspect of time also comes out in

expressions like "wasting time" and "gaining time," or in the positive or negative valuation of the way somebody "spends his time."

9.2.12 AESTHETIC TIME

Beauty in life is far from being a timeless affair. In music it is closely connected with tempo and rhythm. One may attempt to approximate this tempo by means of metronome figures (cf. sec. 5.14 above), but in the actual aesthetic performance of the music these symbols are personally or collectively interpreted.

In the visual arts aesthetic quality is experienced in questions like: What is the physical age of the material? Is the style contemporary? The implied influences turn aesthetic time, which is implicit in aesthetic entities, into something characteristic, something quite distinct from physical or historical time.

In the writing of novels there will have to be an exciting variation in the progression of the story, whereas a chronologically constructed historical narrative is liable to be "boring," that is to say, unaesthetic. The *moment* of a story's dénouement should also make aesthetic sense. In poems it is sometimes crucial whether certain ideas, sounds or rhymes occur earlier or later.

The expression "timeless art," in itself nonsensical, is only meant to indicate that the art in question has always been valued more or less positively throughout the generations and the centuries, something that cannot be said about many works of art from a particular fashionable movement.

9.2.13 JURIDICAL TIME

The meaning of retribution gives an entirely distinctive mode of expression to time in the juridical aspect.

(a) Certain rights can be forfeited through lapse of time and "superannuate," losing their validity. The term of a prison sentence cannot be prescribed in law in terms of a fixed number of months or years. The term is a punishment, which is a juridical figure. To be a *just* punishment, a judge (as a living and deliberating person) must determine its length in each individual case in a balancing consideration of guilt and punishment, allowing for, say, an offender's psychological state, his age, background or culture. Hence criminal laws always mention a *maximum* sentence, which is no more than an upper limit for the judge.

Government laws do not acquire force of law until the time they are published in the official gazette, unless they take effect retroactively from a specified earlier time. All these are *juridical* figures of time, which cannot be identified with their moral aspect, their social or religious aspect.

(b) When does a human person actually come into being? The *juridical* time in question here can be laid down in statute law as a criterion for making abortion punishable or non-punishable, for instance after the first trimester. Similarly, according to the biotic aspect of temporal human generation, the beginning of organic corporeality can be hypothetically assumed and legally laid down as the moment when sperm and ovum unite.

In both instances we are dealing with no more than one particular (in this case juridical) temporal *aspect* of human life, and not with full humanity itself. A full human being does not have a moment in time when it comes "into being." Everybody knows that the date and hour of *birth* are not this moment either. *Complete* man has a genesis only in the sense of a (supra-temporal) *origin*, namely in God's creation. Here, Christ (God *and* man) was created as the first creature (the "alpha"); and created *with him*, because "in Christ," was man, the first Adam, as was the rest of creation (Col. 1: 15, 16). This "origin" should not be interpreted as a "starting-point" in time.

(c) The *juridical* moment when a marriage is dissolved always follows some time after the *moral* termination of a love relationship in a marriage, something which cannot be located in clock time. For the love relationship is what makes *the marriage as such* possible and qualifies it. The beginning, decline and end of the love relationship, which makes or breaks a marriage, cannot be pinpointed to a specific date or moment. Both require a certain amount of time, a period which cannot be circumscribed by a date.

(d) Similarly, the juridical point in time when the age of majority or "legal age" is reached is merely a very rough approximation of biotic, psychological, social or economic adulthood. This *point* (!) in time, when majority is attained, with its attendant change in public rights and duties, also has a typically juridical meaning, namely, within the context of a public legal community. So this point in time is of a juridical nature only and cannot be understood on the basis of physical calendar time, biotic time, psychological "maturity," or social or economic "independence." Each of these factors differs from individual to individual, but the just notion of "equality before the law" requires it to be stipulated in law when the legal age is reached.

9.2.14 MORAL TIME

In the love aspect the distinctive nature of time is expressed, for instance, in the figures of haste and patience in love, or the lack thereof. It also operates in "taking time" for one's fellow man, especially in situations where help or attention is urgently required. "Love takes time," as the saying goes.

This time of love also manifests itself in various "periods" and in the relation between them. For there is (at least in the Christian custom of several centuries) a progression of the time when two people get to know each other before they get engaged, of a time of engagement before the wedding, of the wedding day before sexual consummation. Again, this traditional progression in moral time does not admit of fixation in physical clock time or calendar time. Viewed from the normative side, it is a *principle* which must freely and voluntarily be "positivized" as the partners give shape to their love relationship. More on this later, in the chapter on "praxeology" (commonly called "philosophical ethics").

9.2.15 RELIGIOUS TIME

Time in the aspect of religious faith has, once again, an entirely different and completely distinctive nature.

(a) It is *the distinctive nature of faith to be oriented to what transcends all time*, that is, to God, to His revelation, to God's work of creation and providential ordainment, and to the "end of the age," to "eternal" salvation. But faith is also directed at angels, at heaven and hell, at God's plan for our lives in judgment and redemption. This faith content affords a practical perspective on the totality of cosmic time, its first beginnings and its consummation at the end of time. It also gives content and direction to our worldviewish conception of time, that is to say, of all its concrete phases.

In faith, but *only in faith*, do we also gain perspective on what Scripture calls "the fullness of time" and on our philosophical translation of this reality as the "supra-temporal concentration point of all time."

The first word in the Bible reads: *"In the beginning* God created the heavens and the earth." This "in the beginning" is taken up again and made more explicit in John 1:1 with the familiar words, "In the beginning was the Word." It is an expression that also occurs in many mythologies, and there, too, it refers to a "primordial time," a time which is not some moment long ago but which remains in force in the present and at all times. The famous mythologist Mircea Eliade always talked about *"in illo tempore"*—in that (primordial) time.

From out of our religious experience of time we are oriented to the "end" of time, when Christ will return. Faith has been called the window through which we, living in time, can view the eternal God and the supra-temporal fullness of Christ, of ourselves and of all creation. Epistemologically we say that, although we cannot conceptualize these revealed divine and non-temporal matters, we can have an *idea* of them, a religious idea, a "vision" (the term "idea" comes from *idein*, to see). In religious time we also experience all our other experiences of time as relating to the eternal God and His eternal doings.

(b) We know, not in the sense of calendar time but in the specific sense of faith and the time of faith, that our heart must "first" be opened by God's Spirit before we can believe and accept God's Word. Certain forms of mysticism try to locate this work of God somewhere in man's time of life as a separate stage or moment, as a "rebirth" which must be behind us before we can move on and seriously devote ourselves to (the call for) faith in the message of the gospel.

In the sense of faith, to be sure, *the gift "precedes"* the act of faithful obedience, and being born again precedes the new life. In acknowledging this truth, however, faith reaches out to a knowledge of what is beyond our (logical) understanding and powers of the mind, since it points to God's activity beyond time and within time, an activity that does not exclude but *includes* human responsibility. In the history of the church, the wish to talk about these "spiritual" things and systematize them in terms of *time* has led to endless theological controversies regarding the "order" or proper sequence of calling, regeneration and conversion, justification and sanctification.

These controversies remind us that we should not try to systematize or fix the knowledge content of these divine works in *chrono*-logical processes. All theological positions on this topic can base themselves (though incorrectly) on the Bible, precisely because the Bible is not interested in this chronology and sometimes talks one way, sometimes another, about the temporal sequence of the Spirit's work. After all, faith knowledge of these matters relates to what lies beyond time (*chronos*) with its "earlier" and "later."

Thus the so-called *"order of salvation"* is not *an order of time*. Rather, in faith, and thus in the time of faith, it is a figure of speech that is projected onto the work of salvation in Christ, the supra-temporal redemptive work of the eternal God. To talk about the *ordo salutis* as if it were an order of time in God's work is theologically irresponsible. In the supra-temporal or full-temporal sphere, in what Scripture calls the "order of Melchizedek," all historical points of time with their past, present and future are *one* in Christ.

From the sixth century onward, scholasticism talked about eternity as an "eternal present" (*nunc aeternum*). This is of course a logical contradiction, yet a justifiable one if it is not taken literally or as a definition but rather as a *metaphorical religious idea* about that which cannot be defined in the categories of time. The same applies to Bultmann's expression "eternity here and now." All this is quite common in mythical (religious) language, and it is familiar to a Christian's faith life. But Christian *theology* cannot handle it because much of this theology is rooted in a rationalist tradition which has no room for the reality of a temporally transcendent "fullness" of time. Hence it has no room for a creation of all things "in Christ," as the Scriptures nevertheless teach us.

(c) In religious self-reflection and self-knowledge we transcend intentionally, that is purposively, our entire temporal mode of existence. That is to say, we transcend it in the *concentration* of our entire existence in the supra-temporal focus of our life, in our "heart." For there, in this *radix* (i.e., root) of our existence, we make the radical choice as to the religious direction of our life. That comes to expression in time as a *religious choice* in the borderland between time and supra-temporality.

(d) In theology this distinctive character of religious time in the religious aspect of cosmic time has led to many studies and theories regarding "theological time." Some important names here are Plotinus, Augustine, Boethius, Martin Heidegger, Karl Barth, Rudolf Bultmann, Karl Heim, Oscar Cullmann and Hendrikus Berkhof. Sadly, the theological problem of time has so far remained virtually beyond the purview of Reformed theology.

9.3. Time and eternity

9.3.1 A "boundary problem"

The difference between time and eternity is a boundary problem for philosophy, one to which it cannot give a *philosophical* answer. Theologians have tried to define eternity in categories of time. They have said, for instance, that eternity is an infinite *time,* or (like Boethius, 480-524) an infinite *present,* an eternal *now* (*nunc aeternum*).

But all this is highly disputable from a logical point of view and for this reason alone scientifically unsound. We cannot give a scientific definition of eternity, since it is God's eternity. To *define* is to demarcate, to indicate *fines* (Latin for boundaries). What we know about eternity in *faith,* hence with faith knowledge, we can only describe *analogically,* metaphorically (with an *"analogia fidei"*). Only in this way can we feel at peace, faith-wise, with the non-theological *practical figure of speech* that eternity is a never-ending, ever-lasting "time." We can never speak of that which exceeds and lies beyond time except in terms of time.

Thomas Aquinas thought he had to distinguish between God's eternity (*aeternitas*) and the created eternity (*aeviternitas*) of creatures like angels or human souls, the difference being that *aeviternitas* has a beginning and *aeternitas* does not. This historical attempt to formulate the difference between time, supra-temporality and eternity is understandable. Indeed, there is an essential difference. *For we cannot talk scientifically about time without being aware of a contrast with what is non-time.* If "everything" were time we could no longer say anything characteristic about what time is. Compare it with the problem about the notion of history: if *everything were* history we could not talk meaningfully about the history *of* something which *is* not itself history—for example art, economy, language, law—but which does *have* history.

Scientifically, however, we can do no more than show that a theological definition of eternity or supra-temporality is an impossibility. Only *through faith* do we understand that the eternal God can in no way whatsoever be conceptually known by means of creaturely categories. His "eternity" cannot be "defined" in the temporal categories of human thought. For a thousand (creaturely) years are like one day to God, and one (creaturely) day can count, so to speak, for a thousand years with God. In short, God is far exalted above creation and above creaturely time. All so-called scientific theologizing about the "concept of eternity" breaks down in the face of this reality.

9.3.2 ETERNAL ELECTION AND REPROBATION

Similarly, theology cannot, strictly speaking, address God's works in His eternal election and reprobation. These works of God can only be embraced in faith. It goes without saying, however, that this faith is not always sound or fully biblical. Human faith is often weak and inadequate. Not infrequently it has also suffered damage from theological influences (intellectualism, rationalism, mysticism) or (partly as a result of this) from a scepticism thanks to which people reject the faith "because we cannot know anything about it anyway, let alone know *for certain.*"

But Scripture does not talk about divine election as an isolated and secret act. That would be pure abstraction. Scripture talks about God's electing love "in Christ" (Eph. 1), and that in a pastoral context. This means, among other things, that *only in Christ,* in His person (God *and* man) and in His work, does the electing God reveal himself to us and in this way asks us to respond in faith and offers us comfort and assurance. "Speculation" alone introduces a separation here between the eternal counsel of God and God's work in time in Christ, between God's work and our human responsibility.

Chapter Ten – Anthropology: The human heart

CHAPTER TEN

ANTHROPOLOGY: THE HUMAN HEART

10.1 THE PROBLEM OF UNITY

10.1.1 COSMOLOGY AND ANTHROPOLOGY

So far we have dealt in broad outline with (a) the theories of *modalities* and *entities*. Next we discussed (b) *the problem of time*, during which we already began to make a transition to (c) *anthropology*. These are three extensive theories of Reformational cosmology, of which, properly speaking, the theory of time still belongs in part to the philosophical "prolegomena," the foundational issues of philosophy. As we now turn to anthropology we will have to refer back to the theory of time, just as, conversely, in the theory of time we had to anticipate anthropology.

The theory we wish to explore in this chapter is the most important component in the indivisible systematic whole of Reformational philosophy. We made mention of it above, in sec. 3.1 and 3.2, but we have not yet examined it. This third theory comprises in the first place just one fundamental idea: namely, that the cosmos (with everything in it, and that is the sole subject of philosophy) is a *unity* by virtue of its *transcendent center*. It is not just a quantity within which there is a universal *coherence* between the diversities, but in this cosmic coherence there is also a *unity*, and specifically a *central time-transcending unity*.

This central point, this central unity is *Christ*, the living Christ as revealed to us in Scripture. It is a unity that we cannot know conceptually, but we know it religiously (we can also say: we know it as an idea, not as a concept). It is the answer of faith to questions of philosophy that necessarily arise in the course of scientific inquiry and appear there as boundary questions, questions that cannot be answered by philosophy itself.

Christ is primarily the *original unity* (Col. 1:16 and related places). He is, with God the Father, the Creator and bearer of the entire cosmos which was created *in* Him. But Christ is also, as the second Adam, Head of the new humanity. — These are, by the way, exclusively faith statements, affirmations of God's revelation in the Word; they are not philosophy. *I am not sure I agree*

In faith we also confess that the earth is the center of the universe. Of course, not in the scientific sense of astrophysical cosmology, but in the *religious* sense, which we can only experience *in faith*. This statement, too, is not a philosophical but a pre-theoretical, worldviewish remark, and as such religiously qualified.

 I disagree

The fact that planet Earth is the religious center of the universe is due to its unique position as man's dwelling-place. That is why man, again seen from the religious totality perspective, is the *"spiritual"* center of the earth, and thus of all creation.

10.1.2 CHRISTOCENTRIC OR ANTHROPOCENTRIC?
AN INCORRECT QUESTION

After what we said in sec. 1.7.7 about the Christocentric and anthropocentric character of Dooyeweerd's Reformational philosophy, it should suffice to emphasize once again that both terms are not in opposition to each other but mean essentially the same thing. The only difference is that "Christocentric" indicates that this philosophy in its *non-philosophical religious basis* starts from the creation and the existence of the cosmos in and through Christ. The term "anthropocentric" points, *in the manner of theoretical philosophy,* to the concentration of all reality in man, in particular in Christ as man. In both cases, in faith and in philosophy, more is seen of reality than non-Christian science can ever perceive. The depth dimension of reality eludes it because by means of an artificial theoretical distinction it separates faith from scientific thought.

10.1.3 LANDMANN ON THE PLACE OF PHILOSOPHICAL ANTHROPOLOGY

In the introduction to Michael Landmann's vast anthology of the history of philosophical anthropology we find an indication as to the relative importance of this voluminous work.[64] Landmann rightly

---

64. Michael Landmann et al., eds., *De Homine: Der Mensch im Spiegel seines*

begins by remarking that, long before philosophy had developed, man had an *image* of himself. Human beings, precisely as *human beings,* always lived within "an horizon of self-understanding, an understanding not just of his own person but just as much of man as such."[65]

For our part we call this man's *pre-theoretical view* of himself and of humanity. We want to treat this more seriously than is customary and place particular emphasis on it.

The practical, non-theoretical view proves to be decisive for any *theoretical* reflection on man that is made possible by it. It can be seen as a non-scientific *"conception"* of man or a *"conviction"* about man, one that is often formulated ad hoc and piecemeal, close to life, in concrete situations. It comes out in proverbs and sayings, habits and customs, novels, personal mottos, heraldic devices, etc. This non-scientific *worldview* forms a structural part of, or rather is a manifestation of, people's total "temporal" *attitude to life,* their *ethos,* which inheres in human identity as a depth layer in all human actions, as we will clarify in the next chapter.

When we come to discuss epistemology (chapter 14), as a follow-up to what was said in sec. 1.6.3, we will examine what the relationship is between theoretical and pre-theoretical insight into human existence. Our conclusion will be that the pre-theoretical necessarily precedes the theoretical and *grounds and guides* it. This also means that a worldview is not a primitive "philosophy" of unlettered people while scientific philosophy represents a better or "higher" form. We have here an issue that closely parallels the relation between (practical) faith knowledge and (theoretical) theology, which will be discussed later as well.

10.1.4 BRUNNER ON THE PRIORITY OF THE PRE-THEORETICAL IMAGE OF MAN

Emil Brunner has made the insightful remark that what gave Darwin, Marx, Nietzsche, Freud and others so much influence on the life and thought of the masses and on political power relations was *not* their *scientific theories* about "the origin of species," about capital and surplus value, about the subconscious and the psychotherapeutic

---

Gedankens (Freiburg, 1962); 619 pp. Trans. by David J. Parent, *De Homine: Man in the Mirror of His Thought* (Ann Arbor, 1979).

65. Ibid., p. xi.

method, and so forth.[66] Rather, the world-historical influence of these great thinkers lay in the *pre-theoretical*, intuitive, prophetic or visionary *image of man* from which they started or by which they were inspired, even before this practical image of man was systematized into a more or less scientific anthropology.

10.1.5 Landmann on the pre-theoretical view of man

Landmann is right in recognizing *the great importance of one's conception of man* (be it scientific or not). He writes: "The conception of man involuntarily affects everything we think, do and generate." Further on: "In short, the collective cultural domains of a people and an era contain a tacit and often fragmentary human self-understanding, one that we might call an *implicit anthropology*." Given his immanentist standpoint, Landmann calls this "implicit anthropology" an extremely important "determinant" that governs everything in our lives, "perhaps even more important than the religious determinant, which intellectual historians have long considered the most fundamental of all. For how we see the gods depends first of all on how we see ourselves."[67]

According to Landmann, therefore, this is how *fundamental and compelling* anthropology is "before it turns" theoretical. In his view, this has an effect on what people believe religiously, but also on scientific philosophy: "Just as every cultural product bears testimony to a view of man, so too does philosophy."[68]

Such are the views of Brunner and Landmann, but we could mention dozens of other authors who have similar convictions about the importance of pre-theoretical "anthropology," the practical view of man. Sadly, recognition of its importance often goes together with its simultaneous classification *below* scientific anthropology, which is considered even more important. This is again a clear symptom of the idolatrous overestimation of science which characterizes our Western culture. It disregards the differences in structure and value between the two, as we will argue at greater length in connection with epistemology.

---

66. Emil Brunner, *Der Mensch im Widerspruch*, 3rd impr. (Zurich, 1941), pp. 21–25. Trans. by Olive Wyan, *Man in Revolt: A Christian Anthropology* (London, 1947).

67. Landmann, *De Homine*, p. xi.

68. Ibid., p. xii.

10.1.6 THE CHRISTIAN ANTHROPOLOGY REGARDING HUMANKIND

10.1.6.1 HUMANKIND AND THE ANIMAL KINGDOM

Like every genuine philosophical theme, anthropology focuses on totality and unity. In this way it arrives at the notion that there is a reality known as *humankind*. This word refers to a unique commonality, a common bond that is typical of all human beings as distinct from other creatures, in particular animals. There is no "kingdom of man" *debatable* as there is a "kingdom of animals"; *humankind* is a "spiritual" *totality and unity*, which cannot be said of the animal kingdom. This bothers no one in everyday life, but theoretically the big question is: What does this common bond consist of, this "unity and totality"?

Undoubtedly people are fascinated by the fact that all human beings, precisely as human beings, have some things, or even a great many things, in common. But if one looks for this universal commonality or equality in the *external form* only, one's biology runs into problems about the so-called *dividing lines* between the different human races as well as the *boundary line* between humans and other primates. And if instead one locates the defining feature of humankind in *culture*, one can point to profound cultural differences within the human race, differences which defy any notion of unity and equality.

The whole theoretical problem of the differences and similarities between humans and animals can be a boundary problem precisely because there *is* a boundary. But no *science*, which qua science is bound up with the *aspectual* approach to our *temporal* mode of existence, is able by itself to indicate a *definite* and *fundamental* boundary between a kingdom of man and the kingdom of animals. (The same applies *mutatis mutandis* to the boundary between the plant and animal kingdom.) The special sciences remain tied to the temporal aspects of reality and at most will observe a different number of *subject functions* in human beings and animals. Restricted to an aspectual approach, the sciences can go no further than to pose their *boundary questions* without being able to answer them.

Thus the evolutionism debate cannot be decided on an abstract scientific basis, because science *cannot* answer boundary questions on its own using its own resources, including its own boundary questions. At bottom, these boundaries are the boundaries drawn in the divine order of creation, and as such, as God's creative works, they are not accessible to the human mind, let alone fathomable or "definable." We are dealing here with the "wonders" and "mysteries" of God's works, and thus with God himself. Scripture contains many hymns to the great and *wondrous* works of God in his creation and to God himself. "Wondrous" here does not mean unnatural or supernatural. On the contrary, it confesses how mysterious and unfathomable to the human mind are God's works and God's active presence *in the created world*. Not until the Christian faith has answered the preliminary questions of faith and philosophy that are structurally present in every special science is it possible for theory to address the boundary questions.

In reality, faith (including non-Christian faith) never stands dualistically *alongside* science, but asserts itself—usually without intending to—right *inside* the scholarly debates about the boundary questions, if only by pointing to Christ and to the order of creation given in him. But almost all debates about the relation between faith and science have already incorporated that dualistic "alongside" in their framing of the problem, after which the debates are as interminable as they are unfruitful.

It is true, of course, that man has more functions and also a different community structure as compared to animals. But which ones? And where exactly does the boundary lie? Or is there a vague borderland between the psychical and the logical-analytical? We are familiar with the traditional idea that man differs from animals by being *endowed with reason*, by being a "rational animal." But modern thought, rightly in my view, increasingly questions the presumption of this demarcation. The more so if Willem Ouweneel is right in proposing that the psychical law-sphere be split up into two separate aspects, the passional and the instinctive.

But though I believe it is still possible to indicate a boundary some-where between humans and animals, that boundary would not represent the definitive, the *most characteristic*, distinction between humankind and the animal kingdom. For within the animal kingdom we also distinguish between higher and lower species that hardly bear any external resemblance to each other (think of a single-celled bacterium and an elephant). What could be the objection, then, to classifying man among the animals, albeit with "smooth transitions" that evolved into the "highest species"? There is no cogent scientific argument against this (in terms of non-Christian science), but it cannot be proved either—at least not by *immanence* thought which believes that its rationality can and should confine itself to the temporal world.

But that, of course, is an uprooted rationality and a horizontalized view of reality, which do not and cannot do justice to reason itself nor to reality as such.

10.1.6.2 MAN'S RELIGIOUS CENTRALITY

The most characteristic feature of humanity according to Reformational anthropology lies in the *religious centrality* of man and *mankind* within the totality of reality. What animals lack in their religious relation to God is a spiritual fellowship, which the Bible comprehends in what it calls *covenant*, or *kingdom of God*, or *body of Christ*. In this kingdom of God the central position on the side of creation is occupied by *human-kind*, not the animal kingdom, even though via man the animals are fully involved as "objects" (with all their object functions).

Humankind has a head, is spiritually concentrated in the "head of the covenant," who first (that is, "in the beginning") was Christ, the "alpha," the "firstborn of all creation." *In time*, that is, in temporal reality, Christ was represented by Adam and later for a short while by Jesus of Nazareth, not separate from but *rooted* in his supra-temporal fullness, which should not be interpreted as relating only to an abstract divine "nature" of Christ.

This spiritual covenantal fellowship, in which man participates in the heart of his existence, is not a relation *added after* the creation (as for example Schilderian theology would sometimes have it), but is the *deepest level of* created human life itself. It is on that level that the *fundamental direction* of a man's life is determined in the subjective choice of a positive or negative orientation to God-in-Christ.

This deepest level is not an imagined "thing," nor an interpretation or an imposed "meaning," nor yet an "added value." It is a fact. It belongs to the *integral structure of being human*. It is not an *addition to*, but as we said: a *dimension of*, a *level in* being human. Denial of it is horizontalism, an uprooting (and thus a reduction) of man and cosmos, a "demythologizing" of the biblical revelation, as if human-kind were not (or could not be) created "in Christ." It has its existence in Him precisely for this reason.

Christ also repeatedly calls himself "the beginning," the Alpha (Rev. 2:8; 3:14; 21:6; 22:13). But He also calls himself the Omega, the last. In both cases we can add the explication: "of all creation." This metaphor of alpha and omega is not at all meant chronologically; rather it is unchronological or even chrono-unlogical. After all, what can it mean that Christ is the first and at the same time the last? One might ask, with reference to comparable words: What can it mean that Christ is called both the root and the offspring of David (Rev. 22:16), thus the root from which David "later" sprang but at the same time the offspring from which Christ "later" issued?

Indeed, we can never solve this conundrum chronologically—simply because here again neither "chronos" nor "logos" exists on its own or is determinative by itself, and because the supra-temporal unity and fullness of all time and of all truth is given in Christ. "In Christ" the believer, not only as a believing person but first of all as an *existing* person, shares in this "supra-temporality," so that he can say in one breath: I believe in the resurrection of my body on the Last Day, as well as: I have already been raised from the dead "with Christ" around the year 30 A.D. This is not "dialectics," not an internal contradiction, but the *fullness* of all times and places, which does manifest itself chronologically in time but also transcends it.

10.1.7 THE HUMAN EXPERIENCE OF UNITY

We deliberately paid attention first of all to the idea of *humankind,* in order to be able to show in advance that Reformational anthropology does not see humankind as a sum of individual human beings who as such are primary. On the contrary, intrinsic to being human is that each human being *forms part of* the "spiritual" fellowship mentioned above. To put it somewhat schematically: Every person shares in that spiritual fellowship in Adam and/or in Christ. This having been said (as a prolegomenal statement of faith), we can now go on to look more closely at *the temporal structure* of humankind.

In everyday life we human beings experience ourselves as a unity. We express this in the word "I". We do not say: my hand writes, but *I* write. Not: my legs walk, but *I* walk; not: my mind or thought thinks, but *I* think; not: my faith believes, but *I* believe. Yet there is also the everyday experience that we do not *identify* ourselves wholesale with what we have: I *am* not my body, but I *have* a body, and I know that one day I will have to leave my body. One of the images the Bible uses for this is that of an earthly tent which will one day be taken down (2 Cor. 5:1, cf. also the other images in that chapter).

Philosophy has always tried to understand this experience of unity, with or without a belief in immortality, by hypothesizing that there are two substances in man, material and spiritual, or body and soul. This dichotomy, this so-called dualism (also called "duality") of body and soul, was sometimes reformulated as a threefold division: body, soul and spirit. Man's unity would thus be a duality or a trinity.

This dichotomy or trichotomy can be appreciated as representing a tiny spark of truth, but no more than that. Each is a theoretical *misinterpretation* of the general human experience that a human being is aware that he is not wholly exhausted by what he *has* and experiences with his senses, and that he himself is differentiated from that in his I-ness.

Underlying the dualism of matter and spirit or the trichotomy of body, soul and spirit were two different philosophical views of reality. Rejecting this internally contradictory combination of two or three substances, of matter, psyche and spirit, Reformational philosophy repudiates every notion of substance and its possible sequel in a distinction between essence and phenomenon. It teaches the *many-sidedness* of the existence of all things in the order of creation, and its "spiritual" *root unity* in the cosmic center that resides not in reason but in the human heart with its "*spiritual*" participation in *humankind* in Adam and/or in Christ. That is why we call our cosmology *anthropocentric*, and fundamentally speaking it is also *Christocentric*, because we were created "in Him."

This unity is not rational in character, but "spiritual," knowable only in faith and therefore not scientifically *demonstrable* or able to be conceptualized and captured in a definition. Science and philosophy can do no more than accept a kind of human transcendence in the "I" or "center" of the human person, a *theoretical hypothesis* which is rightly based on practical life in which man experiences himself as a central unity and identity amidst all diversity, tension and change in his existence in time, an experience which we express practically in the word "I".

10.1.8 THE HUMAN "I" AS TRANSCENDENT
CENTER OF UNITY

But no sooner do we start to focus separately on our "I" and begin to ask how this "I" relates to the various things we have and in a certain sense are, and then ask what this "I" actually is, than the *central anthropological problem* is born. This is a philosophical problem which poses no difficulties in everyday life, a problem which the vast majority of people, including Christians, do not even know, and do not need to know either. Yet it is a problem which, as a *theoretical* problem, is of the utmost importance for many special sciences, not least for theology. Reformational philosophy answers the question whether man is a unity, and if so, what this unity is, by stating that this unity resides primarily in the *heart* or *I* of the individual human being—though not in an isolated heart. We will come back to this.

For Dooyeweerd, the discovery of the heart as man's transcendent root unity (instead of the "Reason" of scientific thought that traditional philosophy put in this place), was the great turning point in his thought.[69] The most important feature of his entire philosophy, if not to say its very foundation, stands or falls with his concept of the heart. Here lies the criterion, the breaking-point between what he called "immanence philosophy" and Christian transcendence philosophy. We therefore need to address this point in greater detail.

Starting from the practical experience of life, we see that man relates everything that plays a role in his life *to his I*. Whenever a person uses the word *I* he is referring to himself as the one who talks, walks, comes, goes, does, sees, feels, thinks and believes, as well as the one who in multiple ways experiences things and people around him. All these possibilities of being human are concentrated in his person as a *unity*.

It is highly remarkable that man can so talk *about* himself *as if* he sees or knows or thinks something opposite himself that is not him-self. In psychology a distinction is therefore often drawn between the "I" and the "self." Man can see all his concrete life experiences as *something of* himself, and yet not as *identical with* himself. *He himself* adopts a position (sometimes consciously) above or opposite it. He therefore calls them (outward) *expressions* of life.

Naturally, the Bible too is familiar with this well-known phenomenon and attaches a commandment to it: *"Keep your heart with all vigilance, for from there flow the springs of life"* (Prov. 4:23), or *"My son, give me your heart"* . . . (Prov. 23:26). It is thus that Dooyeweerd, not in a theological exegesis

---

69. Cf. what he writes in the preface to his main work, *Wijsbegeerte der Wetsidee* (1935), 1:v. In *A New Critique of Theoretical Thought* (1953) this passage reads: "The great turning point in my thought was marked by the discovery of the religious root of thought itself, whereby a new light was shed on the failure of all attempts, including my own, to bring about an inner synthesis between the Christian faith and a philosophy which is rooted in faith in the self-sufficiency of human reason. I came to understand the central significance of the 'heart,' repeatedly proclaimed by Holy Scripture to be the religious root of human existence. On the basis of this central Christian point of view I saw the need of a revolution in philosophical thought of a very radical character. . . ."

of these texts but in a *philosophical interpretation* of this phenomenon, talks about the heart as the *concentration point* or *focus* of our entire existence. The heart is not a thing, and certainly not a separate thing. Nor is it one function (for instance the emotional function) alongside other functions.

Nor can the heart *anthropologically* be called a *part* of man (as it can from a biological perspective). The *whole* of man comes with it, is concentrated in it at "one point" (another metaphor!). Even his *history* is summed up in it, for the heart contains the *identity* of a person, who is *the same* person from birth to death. In the identity of his heart a person transcends his own diversity in the separate years and periods of his life: *"Also He has planted eternity in man's heart . . ."* (Eccl. 3:11), but still he remains human and does not in any way become divine. In fact, the words in Ecclesiastes are followed by: *". . . yet he cannot find out what God has done from the beginning to the end."*

The heart, then, is no more than a *figure of speech.* In non-scientific usage we can therefore be flexible and contemporary, or we can also use the terms spirit and soul. All that matters in anthropology is a right understanding and interpretation of these words, and the avoidance of their classical or modern philosophical explanations.

10.1.9 MAN'S UNITY IS "SPIRITUAL," APPROACHABLE ONLY IN AN "IDEA"

The unity of man, which Reformational philosophy sees as a *transcendent* unity, is therefore not a *logical* unity and cannot be logically proved, cannot even be grasped in a concept or "defined." It is a unity that goes beyond all diversity, including the diversity contained in any logical concept. Hence we can only talk about it in a figure of speech. That is to say, we can employ a metaphor to point to it or evoke a vision of it, but we cannot grasp it in a concept, cannot capture and comprehend it in a definition. An "I-concept" is impossible. Since Plato, epistemology talks in this connection about an "idea," a vision, an intellectual insight.

That is why we do not talk about the *concept* of unity but about the *idea* of unity. The human I is not a thing, is not something separate, is not a substance, but it is the *fullness* of a person's entire life, even including their existence before conception and birth and after their death.

Thus we can also use the image of the *focus* of a lens. All parts of the lens, and all the rays of light that pass through it, are oriented to a point that lies *outside* the lens itself, the so-called focus; yet this focus

There seem to be many dualist tendencies in what he is saying. He is trying to overcome it but fails to do so.

INTRODUCTION TO THE REFORMATIONAL PHILOSOPHY OF HERMAN DOOYEWEERD

is the focus *of* the lens, forming an essential "part" of it. The focus is not a thing, nor an "imaginary" reality, but a genuine reality which governs the entire form and function of the lens.

Another image is that of the white ray of light containing all the colors of the rainbow, undivided, as in a unity. Only through a prism can these colors be separated; but if the white ray of light disappears all the colors disappear too: they cannot exist apart from their connection with the source. In this image, time can be understood as the prism through which the supra-temporal unity disperses into the concrete multiplicity and diversity within time.

Yet another image is that of the hole in the center of a wagon wheel. All the points on the circumference of the wagon wheel and all the spokes are oriented to the central point of the circle. But this central point itself is invisible; it is a hole, substantially and in itself a nothing. At the same time it governs the entire structure of the wheel: all the spokes point to it and in principle converge in it. Using another inadequate term, we say: the human heart is a *"spiritual"* center in which our entire concrete mode of existence comes together, converges, is *centered*. Our existence is also represented in this center when the mode of existence is *not yet* or *no longer* in time. For we are more than just our temporal mode of existence, something which the Christian tradition has always believed and realized, be it often formulated in an infelicitous and pagan fashion in an expression like "immortal soul."[70]

10.2 HEART AND LIFE

10.2.1 THE HEART IS NOT AN ISOLATED CENTER

As we already said, the heart should not be understood as a separate thing or part that leads a life of its own more or less. Rather, the heart is a concentration point that gathers up the *fullness* of life. That is why Dooyeweerd could write at one time that the heart "in itself" is *nothing*. Abraham Kuyper in his day used the no doubt biblically inspired image of "root unity," an image gratefully adopted by Dooyeweerd. The entire fullness of life with all its diversity is summed up—concentrated—in the heart, just as a root basically contains everything

---

70. Cf. the book by the noted New Testament scholar Oscar Cullmann, *Unsterblichkeit oder Auferstehungsglaube?* [*Immortality, or Faith in the Resurrection?*] New edition 1968. He argues there that the Greek idea of the "immortal soul" cannot possibly be reconciled with the New Testament.

that emerges from it above ground. This gives our concrete temporal experience of life, our walk of life, its religious *direction, in principle* in a twofold sense of the word: with the main tendency towards God, or with the main tendency away from God. This *connecting bond* of heart and life is like the source and at the same time the stream that springs from the source. They are not the same, yet cannot exist without each other. The same water flows in both.

10.2.2 THE HEART'S "SUPRA-TEMPORALITY," TRANSCENDENCE, OR FULL TEMPORALITY

Dooyeweerd caused a great deal of misunderstanding and opposition by using the term "supra-temporality" and speaking of the "supra-temporal heart." Incomprehensively, some have interpreted these terms squarely in contradiction to clear statements on his part. In using this term he was not referring to something like timelessness, as if the human heart has no part in our concrete existence in time. He never intended any such dualism. Supra-temporality in the sense of Reformational philosophy does not mean timelessness, but primarily *being more than temporal,* transcending time. It stands for *non-absorption* in— for not being exhausted by—the transience of all that exists in time, but the other way around: time and all temporal existence find their *fullness* and *concentration* in the *transcending center*: the human heart. The objection that this idea theoretically "duplicates" the cosmos is also a complete misinterpretation.

The "heart" is not foreign to time: it *lives* in time, it *manifests* itself in time; but it is also "more": *as unity and totality* it transcends time (together with all its temporality and diversity). Because this totality of the transcendent center incorporates time, supra-temporality might also be called *temporal fullness,* a term not often used, or else *"full temporality,"* as Willem Ouweneel prefers, rightly in my view. This term also recalls the New Testament idea of the "fullness of time" (or of "the times"), an idea which denotes much more than a historical chronological period with certain typical historical situations or "favorable factors."

Scripture never makes a separation between the supra-historical unity and concentration "in Christ" and the history that takes place in temporality.[71]

---

71. Applied to the church and its history, the church historian Hans Rückert wrote in 1953: "The mistake of the last great period of Church History is that it cut itself

10.2.3 THE THREE CENTRAL RELATIONS IN HUMAN LIFE

At the same time, however, the fullness of man's existence also includes his relation to *God*, to his *fellow-man* and to *himself* as participating in the world in and around him. These are the three central religious relations in which man stands. This fact alone makes it clear that the human heart cannot be theoretically isolated or substantialized. The very center of his existence also involves his relation to God, his relation to his own corporeality, including everything that takes place in it and with it, and his relation to the human race. So all these relations are involved, regardless of the way in which they are *religiously* oriented, realized or subjectively experienced.

10.2.3.1 MAN'S UNIQUENESS AND IDENTITY.
THE I-SELF RELATION

10.2.3.1-1 HUMAN IDENTITY AND ITS INTERLACEMENT IN TEMPORAL REALITY

Man's relation to his own body involves at the same time his relation to the so-called material world around him. It is with his organic corporeality that man is interwoven with this world, encapsulated, or to use a Dooyeweerdian term, "enkaptically interlaced" (cf. sec. 7.3.12 above).

To an important degree the same natural laws apply to minerals, plants, animals and human bodies. But man alone relates all these so-called material phenomena also subjectively to his *I-ness*. He experiences these "material" phenomena as something *of himself*. It is he himself who manifests *himself* in these aspects and entities of the temporal cosmos. As a result, man feels and experiences a many-sided participation in the world around him, in which he lives and feels at home. And yet he is equally aware of his own uniqueness and identity in this world, as is already suggested, for instance, by his footprints or fingerprints.

It would be foolish to say, however, that the personal identity and uniqueness of a human being resides in his fingertips, or in any

---

off from theology to become an autonomous historical discipline. This dissolved the concept of church, theologically speaking, since only the church's empirical manifestation and social structure were now examined. Yet this one-sided approach is in conflict with the church's self-understanding, which is *at once supra-historical and historical* . . ." Quoted by R. Slenczka, in Christian Henning and Karsten Lehmkühler, eds., *Systematische Theologie der Gegenwart in Selbstdarstellungen* (Tübingen, 1998), p. 84 (emph. mine, A.T.).

part of his body for that matter. It is the unintentional effect of an uprooted and materialist view of man that induces a writer to say that a Christian need not object to organ transplants except for the transplanting (if possible) of a brain or genitalia.[72] This is essentially a horizontalist view of man that seeks man's uniqueness and identity somewhere in certain organs within his temporal corporeality.

10.2.3.1-2 THE BIRTH OF A HUMAN BEING IS NOT HIS ORIGIN

The same deficient anthropology is found in the view that the fusion of an egg cell with a sperm cell produces not just a human organ, but a new *human being*. This leads, by logical inference, to the well-known and over-simplified proposition "abortion is murder." But the origin of a human being, his fullness and uniqueness and thus his totality, cannot be scientifically established or bio-technically grasped. That would betray a positivist-rationalist attitude of thought. The *origin* of a human being is not the same as his *beginning* in time.

Human origin *remains a religious mystery,* and we should not presume to pass a ("scientifically reliable") judgment on the "point in time" (??) when a human person comes into full being. For the origin of a person does not lie in time, unlike the origin (in the sense of "beginning") of the human body. The *origin* of the total human being *transcends* all temporal knowledge, understanding and control, just as it transcends his corporeality as a whole, including all the "genes." Man's origin resides in his (scientifically inaccessible) supra-temporal and thus supra-corporeal center, in his "heart," in his *createdness, in Christ as the alpha, the beginning.* And no different is the end of man's temporal mode of existence: it is a given already now, in Christ, the alpha *and the omega.*

10.2.3.1-3 THE JURIDICAL AND MORAL ASPECT OF A HUMAN BIRTH

However, what we can do for the situation of a birth or impending birth in our *temporal mode of existence* is to formulate juridical and moral agreements or enact laws in human society, and in this way construct a *practical normativity*. In part this is even mandatory, given the brokenness of life and the many possibilities of ethical lapses.

---

72. Cf. R. Seldenrijk, in *Bijbel en Wetenschap* 20 (1996); J. Douma, *Rondom de dood* (Kampen, 1984); series Ethische bezinning, vol. 10.

But any *argument* one might wish to mount in these cases will have to respect the mystery of the point in question and will therefore have to refrain in our legal system from restricting or enlarging, on religious grounds, freedom of belief and freedom of choice. Rules can only be drawn up for the various sectors of the public sphere on public-moral and juridical grounds, but these rules should not presume to represent the whole will of God for the private spheres of marriage or family life.

10.2.3.2 SOLIDARITY

The same holds for the relation to our fellow-men. A human being cannot but live together with other human beings, as the very process of his generation and his birth already make clear. Yet "solidarity" (*medemenselijkheid*) is not just a temporal given; it has not only a moral, juridical, economic and social meaning, etc. in time. Solidarity also belongs, anthropologically speaking, to *the religious, full-temporal center of man's existence.* This bond not only consists of a number of temporal social or moral structures, but it is in a *spiritual* community that man practices solidarity in these social structures.

This community is *humanity* in its entirety. It is a supra-temporal fullness, a spiritual bond, a religious community which *expresses itself in time* in many types of social relations, partly shared lifestyles, behavioral patterns, habits of thought, funds of knowledge, and so on. This *religious* community should not be mistaken for a community of faith (on which more in sec. 12.3.4 below). Since the fall and the substitution of its temporal head Adam by Christ as the "second Adam," this community of humankind as a whole is a *religiously divided community,* an "old" and a "new" humanity.[73]

10.2.3.3 RELIGION

Finally—or rather, first of all—there is man's relation to God, the relation between God and humanity. By using the word *relation* I seem to be expressing myself neutrally here. Indeed, all people are related to God, without exception. God, who is the Creator of all people, revealed himself

---

73. On the philosophical and to some degree theological debate that this idea has sparked, see the article by D. F. M. Strauss, "The central religious community of mankind in the philosophy of the cosmonomic idea," *Philosophia Reformata* 37 (1972): 58–67.

normatively in words and works and obliges all people to believe this revelation and to live accordingly in loving fellowship with God. In a literal and strict sense, atheism and godlessness do not "objectively" exist, for God *is*, whether people believe it or not, or whether people want to know it or not. Through his creation God *established* his relation to the creature, the relation which in practical, non-philosophical language we call religion, or covenant, or the kingdom of God. God is always actively present in the order of creation. By "atheism" or godlessness we merely mean the anti-normative subjective denial of God's existence, not its creaturely possibility in the active presence of God.

The above anthropological view is at odds with every theoretical spiritualism, psycho-monism or existentialism, which see man as a spiritual and "free" subject, inwardly above and outside of matter, or as a subject elevated above his temporal corporeality. Reformational philosophy teaches instead that as long as man lives on earth he is there corporeally, and no "spiritual" function can be conceived as absent from this corporeality. Still, expressions in Scripture, for example that our "earthly tent" is taken down (2 Cor. 5:1), or that we need not fear those who can only kill the body (Matt. 10:28), or that Paul desires to leave his body and be at home with the Lord (2 Cor. 5:8), do show that the *core, the crux* of our human existence does not lie in this temporal mode of existence itself.

Only the mental attitude of an anthropological dualism can misinterpret this as a *depreciation* of time or of earthly corporeality. Our own corporeality always remains with us in a certain way, either *in* time, *or* (differently) *in "supra-temporal" fullness!* This is theologically crucial to the theory regarding our belief in "the resurrection of the body," regarding the spiritual or heavenly and glorified nature of our resurrection body (1 Cor. 15:35 ff.), regarding our belief in the presence of Christ in the Communion bread, regarding *our* death, burial and resurrection with Christ, and regarding various other subjects in theological doctrine.

10.2.4 RELIGION AND FAITH

Above, in sec. 10.2.3.2, I drew attention to the difference between the full temporal *religious* community of humankind and a typical community of *faith*. This has to do with the totality character of religion, which as a relation to God encompasses our total human mode of existence. We can therefore distinguish this community from the various communities or social relationships in our concrete earthly mode of existence which together are religion's *field of expression in time*. For none of these social relationships or structures is totalitarian. Each is typically, modally qualified. All of them, together with the whole of our temporal life, originated in time and will also perish with time.

So there is no specific *religious sector* or *religious sphere* in human life, because life is *entirely* religious, that is to say: stands in relation to God. Religion as a relation to God is not something that has been added to being human, but is constitutive of being human. No human being can exist without religion.

There is, however, as one of the concrete manifestations of religion in human life, a typically "religious" (usually liturgical) *sector* of life qualified by the faith aspect, the sector in which we find, among other things, organized church life. But "church" is no more than an (important) *sector*; it is a part of life, not a totality that "really" ought to encapsulate everything in life, or guide and govern it with authority. Such a traditional (in essence typically Roman Catholic) view of the institutional church continues the pre-theoretical dualistic scheme of "nature and grace," "church and world" or "church and culture," "church and state," "faith and science," and many related dualisms. In practice this view leads to a strong overestimation of our church communities and to untenable pretensions of "the church" over against other forms of community. "Political theocracy" is one example of this.

In theology this overestimation of the temporal institution of the church in relation to other social structures (within the kingdom of God) is often (though usually unconsciously) defended by means of a platonically tinged Neo-Kantian philosophy of values. Its humanist, non-Christian character is not recognized, so that "the highest value" is awarded to the church, which people are loath to put on a par with other social structures. It is a clear example of how the Christian faith is scholastically connected with a non-Christian worldview (in this case the worldview of modern humanism), borrowing its vocabulary from the philosophy of values not just in practical usage but precisely in theological discourses.

10.2.5 THE RELIGIOUS CONCENTRATION OF THE COSMOS IN MAN

10.2.5.1 THE INTERNAL STRUCTURAL CONNECTION BETWEEN MAN AND COSMOS

Already in the opening section of this chapter I remarked that man is the religious center of creation. All non-human creatures, too, exist *"unto God,"* but *via* man. This is the *religious determinant* of all creation. Article 12 of the Belgic Confession puts it this way: God gave "every creature its being, shape, form and several offices to serve its Creator," and God "upholds and governs them . . . for the service of humankind, to the end that man may serve his God."

This perspective of the religious orientation of all non-human creation to man, and via man to God, is not an isolated belief about the cosmos, separate from the cosmos itself. It is an inalienable "part" (or rather "property") *of creatures as such* that they are an *object of faith* (cf. sec. 6.4 above) and *therefore* not intrinsically separate from man or over against man. This is evident in the structural blueprint of reality, as we already discussed in connection with the subject-object relation.

The orientation of non-human creatures to man is also evident in God's judgment on human sin. Not just the earth was cursed ("for your sake," Gen. 3:14–21) but the "heavenly bodies" are also involved (2 Peter 3:7,10), just as the great work of reconciliation involves the entire cosmos at the restoration of all things (Isa. 11; Matt. 23:29–31; Col. 1).

The fact that this entire relation between God and cosmos proceeds via man (fundamentally via Christ, the alpha and omega of all creation) is likewise evident in the very special and unique position of Adam. Adam is the religious head of the covenant: all humanity is centrally *comprehended* in him and not just *represented* in a juridical or forensic sense. Christ who comes to earth in Adam's place therefore functions as a "second Adam." Even those who have not been "incorporated" in Christ through faith nevertheless remain *religiously determined* by their relation to Christ, albeit in the negative sense of *not believing* in Christ and therefore believing in something or someone else: in an idol, which is a *structurally necessary* alternative to the only true Creator.

10.2.5.2 MAN IN THE COSMOS AND THE COSMOS IN MAN

According to Max Scheler in his well-known essay *Die Stellung des Menschen im Kosmos*,[74] the task of philosophical anthropology is to investigate the place man occupies in the whole of the cosmos. Inevitably this entails looking at all kinds of connections between man and the non-human. Well, everybody is quite willing to speak in philosophy of man's *bond* with the cosmos. But for the reasons discussed above, the term "bond" is too little and too weak a term.

The bond between humans and the non-human creation should not be interpreted as an external coupling, in the way that a locomotive is coupled to a train and can be uncoupled. Nor is it a fantasized mental object which we ascribe to man and world, a subjective and speculative notion. This bond, rather, is an internal structural *centeredness* of the cosmos in *man*. The whole of creation, both *via* the law-side and according to the subject-side, *via* its own religious *center in humanity*, is internally directed to and connected with God. Not of course in a pantheistic or mystical sense (that would be unbiblical metaphysics or ontology), but "in Christ," and thus actual and knowable through faith alone.

In our Christian philosophy we call this the *religious law of concentration* by virtue of which all things refer to man, and via man to God, *with and through their very structure. All* things are from God, but also *unto* God! Not only is man himself an "image of God," but all creation participates in man and in his relation to God. By virtue of being created, "all things" are oriented to God "in Christ" in a mutual relationship, in which God's glory is expressed in "the works of his hands." Man is indeed man-in-the-cosmos, but we can say, and may even say in the first place, that the cosmos is in man.

10.2.6 CREATION'S "OPENNESS" AND "MIRACLES"

The above is also important for seeing more clearly what it means when we protest against a closed worldview. A closed worldview not only sees non-human things as separate from man, but also regards this world (sometimes including man) as being enclosed within the aspects that are to be scientifically analyzed and causally determined. The world, including all the processes in its history, can then be compared to a self-enclosed *thing*.

---

74. Darmstadt, 1928. In English: *Man's Place in Nature*, trans. by Hans Meyerhoff (Boston, 1961); or *The Human Place in the Cosmos*, trans. by Manfred S. Frings (Evanston, Ill., 2009).

By contrast, Reformational philosophy recognizes an *opening process* which is given with the nature of creatures but which has largely closed and shut down through sin. By the grace of God's *work of upholding and redeeming* creation, this opening process has been provisionally but fundamentally re-opened in the direction of *meaning* and *meaning-fullness*. This means that development—the process of opening or unfolding—can continue, though it does not always take place in a religious orientation to God.

In the history of the manifestation of God's kingdom on earth we see this dynamic openness of creatures shining through time and again. Central to this are the "signs and miracles" performed by Christ during his sojourn on earth. He healed the sick who had been written off as incurable, he walked on the water, multiplied loaves, raised the dead, and predicted that his apostles would perform even more and even greater miracles (Mark 16:17–18). This did in fact happen, especially in the first period after Pentecost. It continues today, for instance in faith healing and many other answers to prayers. For the "signs and miracles" are always connected with active *faith*.

We rightly associate these wonder-full phenomena first and foremost with true faith; however, the false faith of magicians, hysterics, the demon-possessed, the Antichrist, and the like, is equally capable of performing so-called miracles. Faith as such, as a human structure, has a leading function in relation to all functions in the preceding aspects. Via their anticipatory structure these are "opened" or "disclosed" in the development of culture.

The miracles already occurring in time are therefore also "signs." They are signs not only of the powers of faith, but especially signs of the future, when creation will be wholly restored and opened up to the service and glorification of God. Via the leading function of faith the cosmos will disclose its riches and man will be able to demonstrate his dominion over the cosmos in making it serviceable to God's "honor and glory." At the same time, when this faith is directed to idols instead of to the only true God, those idols will poison the factual structural disclosure and bring about the utter degradation of creation under the regime of the Antichrist in the end time.

It is wrong, therefore, on the basis of the *closed worldview* of a causally determined reality, to talk about miracles as "supernatural interventions" by God. There is nothing supernatural about miracles. They just seem supernatural because we are used to the modern concept of a world and a humanity that are closed off in their temporal aspects and can be scientifically explained in terms of causal forces and objectives. Theological "supernaturalism" wanted to break out of this deterministic view, but on account of its traditional ground-motive of nature and grace this did not lead to a different and radically Christian view of reality. By contrast, Reformational philosophy sees the creative dynamics of the opening process in the direction of God ("created unto God") as taking place via people with a vibrant biblical faith, people to whom "all things are possible" (Mark 9:23; Matt. 17:20).

10.2.7 MAN: IMAGE OF GOD

The biblical revelation that God created man in his image and likeness inspires and supports the philosophical idea of the human heart as the original unity of temporal human life. It is in fact *man himself who gives form and shape to his concrete life in time.* The humanist idea of the *autonomous human being* who creates his own life, his own culture and his own history is fundamentally unbiblical, but it does contain one element of truth. The one element of truth is that man himself, in his I, in his personal *center*, is the creaturely, subjective *origin* of the *concrete subjective content* of his existence. Man is a "creator" of his life, though "creator" between quotation marks.

He who is the *image* of the real Creator is not, properly speaking, a creator himself, but he is allowed to be a creaturely representation of Him. For the entire normative *framework* of his life, which makes human life possible and forms part of it, is an element in it: this framework is the *divine* law-order. Within and through this framework man is called by God to live his life under the one central law of *love of God* and *love of neighbor*, to be in all his doings the image of God's love and the image of God's justice, of God's wisdom and of anything created in which God chooses to manifest himself. In short, in the entire cultural opening up of creation all creation is allowed to mirror, radiate, represent and reflect the glory of God and the rule of Christ and all those who are His.

186

Chapter Eleven – Anthropology: Human Acts

CHAPTER ELEVEN
ANTHROPOLOGY: HUMAN ACTS

11.1 FUNCTION COMPLEXES AND THEIR INTERLACEMENT

11.1.1 HUMAN CORPOREALITY IN TIME

Reformational philosophy's radical break with the dualism of soul and body in the philosophical view of man gives the term *body* a very broad meaning. The body is now man's *entire temporal mode of existence*. Not just the "material" but also the "spiritual" aspects of human existence are aspects of human corporeality. The "human body" is the sum total of all man's aspects and concrete functions in his temporal mode of existence.

Having broken with the scheme of matter and spirit as the two elements of creation, we do not like to talk about material and spiritual functions. If we often conform to this usage for the sake of convenience, we sometimes enclose these words in quotation marks as a sign that we really want to distance ourselves from these terms in philosophical (or other scientific) discourse. Instead of "material" functions we prefer to speak more precisely and discriminatingly of physical, biotic and psychical functions. Instead of "spiritual" functions we prefer to talk about "functions of consciousness" or, more precisely and judiciously, about logical, historical, lingual, social, economic, aesthetic, juridical, moral and pistical functions— thus nine kinds of functions, of which not one is possible, however, *without* its foundation in the physical, biotic and psychical.

11.1.2 BODY AND SOUL

Yet we do not go to the other extreme, like schools of thought that are inclined to say: man *is* his body. The great diversity of functions are and remain functions *of* the total human being, who is a unity but who precisely as a total unity *is not exhausted* by his temporal modes of existence nor by the sum of his functions. Man *transcends* his functions, that is to say, he goes beyond them: from the center of his person, in his "I," his self-hood, his self-consciousness, he can spiritually and contemplatively distance himself from their concrete form. He is very much alive to the fact that after his death this entire complex of functions goes down to the grave, to "return to dust." He must completely lay down his concrete life on earth, his "function mantle" as Vollenhoven called it. According to 2 Cor. 5:1, when this "earthly tent" is taken down we have a heavenly "building," an eternal house, which we cannot philosophize about. Perhaps we can do so once we have moved there, who knows. Paul begins to refer to it already as a "spiritual body" (1 Cor. 15:44), an image of the heavenly Christ (v. 49).

It is this religious truth that Christians have been in the habit of professing partly in terms of Greek philosophy, that is, in terms of an immortal soul and a mortal body, as spirit and matter. Already in pre-Christian Antiquity this philosophical language had entered the everyday life of the Western cultural world. The writers of the Bible, too, repeatedly used this terminology in their practical everyday language. That is why we will not fight these words as such, provided we take them in a biblical sense and avoid putting a philosophical theory of man in the mouth of the Bible writers (and thus of the Holy Spirit). But instead of soul and body we prefer to use the words "heart and life," which are also biblical words but which do not savor of a pagan view of man. That view sees man's continuing existence (his "immortality") as being borne, not by God, but by a spiritual substance, the *soul*. As a substance, this so-called spiritual soul is considered *as such* to be the basis or vehicle of "immortality."

II.1.3 THE BODY: AN ENKAPTIC WHOLE OF PARTS AND SUBSTRUCTURES

II.1.3.1 THE FOUR SUBSTRUCTURES

As we have emphasized, scientific philosophy, unlike practical worldviews or ethical teachings, is largely a *structural theory of temporal reality*. In cosmology we needed to distinguish modalities and entities. We will now apply this distinction to the temporal structure of human life, the body. As announced in sec. 11.1.1, we will take the word "body" in the broad sense of man's entire temporal mode of existence. Thinking, loving, believing, and so on, are equally corporeal or bodily activities, which at the same time engage all other modal aspects of reality.

Within the framework of the cosmological totality view, our anthropology distinguishes four substructures, each of which has the character of an entity. These four are: *the physical substructure, the biotic substructure, the psychical substructure,* and *the act structure* (see Appendix, Figure 4). Each of these substructures in turn is characterized or qualified as an entity by its highest aspect, except for the act structure, to which we must devote a separate section.

As entities, these substructures have a certain degree of relative independence, combined with many possibilities of reciprocal influence. This explains, for instance, the success of the many chemical drugs that can influence organic functions or later functions like feeling, thinking, language, and so on, via our physical-chemical substructures. Another example of the connection between these substructures (in this case the organic and sensitive ones) is the phenomenon of a toothache: an organic inflammation causes a non-organic sensation—pain, or an aching feeling.

11.1.3.2 FOUNDATIONAL ENKAPSIS
The mutual relation between the substructures of the body is that of the so-called foundational enkapsis, that is to say, the substructures are *successively encapsulated* in the whole in a non-reversible order. We have already discussed the difference between enkaptic relations and part-whole relations (sec. 7.3.13). The difference was that *a part-whole relation* exists within and between entities which (a) cannot exist independently, and (b) are qualified by an identical function. Thus lungs and liver, heart and kidneys are *parts* of the organic substructure. Each has its own structure and function, but only within the organic *whole* of the *body as a biotically qualified substructure.*

Some organs in this whole, like the nervous system, serve to found the psychical or sensitive substructure. At the same time this entire organic substructure depends on the physical elements in the physically qualified substructure. The organic is embedded in this as in a basic layer, a foundation. On the other side, the organic substructure is encapsulated as a basic layer in the ("later," "higher") psychically qualified substructure. This "organism" contains the foundations not only for the sensitive functions such as hearing, seeing and touching, but also for the emotions.

Conversely, emotions, emotional experiences, thoughts, gestures and actions can also express themselves in the outward forms of our organs, such as frowning, turning pale with fright, shedding tears of sorrow, getting goose pimples from fear, breaking out in a cold sweat, wrinkling one's forehead from worry, and the like. One might call this the retroactive force of the sensitive functions.

The internal interlacement of these *enkaptic relations* among the four substructures is so intensive that influence is exerted in both directions. This is also the basis of "psychosomatic" medicine in which treatment for certain diseases is often not, or not only, sought in chemical drugs, that is, from below, but instead in *psychical* changes through, for instance, therapeutic counseling, occupational therapy, changes in the social environment, and so on. All kinds of organic diseases and defects are clearly due to "psychical" causes. Certain diseases are notorious for this, like particular forms of rash, stomach ulcers and asthma. In those cases people will say that it is because of tension, "nerves" or "stress"; and the "medicine" is often rest and relaxation, or improved relations in the workplace or with other people.

II.I.4 Birth and death in light of the "order of Melchizedek"

The new Reformational view of man also has consequences for the view of life and death. Philosophical anthropology can say little about this subject, but the little it says is important and fundamental, for this subject takes us to the boundaries of our temporal human existence. We can look beyond these boundaries through faith alone, by means of God's revelation about the meaning of our humanness.

The question of meaning is always a threefold question, the three subquestions of which cannot be considered in isolation. The three subquestions are those of the *origin*, of the fundamental *mode of existence* (in the law/subject correlation), and of the *destination* of our humanness. Consciously or unconsciously, the answers to these questions form the substrate of every genuine philosophy. They may be Christian or non-Christian answers.

We have said repeatedly that our humanity is not exhausted by our temporal mode of existence, by our life "in time." Christians are familiar with the belief in the resurrection from "temporal death" and eternal life. Christians are less familiar with the equally biblical idea that the conception and birth of a human body is not the absolute beginning of its existence. For even before all temporal existence came into being we were *created* "in Christ," in Him who is "the firstborn of all creation" (Col. 1:15–16), the alpha and the omega (Rev. 1:8; 21:6; 22:13), "the first and the last" (Rev. 1:17)—in Him who encompasses the entire alphabet of created reality.

What Scripture says about this in various contexts is usually "located" by theology in God's eternal counsel. After all, the demythologized and thus partly secularized and horizontalized Western *view of reality*, in which God is no longer present, thinks according to the scheme of creaturely time and divine eternity, with nothing in between. Not even Christ as God-*and*-man! In this context, however, a Christian philosophy has to talk about supra-temporality, about "supra-temporal unity and fullness," namely "in Christ."

So we continue to base ourselves on the scriptural idea that we were truly created "in Christ," just as we confess that when Adam lapsed into sin we too were there and sinned "in Adam," if not "in the likeness of Adam's transgression" (Rom. 5:14). Adam's transgression took place *not only* (!) within the temporal order in paradise, but primarily in Adam's heart, out of which, also in his case, flowed the "springs" of his life (including his concrete deeds). This was not just in the ("supra-temporal") *fullness* of his personal life, but also in the fullness of *time*, in which all people as well as all the temporal moments and periods of people's history are concentrated together, as in a depth dimension.

This is what Scripture sometimes calls "the order of Melchizedek," that strange man from Genesis 14 who is introduced in Hebrews 7 in mythological fashion as someone "without father or mother or genealogy, and having neither beginning of days nor end of life . . ." That is to say: the ordination of Melchizedek as both king and priest is not an ordinary ordination. It is not an order in which, say, family ties or a predecessor's death play a role, or an order to which calendar time or chronology applies. It is, rather, an order in which present, past and future are not lined up in succession but are all "from eternity." It was an order in which Christ (God *and man*) was also the "root of David" (Rev. 5:5), and not just the other way round (David the root of Christ because Christ is also called the great son of David)!

That is why God could say to Jeremiah that he already knew and chose him before his temporal existence that started with his conception and birth (Jer. 1:5). In his high-priestly prayer Jesus, too, talks about the work of salvation in a way which to our Western minds confuses present and future (John 17:11a, 12a). This work of salvation indeed transcended its temporal, historical forms, as we experience faith-wise, for instance, in Holy Communion, when we eat and drink the body and blood of Christ in the year 2000 A.D.—not in a manner of speaking but in reality.[75]

In this full-temporal order ("supra-temporality") there is no order of salvation in a chronological historical sense either. In this order, all God's salvific benefactions past and future (election, justification, sanctification, renewal, resurrection of the body, consummation) are one, and are "simultaneous" *in Christ* (2 Cor. 5:17; Rom. 6:14). Christians may already now live by faith in what C. H. Dodd, using an oxymoron, calls "realized eschatology."

This internally contradictory expression, adopted by many New Testament scholars, can't help but replace the more correct insight that in our "heart," in our transcendent unity and fullness, we participate in the fullness of Christ and express this in our temporal life. In this context we can also point to the equally contradictory expression: "become what you are." In every theology that wants to remain faithful to what Scripture says, temporally immanent thought, when it fails to acknowledge temporal transcendence, is constantly forced to come up with illogical constructions.

Thus the conception and birth of our temporal mode of existence as well as our "corporeal death" are only a beginning and end in a temporal, historical sense, but not in *full* reality. We are more than time and history. We transcend and concentrate our temporality in our heart, our "I".

---

75. This cannot be explained by theoretical constructions like the Roman Catholic doctrine of transubstantiation, nor by the Lutheran doctrine of consubstantiation, nor by the idea of pure symbolism, as in Zwingli, nor by the compromise of "sign *and seal*," as in Calvin. "This is my body" should be *maintained* in all its simplicity and *believed* by us in that way. It means that, to the eye of faith, Christ with his work of reconciliation is corporeally present in bread and wine, a reality that would be sold short by the addition: "in a manner of speaking," i.e., not really.

11.1.5 SPIRITUAL DEATH AND NATURAL DEATH[76]

Traditionally, Christian theology rightly draws a distinction between natural and spiritual death, also referred to as "temporal and eternal death." Yet there is a reluctance to see "natural death" as actually "natural" in the sense of belonging to the creation ordinances. Does not Scripture say: "the wages of sin is death" (Rom. 6:23)? But the connection with the previous verse shows that Paul is not just referring here to "temporal" death (though that too), but to the death which involves the entire human being—to death in the fullest sense of the word, death "for time and eternity" in both the temporal and the "supra-temporal" order. As for our natural, "physical" death, this in fact belongs (for those who are in Christ) only to our *temporal* mode of existence, and remains temporal. It is part of our temporary "earthly tent."

To be sure, all the suffering and misery that we experience in this *time period* (our earthly time of life) should also be seen in connection with sin, as part of its "wages." Those wages include our death, which we rightly call our corporeal or "temporal" death, even the "last enemy" (1 Cor. 15:26). But there is more. Death also belongs to God's good creation. All organisms are created in such a way that they are structurally comprehended in the temporal process of birth, existence, decay and death.

But the *way in which* we die and experience the process of dying is a consequence of sin and God's judgment upon it, such that, just as in the prime of our life, death comes with all kinds of imperfections, major or minor infirmities, pain, illness, anguish, and the like. Like our entire earthly existence, however, "temporal death" is "natural" in the sense of *creaturely*. And on the new earth our bodies will probably be structured in a different way. Paul says that what is raised will be a "spiritual body" (1 Cor. 15:44–49). This could already be observed in the risen Savior before and during his ascension.

Our "spiritual" death, however, entered the world when we broke the covenant, that is, the religious bond of love with God. This already happened when we sinned "in Adam"—that is to say, in the supra-temporal order in which all our earthly existence was present in concentrated form and summed up in our heart and in our head, Adam. Only "in Christ" have we been saved from this total death

76. Cf. also Appendix, Figure 2.

(including our corporeal death!) and are we reconciled with God, as will be made manifest in the resurrection at Christ's return. But we have reached this point *already now,* in Christ: "Therefore, if anyone is in Christ, he is a new creation; the old has passed away, behold, the new has come" (2 Cor. 5:17). That "spiritual" or "eternal" death was at bottom the separation from God's love, the breach of the covenant.

II.2 THE ACT STRUCTURE AND ITS DEPTH DIMENSIONS

II.2.1 ACTS DO NOT HAVE A FIXED QUALIFICATION

The three substructures of the temporal human mode of existence provide the foundation for the fourth, the typically human. This is the "act structure." By "acts" Reformational philosophy understands internal acts, as distinct from their manifestation in concrete *actions*, which are also visible externally. All human *acts* start from the heart, the selfhood, the spirit, the soul, or whatever one wishes to call it. As a person a human being expresses himself in his actions, which manifest his freedom and his imaging of the Creator.

It is by means of *a great variety of* internal acts and external actions that a person gives form and content to his life. Hence the entity structure of acts as such does not have a fixed qualifying function. Naturally, acts as concrete entities, just like concrete actions, always have some qualifying aspect by which they can be distinguished from one other, as for example an economic, a historical or a juridical act or deed. These qualifications can be different in each particular case. The act structure qua structure is the entire field of expression of the human person, the entire field of his typically human possibilities and functions.

Within the complicated enkaptic whole of the human body, however, the act structure as such is *characteristic* of man, is *qualificatory* for man: animals probably do not have an act structure but at most the *psychical functions* of their sensitive substructure. The fairly fixed and not very individualized behavioral patterns of "nobler" animals do resemble human actions and their dispositions but lack their essence: freedom of choice and accountability.

11.2.2 DEPTH AND SURFACE, INWARD AND OUTWARD

Our everyday language is full of expressions indicating that we make all kinds of distinctions in life which do in truth refer to something real. If we say about a person that something touches him deeply, or about somebody else that he is a shallow person, we have made the distinction between depth and surface. "Still waters run deep," as we sometimes say. This distinction also has something in common with that between inward and outward.

Scripture too talks about inward and outward man[77] and says of the human heart that it is unfathomably *deep*.[78] We are dealing here with *depth dimensions* or *depth layers* in human life. These are far less easily observed and known; in fact, they are known only *indirectly*, via our actions and our explanations of them. Scripture also points out that God searches and knows our *heart* and that Christ knew what went on in men's thoughts, that is to say, in their invisible innermost selves.[79]

In the human act structure our anthropology distinguishes *three depth layers* or *depth dimensions*, which we will briefly look at in the next section. In doing so we will, by virtue of this anthropology's philosophical character, continue to see the temporal act structure within the totality framework, and so as a temporal and corporeal or bodily mode of existence which grounds its own creaturely totality and root unity, as well as the "spirit" in which it realizes itself, in the human heart, the self, the "I".

11.2.3 DEPTH LAYERS IN THE ACT STRUCTURE

Moving from the outside to the inside or looking from the top down, we distinguish three depth dimensions referred to above: 1) concrete acts; 2) their dispositions; and 3) ethos. For all human actions, ethos is the foundation in which they are rooted. We will make a few brief introductory remarks about each of these three. See also Figures 4 and 5 in the Appendix.

11.2.3.1 ACTS

We get to know a human being from his *exterior*. This already starts with the external shape of the body and the facial expression. But

---

77. 2 Cor. 4:16.
78. Cf. Ps. 64:6; Prov. 25:3; Jer. 17: 9, 10.
79. Ps. 139:23; Luke 5:22.

we can be very wrong about such external features, even if they do provide some indication. More headway can be made if we take into account a person's concrete life expressions in actions, words and patterns of behavior. We know from everyday experience, however, that conscious human deeds do not come out of the blue but "from inside." They are based on the *aim* or *intention* to realize an action that has been preconceived in the imagination. In our imagination we even anticipate the action, resulting in the *exercise of our will*, our *decision* to act.

All this takes place beneath the surface of our life, inside its exterior. There, anthropologically speaking, lies a basis of human action. In contrast to dispositions and ethos, this basis, this depth level lies very close to our "superficial" concrete external deeds, but they are still *internal and intentional* "acts."

11.2.3.2 DISPOSITIONS

Yet these acts, which form a structural substructure in man's temporal corporeality, are also themselves internally layered or articulated, an articulation that requires further analysis. We know, again on the basis of everyday experience, that someone's deeds, sometimes including their explicit immediate intentions, cannot be sufficiently gauged by means of our practical insight into human nature. In everyday life it is enough some of the time, but very often it is not. We can make further headway in assessing another person if we also consider his "character."

11.2.3.2-1 CHARACTER TRAITS

In a person's character we meet the intentional acts mentioned above in the form of various *habits and other behavioral patterns* which are more or less *enduringly* present, thus as relative *constants*. Hence we can predict with some probability how specific people will react to given circumstances or to certain activities by their fellow-men. We call these patterns *dispositions* or character traits. They lie somewhat deeper than the acts which are *anchored* in them and for which they are available as a necessary motive force. Via these acts they become public only in complete actions or other activities.

In this way we know how a particular person will probably react to a variety of circumstances. His internal "inclinations" have a certain degree of consistency. It is not without reason that we speak of character traits or personality characteristics. If we have known someone well for a fairly long time, we can say something about what is "characteristic" of him: his "tempo," his introversion or extroversion, his usually cheerful, even-tempered or else somber "mood," his radical or instead his laid-back personality, and so on.

11.2.3.2-2 SKILLS

Another type of disposition is formed by *skills*. A pianist has the ability to play the piano, and this ability, this know-how, is relatively continuous. It continues to exist even when he is asleep or when illness prevents him for a time from playing the piano. The same can be said of all kinds of other specialized knowledge or skills.

11.2.3.2-3 SOCIO-CULTURAL DISPOSITIONS

All kinds of *social relationships* also have this dispositional depth level and form still other types of dispositions. Precisely social relationships predispose or promote the behavior of the members in certain respects. A member of an orchestra can be expected to perform musically in this particular form of collaboration, but he is not therefore expected to be good at playing soccer as well. The social structures of which people form a part also belong to this relatively *continuous* depth layer of dispositions which remain potentially present even if the corresponding acts and deeds are not actually performed. In the behavior of children we can often recognize the behavior of parents, teachers, pop stars, and so on. Or we recognize in the behavior of one person a whole people or a regional culture. In "multicultural societies" (for instance in large urban communities) these socio-cultural dispositions are often recognized quite easily.

Like the more personal character traits, these social structures, too, have something normative about them. I will clarify this later, but already now I would explicitly want to include the entire depth layer of dispositions in human behavior when talking about the normative character of the act structure as such.

11.2.3.3 Ethos, the religiously determined attitude to life

11.2.3.3-1 The last (or first) depth level in human life

Meanwhile, we are very much aware that in using the word *character* or in knowing about social, cultural or economic *determinants* we have still not revealed the deepest part of man. A large part of our dispositions are in fact more or less easy to control, or to unlearn, or even to "suppress." As human beings we can control *ourselves*. That is altogether different from the psychological technique that animals also employ, for instance in their hunting territory or in their interaction with people (as in "animal training" for example).

Self-control helps us to prevent dispositions from controlling or causing our actions and deeds in a deterministic fashion as it were. That is why we call the human act structure a *normative structure*. It determines our activities, yet not autonomously, inasmuch as it merely offers *starting points* and *structures* for the free realization of *principles* in the divine creation order.

But does man have an inner need or inclination to take any notice of this? In a biblically directed faith we know that something more and different is required than voluntarily and obligingly conforming to the traditions of our social milieu. In a humanist-driven faith as well, people are aware of this and rightly talk about mentality, cultural conditioning, solidarity (as a rule interpreted solely in terms of morality), and the like.

We are touching here on what may be called, in our temporal mode of existence, the deepest layer of our (temporal) humanity, the first or last depth level as seen respectively from the heart or toward the heart. I for my part choose the word "ethos" for this, by which I mean a person's *basic attitude*, his *total attitude toward life*, his *"ground-motives,"* his *mentality*, or whatever one is accustomed to calling it. We can also speak here of the religious *color* of a person's life (which should not be confused with the religious *direction* of his *faith*, though it can at times give a clear indication of it). So defined, ethos too can be learned about, namely through observation, inquiry, empathy and sympathy. In the present inquiry we will be able to distinguish some *main types* of ethos, as Dooyeweerd for instance did in his theory of the four "religious ground-motives of Western culture."

All the same, we are here *approximating* (and no more than that) the depth of the human heart, which is no longer accessible to theoretical-scientific inquiry by anthropology, or even entirely accessible to practical wisdom and knowledge of human nature. Nor can ethos be categorized simply under the *temporal* human mode of existence in which it manifests itself outwardly to some extent ("from the heart flow the springs of life," Prov. 4:23) and to which scientific anthropology must confine itself. Hence we distinguish the heart itself from ethos as its primary expression. Ethos is the *basic layer* in man's entire *temporal* mode of existence, the *borderland* in the direction of the transcendent, the *first* level of the "normed" expressions of life. It is the *fundamental attitude* that can be recognized with greater or lesser clarity through the entire breadth of life. It therefore has various types, which we can call types of ethos.

II.2.3.3-2 ATTITUDE TO LIFE AND VIEW OF LIFE OR WORLDVIEW

It is *directions in life, attitudes to life* which not only govern our thought, including our practice of science, but which determine the fundamental attitude in all our doings—communally in social relations and structures as well as personally. It is therefore virtually impossible for individuals to escape the influence of community institutions, cultural practices, mentality traits, and the "spirit of the time."

Accordingly, the different *types of ethos*, to be discussed below, are closely connected with the various larger or smaller regional cultures. Anybody with any experience knows about the difference in mentality between people from, say, the Far East, from the West, and from developing countries in the South. In the final analysis these large cultural differences are to some degree also connected with the various types of religions and religious norms. The word combination "religio-ethical" is therefore acceptable and applicable to ethos and the structure of ethos as it functions in time. Anthropologically speaking, ethos is the borderland between a man's heart and his entire temporal mode of existence: ethos belongs to that borderland but is primarily and directly "inspired" from the heart. Though the Christian attitude to life, for instance, may not be entirely the same among all Christians, yet their fully religious orientation is the same, because through their faith they partake of Christ in the heart of their being.

Once we set out to *formulate* the various attitudes to life in our daily existence, we speak of view of life or worldview. This is not yet philosophy as such, but it does form the basis for philosophy. The view of life or worldview itself, however, is practical in nature (cf. chap. 1) and is *qualified by faith*, whereas philosophy is theoretical in nature and is therefore *qualified by logic*.

II.2.4 TYPES OF ETHOS

Just now we mentioned that various types of ethos can be distinguished. In line with Dooyeweerd, who distinguishes four centrally religious "ground-motives" in our culture, I would like to outline five "ethos types," albeit in a provisional manner. A closer examination of these types goes beyond the scope of this book because they require in-depth historical studies. Hence they are only mentioned here, with a few added words by way of clarification.

II.2.4.I SECULARIZATION

II.2.4.I.A PRIMARY SECULARIZATION OF RELIGION: BREACH OF COVENANT

Man was created in a religious bond with the Creator and with a proper realization of this bond. Interpreted in terms of religious content and in the light of Scripture, we can refer to this bond as the "covenant" between Creator and creature.[80] This bond is not broken by sin, but *within* the enduring *structural or normative* (real, not just "formal") existing bond, man turns away from his Creator and starts to deify something in creation and substitute it for God. Particularly in less open regions and cultures, this usually involves various religious rituals, (pseudo-) word revelations (e.g., myths, oracles, magic, etc.), priests and prophets, religious wars, and so on—in other words, from a Christian point of view, some or other "pseudo-religion" or caricature-like cult of God. This could be called *primary secularization*. We can also say: *breach of covenant* is the religious origin of *the ethos of secularization*.

A "pseudo-religion," owing to *its very nature as a religion*, in principle governs all of life—religiously, historically, socially and personally. Those

---

80. Linguists interpret the word "religion" in different ways. Many link it to "ligare," to tie, bind, connect. In our usage "religion" is primarily the *relation* between God and creature. In terms of religious content this linking relationship can be interpreted as "covenant."

structures of creation that we call religion and cult are therefore not empty "formal structures," even less "language-games," but by virtue of creation they contain a divine power of *principles* by which the *direction* of life is already *normatively* indicated. For we were all created *"unto* God."

II.2.4.I.B SECONDARY SECULARIZATION OF RELIGION: DEMYTHOLOGIZATION

A great change occurs in a given culture when religion in its traditional *religious forms of expression* weakens, is suppressed, or even disappears. One might call this process *secondary secularization*. In "primitive" cultures it mostly starts very practically through contact with or domination by other peoples or tribes. As regards Western culture, however, a chief factor in the disintegration of traditional religion in pagan Antiquity was the rise of science. Perhaps a better way of putting it is this: the emergent sciences *linked up* with the religious *process of secularization* already underway in paganism, and offered an alternative religion. The familiar myths, which after all provided the (pagan) *religious norms* and determined the content of (pagan) *religious faith*, were disqualified as priestcraft or poetic imagination.

This main feature of pagan, *secondary* secularization, wherever promoted or reinforced by the emergent sciences, is therefore the *demythologization* of religion. This means that the myths are no longer sincerely held, that the relation to myths becomes indifferent, skeptical or folkloristic, and that more truth, certainty and fulfillment is expected from the sciences insofar as they no longer take into account any gods, spiritual powers, mythological stories or divine presence and activity in everyday life. As a result of this demythologization, in a long and gradual process, sometimes over centuries, the concrete reality with which *science* should occupy itself is experienced and regarded in a more or less radicalized way as if there is no longer anything divine, anything demonic, or anything supra-temporal in this reality.

The process of demythologization caused undeification, horizontalization and substantialization in the everyday view of reality. In this way it also brought about a separation between the workaday world and the supernatural, if indeed people kept any faith in it at all. Those who retained a modicum of religious belief now faced a different, metaphysical or *supernatural* world, one in which they no longer participated. It was "another world."

Demythologization also led to the demise of pantheism. What we do see from time to time was that many people later, in a reactionary and secondary pantheism, returned to an alternative *philosophical* "*re*mythologization." To the extent that people still believed in divine creation (and almost all pagan myths still do) they regarded these gods or divine powers as beings from a transcendent "supernatural" world, the world of the "immortals," an "*other world*," one *separated* from our world. This resulted in the *dualism* of nature and the supernatural, which became so ingrained in Western thought that the Christian church and theology adapted their worldview so as to embrace this dualism as something self-evident. Thus breach of covenant and demythologization are the two combined motive forces in the great, global process of secularization.

II.2.4.2 FORM AND MATTER

The dualism that distinguished but at the same time divorced the natural from the supernatural world continued to determine the world-view of paganism after the process of pagan secularization. This was the case even where paganism, in part and in particular through religion, differentiated itself into *contradictory directions* in terms of mentality and attitude to life. If Dooyeweerd is right in his more precise description, such an attitude to life can be characterized as being governed by two internally contradictory basic religious attitudes. He formulated this as *the Greek ground-motive of "form and matter."* Not being an expert, I am not sure whether this is a correct description, though I do believe much can still be said for it even after the critique of Professor Bram Bos.[81] I see the first ground-motive proposed above, that of (primary and secondary) *religious secularization*, as structurally preceding the four religious ground-motives mentioned by Dooyeweerd.

---

81. See A. P. Bos in his *In de greep van de titanen; inleiding tot een hoofdstroming van de Griekse filosofie* [In the grip of the titans: introduction to a main current in Greek philosophy] (Amsterdam, 1991). His criticism of Dooyeweerd's theory of the Greek ground-motive of form and matter seems plausible because current scholarship no longer credits what Dooyeweerd took to be the religious origin of the ethos type "form and matter." In my view, however, this does not seriously detract from the correct element in Dooyeweerd's description of the divided Greek ethos with its "ground-motive" of "form and matter." Cf. also Bos' criticism in his "Dooyeweerd en de wijsbegeerte van de oudheid," in H. G. Geertsema et al., *Herman Dooyeweerd 1894-1977. Breedte en actualiteit van zijn filosofie* (Kampen, 1994), pp. 197–227.

11.2.4.3 THE CHRISTIAN GROUND-MOTIVE

Though the two pagan ground-motives (those of secularization and form/matter) continue to manifest their power and efficacy in Western culture to this very day, the irruption of the Christian religion at the beginning of the Christian era introduced *a new spiritual direction.* This spirit or attitude to life—this ethos—is *in principle* entirely governed by the power of Christ and his Holy Spirit. Via the Word revelation Christ teaches us to experience and regard life as being created by God in Christ, as fundamentally corrupted in Adam's fall, and as completely renewed, recreated and fulfilled by Christ with his Holy Spirit. Through faith in this word revelation, and thus in religious surrender to Christ, we personally share in this new world and this new humanity, of which Christ himself is the Head. Just as "in the beginning," from supra-temporal "primordial time," He also is and was and ever will be its "root."

11.2.4.4 NATURE AND GRACE

In the first centuries of the Christian era the church of Christ found itself in a pagan world in which the believers had to live their lives. There were enough shared elements in human existence to make this possible by and large. But it was impossible to prevent spiritual enmity—a religious "antithesis" between the kingdom of God and that of Satan—from being widely expressed in violent persecution or arrogant negation and ostracism. In practice this gave rise to the problem that would later be debated under the theme of "church and culture" with its many parallel and related terms, like the theological theme of "particular" and "common" grace.

The spiritual conflict was articulated by the two camps in two basic worldviews. The school of the "apologists" tried to give an account of the Christian faith and its practical meaning for everyday life. Many Christians went beyond witnessing by trying to demonstrate to the pagans that the Christian religion was also more rational than the traditional pagan religion, in any case was not irrational. Some Christians engaged in direct debate with philosophers, such as the Stoic Christian philosopher Aristides of Athens (first half 2nd century) and especially Justin Martyr (died c. 165), who before he became a Christian was heavily influenced by the teachings of Plato.

In this way nascent Christian theology, too, was from the outset influenced by Greek-philosophical patterns of thought, strongly supported and inspired by the nature/supernature dualism that had long influenced pagan life and thought. The difference now was that the "supernatural" was preferably not, or at least not only, seen as the world of gods, spirits and immortal souls, but primarily as the area where God's grace or the church was active.

This whole development gave birth to thought based on the nature-grace scheme, thought which today is widespread and deeply rooted in Christian theology all over the world. It characterized all of medieval theologizing but continues to exert a powerful influence even today in the theology and worldview of orthodox Protestants. It is an "ethos," an *attitude* to life and thought.

To be sure, there have been plenty of Protestants to critique Roman Catholic nature/grace thinking. Yet, purely theologically, this dualism is proving insurmountable. Despite countless attempts to overcome it, it is always adopted again in a diluted form and then defended with the term "duality" in place of dualism. Although everybody is opposed to a dualism, a "combination" of nature and grace into a duality or "bi-unity" is and remains a dualism: it will never become an original unity; the two-ness remains presupposed.

Two of the most prominent manifestations of this stubborn dualism are seen in the problems of *church and state* and *faith and science*. Thinkers traditionally posit a "tension" between them—a dubious tension at best. In "theological anthropology" this resonates in the interminable "tension" between intellect and feeling, between "knowledge" and "firm confidence,"[82] between doctrine and experience of God, between "head and heart," and similar "dualities." The traditional theological view of the nature of faith—in other words, the prevailing philosophy of theology—is partly to blame for this.

The standard way of resolving all those tensions is still sought in *balancing* the twin one-sided positions, rather than in grasping the deeper or higher fullness, unity and identity that are seen individually in the human heart and socially in the spiritual communion of the one "body of Christ." That is a deeper level than the level of the aspectual multiplicity of "elements" or "facets" which as "one-sided" positions compete with one another or else are supposed to harmoniously "complement" each other. True enough, harmonious balance is neces-

---

82. Heidelberg Catechism, Lord's Day 7.

sary and normative in life, but it is hard to achieve if we cannot *start* from the spiritual unity of all this temporal diversity in the totality or fullness of the human heart in its participation in the universal communion in Adam or in Christ.

11.2.4.5 NATURE AND FREEDOM (SCIENCE IDEAL AND PERSONALITY IDEAL)

The secularization of Christianity, which emerged in a new wave in movements like Humanism and the Renaissance, brought to light what is provisionally the last ground-motive of life and thought in our Western culture, marking the important turn to the "Modern Age." Initially Dooyeweerd labeled this ground-motive the science ideal versus the personality ideal. After further developing the theory of ground-motives, he mainly used the term "nature and freedom." In my view, the earlier formulation remains valuable because it focuses more clearly on the practice of life.

11.2.4.6 NATURALIST TENDENCIES VERSUS FREEDOM IDEALISM IN HUMANIST SCIENCE

Because humanist philosophy, and Western thought in general, did not discover the real transcendent center of human existence in the heart, this thought remained trapped in the traditional dualism of matter and spirit. This also influenced modern variations of the dualism between nature and freedom, materialism and spiritualism. Thus leading scholars even today say that anthropology should stop searching for the unity of man. All this is mere speculation, they contend, since the observable and verifiable hard facts indicate that man is a bundle of contradictions, and nothing can change this. Most probably, there simply is no central, all-embracing and therefore in principle all-governing unity. We know man only as an internally contradictory being.

This idea is developed in various ways, as for instance in Freud, who sees man as an internally contradictory bundle of three principles: the pleasure principle, the nirvana principle of the death wish, and the reality principle. This contradiction is, so to speak, a technical glitch in the evolution of man.

An opposite view is held by people who stand in the tradition of German philosophical idealism and who secularize and absolutize human freedom while denying his corporeal restraints (or determinants, as they prefer to say) or at least disqualifying them as not being part of man's authentic self. This existentialist and personalist approach plays an important role in present-day theological hermeneutics and exegesis. Even now that Bultmann is less fashionable, his method of "existential interpretation" is still important in much current theology, despite his anti-mythical line of reasoning.

Nowadays, when "fundamentalists" become somewhat detached from their rationalist traditions, they almost automatically revert to this present-day dialectical, personalist or existentialist way of thinking, since they lack a Christian philosophical alternative (or because they do not take this alternative seriously). Their uncritical intention is to bring theology up-to-date and make it practical, "socially relevant," satisfying emotional needs and giving answers to "today's questions."

But the conflict between nature and free will cannot be resolved by humanist thought, because it recognizes neither (a) a harmonious coherence in the order of creation, nor (b) its transcendent unity in God's revealed will (the love command) in which alone human freedom is true freedom through faithful submission to God's will. More on this in the later chapter on "praxeology" (my term for philosophical ethics, theoretical teaching for life, or theory of action).

II.2.5 SCHOLASTICISM

As mentioned, the development of the modern ground-motive did not mean that the previous ground-motives stopped exerting their influence. In this context Reformational philosophy has given a relatively new meaning to the concept of "synthesis" and especially to the term "scholasticism" by not focusing in the first place on the *method* of theologizing in the Middle Ages (the scholastic *organon*) but associating these two terms with the *combining of the biblical ground-motive with a non-Christian ground-motive.* Scholasticism therefore involves much more than the making of sharp and subtle distinctions and the setting up of strictly logical constructions. The intellect can be used wrongly in science, but never too much. Hence Reformational philosophy feels no need to compensate scholasticism with some measure of emotional or experiential mysticism. Both should be avoided, not just as one-sided positions but as two erroneous paths.

Besides *medieval scholasticism*, therefore, in which Christian thought was in part determined by the thought of *ancient* philosophy, our philosophy also distinguishes *modern scholasticism*, in which Christian thought links up with *modern humanist* patterns of thought, patterns that are at bottom religiously inspired by the dualism of nature and freedom. The reason we oppose modern scholasticism is particularly because its forms and habits of thought have become a permanent feature of our modern culture, either expressing man's hidden ideal that *life should be governed by science* (including political science, technology and economics), or else championing the diametrically opposite ideal *that the personality should be free to realize itself* in the quest for its identity.

11.2.6 "Dialectic"

Three of the five ground-motives or types of ethos can be said to be "dialectical," that is to say, they are internally contradictory and their internal poles call up and compete with each other. This means that they inspire and stimulate life and thought in contrary directions. Consequently, they are the deepest source of all contradictions and conflicts in worldviews and life ideals as well as in scientific paradigms or attitudes of thought.

By its very nature, this "dialectic" does not occur in the third, biblical ground-motive of true religion. The same applies to the first ground-motive, that of *secularization*. But the only thing that can be said about the latter is that it is *antithetical*, since it is a (doomed) attempt to divorce life and thought from religion by replacing the "immortal gods" and other godlike powers by human (scientific) reason.

11.2.7 Ground-motives are not intellectual schemas

It should be clear that the religious ground-motives or ethos types are by no means to be identified with theoretical schemas or theological classifications. They are total and central *communal attitudes* in life and thought, supra-personal spiritual motives and powers. We cannot treat them purely theoretically as intellectual motifs or presuppositions, nor modify them to fit this purpose or otherwise grasp them with our understanding. *It is the other way round.* These communal attitudes and ground-motives, these *attitudes* to life and (therefore) to thought have *us* in their grasp. They guide or determine the basic direction of our life and thought, and as regards thought: they first of all control the way we analyze, think and experience reality in everyday practice, and thence also our theoretical-scientific thought. They lead our thought time and again to the same or related dualistic, "dialectical," "high-tension" problems.

That is why the "theme" or the "problem" of nature and grace cannot be *theologically reasoned out* and critically resolved, as theology often tries to do. Such a critique touches on *only one* of the many possible manifestations of this religio-ethical dualism, namely its *concepts*. In doing so this critique stays on the surface of life. A theoretical schema like that of nature and grace can only be theoretically-theologically overcome, step by patient step, by starting from the *religious depth* of the true knowledge of God and the self and by applying a corresponding worldview and philosophy—particularly by positing the Christian faith regarding *the creation of all things in Christ* and *the universality of the kingdom of God.*

II.2.8 THE WAY TO OVERCOME RELIGIOUS DUALISMS

We will have to take up this idea again when dealing with various theological problems, particularly the problem of (how we practically view) the relation of church and state, the relation of faith and science, or the relation of the Christian life inside and outside the church. These themes will clearly show whether or not our thought is trapped in the religio-ethical dualism of nature and grace.

The nature-grace dialectic also asserts itself in the main schools of thought in the sciences, including theology. As we argued above, it cannot be resolved *scientifically* by improving our logical thinking or substituting some basic schemas or categories, but only by profoundly altering our *spiritual attitude,* our *ethos.* Only then, from a different attitude of thought, will we be able to "see" why those whom we do not wish to regard as dishonest, wicked or un-Christian, or as dull and less intelligent than ourselves, nevertheless *cannot* be convinced by our irrefutable logical arguments. Indeed, people's insight or vision is anchored deep down in their ethos.

With this in mind, Dooyeweerd drew a sharp distinction between what he called a "theoretical dialectic" and a "religious dialectic."[83] Apostate religions always idolize or absolutize one or more aspects

---

83. Cf. *A New Critique of Theoretical Thought,* 1:64.

of reality. This inevitably invites a reaction in the form of a similar idolatrous absolutization of other, neglected aspects. Thus arises the "dialectic," the war among non-Christian religions; but this process is also at work within Christianity itself to the extent that—first deep within and then in thought and terminology—it enters into a combination with non-Christian thought. It then goes on, again inevitably, to split up into self-absolutizing schools of theology and self-absorbed church denominations—calamitous divisions that are euphemistically called "one-sided positions."

11.2.9 SYNTHESIS

The interrelation between the above-mentioned ground-motives or attitudes to life (types of ethos or mentality types) cannot be described simply as a chronological sequence in which they succeed one another as paganism, Christianity, Catholicism, Humanism and Protestantism. On the contrary, every ground-motive, even when no longer dominant in a given cultural era, retains its power and influence. Thus in philosophy and theology Christianity has almost always, to this very day, traditionalistically adopted the secularized and substantialized view of reality from (long obsolete) religious paganism. We can illustrate this by means of two examples.

11.2.9.1 SUBSTANTIALISM

Early Christian theology combined (externally) the pagan view of nature with the Christian faith by *adding* (externally) the religious truths of God's creation and providence. In terms of faith this was good and important. However, as a result of this addition no change was made to the persistent pagan philosophy in which the internal structures of reality are regarded as "substances" or functions of it. And in the reaction to pagan pantheism—a reaction that sometimes goes to the other extreme of deism—God was and continues to be omitted from the reality structures of creation, so that we can still speak of an undeified and consequently uprooted, horizontalist, secularist view of reality in Western habits of thought, including Christian theology. Theologians demonstrate this time and again when they employ certain conceptions about creaturely realities such as levels in the structure of man, relations in and between social structures (for example, "church and state"), the nature of faith, the relation of heart and functions ("body and soul"), truth and history, the concept of truth, the connection between justice and morality, faith and politics, and so on. In particular we should mention here the tradition of "theological ethics."

The modern humanist ground-motive of substantialized nature versus autonomous human freedom uses, as regards the motive of *nature*, the pagan "demythologized" view of nature or reality in some or other modern version. And its *freedom or personality* motive cultivates a secularized form of the biblical idea of freedom through all kinds of "normlessness."

II.2.9.2 HORIZONTALIZATION

Present-day Christian thought in the field of science clearly demonstrates the effects of all four non-Christian ground-motives in the great diversity of its schools. Yet also in the field of science it remains the calling of Christian scholars, according to Romans 12:2, to be transformed by the renewal of "the Christian mind" through the hard work of uncovering, analyzing and purging non-Christian, especially modern, philosophical elements.

In particular it will be necessary to fight against the *horizontalization* of the outlook on reality owing first of all to the *negation of the transcendent fullness* of temporal reality in Christ, in whom the believing Christian participates in his heart through the Holy Spirit; and secondly, owing to the negation of God's immanence in creatures through his creation order (including his Word revelation), his will and law, through which he created all things and still upholds them, carries them and directs them.

CHAPTER TWELVE–
PHILOSOPHICAL SOCIOLOGY

CHAPTER TWELVE

PHILOSOPHICAL SOCIOLOGY

12.1 SOCIOLOGY AND PHILOSOPHICAL SOCIOLOGY

By way of introduction to this chapter and to avoid possible mis-understandings, I need to make a few preliminary remarks in which to define what I mean by sociology.

12.1.1 PHILOSOPHY AND THE SPECIAL SCIENCES

By sociology I understand a special science or academic discipline, a *vakwetenschap*, so not a totality science like philosophy. The relation between philosophy and sociology is governed by the nature of the connection between philosophy and the special sciences in general. Among other things, philosophy analyzes the fundamental concepts of every special science, and specifically their place among and connection with the fundamental notions of the other special sciences. This takes place within the framework of a general systematics, hence on the basis of the theory of modalities and entities, with a focus on the totality or transcendent root unity of existing reality.

12.1.2 SOCIOLOGY

Broadly speaking, we can say that special sciences analyze a part of concrete reality from the viewpoint of one of the modal aspects that we learned about in cosmology. Reformational philosophers (in particular D. F. M. Strauss) sometimes say, rightly so, that the modal aspects form the *gateways* to the scientific study of reality. The main feature of science is indeed not pure "abstraction" but typical *modal abstraction*: first the theoretical isolation of a certain *aspect*, and then the analysis of something concrete from the perspective of this aspect. This feature alone makes a special science possible and gives it its defining character.

Now then, in the theory of modalities we also encountered the social aspect. Its nucleus can be referred to as "sociation and intercourse."

These words should not be taken as referring to concrete phenomena, but to *the core fact* that man can never be absolutely isolated, that he always lives together in various ways with others and is involved in relations, regardless of the way in which these relations are in fact experienced. So in a literal sense we could also refer to all this as "solidarity" (*medemenselijkheid*: fellow humanness). In today's usage, however, the term solidarity tends to have a typically moral thrust, and that is not what is meant here. For that matter, the word social, too, often has this moral connotation in everyday usage: we regard somebody's behavior in "sociation and intercourse" as antisocial if he is inconsiderate of his fellow-men in a *moral* sense.

Thus in the special science that developed during the theoretical investigation of concrete human social phenomena, namely in "positive or empirical sociology," the social aspect is the limited perspective from which various concrete relationships in society are analyzed and, for instance, statistically processed. For this reason as well, the worldview term "solidarity" is not suitable for indicating the core or nucleus of the social *aspect*, because it is far too broad and refers more to the *concrete* human being or to humankind. In our context the term "social" lends itself much better to strict demarcation and scientific definition.

12.1.3 Why various special sciences encroach on each other

Many special sciences, particularly in the humanities, adapt too strongly and uncritically to current everyday usage, with the result that in practice the special sciences show much needless rivalry and mutual encroachment, once given their lack of a well-defined and consistent definition of the boundaries of their specific science. Turf wars can be prevented, however, through greater methodological precision. The theory of modal aspects can offer a remedy here for the existing confusion about disciplinary boundaries.[84] The problem can become particularly acute when university administrators lump together (or break up) all kinds of "social sciences."

---

84. *(Ed.)* See the prize-winning essay by Johan Stellingwerff, in part reproduced in his *Inleiding tot de universiteit; de samenhang der wetenschappen en de wetenschappelijke bibliotheek* [Introduction to the university: the coherence of the sciences and the academic library] (Amsterdam: Buijten en Schipperheijn, 1971), pp. 215–39.

The problem of transgressing the boundaries of other disciplines, therefore, does not just occur in theological ethics, which in a certain sense has become notorious for its encroachments on the fields of politics, economics, genetics, the environment and morality. We need not discuss this problem at length here, but a few examples may suffice. Famous in the history of jurisprudence is the problem of the difference and connection between law and morality. In the Roman Catholic tradition, law resides under moral philosophy. This is a broadly held view, also outside of Christianity. Similarly, many sociologists pose as moralists because they cannot or will not distinguish between the social and the moral, a deficiency we also find in everyday language.

Theologians, too, often treat a select number of fundamental questions of law, morality, economics and solidarity as part of their discipline, in particular as part of theological ethics, and they believe the results they offer are normative. A few decades ago we had a spate of "theologies of . . .": theology of liberation, theology of money, theology of law, theology of labor, theology of peace, theology of the environment, theology of education, theology of medical care, theology of language, theology of history, theology of art, of death, of economics; and the list goes on.

In our time there is a trend to replace the word theology here by ethics, because it is held, very traditionally, that anything having to do with norms, that is, with good and evil, is a matter of ethics. The Roman Catholic tradition mentally adds that ethics therefore is ultimately a matter for pope and magisterium, for the church and its teaching authority. The Protestant tradition mentally adds that it is therefore a matter for theology and for (theologically inspired and theologically based) ecclesiastical publications and "pronouncements," messages from the church to the government and the general public.[85] Both traditions labor under a view of reality that manifests itself in a certain view of society, a view that we now want to discuss from a critical Reformational perspective.

---

85. The common source of both traditions is the scholastic framework of nature and grace. It affects theology whenever the kingdom of God on earth is primarily, if not exclusively, equated with the church as the community of believers administered by the official clergy. The church, so defined, is then set over against either the state or society as the "natural community." Both traditions labor under an unbiblical conception regarding reality or "nature."

12.1.4 PHILOSOPHICAL SOCIOLOGY OR PHILOSOPHY OF "POSITIVE SOCIOLOGY"

As we said, the task of philosophical sociology is to analyze the modal and entitary basic structures of social relationships in the context of a totality view of their diversity, coherence and unity. Primarily this includes a further analysis of the social aspect with its many anticipations and retrocipations, as well as the classification of concrete social structures (entities) into various types and the analysis of their internal substructures. In the survey following sec. 12.2, we will (have to) confine ourselves to sketching the basic structures of the main forms of human social intercourse and sociation.

As we do so we are staying within the boundaries of philosophy but moving from general philosophical systematics to the specialized philosophy of positive sociology. The latter often goes by the less accurate name of "social philosophy."

12.2 HUMANITY AND SOLIDARITY

12.2.1 HUMANITY IS A UNITY

The philosophical anthropology discussed in the previous chapter also gives rise to a new conception of human society. However, for this subject, too, we cannot draw enough attention to Reformational philosophy's insistence on maintaining the integral and consistent character of its *totality view*, where "totality" is taken only in the sense of all-embracing reality, reality insofar as it is accessible to scientific analysis, in other words "earthly creation" (Vollenhoven). Every philosophy, qua totality science, even if it does not consciously accept Dooyeweerd's definition of philosophy, is concerned primarily ("worldviewishly," "prolegomenally") with theoretical insight into the totality as unity and as unity of meaning.

Philosophy therefore focuses on the totality as embracing all that is temporal and theoretically accessible, but including the tendency towards its supra-temporal concentration in a unity, a unity that is already known religiously but still needs to be discovered philosophically. It then turns out that the content of this unity cannot be discovered by philosophy but is accessible only to some or other faith. For the unity of the human race does not reside in our corporeal descent from one progenitor or from one human couple. This organic relation may in fact exist, but it is not the most important thing, just as organic corporeality is not the only or the most important thing about human existence. The unity referred to is a *transcendent* unity which is also an *original* unity. It can be understood only in the biblical belief in creation as the supra-temporal unity in Christ, in whom all things were created. In Him, the first creature, all mankind was present "at the same time" (literally: "in no time")[86]—like the rest of creation, for that matter, since "all things" were created in Him,[87] were "supra-temporally" concentrated in Him. Moreover, they were so created "in the beginning," "*in illo tempore*" (Eliade).[88] He is the original unity, the "root." For in our pre-theoretical religious language (thus not in philosophy as such) we talked about God's covenant with man, of which Adam was the first head, the representative of the entire human race. In the Christian faith we therefore already know from the Bible that from a pre-theoretical point of view there are strictly speaking no individuals who exist as independent isolated units. By virtue of mankind's created structure Adam's fall was *our* fall, and Christ's work of reconciliation is made our work by God's grace. (The confessional term "as if" says too little here.[89]) For this reason human-ity as a unity is not an abstract product of thought, nor a "metaphysical

---

86. The term "pre-existence" is inadequate here, though it can sometimes be used metaphorically.

87. Unfortunately, the New Testament deepening of the Old Testament revelation regarding creation has not yet been incorporated in conventional theology. This is primarily due to the fact that Christianity did not yet have a philosophical alternative to the classical philosophy of substance thinking. One of the things it still lacked was the distinction between creation ("in the beginning") and genesis (in time). As a result, the theoretical hypothesis of evolutionism, for example, could often only be disputed in a biblicistic (i.e., theologically positivistic) manner, thus less than convincingly. More on this in chapter 14 on epistemology.

88. Eliade's expression is his description of that which is (in well-nigh all creation myths throughout the world) the typically supra-temporal "beginning of days" that "precedes" all time but also remains active within it: namely, the reality represented by the phrase "in the beginning" of Gen. 1:1, the primordial time, the *Ur-Sprung* (Origin). It is often interpreted as "cyclical" because it features an "eternal return of the same" (Nietzsche), but in my opinion this does insufficient justice to the typically supra-temporal element in the mythological creation stories of countless peoples. This element alone goes to show that the pagan myths are genuine (pagan) *religious* stories, directed at "things that are not [nor can be] seen." Cf. Heb. 11:1.

89. Cf. Heidelberg Catechism, Lord's Day 23: "God grants and credits to me the perfect satisfaction, righteousness, and holiness of Christ, *as if* I had never sinned nor been a sinner, *as if* I had been as perfectly obedient as Christ was obedient for me" (ital. added, Editor).

speculation," nor yet a logical sum of individuals, but a human *race*, a real unity with a time-transcending center, a spiritual, "supra-temporal" root community which is always present in a "head," is always "re-present-ed," namely in Adam, or in Christ as the "second Adam." In them we were or are *really present*.

But these fundamental biblical truths cannot be convincingly demonstrated by any apologetics. At most (and this is not unimportant) we can point to all kinds of pagan myths which, though flawed, likewise refer (in a *falsified* manner) to an original unity of mankind. Only in *religious* surrender to our God who reveals it to us can this central unity and solidarity of mankind be cognitively appropriated, and can it be clarified in a testimony of faith by means of a metaphor (for example, "a body," or a vine with branches).

12.2.2 THE SPIRITUAL BREACH IN THE UNITY OF THE HUMAN RACE

If only from a scientific point of view, theoretical sociology, either philosophical or scientific, cannot escape reflecting on the fundamental, truly universal questions about the meaning of human society. The prolegomenal reflection on preliminary philosophical questions which this requires is the area where faith (of whatever kind) and sociology as a discipline necessarily encounter and influence each other. From the perspective of the Christian faith we must therefore first say something about the spiritual breach mentioned in the heading of this section.

The apostasy from God, which started empirically with Adam's fall,[90] but also the restoration of reconciled fellowship with God in Christ, involved the entire human race. According to the word of Scripture, Christ is, normatively speaking, a "propitiation [atoning sacrifice] for our sins, and not for ours only but also for the sins of the whole world" (1 John 2:2).[91] Even the non-human is involved in this. "All things" on earth and in heaven are "united under one Head, that is Christ" (Eph. 1:10) and are reconciled unto Him (Col. 1:20).

---

90. Not Eve's, though she sinned earlier in time than Adam. Our chronology does not apply to the supra-temporal reality dimension of Adam's conduct in his office as "head" of humanity.

91. Theological universalism is wrong in invoking this text: philosophically speaking, it equates the norm for faith with the subjective response of faith.

Meanwhile, this deepest and integral unity of the human race was ruptured, and as a result not all people subjectively share in this restoration. Not because they have no relation to God-in-Christ, but because they experience and realize this normative relation in unbelief. But what is normal—what is "natural" in the sense of normative—is that humanity received a new root of life in Christ, a new Head, a second Adam, who became historically manifest in the "incarnation of the Word." The original "head" function of the first Adam has been cancelled for Christian believers. The rule they are now under is: "Therefore, if anyone is in Christ, he is a new creation; the old has passed away, behold, the new has come" (2 Cor. 5:17).

These positions or functions of the first and second Adam are characteristic of the spiritual depth dimension (independent of place or time) of all human life, including the cultural products and social relations formed by man. They refer to life's religious determinant, that is, to the concrete relation of man to God which includes the whole of human life (and so not just the domain of faith and worship). In this "supra-temporal" dimension of reality the *social* unity of all believers, too, is anchored in Christ, in "his Body," or to put it differently: our social unity as believers is the (supra-temporal, "transcendent") *fullness* and perfection of all (temporal) sociality. This is not an ideal reality of *thought* in the style of Plato, but genuine reality, of a supra-temporal ("spiritual") nature.[92]

---

92. This spiritual, supra-temporal depth dimension was also where Adam's fall (in his heart) and Christ's work of redemption took place. We should therefore restrain ourselves somewhat when insisting, in an uncompromising rejection of Higher Criticism, on the historical character of Adam's fall or the redemptive facts of Christ's life on earth and on Calvary. That historicity is only too real, but its meaning and impact reside not just in its *historical time aspect*, however essential that is, but primarily in its fullness and supra-temporality, in the "spiritual depth dimension" just mentioned. Something of this was understood by theologians like Gerhard von Rad, Rudolf Bultmann, Karl Barth and many others who followed in their footsteps. They sometimes expressed this by distinguishing *Historie* [the objective history of the historians] and *Geschichte* [the eschatological events of existential significance]. But the elaboration and application of this distinction is often highly disputable, owing to the lack of a Christian-philosophical alternative to the fundamentalism they rightly criticize which mostly adopts a rationalist (positivist) outlook on history, historiography and historical science, involving a view of historical facts as though they were the "positive data" of natural science. We see a comparable phenomenon in the latest re-evaluation, partly *contra* Bultmann, of the "biblical myths."

12.2.3 SOCIAL RELATIONS ARE THE TEMPORAL STRUCTURES OF SOLIDARITY

In the modern humanist view of society, man has been theoretically (not, of course, in reality) torn loose from society in *subjective, inner* freedom. In principle, or at least in intention, he stands free and sovereign in and above (and at times even opposite) society. But neither philosophically nor worldviewishly does this humanist conception do justice to the reality of solidarity (in the sense of sociality).

Certainly this sociality can be acknowledged as an *"anthropinon,"* that is, as a characteristic feature of man. For this solidarity or sociality is an empirical fact that makes clear that also man's personal life partly consists and largely functions in *interpersonal relations*. In humanism as a practical view of life—and that is what we mainly deal with every day in the media, in politics, in public opinion, and so on—we still often do run across this insight, partly in connection with the moralistic interpretation of the term solidarity, namely as "humanity" or the quality of being humane. But then "humanity" has been separated from God's law of creation and re-creation and is experienced in the form of an absolutization of love of neighbor.

Social relations do in fact largely make up human life, just as our arms and legs, our senses, and so on, partly make up—*constitute*—our temporal human existence. Granted, our human existence is not totally exhausted by these temporal structures of our corporeality or this sociality. That is the element of truth in the individualistic theory of man mentioned above. In the center of his existence, it is true, man *transcends* his entire temporal mode of existence, including his social relations. He is neither absorbed by time nor submerged in time and his temporal relations. Nevertheless, not even in the supra-temporal concentration point of his heart is man ever alone or solitary, as we discussed in sec. 12.2.1 and 12.2.2.

In temporal life, however, various kinds of social relations constitute the *structures* of the human mode of existence. Social relations are not just casual garments that can be put on or taken off at will. Nor are they *role patterns,* as many modern sociologists like to say. Roles are played on a stage, and the more an actor can be himself in a certain role, the better his performance of the role will be. But this is not always the case. Roles are more or less external patterns of behavior and are mainly acquired through studying them. By contrast, the social relations or structures in which man lives are for a large part not external role patterns but very real human "building blocks"— or rather, structural elements—of the temporal life that is always a life in which the various individual human modes of existence presuppose and need *each other* and in which they *manifest* their personal individual identity. This identity does not exist by itself without the forms in which it expresses itself.[93]

So there are no so-called free autonomous subjects above or opposite the structures of society. The latter are the temporal structures of *life* for each and every human being. Viewed according to the transcendent fullness of life in the "body of Christ" (or "in Adam") as well as according to the entire mode of existence in time, man is never totally alone and by himself. He is always bound up in *solidarity*, both in various temporal relations and in the sense of the fullness of life in Christ and His church as the *"new humanity,"* or else in the equally supra-temporal community of the human race in Adam. This twofold transcendent fullness, between which there exists a religious "antithesis," manifests itself in time in many social relationships and behaviors, the chief ones of which we will now discuss.

12.2.4 INTERNAL DESTINATION FUNCTION AND EXTERNAL GOALS

Social forms are concrete phenomena in the world of experience given to us to live in. They therefore have an entity structure. In the theory of entities we explained that all entities contain a leading or qualifying aspect, which is also called the destination function. In the case of societal structures it is crucial to distinguish carefully between this leading and qualifying internal structural function on the one hand, and on the other the possible *external goals* to which the social form in question may be made serviceable. We will underline this and provide examples of it as we discuss a number of societal relationships.

---

93. In my view, therefore, the vogue of "searching for one's identity" does not lead to profound self-knowledge, but testifies rather to dissatisfaction with one's own concrete existence, for which a remedy is sought in a self-centered way.

12.3 Principal types of societal relationships

12.3.1 Marriage

12.3.1.1 Marriage has an entity structure

In the theory of entities I drew attention to the fact that every concrete existing reality has an *identity structure* in which all modal aspects are bound up into an entitary unity of a certain type. This type is determined first of all by the *leading* or *qualifying* function and, in close connection with this, by the *founding* function. The same applies to all societal relationships, of which marriage is one.

12.3.1.2 Defining the structure of marriage

Marriage can be defined as the binary love community between a man and a woman for the duration of life and on the basis of gender difference.

In the light of this definition a polygamous marriage is not one marriage with several women, but a plurality of simultaneously existing marriages that one man has contracted with several women.

12.3.1.3 Marriage's leading function

Although marriage functions as an entity in all modalities, its functioning in the moral love aspect is what gives direction and meaning to the whole. This distinctive total entity makes abstract modal love a typical "marital love." Marital or conjugal love remains typical for a marriage, both normatively and in principle factually, and despite all shortcomings also in a "good marriage." The actual character of the marital relationship is therefore *structurally qualified* by typical marital love, also in the subjective factuality, either positively if things are relatively normal or negatively if love cools off, is lacking, or turns into its opposite. Marital love *ought* to leave its mark on the total life of the marriage in all its functions. It forms the *internal destination function* of marriage.

This quality lends a certain cast and color to everything in marital life: the economic spending of usually limited means (of subsistence), juridical functioning in doing justice to each other, the social intercourse of doing many things together (eating, drinking coffee, sleeping, planning a vacation, walking), the way of talking and behaving in each other's company, furnishing a house together and other joint activities, in short, the whole way of associating with each other in the marital relationship. It is the marital style that is qualified by that special subtype of neighborly love, namely marital love.

Marital love as a type should therefore be distinguished from other types of love like parental love, love of country, friendship, comradeship, human love of animals, love of plants, love of a hobby, and so on.

12.3.1.4 INTERNAL DESTINATION FUNCTION AND EXTERNAL GOALS

We already referred to the difference between goals and destination in sec. 12.2.4. It implies that we should fully acknowledge the inner nature, the distinctive worth and significance of marriage as a meaningful form of life whose meaning and destination does not depend on external goals to which a marriage may make itself serviceable. A well-known example are the Curies, where husband and wife, individually and together, wished to devote their lives to science. Other examples are well-known from history. German National Socialism bred a spirit and a worldview in which all life, in particular marriage and procreation, received their true meaning only from the *folk* community. Many sects often regarded marriage as a procreative institution serving the community of faith with natural growth. Until the last world war this was also very much the prevailing opinion in Roman Catholicism. For this reason alone, any kind of birth control was condemned. Life was to be subservient to the enlargement (the "increase") of the Church. This view was also found in certain strands of Reformed Protestantism.

Of course, if there are good reasons for doing so it can be entirely legitimate for a social relationship, including a married couple, to pursue *external* goals like the ones above. But this should not be done at the expense of the real, internal destination of such a relationship, which as a part of God's creation has its own law of life—its own value and meaning—first of all in and of itself.

12.3.1.5 THE SEXUAL FUNCTION OF THE MARITAL STRUCTURE

Our definition of marriage located its founding function in the gender polarity of man and woman, so in the biotic modality.

For this reason a homosexual friendship can never be called a "marriage," and any civil recognition of this relationship in a contract or by some other legal instrument cannot transform it into "another type of marriage," no more than its consecration by a clergyman can. To legislate "equality before the law" of a *civil union* and a marriage is a simplistic solution. The equality that applies here only concerns a number of *legal* rights and duties, and whether the state should move in that direction is a matter of *political* decision. However, public opinion makes little or no distinction between law and morality and is therefore readily inclined to assume the issue concerns a moral decision. But not everything having to do with good and evil is for that reason an issue of "morality" or "ethics." Political decisions (correct or incorrect) are therefore not necessarily moral or immoral, but remain juridically qualified. The moral norm is not the principal norm for politics, no more than the religious norm is. As we will see further on in this chapter, the public national community is first and foremost a *legal* or *juridical* community.

12.3.1.6 DIVORCE

Finally I want to emphasize in this brief sketch that the sexual *founding* function of marriage is not its *leading* function. Any problems in this area, of whatever kind, should be dealt with under the guidance of marital love and solved in the spirit of this love, with or without outside help. Every attempt at reversing the relationship between founding and leading function will inevitably result in disappointment. Where love and troth no longer put a decisive stamp on a marriage, all the rest will be directly threatened and the *internal dissolution* of the marriage will be imminent. Once this internal dissolution has become a fact, it is the state's *task* to *legally* sever its external connection with this factually defunct marriage in a divorce procedure.

12.3.1.7 MARRIAGE AND STATE

The task of the state with regard to broken marriages should not be deemed wrong or called a compromise, but is a fundamental task of the state, a typical legal task. The state is not called on to pass a moral or religious judgment on a concrete case such as a divorce, whatever a "theocratic" political ideology might wish. Government must perform its own typical, limited task within the *public legal system*. It is no different from the churches, which have been able to assume their own limited task, different but comparable, with regard to the marriages of their members.

Much traditional Christian social theory still looks upon marriage as a legal matter for the state, sometimes even as a matter for the church. Both views are based on an incorrect equation of marriage with one or more of its external *connections* with some other social structure such as nation, tribe, state, faith community, economic class, intellectual group, and so on.

12.3.1.8 MARRIAGE AND CHURCH

The *external* connection of a marriage with a church community may lead to rules which the church community draws up on its own, without having to follow public legal forms. Unless the signs are deceiving, the law in our country that forbids churches to "solemnize" any marriage that does not yet have civil status will soon be a thing of the past.[94] The same goes for the traditional but erroneous opinion that as a Christian you are not yet married until you have been married "in the church" or, as Roman Catholics say: "before a priest." In orthodox Protestant churches, too, we are gradually seeing that what used to be called "solemnization" or "consecration" in the church is being replaced by the congregation's intercessory prayer in an ordinary church service. There is nothing wrong with that in principle; to use old-fashioned terms: it is an example of "sphere-sovereignty."

12.3.1.9 AUTHORITY, EQUALITY, EMANCIPATION AND PERSONAL FREEDOM IN MARRIAGE

A few words in this context on public opinion today. We are living in the atmosphere of modern humanism which to an overwhelming degree determines the spiritual climate of our times. Now then, in this atmosphere almost all power and authority are suspect.

Yet in a marriage, authority is just as essential as conjugal love. Not only Scripture mentions it, but everyday practice shows that in any close-knit *community*, also in a marriage, there is in fact an *authoritative* agency (no matter who exercises the authority). Where such an authoritative agency is lacking, we can no longer speak, in a

---

94. *(Ed.)* Dutch legal practice in medieval and early modern times provided for marriages to be consecrated in a church service. The introduction of the French Civil Code in 1809 (left unchanged by the revised Code of 1848) made marriage a civil contract, formally entered into and registered at city hall. Churches adjusted by having marriages of its members officially "solemnized" in a church service following the civil ceremony.

sociological sense, of a "community" but are forced to use different terms, like "partnership," "friendship," "relationship," or the like.

Only the *types* of leadership and thus also the styles of leadership differ widely from community to community. Even within the same community, such as a marriage, authority can still be very different in individual cases. Such matrimonial arrangements can never be laid down in a generally valid codex. And a good thing too, for otherwise the order of authority in a marriage would immediately be threatened by a kind of "juridification," a distortion that can severely undermine marital love. The less the question of authority has to be discussed in a marriage, the better the marriage. Where marital love is decisive for how a marriage is experienced, authority in marriage will usually not become a topic of negotiation, let alone a subject of dispute.

12.3.1.10 FEMINISM

The feminist struggle for freedom and equality is on a par, from an ethical-mental point of view, with the original idea of so-called radical democratization. The latter *can* have a healthy meaning, but usually it expresses an inner aversion to any and all authority that has not been inwardly and autonomously consented to by those subject to it. In that case authority is not called authority but simply "consensual power."

"Authority" thus understood (hence based on consent) is in fact present in many extra-social structures. Artists and scientists who are exceptionally gifted can acquire a kind of "authority" and consequently will be imitated from free choice. But that is not a case of organizational or institutional legal authority. It is sometimes called "natural" authority.

Of course feminism is right to react to corruption and abuse of power and authority—just as such corruption and abuse occurred and still occur in various other sectors of society.

Romantic theories about love and marriage, to mention another approach to personal freedom, tend to ignore the fact that nobody can find total fulfillment in one community—neither in marriage, nor in the family, nor in the state. The limits of personal freedom cannot be established by definition or by contract, but every form of society finds them in a process of growth and often realizes them without words or conscious rules. In every relationship every human being has a smaller or larger private sphere which ought to be respected by the other members of the community. This also applies within a marriage.

12.3.2 THE FAMILY

The (nuclear) family differs in character from marriage; it has a different structure. A marriage without children is and remains a marriage, genuine and complete. But very often a marriage is interwoven with a family community, which likewise bears the normative stamp of a love community. But the familial love between parents and children and among siblings is of a different type compared with marital love. Incest can therefore never be justified with an appeal to (voluntary) reciprocal love. Marital love has a unique type of sexuality, which has no place outside of the marital union in any other relationship.

The *biotic founding function* of a family is not gender, as in marriage, but *blood relationship*. While that holds for a *natural* family, it is obviously different for the separate type of an *organized* family with adopted children. In my view, however, that is not a compelling reason to classify the family as an inter-individual voluntary "relationship" and not as a "community."[95]

The leading function of the nuclear family is typical familial love. In the nature of the case, this familial love has three subtypes: the love of parents for their children, the love of children for their parents, and the love among siblings. These three main types are very different from each other in structure, and also in many respects in the way the love is expressed. Together they each have their distinct contribution to make toward realizing typical familial love; again, each individual family can display a style of its own in this.

Thus far we have not yet talked about "variability types" like paternal and maternal love of children. However, these and similar details belong to sociology rather than philosophy.

12.3.3 THE STATE
12.3.3.1 RECOGNITION OF STRUCTURAL PRINCIPLES
VERSUS HISTORICISM

In modern times historicism or historical relativism is the main philosophical opponent of Reformational philosophy, not just in its approach to marriage and family but also in its view of the state, the business firm, associations, churches, and so on. This school of thought says that all

---

95. (*Ed.*) Allusion to the distinction in Dooyeweerd's social philosophy between a family, which is a "natural community" with involuntary membership, and an "interpersonal relationship" in which membership is entirely voluntary.

societal relationships are purely human inventions and constructions which are determined by tradition and can be changed according to our needs and desires. By contrast, Reformational philosophy acknowledges that life in the various societal structures, including the state, cannot be organized at will, just to suit ourselves. Our philosophy recognizes supra-arbitrary *principles,* called *structural principles.* These are at the core of the various concrete types of human society.

12.3.3.2 NECESSARY QUALIFICATIONS

It is therefore too simple, indeed unacceptably reductionistic, to equate the state with "the community." In the course of time this view has been subject to some qualification. In the days of Abraham Kuyper the triad "church, state and society" was a popular improvement in the view of society. Non-Christians often omitted the church or subsumed it under "society," which was sometimes also called "the community." Thus, many upheld and still uphold the division: state and society, or government and people. However unsatisfactory, it was at least an effort at improving what was called, with some exaggeration, the "ecclesiastical unitary culture" of the Middle Ages, or the secularization thereof in "the State" as the all-embracing totalitarian "community." For the sake of convenience this nomenclature may have a place in everyday language, but it is fundamentally and scientifically inadequate and unsound.

To be sure, the state is a community. It is one community among many other, non-state communities and social structures; but the state is not *the* community, no more than "civil society" is. The traditional universalistic view of the state soon comes to conceive of the state as a total structure embracing the whole of society, a view that leads to an overestimation of the state's task and a transgression of the bounds of its authority. A state can overreach itself when it tries to regulate private morality, or personal religion, or the life of private associations.

The history of political states and constitutional law tells of a centuries-old struggle against state transgression and its apparent omnipotence vis-à-vis individal citizens or non-state communities and structures. This has also been the issue during various revolutions in their struggle for so-called "human rights" against the absolutist tendencies on the part of governments. On the other hand, an ideology regarding "human rights" is often just another absolutization, either of an individualist or anarchist type, or of a type championed by "radical democracy."

12.3.3.3 THEOCRACY

Christians were often no better equipped than revolutionaries in the struggle against state omnipotence. Proceeding in a "theocratic" spirit, they professed God's omnipotence and defined the government as God's servant, all the while lacking clear insight into the fundamental limits of the state's task. A typical example is the regulation of public morals. The correct idea that government, too, is bound to obey God's commandments in fulfilling its task and is obligated to uphold public morality is narrowed down by "theocrats" to specific precepts mentioned in Scripture, even as they ignore the limits that the order of creation imposes on the power of social structures like the state.

On many issues the Christian political parties in Europe have never been able to move radically away from the influence of the traditional scholastic division of society into the spheres of nature and grace. This is evident in all kinds of dilemmas that are still current, like church and state, Christ and culture, church and society, and so on. One of the roots of this dualism is a lagging religious development in understanding *the creation as the kingdom of God*. As a result, the church, but not the state or a sports club, is seen as belonging to the kingdom of God.

12.3.3.4 DEFINITION OF THE STRUCTURAL PRINCIPLE OF THE STATE

The structural principle of the state can be defined as follows: the state is a *public legal community* of *government and citizenry*, historically based on a monopoly of the power of the sword within a defined territory and charged with the administration of public justice as its leading destination function. From an aspectual point of view, this can be summarized thus: the state is historically founded and juridically qualified. "Power of the sword" and "administration of justice" are entitary substructures of the state community.

12.3.3.5 THE INTERNAL DESTINATION FUNCTION OF THE STATE

The leading or qualifying aspect or function proper to an entity, you will recall, can also be called its *internal destination* function. That function is distinct from any *external goals* to which a social structure can make itself serviceable. A company can earmark much of its profit for a charitable goal, but its internal operational management will have to be focused on the leading economic principle if the company is not to go out of business very quickly. A marriage, too, can outwardly place itself entirely in the service of science, or make itself subservient to the state or to a church, but *internally* the marital community will fail if *typical marital love* is no longer the leading *internal bond of the community.*

Thus the internal destination function of the state should be seen in the *public administration of justice*—so not, for example, in the promotion of economic prosperity, the distribution of wealth and income, or public welfare, not even for the sake of the "public interest" if that is taken to be more than public *legal interest*. Exactly there, in principle, lie the limits of state authority. The state should be a constitutional state on the power base of monopolized armed force. Incidentally, "public legal interest" may have to include much that does not at first sight seem to be *legal* interest. But it is the task of politics—of government, parliament and political parties—to apply this basic principle in concrete cases.

12.3.4 THE CHURCH
12.3.4.1 SOCIAL PHILOSOPHY IS NOT THEOLOGY
Whenever philosophers start talking about the church every theologian pricks up his ears, and rightly so. It is one of theology's tasks to develop a biblically founded theory of the church, of its offices and functions, its history and internal church law, and so on. Such theological theories on the basis of an exegetically grounded ecclesiology or systematic theory of the church do not belong to the task of a Christian philosophy.

However, (social) philosophy, and particularly *philosophical* sociology of religion, investigates the general structural principles which make possible every typical community of faith, including non-Christian ones, and which at the same time establish its norms. Its approach is therefore not from the perspective of faith or theology but from that of philosophy. Philosophy, after all, analyzes the functioning of all communities in all cosmic aspects, more precisely in their *diversity and coherence* of functions.

In doing so, however, philosophy must not disregard the religious depth of these functions in their totality or root unity. It must witness to it (whether that witness is Christian or non-Christian) from a specific *religious basis*. Sadly, however, this is unusual in our Western tradition of science, both in philosophy and in sociology. Both fields are thought to deal with so-called "purely empirical data."

This last task was already discussed in the prolegomena (chapter 2). It means that philosophical activity is guided by pre-scientific religious convictions (not to be confused with theology). As a structural theory, however, philosophy must confine itself to the general basic structures of reality and see them in their typological diversity and their cosmic coherence, from the perspective of their unified totality in origin and destination.

12.3.4.2 THE DISTINCTIVE NATURE OF THE CHURCH AS A CULTIC COMMUNITY OF FAITH

All organized communities are founded in the aspect of historical formative control or power. In the case of the church this involves primarily, though not exclusively, the power and authority of ecclesiastical offices: that is to say, the formative power of a shared faith establishes an official organization for worship, the "cultic community." This is the primary form in which the common task and call to worship God can be fulfilled in thanksgiving, adoration and praise, in instruction and nurture in the faith, and in missional activities. Naturally this does not take away the vocation of church members to assert their faith in non-church life too, both personally and in all kinds of social relations or groups. Indeed, this is inherent in the missional function.

All this is only possible on the basis of a shared faith that needs to be organized in the institutional church; that is, it is only possible on an organizational power base of communally held and officially upheld confessional standards. The task performed by ecclesiastical authorities does not represent the *destination* function of the church: it is the church's *founding* function, required to carry out its internal *destination* function, namely, to be a *community* of *faith* for the purpose of glorifying God and communing with Him in faith, thanksgiving and worship, and to bear witness of Him in outreach.

The internal destination function of the church therefore lies in the exercise and mutual encouragement of faith as the vital connection with and surrender to God. Accordingly, the primary task of the Christian church is to organize worship services for the ministry of God's Word through proclamation and the administration of the sacraments. From this follow various secondary tasks that are required to fulfill this primary task. We can think here of preaching, catechesis, liturgy, pastoral work, the exercise of church discipline, works of mercy and charity, training for the ministry, youth counseling and care of the elderly, evangelization and mission, and so forth.

12.3.4.3 COMMON MISCONCEPTIONS OR AMBIGUOUS STATEMENTS

This very brief description implicitly *rejects* a number of common misconceptions or ambiguous formulations about the church. I mention the following:

    a. the institutional church is the total community of all true believers;

    b. the church consists of the church-as-organism and the church-as-institution;

    c. the church embraces both the visible and the invisible church;

    d. the church is the same as the kingdom of God, or at least as the beginning of its realization on earth;

    e. the church is the body of Christ;

    f. the church is the same as "the church of Christ" mentioned in the New Testament;

    g. there is only one true church on earth;

    h. the church has the mandate to direct and guide the entire life of its members, both in their private life and in all their social relationships;

    i. the church has the mandate to pay critical attention to politics, public morality and social developments by means of publications (including the spoken word) and by assisting in the regulation of these areas;

    j. the church arises from "particular grace" or "special grace" and represents "holy ground," a "sacred terrain," whereas the rest of life arises from "common grace" and is "profane";

    k. the church is the earthly embassy of Christ's heavenly kingdom: it is the earthly address of Christ, while its office-bearers are his ambassadors;

    l. the church is the source and sponsor of ecclesiastical theology;

m. ecclesiastical theology is able, in the academic subjects of exegesis, dogmatics and church law, to deduce "the" truth directly from Scripture, without depending on socio-philosophical categories;

n. and the list goes on.

Much more could be mentioned in this context. The worldview of our Christian tradition continues to labor under the powerful influence of scholastic dualism.

12.3.4.4 THE MISCONCEPTIONS ANSWERED

We now offer our critique point by point. In doing so, however, we should not weigh every word or expression that believers use in their language of every day, because that language cannot be scientifically precise, nor is it intended to be.

Ad a. To say that the institutional church represents the total community of all true believers is tantamount to absolutizing the church on earth. An ecclesiastical institution is a phenomenon in time. The "total community of all believers" is the community in Christ; it is our *transcendent* unity. It includes the dead, whose lives are "hid with Christ in God" (Col. 3:3), and it includes the unborn, who have already been created in Christ (cf. Appendix, Figure 2).

Ad b. What is commonly designated as representing the church-as-organism (as opposed to the church-as-institution) is not a church but some non-ecclesiastical community, organization, association or group composed of Christians. Similarly, most so-called "church" periodicals are not official organs of any particular church but are owned privately or by an association. "Church papers" are usually ordinary "Christian" journals for which no *church* bears any responsibility, even if the entire contents is written by ministers. For the sake of convenience many Christian associations are called "interchurch" or "interdenominational," but only to indicate that membership is not restricted to membership in one particular church. Often therefore the typical activities of such an "interdenominational" organization are not of an ecclesiastical nature.

Ad c. The distinction between visible and invisible church is usually meant well, but its formulation is deficient. The "invisible" church, which cannot be physically seen, refers to the spiritual unity and solidarity of all believers in Christ. For that matter, what is most typical of the church, that is, faith, cannot be seen in the "visible church" either. Even visible and audible religious worship, complete with a liturgy, can be something that has nothing to do with a Christian "church" but may, for instance, be a heathen cult or the folkloristic custom of an internally dead Christianity.

Properly speaking therefore, the expression "invisible church" refers to the spiritual unity of all believers in Christ (see also above under a). This community can also be called "the body of Christ," a biblical expression which has more than one shade of meaning. Other expressions that refer to the same are: people of God, the church of all times and places, the gathering of the elect, the fellowship of Christ. This "spiritual" community is in fact the *transcendent depth dimension* of what we see in time and experience in various ways as the church and equally as the whole of the Christian life.

Ad d. The kingdom of God is the entire creation, though we still find much power of the devil in it, and much disobedience to the King. The "restoration" that came with Christ was not (in an abstract ontological sense) a *new* creation, in the sense of a *different* creation, but a fundamental, concrete purification of the creation which God had not abandoned. The concrete earthly beginning of this restoration is present in everything that lives in and from Christ, and these are not just the typically ecclesiastical or religious phenomena, but everything that can be called "Christian." Equating church and kingdom is therefore a mistake.

Ad e. It is proper to say that the church is the body of Christ, so long as it is not understood as a theological definition. *Theologically* speaking, we should distinguish the earthly temporal church from its (own) *spiritual depth dimension in Christ*, of which it is a temporal manifestation; otherwise a temporal church organization will be absolutized or deified. On the other hand, *religiously* speaking we need not object to the statement, because as a religious statement it does not separate the concrete temporal church from its root "in Christ."

Ad f. It is also quite proper to say for practical purposes that the church is the church of Christ spoken of in the New Testament, so long as the previous point is observed.

Ad g. To speak of "the one and only true church on earth" confuses or identifies the norm with subjective reality. Moreover, it fails to appreciate two facts: the factual brokenness of the church in time, and the factual unity of the church which cannot possibly reside in an earthly organization but must rest in Christ. The expression implies that the supra-temporal dimension and fullness of the church is not recognized as a factually existing "supra-temporal" reality "in Christ," in which any concrete real Christian church on earth *participates*.

Theologically speaking, both facts, that of the church's unity and that of her brokenness, are a blatant contradiction if this unity is not seen as a supra-temporal or "full temporal" ("spiritual") unity or "root unity" in the one divine-and-human person Jesus Christ.[96]

Ad h. For the church to act as the moral conscience of its members is at odds with the limits of the church's authority as an organized cultic community. The Word of God, not the ecclesiastical forms of it in doctrine and proclamation, is normative for all of life. God's Word itself (in tandem with God's revelation in His works) has totalitarian authority, not the church and its administrative organs.

Ad i. The church's vocation in public life is not to act as the moral guardian of society but to proclaim the full gospel as well as various *principles* of God's will for human society. It is not the church's vocation to encroach on the prerogatives, authority and vocation of other social structures. Not the church but Christian believers may be called upon to help in giving concrete shape to the principles of God's will in various sectors of life. In modern times these sectors call for work by professionals, work for which the church has neither calling nor competence: think of the world of the arts, economics, politics, medicine, science, and so forth.

Ad j. The church arises from the creation and is therefore called to holiness in the sense of being obedient and dedicated to God within its own normative structure (and structural limits). But the same holds for every other form of community on earth. Specific churches can sometimes be as unholy as brothels or drugs-selling coffee shops—just as, conversely, a soccer club of Christian soccer

---

96. This recalls again the notorious theological misunderstanding that Dooyeweerd's philosophy introduced a new dualism by distinguishing time and supra-temporality ("full temporality"). Many held that this was a "duplication of reality" along the lines of Plato's two worlds. This objection is easily met by recalling Dooyeweerd's frequent use of the term "concentration point."

players can be "holy." The theological distinction of general and particular grace has practical value but needs to be used very critically in view of much misunderstanding and abuse in the past.

Ad k. Is the church the address of Christ's kingdom on earth? This idea fails to recognize the kingdom-like character of the entire creation and the limits of authority which God has imposed on its various social structures. The correct starting-point that our life should be guided by biblical faith and that the church has the important task of shaping and supporting the faith of its members on the basis of Scripture is here stretched to such an extent that the church organization and the activities it sponsors are made absolute. This also involves a failure to recognize that the leading of God's Spirit is promised to *all* believers.

Ad l. Can the church lay exclusive claim to doing theology? This is a widely held idea, propagated in particular by Karl Barth. It is based on fallacious theories of knowledge and science, which will be discussed below in chapters 14 and 15. Theology is sometimes a very useful handmaiden for ministers, but it can also become a temptation to err in one's theory or to overestimate the church and the office of minister, as if theology represents a better quality of faith.

Ad m. To claim that the theology done by the church needs no philosophy in order to discover biblical truth falls in the same error as the previous claim. I mention only a neglect of the distinction between various *types of concrete truth*[97] and their transcendent unity and fullness in Christ, who says that He *is* the truth and not only speaks it and does it, and who also summons us to "walk" in it. But in our Western culture, particularly in science, the idea of truth has been rationalized to mean only logically qualified aspectual truth, mere "correctness."

12.3.4.5 NATURE AND GRACE

Ad n. Numerous traditional or journalistic expressions like church and culture, religion and politics, faith and science, general and special revelation, common and special grace, church and world, "sacred divinity" and profane sciences, natural and supernatural (or "biblical")

---

97. Scientific—including theological—truth, religious truth, moral truth, artistic truth, economic truth, historical (factual) truth, etc. (see below, sec. 14.1.5 and 14.2.6).

theology, and so forth, are all stamped in their meaning and use by a specific worldview. This worldview has created a terminological framework within which our thought is guided and suffused as if by a firm paradigm or ground-motive. The worldview in question can be briefly characterized by the term dualism, specifically nature-grace dualism, comparable to and often combined with the nature-freedom dualism of humanism. This bipolar, internally contradictory dualism almost always tries to overcome its difficulties by claiming that it is not endorsing a *dualism* but merely recognizing a *duality*. This then leads to the basic religious pattern of "*synthesis,*" the combining of Christian with non-Christian life and thought, often defended via the idea of "common grace."

The historical preponderance of this thought pattern is so great that it takes many years to shake loose from it even after coming to the realization that this dualism is unbiblical. Time and again we discover that remnants of it have remained present and powerfully active in our intellectual tradition. This can also be explained from the very nature of this particular dualism, which is much more than an intellectual framework that can be refuted with logical arguments. On the contrary, it is a deeply lodged mental *attitude*, a *disposition*, and a *community ethos*.[98] Dooyeweerd was in the habit of speaking of a "religious ground-motive," which he also called a community motive.

12.4 PRINCIPLES OF INTERCOMMUNAL RELATIONSHIPS
12.4.1 THE CONCEPT OF SOCIETY

We pointed out in the foregoing that the concept "society" should not be defined as the sum total of all the social forms that are not state or church. For the sake of convenience we can use the concept this way in everyday language but without presuming it to be scientifically sound. More positively, society should instead be defined as an *external interwoven coherence of all the communal forms and relationships occurring in the human world.*

From its inception, social philosophy has had a *totalitarian* view of society. From the perspective of Reformational philosophy this is understandable, for if the *transcendent* spiritual unity of the human race is not recognized, one of the temporal social structures of

---

98. Cf. the anthropology in sec. 12.4.4.3 and 12.4.4.4, and Appendix, Figures 3 and 4.

humanity will inevitably be absolutized into the single dominant community. This lies in the nature of human life and thought, in both of which, anthropologically speaking, a *concentration law* is operative by virtue of our being "created unto God in Christ." That is to say, life and thought themselves contain a tendency towards one all-embracing unity.

Traditionally the state, the political community, has been seen as the largest, all-embracing total structure of life. According to most Greek philosophers, it was only in the state that man truly became man; that is also why they regarded the state as primarily responsible for the raising of children. Reformational philosophy, however, starts from the creation of all things according to their nature, "after their kind." A distinctive nature brings with it a unique vocation and task, as well as specific limits. This means for the study of society that it is an interwoven coherence of many differently qualified, distinctive social relationships that stand in a certain relation to each other. Each of these structures has its own structural principle, an entity structure which is also an identity structure. Despite their interwovenness these basic structures retain their distinctive identity, and their distinctiveness must be respected.

Before discussing these interrelations, we first need to say something yet about structural principles in general, adding to what was briefly said above about the features of marriage, family, state, and church.

12.4.2 SOCIAL STRUCTURES ARE PRIMARILY STRUCTURAL PRINCIPLES

The slogan that the structures of society need to be changed was fashionable for a time in the turbulent sixties and seventies of the previous century. At first sight—that is, from a rather superficial per-spective—this is incompatible with Reformational philosophy which is mainly focused on analyzing the constant, unchanging basic structures of reality.

Our philosophical focus has occasioned the oft heard criticism that we stand for a static system that merely charts existing conditions in society and is opposed to fundamental changes in "the structures." This criticism suffers from a fundamental error, for we teach that the constant and unchanging structures of social relationships are structural *principles*.[99] "Principle" means *beginning*, a beginning that

---

99. Cf. also sec. 7.3.8 above and chap. 13 below.

calls for subsequent development, for continuation and progression. We are in fact dealing here with *starting*-points which normatively indicate the *direction* and partly also the *content* of the way in which concrete subjective life in the various social structures *ought* to be realized (or "positivized," to use a juridical term).

Thus these "positivized" principles, and therefore the *concrete* structures of society, are not in fact as constant as their starting principles, since they are involved in progressive, conservative or reactionary changes in subjective historical developments. As *concrete "structures"* they are only constant in a relative sense, namely insofar as real, constant structural *principles* have *subsequently* received concrete and variable form in them. *Principles* can be compared with dotted lines that are filled in when the principles are concretely realized.

Let me clarify the point further. As normative structural *principles*, the marriage structure, the state structure, the company structure, the church structure, and so on, do in fact have a constancy, exhibit something unchanging. To put it in technical language: structural principles are the *"transcendental conditions"* that make *possible* the concrete realization of life through and within the framework of these structures. The subjective realization of *life itself*, however, by no means always takes place in (complete) conformity with these normative, guiding structural principles.

Another point in the criticism mentioned above is that it often forgets that Reformational philosophy has always presented its theoretical results as "provisional." It is aware of the fundamental fallibility of scientific thought and is therefore keen to hear reasoned criticism (not based, as so often, on inadequate knowledge), in the hope that its response to this criticism will in turn be taken seriously.

12.4.3 STRUCTURES AS CONTINUOUS SUBJECTIVE FORMS OF LIFE

Deviations from normative structural principles or resistance to them are the cause of many abuses in marriages, families, churches, business firms and political communities. These abuses may become enduring and may even be backed up by laws, regulations, traditions, customs, styles, practices, and so forth. If *these* are regarded as "structures" also, there is every reason to discuss which structures should be changed and how.

However, in opposition to the modern spirit of *subjectivism* and *historicism* we do need to insist that man cannot give shape to life and alter society *at will.* Man is held to the dotted lines and chalk marks which the divine law-order has traced for us and which we must bring to light and analyze in science, or which we intuitively fill in with greater or lesser wisdom through our life practices, whether or not guided by the Spirit of Christ.

Accordingly, some thinkers distinguish between structures *for* and structures *of.* In that case the structures *for* life are what I have been calling the structural principles, while the structures *of* life in this line of thinking are the concrete man-made forms of life, forms which are shaped by tradition, personal preference, collective style, customs, and so on. These often stand in need of change because they are always to some degree deficient and sometimes founder in the face of reality, which remains primarily governed by unchanging structural *principles,* by governing conditions which in the long run cannot be violated with impunity. "The dock turns the ship," as the Dutch say: reality will catch up with you. History is full of actions and reactions, of conflicts between progression (or progressivism) and conservatism or even regression.

12.4.4 Principles of intercommunal relations

One of the most fundamental problems of philosophical sociology is that of the mutual relations between concrete social forms in our pluralistic society. The answer of Reformational philosophy to this problem is, put succinctly: throughout their social interlacement the social structures *retain their distinctive responsibility.* This is a more precise wording of the nineteenth-century concept of "sphere-sovereignty" formulated by Groen van Prinsterer and broadly applied by Kuyper. To understand this answer properly, we should see it in contrast to what was generally thought in non-Christian society throughout the centuries.

12.4.4.1 The part-whole relation

The earliest answer which philosophy gave to the above problem was that of the totalitarian Greek *polis* (city, including surrounding villages), from which our word *politics* is derived. This city-state was regarded as *the whole* of society and all other societal forms were seen as *parts* of it. The nature of the part-whole relation was already discussed in sec. 7.3.12.d, where its main feature was that the whole decisively determines the functions of the parts; the parts depend fundamentally on the whole in their functioning.

Thus, according to the conception in Antiquity, all human society in principle is guided and overseen and governed by the state. In more primitive, undifferentiated societies such total power belongs self-evidently to the patriarch. But as soon as the cultural-historical process of development gets underway, which is also a process of *differentiation*, we see the rise of a pluralistic society in which the individual nature that is proper to very different forms of society asserts itself. This gives rise to tensions with the absolute and totalitarian power at the head of the family or the state. Protests against this power mark the beginning of the development of what are later called "human rights," primarily in opposition to state omnipotence.

12.4.4.2 REACTION AND PROGRESSIVENESS

In modern times a totalitarian state, whether governed dictatorially or democratically, is a reactionary phenomenon that runs counter to the historical law of cultural development and its principle of the differentiation of tasks and authorities. It is therefore not progressive but reactionary when, in an orthodox socialist approach to state and society, an increasing number of tasks and powers are doled out, looked after or downright taken over by the state. Nor is such statism realistic in a modern, strongly differentiated and individualized society. Current trends in favor of "privatization" can be seen as a reaction to socialist "collectivization," which has clearly shown great disadvantages. "The dock turns the ship." However, a "reaction" not based on healthy principles of its own is soon liable to go to the other extreme.

A comparable process is also taking place in churches of which an increasing number of members are moving toward a more developed faith, which can also mean a more strictly personal and maturing faith. This process often causes tensions with official creeds, church orders and other ecclesiastical or theological authorities, in particular when the individuation process is driven by growing secularization or changing beliefs. However, this last is not necessarily present in a process of individuation that is in line with the historic faith and stays loyal to the church. Indeed, a more dangerous spiritual threat today is posed by a folklore-like collectivization of religious life steeped in traditionalism.

12.4.4.3 THE ROMAN CATHOLIC DOCTRINE OF THE TWO SWORDS

In the course of the Middle Ages the all-powerful and totalitarian-like state of Antiquity found a counterweight in the church institution centered on Rome. Church and state became each other's rivals. Like the state, the Roman church was centralist and totalitarian in its aspiration and organization, with the pope as its head. This struggle for supremacy lasted for centuries. On the basis of Luke 22:8 the Church of Rome—most famously Boniface VIII in his bull of 1302, *Unam Sanctam*—defended its claims with the "doctrine of the two swords."

This doctrine taught that Christ, who has all power in heaven and on earth, has delegated this power to his vicar on earth, the "head" of the church. The pope rules in two ways, with two swords, a spiritual sword and a secular sword. The spiritual sword he wields himself or else delegates it to the hierarchically structured church which holds sway over the faith and life of the believers. His secular sword the pope delegates to the emperor, who rules over virtually all non-church life on the pope's behalf and at the pope's behest, making the emperor ultimately accountable to the pope. This is a centralist and totalitarian view of the church, a view that survives in diluted form among those Protestants who advocate a "theocracy."

12.4.4.4 THE SUBSIDIARITY PRINCIPLE

Over time, Catholicism became aware of the dangers surrounding the idea of the totalitarian state. Modern Catholic social thought therefore developed the so-called subsidiarity principle, which was given the imprint of official doctrine by the encyclical *Quadragesimo Anno* of 1931. This philosophical principle entails that "higher" communities must abstain from activities which "lower" communities can perform for themselves, and that lower communities should abstain from activities which individuals can perform for themselves. In positive terms this means that the lower communities should help ("subsidize") persons to exert themselves and initiate action, especially if in the judgment of these communities these persons are failing in their task. And a higher organ has the same subsidiary task in relation to a lower.

Our criticism of this line of thought is that it fully upholds the scheme of whole and parts, even though it uses the terms higher and lower communities. Moreover, the criterion for deciding which are "higher" and "lower" is often the *number* of members. Also, the principle maintains the scheme of nature and the supernatural, for though in natural life the hierarchical order of lower and higher communities is presided over by the *state*, it is the church that functions above the whole of nature, including the state, as the institution of supernatural grace that is the custodian of the entire kingdom of God.

In this scheme, all power and authority are always exercised by the higher over the lower, according to *the criterion* whether the lower is functioning adequately or inadequately *in the judgment of the higher!* Accordingly, church and state can freely interfere with any aspect of human life. In principle this has enormous consequences for the raising of children, for business and industry, and for all kinds of cultural activities. The limits of authority are determined by mere size and power, with the aid of sociological thought according to the scheme of whole/parts and higher/lower that is mistakenly applied here.

12.4.4.5 FUNCTIONAL DECENTRALIZATION

Democratic socialists have likewise become aware of the dangers inherent in a totalitarian conception of the state. Some of them have therefore developed the theory of functional decentralization. But this principle, too, starts from the scheme in which the state is the whole and the other social forms, summed up in the term "society," are its parts.

As we discussed earlier, this scheme is quite justified when applied to *similar kinds of* relationships. Thus municipalities and provinces can in fact possess a limited *autonomy*, and various state functions can be decentralized and served by these public-legal political subdivisions, under the hegemony of the state as a whole. A similar level of autonomy can obtain in federations of trade unions and in all kinds of other nation-wide organizations with regional and local branches. But in all these cases the functions of the parts derive their powers, limits and content from the whole.

The situation is altogether different when the autonomy principle is applied to the relation between *different kinds of* communities. In that case families, business firms, universities, churches, associations *cannot* exercise their *own proper* task and social responsibility, since *decentralization* means that a higher and central part determines what the lower part is allowed to do and within what limits. In this thinking, too, there is no fundamental resistance to totalitarian tendencies, though it does usefully moderate them.

12.4.4.6 DIFFERENTIATED AUTHORITY: SPHERE-SOVEREIGNTY

Against all these dangerous principles Reformational philosophy maintains the principle of differentiated responsibility for all the individual life-forms which according to the Christian confession of faith were instituted when God created all things "after their kind" (cf. sec. 4.4). In the normative structural principles of social forms we have attempted to define their unique nature and so indicate the intrinsic limits of their task. Their powers are subject to these limits and their responsibility is first and foremost defined by the same limits. More can be said about the whole subject, but this is the main principle, the boundary idea. We will further discuss it in the following chapter on praxeology.

Chapter Thirteen – Praxeology

CHAPTER THIRTEEN
PRAXEOLOGY

13.1 THE PHILOSOPHICAL THEORY OF HUMAN PRACTICE [100]
13.1.1 THE TERMS PRAXEOLOGY, THEORY OF ACTION
AND ETHICS

The word "praxeology" has gained currency in the last twenty-five years or so. Literally the term means the *logos* of *praxis*, the theory of practice. As such it is a useful term which we are happy to adopt for that part of scientific anthropology that is focused on the *structural analysis of human practice*. Praxis here refers very generally to the human practice of life in its *totality*, both inner and outer, individually and in all kinds of social relations. Praxeology is therefore a part of philosophy, which is after all the science of the totality.

Nowadays various "behavioral sciences" will also use the term "theory of action." Since human practice largely involves human *action* (though it is not exhausted by it), it is natural to ask what the relation is between praxeology or theory of action and what has traditionally been called "ethics." Since Aristotle, *ethics* has been called the theory of good action, with all its problems of good and evil, conscience and freedom, norms and values, virtues and morals, happiness and meaning, pleasure and utility, and so on.

First some brief historical information is called for. Historical information necessarily uses systematic concepts and selection criteria,

---

100. A more extensive and documented discussion of the subject in this chapter can be found in my "Praxeologie als wijsgerig thema" [Praxeology as a philosophical theme], *Philosophia Reformata* 55 (1990): 48–73, and "Normativiteit" I, II and III, *Philosophia Reformata* 57 (1992): 3–38; 60 (1995): 147–64, and 61 (1996): 61–84. More succinct treatments appear in my "Christian Alternatives to Traditional Ethics," *Philosophia Reformata* 38 (1973): 167–78; "Toward a Reformational Philosophical Theory of Action," *Philosophia Reformata* 58 (1993): 221–36; and "De betekenis van Dooyeweerds wijsbegeerte voor de theologische ethiek" [The significance of Dooyeweerd's philosophy for theological ethics], in *Herman Dooyeweerd, 1894–1977. Breedte en actualiteit van zijn filosofie*, ed. by H. G. Geertsema et al., eds. (Kampen, 1994), 172–96.

and so cannot truly be philosophically "neutral" or be couched in religiously neutral terminology. We therefore candidly admit that we will look for historical information in the light of the Reformational view of reality and conception of science.

13.1.2 THE ROLE OF ETHICS IN PHILOSOPHY

Although Aristotle (mid-4th century BC) was the first to talk about ethics as a science, the activity itself had started a few generations earlier. In philosophy, ethics began more explicitly with Socrates. In saying this we mean that since the Sophists (second half of the 5th century BC), and especially Socrates, philosophers were no longer solely concerned with how the world is constructed as a totality (what its essence consists of, what its unity resides in, and how it was generated), but they also started to address all kinds of *practical* problems in everyday life. It began with politics, justice, education, but soon went on to human virtues and vices, the significance of the human conscience, what to do and not to do in various situations in human society, in marriage and family, in friendship, in religious matters, in business and technology, in the development of one's personal lifestyle, and so on.

From the outset this ethical inquiry also dealt with problems that went deeper and were more comprehensive yet still practical, such as the ultimate *goal* of everyday living, norms for human life, traditions and freedom, happiness, the attitude to suffering and death, time and eternity, origin and destination. In short, the new phenomenon of theoretical thinking did not recognize people's *religiously determined worldview* for what it was and instead recommended it as *scientific ethics*, whose goal it was to provide overall guidance for the practice of life, to be a "guide to life," the *dux vitae* (cf. above, sec. 1.5 and 6).

Not much has changed since then. Present-day philosophy partly consists of somewhat scientific (that is, genuinely philosophical) but above all practical, worldviewish meditations on politics, morality, the environment, medical ethics, economics, and everything of current interest in certain quarters or particular cultures. In short, philosophy today is very much focused on the practice of life. As in its first centuries, ethics has the pretension to be a scientific alternative to *religious traditions*—in the case of Christianity, to the church's proclamation. That proclamation, after all, likewise has a practical content.

13.1.3 WORLDVIEW OR PHILOSOPHY?

At this juncture already I would like to make a critical comment from the perspective of philosophical systematics. In all these practical and/ or deeper questions about life we find that philosophy very quickly comes close to faith, religion and worldview, sometimes at the expense of its own character as *science*. Precisely in relation to these subjects it is *scientifically important* to distinguish clearly and consistently between *religion, faith, cult* or *worship, attitude to life, worldview, theology, wisdom* and *philosophy*. One of the difficulties here is that our Western intellectual tradition and public opinion even today fail to make these distinctions, or if they do, often draw them incorrectly. Many popularizing writers lump all these different categories together.

This tradition is understandable because these matters may in fact be closely connected and cannot be properly and clearly distinguished when intellectual thought is still at a less differentiated stage. But it is regrettable that for the sake of convenience (or from other motives we won't enter into now) many scholars follow this usage without question. This need not be a problem in everyday language, but in a *scientific context* much confusion can be avoided if these terms are used as unequivocally as possible.[101]

The tradition is also understandable on account of the next two points, which are crucial here. First, philosophy and worldview share an important feature: both are focused on the *totality* of our existence. Second, this shared feature cannot and should not nullify the difference: a worldview is practical and meditative and ultimately led ("qualified") by a conscious or unconscious faith, whereas (genuine) philosophy is theoretical, scientific, analytically qualified, though not without a worldview as its basis.

13.1.4 PRACTICE AND THEORY, AND THE NEED TO DISTINGUISH THEM

Failure to clearly recognize the difference between philosophy and worldview leads to the same situation in philosophy as has developed in theology: a tendency towards the presumption of being charged with a supreme task to lead and govern. The age-long struggle between pope and emperor was only one, if very significant, symptom of this.

---

101. Unequivocal is a juridical form of disclosure and deepening and thus fosters the development of science and scientific language.

Officially the Roman Catholic Church's claim to prescribe popular morality is still fully upheld, and is echoed by the mainline churches in Protestant countries, which from time to time feel called upon to make official pronouncements on various (albeit selective!) public policy issues.

The question is also highly relevant in the domain of scientific theology where all these phenomena are often encountered. Sloppiness is disastrous here and leads to countless misunderstandings and conflicts. The short-sighted and anti-intellectual aversion to philosophy in some circles of orthodox theologians virtually prevents any biblical renewal of theology on this score. As a result, it atrophies into conservatism or goes to the other (more or less modernist) extreme, given the lack of alternative theories with which to counteract both tendencies.

The intuitive awareness that there is a difference between theory and practice urgently needs to be theoretically explored, so that scientific discourse can distinguish between worldview and philosophy and grasp the enormous practical significance of this distinction. Otherwise philosophy remains the "worldly" alternative to "theology" and both remain rivals because each regards itself, more or less openly, as *regina scientiarum* or *dux vitae*, queen of the sciences or guide to life—the one with an appeal to pure reason, the other because theory is thought to represent God's revelation. There you have it: nature and grace! reason and faith![102]

13.1.5 The origin of ethics

We will therefore briefly return to the emergence of philosophy. From the outset, like today, this science was full of pretensions. It wanted to offer a *scientific substitute* for the pagan religion that was increasingly unable to stir and inspire people because ancient culture was turning more and more secular. Philosophy posited a *"rational alternative"* to the *guidance and direction* that pagan priests were giving to traditional society by such means as religious education with the help of myths.

According to the first philosophers, the role of providing guidance and direction should not be entrusted to traditional and irrational "opinions" (*doxai*) but to "real knowledge" (*epistèmè*), to science. Science at the time was mainly philosophy, which for many philosophers

---

102. Cf. the eponymous encyclical of September 14, 1998 by John Paul II, entitled *Fides et Ratio.*

included knowledge of pagan theology (such as that of Xenophanes or Aristotle). And the substitution of philosophy for worldview became particularly relevant when philosophy turned away from the big questions surrounding the origin and mode of existence of the cosmos and started to focus its analysis more on the human practice of life. The philosophical question of life's meaning was narrowed down to a search for consolation and happiness in the midst of life's difficulties and transience.

The refocused discipline also came to be called (for a large part wrongly) *practical* philosophy,[103] or sometimes *ethics*, and for long periods and many centuries major schools of thought thus ascribed extraordinary importance to philosophy for the practice of life. When Cicero (106–43 BC) called philosophy *life's guide* he was expressing the public opinion of his day.[104] It is in the same vein that some modern newspapers devote regular features to "philosophy."

13.1.6 AMBIVALENCE IN THE CHRISTIAN PROTEST: THE RISE OF "SYNTHESIS"

When the Christian religion entered the world of Greco-Roman civilization it daily encountered this pagan philosophy and the pervasive influence of its popularized form on everyday thought and action. Its reaction, however, was often very uncertain and ambivalent. Christians were well aware that pagan philosophy, its so-called

---

103. Cf. the habit, still prevalent today, of calling a certain part of scientific theology, which is theoretical in nature, *practical theology*, not so much because its nature is different but because the subject matter is different, *viz.* the pastoral practice of a minister. As if doctrine and the confessions (the focus of dogmatics) are *not* parts of the practice of life! To the extent that a science is genuinely science (and this also applies to theology) it is by definition theoretical as well as systematic. That does not depend on its subject matter, but is its inner nature as a science. It is a certain way—to be defined by epistemology—in which thought approaches something in reality or human practice.

104. Cf. Cicero on philosophy as *dux vitae*: "Augmenting the advent of adversity by our dread and its presence by our sorrow, we blame the nature of things rather than our own mistakes. But we must look to philosophy to correct this fault of ours. . . . Oh philosophy, guide of life, explorer of virtue and expeller of vice! What would have become of us and of human life in general without you? . . . You have been the teacher of morality and discipline. To you we fly for refuge, to you we look for aid, to you we entrust ourselves wholly. . . . Whose help shall we seek but yours? You have granted us tranquillity in life and destroyed the terrors of death." Cicero, *Tuscan Disputations* 5.1.4–5.2.5.

"ethics," could not serve as their *dux vitae*. For this they had the Bible, the Word of God, which they confessed to be a light on their path. On the other hand they also recognized, following Scripture, that pagan nations and pagan philosophy gave evidence of much practical *wisdom*.

Moreover, philosophical ethics dealt with many aspects of practical life that the Bible says little or nothing about. It also generally recognized all kinds of norms not mentioned in the Bible, or not in so many words, for instance that parents should love their children. But philosophical ethics also contained much that ran directly counter to the letter or the spirit of the Bible, especially in relation to the religious cult, sexuality, child-rearing, slavery, and so on. It often paid little heed to the gods (let alone God), or else used the word "god" to refer to "nature" or to deified human *reason* (*logos*), instead of denoting the living God who had revealed himself in Christ. In short, both practically and theologically Christians adopted an ambivalent attitude. This ambivalence has never disappeared and in recent centuries has lurked behind the problem of church and culture, faith and science, common and particular grace.

Ambrose (AD 340-397), bishop of Milan, wrote the first Christian ethics, but both in form and content, and even in the title, he followed the model of a four-centuries-old book on ethics by the philosopher Cicero.[105] In his turn Cicero had popularized the Stoic doctrine of duties in Roman thought, particularly in the version of Panaetius (185-109 BC). This was a theory of duties with which Jewish thought also felt an affinity, in keeping with the legalistic tradition of rabbinical teaching after Ezra.

Ambrose adopted many of these Stoic ideas, though obviously with corrections and additions from the Bible. On the part of Christianity this was therefore a kind of *synthesis*, a combination of Christian faith with pagan philosophy, even apart from the influence of Jewish traditions, which in the Hellenistic period had likewise blended with pagan philosophical traditions.

But there was also tension and conflict. Philosophy was in part experienced—and rightly so—as a *rival* of Christian teaching and theology. Christians soon became aware that philosophy is more than just an "intellectual tool" or a "thought form," as it would be put later.

105. Cicero, *De officiis* [On duties], 44 BC.

To this very day the sense of this rivalry persists, because non-Christian philosophy, particularly in our time, still pretends to offer *life wisdom* and *practical lessons*, and thus *life guidance*, not inspired by faith but directed by rational thought.[106] In particular, most schools of contemporary philosophy pretend to offer "reflection" in the sense of "giving meaning" to life or at least to one's personal life. Its focus is strongly anthropocentric.

This "spiritual deepening" of philosophy (in comparison with rationalism, which has been only partially discarded) is in the ascendant, is perhaps even fashionable. Usually, however, it comes no closer to biblical life and thought than the old rationalist philosophy. At most it does so in a formal sense, using the biblical words of faith though not the faith of the biblical words—just as "religion" is no longer a matter of ridicule in political and academic circles, but is "the *in* thing" in many places. But a curtailment of rationalism alone is not a sound alternative, anymore than irrationalist and personalist "chaos thinking," which tries systematically (!) to be "anti-systematic" and "anti-metaphysical."

13.1.7 PHILOSOPHICAL ETHICS AND THEOLOGICAL ETHICS

At the same time there were also Christians and above all theologians in the age of the Church Fathers who rightly saw that practical life guidance had better not be looked for among the worldly wisdom of pagan philosophical ethics. Exceptions were the Christian philosopher Justin Martyr (c. 100 – c. 165) and Athenagoras (second half of the 2nd century). But the Apologists, as they are called, were in general (at least theoretically) opposed to philosophy. Someone like Tertullian (c. 150 – c. 222) wanted nothing more to do with philosophy. He said that the true philosophy is *theology*. But this mistake was as historic as it was fatal, however sympathetic and understandable it may have

---

106. To the extent that theology accepts the fact of philosophy's claim that it provides wisdom, it rightly experiences this as unacceptable competition for the Christian message. But the addition of a Christian *philosophical* alternative to pagan conceptions of science and wisdom would be even better. This could prevent *philosophy as such* from being seen as an alternative to theology and the Christian message. Meanwhile, vigilance is imperative, since philosophy tends to persist in its old pretensions, now using terms like meaning of life, practical wisdom, philosophical ethics, foundations of norms and values, the discovery of identity, and the like.

been, given the situation. For that matter, Tertullian was strongly influenced by Stoic philosophy in his own theology, or at least in his terminology.

This mistaken approach gave rise to the pretensions—still seen today—of *theological* ethics. Initially it set out to be a Christian alternative to *philosophical* ethics, yet it continued to proceed uncritically from the pretensions of philosophy, claiming to be teaching the true knowledge of life and its normativity. So this claim was now applied to *theological* ethics, with the proviso that since it was Christian it would have to be based on the Bible and *the Bible alone* and not on human reason, as assumed by philosophical ethics.

This last point, however, was a misguided aspiration, though it was not recognized as such by the fathers of Christian theology because they lacked a Christian philosophical epistemology. Sadly, in our time, too, many tend to adopt without question the traditional view that philosophical ethics is based on reason and theological ethics on Scripture alone. Certain orthodox Reformed theologians still say that philosophy (or philosophical ethics) comes from below, theology (or theological ethics) from above. Even Pope John Paul II had to try to qualify this position in his encyclical of 1998, *Fides et Ratio*, though he retained its starting-point, the religio-ethical dualism of "nature and grace."

"Christian ethics should be based on Scripture alone." This sounds rather good at first. In our time this position is often put forward with strong support especially from Barthians, in part on the Reformation principle of *sola Scriptura*. Such a "biblical ethics," it is argued, would be a truly reliable guide to the practice of life. In Reformed churches this scientific error still sets the tone and dominates the debate, with all the implications of legalism that this entails.

Yet this way of thinking turns out to be untenable in practice. Philosophy, on the one hand, talks about many normative matters of which the Bible does not speak at all or only in the Old Testament, or also in the New Testament but there too in culturally outdated forms. On the other hand, the Bible talks about the most essential questions of life, such as questions about life's meaning or purpose, about suffering and blessedness, about fate and responsibility, and so on, questions to which pagan philosophy with its implicit worldview gives very different answers.

There has always been some awareness that the Old Testament part of the Bible cannot be normative for our present-day life in an absolute and unqualified sense. People have tried to solve this theoretically by artificially dividing the Old Testament laws into three kinds: ceremonial, civil, and moral laws. This is a highly reductionist and disputable theory, which usually fails to consider, from the point of view of a Christian *sociology*, the nature and variety of these so-called civil and moral laws.

Moreover, the development of culture has not stood still. A vast process of differentiation has taken place in modern life, certainly in the West. It has brought to the fore, manifest in an unmistakable manner and differentiated in a pluriform wealth of life, all kinds of creational riches which had long remained invisible. It has given rise to all kinds of new social forms of life, new technologies, scientific specializations, social classes and positions, a proliferation of consumer goods, trades, vocations and professions, educational demands, sports and musical forms.

Thus there is no question of the Bible legislating answers to everyday problems in a manner that goes back to Old Testament times or to rabbinical teaching of the intertestamental period (or to Jesuit casuistry of the 16th to 18th centuries). In regard to countless questions in the present phase of culture we can no longer dispense with the expertise, experience and scientific analyses to help us make our decisions about what to do (even though the explosion of scientific knowledge, precisely in the fields of human action, is probably still in its infancy).

13.1.8 SCHOLASTICISM

In this context Christian thought gradually came to distinguish between on the one hand *natural, earthly* life with a matching "natural ethics" of "common sense," and on the other hand *spiritual* life and what it entailed in terms of church and worship, works of mercy and charity, missions and evangelism (and possibly also marriage and family). This scheme increasingly monopolized Christian thought, a thought based on a warped sense of *two kingdoms*: on the one hand a temporal, earthly and material kingdom in which the state ranked supreme in society and virtue ranked supreme for the individual human being, and on the other hand an eternal, spiritual kingdom of religion, faith and church.[107] This last was guided mainly by *theological ethics*, whereas the *earthly kingdom* was increasingly receptive to *philosophical ethics*, with an emphasis that this "natural ethics" (which was not yet recognized as un-natural) was of lesser importance.

This whole development enabled the nature/grace scheme to make broad and deep inroads into Christian thought, of course with multiple attempts (always and inevitably to no avail) at keeping together the "two-ness," those two kingdoms, and not ending up in a *dualism*. These attempts can be roughly divided into three types:

(a) the *supplementary idea*: the kingdom of grace supplements and completes the kingdom of nature (*gratia naturam perficit*);

(b) the *integration idea*: theological ethics is an integrating science whose task it is to integrate Christian thought and the thinking of the non-theological sciences; this is the prevailing idea in theology today;

(c) the idea of *dialogue in peaceful coexistence*: no rivalry or reciprocal attempts at proselytizing and domineering, but just passing information back and forth while leaving each other entirely free.

We are confronted here with a deep and stubborn dualism that can only be truly overcome, both in the practice of life and in the sciences, through faith in *Christ* as the one "in whom" all things were created. The so-called *two* kingdoms are then believed and experienced as the *one* kingdom of God. Within this kingdom of God there are not two *realms* but two *directions*: the total, religious turn to God, and the equally religious turn away from God. And furthermore, there are, in the temporal mode of existence of God's kingdom, a large number of distinct "spheres of life," of which the church, however important, is only one.

13.1.9 WHY PRAXEOLOGY INSTEAD OF ETHICS?

We cannot, in the light of a biblical, Reformational worldview and philosophy, stand by the old distinction between philosophical ethics and theological ethics, *and a possible supplementation of the former by the latter*. Philosophical ethics ignored the light of the divine Word revelation; theological ethics ignored the light of creational revelation, that is, of *the divine norming of life via the creation structures of reality* (including the inscripturated Word revelation itself). Creation faith

---

107. For a more extensive discussion of this theme see my articles on "the question of meaning" in *Philosophia Reformata* 50 (1985): 95–118 and 52 (1987): 41–65.

remained confined to the Old Testament and was separated from its own eschatological and above all New Testament fulfillment. As a result, it was to a large extent *rendered sterile for the practice of life*. Only in a biblicistically elaborated theory of creation ordinances was there, in both Lutheran and Reformed theology, a short-lived revival of scholastic traditions in this regard. This was the case in Reformed circles in the Netherlands in the years 1880–1940, and in Lutheran countries mainly in the years 1930–1950.[108]

Reformational philosophy can no longer work with this combination of "nature and grace." At stake is the unity of the total life in the kingdom of God and, with the unity in Christ, the unity of the full divine revelation in His words and works. At stake is a fundamentally different interpretation of terms like "nature" and "grace": not as two *spheres or sectors of life*, but as two opposite religious *directions* of the one total life of the world and of humanity in the one kingdom of God that was "created in Christ."

Hence science's basic reflection on the world and on the practice of life requires one comprehensive and therefore *philosophic* theory about the *totality and unity of the internally coherent, enormous diversity in the normative structures of human practice*. For this reason we no longer like to use the word "ethics," because it is traditionally associated with two disputable disciplines, namely philosophical ("natural") ethics and theological ("supernatural") ethics. This distinction, as will be clear by now, is unacceptable to us. In our view, what it stands for in both cases is simply unnatural ethics.

13.1.10 THE ANTHROPOLOGICAL BASIS OF PRAXEOLOGY

Moreover, traditional ethics, of whatever type, uses a simplistic concept of good and evil and a simplistic concept of morality and responsibility. It often splits up into schools or subdivisions oriented to the idea of a separate so-called doctrine of goods, doctrine of duties, and doctrine of virtue (summarized in our time as the doctrine of "norms and values"). None of these traditions are acceptable to us, since they *are based on an anthropology* that is not rooted in a worked-out Reformational cosmology. They simply adapt to and mingle with one or more non-Christian philosophical traditions.

Our position must be that "ethics"—or rather, the theory of human

---

108. Cf. my article "Normativiteit" III, *Philosophia Reformata* 61 (1996): 61–84.

practice: praxeology—is a direct *offshoot or extension of philosophical anthropology,* which in turn is founded in an anthropocentric *cosmology.* In this way the study of human practice can retain its *typically philosophical* character embedded in a theoretical totality view. Only thus can it, together with various *discipline-specific philosophies,* furnish a foundation, in a scientifically sound manner, for a range of special sciences which *qua special sciences* include as a legitimate part of their object the specific *normativity* for the type of human action in question.

The question of normativity then cannot and need not be omitted by the special scientist, or assigned to philosophers or theologians. As a rule, neither philosophy nor theology is sufficiently grounded in the particular problems that the special sciences deal with. Christianizing these sciences is quite different from—goes much deeper than—combining empirical sciences of "the facts" with "normative sciences," or supplementing "secular disciplines" with theological ethics. This last idea forms the explicit basis for the prestigious *Handbook of Christian Ethics.*[109]

Prevailing practice merely carries on modern humanist thought which presupposes a *dualism between facts and norms.* It separates facts and norms and assigns them to separate sciences as fields of inquiry. It considers ethics to be "the science of norms and values," while the so-called empirical sciences presumably are the sciences concerned with hard facts.

The Reformational view of the relation between faith and science, and in general the relation between practice of life and science, can only be made scientifically fruitful through an *inner Christianization of the special sciences* themselves, that is to say, on the basis of a Christian philosophical view of reality. Reformational philosophy, after all, takes a different view of norms and values; it is oriented to God's law as the relation between God and creature.

---

109. *Handbuch der Christlichen Ethik,* 3 vols. (Freiburg im Breisgau, 1978–1982); see my critical review article, "Theorieën over ethiek en over de levenspraktijk" [Theories about ethics and life practice], *Philosophia Reformata* 46 (1981): 68–90, and 47 (1982): 69–77.

13.2 THE MEANING OF HUMAN EXISTENCE[110]

13.2.1 THE QUESTION OF MEANING

For as long as there has been a form of reflection called "ethics," people have debated whether human existence with its life and action has any meaning, and if so, what that meaning is. "Meaning" here is usually reduced to something like (ultimate) "goal," "happiness" or "use." But after twenty-five centuries of scientific development it is now time to ask critically and explicitly: is the question of the meaning of our existence a scientific question, or not? In present-day terms: is the question of meaning an existential, practical question or a purely theoretical one?

In the light of Reformational epistemology, which will be briefly discussed in the next two chapters, we can answer that the question of life's meaning can be both: existential or also theoretical. In philosophy these two come together in worldview (see Appendix, Figures 8 and 10). But they do need to be properly distinguished in theory, despite their actual intertwinement. The existential question of the meaning of our lives can easily be asked without theoretical philosophical reflection and is probably asked in this way by almost everybody at some stage. The other way around is impossible. As a fully human activity, theoretical analysis of the meaning question is always embedded in a practical, "existentially" functioning and comprehensive worldview that is religious in nature, whatever its content.

13.2.2 THE PRACTICAL QUESTION OF MEANING AND ITS THEORETICAL SEQUEL

When in the practice of life we ask in general about the meaning of our human actions, in other words about the *meaning of human life as such*, the personal answer for a believing Christian is not difficult. For this answer he does not need philosophy, or theology, or even scientific ethics or praxeology. In *faith* we *know*, even without academic study, that the meaning of our life is to serve and glorify God, to live in love for God and our fellow man. In principle this says *everything* about the meaning of human life. In faith and through biblical pastoral preaching we can learn to think about this in greater depth and learn

---

110. A more extensive discussion of this theme can be found in my articles cited above, "De vraag naar de zin," *Philosophia Reformata* 50 (1985): 98–118 and 52 (1987): 41–65.

to apply and experience it in the practice of our lives.

Grounded in this practice, and constantly guided by faith and the worldview that is led and fed by this faith (both through the church's proclamation and through private devotions and life experience), it is then also possible to explore this question of meaning *theoretically*. Once scientific philosophy is finished with that theoretical work, we will perhaps be able to say *in retrospect* that it has also been of some practical help.

Therefore we will now consider the question of meaning more theoretically. In doing so we will not forget that our concrete everyday life, how we live it, is in effect our existential answer, the answer that *we have already given and continue to give*, consciously or unconsciously, to the question what the meaning of our life is. That does not depend on whether we can also articulate it well.

13.2.3 THE PRAXEOLOGICAL QUESTION OF MEANING

Whenever an answer is given to the question of meaning, either in the existential practice of life or in conscious pre-theoretical reflection and formulation or in scientific philosophy, the answer is always and inevitably *religiously determined and formulated in terms of religious faith*.

For a believing answer to the question of meaning, people will point to God as the Origin and Destination of their lives, embracing his guidance, promises and commandments. Philosophy in its early years (6th century BC) wrongly believed that an answer of this kind—a pagan version of the true answer—could be left out of consideration as *mythology*. The only positive element of truth that we can recognize in ancient philosophy's assessment is its awareness that believing is different from logical reasoning.[111]

In itself this awareness is very valuable, but its value is all but lost if believing is then viewed as an inferior or even bad (or at best a less certain) quality of rational knowing. Later on, and to this very day, Christendom was seriously impaired by this error, so that people again and again turned at least in part to rational (sometimes theological)

---

111. On the other hand, the greatest error in this view was the failure to see that rational thought and discourse is not a real alternative to mythical faith, because people started to believe and worship Reason as the chief mainstay of human life, offering more certainty than mere "belief." Reason thus became the great idol of Western culture.

knowing *instead of* to believing, for the sake of gaining peace of mind, equilibrium, reliable bearings, certainty.[112] Sadly (but no doubt with the best of intentions), traditional theological apologetics has tried to go along with this by defending the Christian faith with a certain degree of accommodation while attempting to demonstrate that believing is not, or need not be, all that irrational. The criterion of truth then continues to be reason. Sometimes apologetics advances the argument that there is a conception of science which is superior to the conventional one, a conception according to which there is most certainly room in science for (a possibly existing) God. Really now!

In philosophical reflection, thus in the theoretical analysis of all created reality (insofar as accessible to such an analysis), the conscious starting-point in asking about the meaning of all that exists should be, as always, our pre-theoretical concrete experience of reality. The first thing we then encounter is a great diversity in reality itself, and on closer examination an extraordinary coherence in this diversity. Concepts like beginning, cause or origin, goal or destination, which suggest themselves as one observes these things, lead one logically to at least *wonder* about a first beginning, a first cause, an origin, as well as a possible end, a goal or destination. If these questions are systematically arranged, the theoretical question of meaning is found to have at least the following components: the question of absolute origin, and the question of ultimate destination.

If now philosophy on its own authority were to give a direct answer to these questions, it would forfeit its scientific character, for no part of its answer could be reasoned in an empirically demonstrable or logically irrefutable way. As philosophy,[113] if it is not to deny its scientific character, it must provisionally confine itself to the question of the *coherent diversity* of empirically reality. And it is in relation to that question that it can, at least scientifically, say something meaningful, something that is open to (partial) verification.

---

112. This is of course not to deny that believing contains an analytical element of knowing, though this is not *typical* for what faith is. More on this in connection with epistemology.

113. So not as the religiously qualified "worldview," on which philosophy always remains dependent and in relation to which it always remains secondary; cf. above, sec. 1.6.3.

13.2.4 THE THREEFOLD PRAXEOLOGICAL QUESTION OF MEANING

This is where the actual scientific *system* of Reformational philosophy *begins*. With the question of reality's coherent diversity it links up with the scientific tradition from the beginning of scientific practice. From the outset the diversity in reality and the coherence in this diversity were the object of wonder and of attempts to explain them. At first these explanations were rather religiously colored, inasmuch as philosophy sounded more or less explicitly in line with the pagan mythical belief in divine forces and titanic powers. The striking order and regularity, even in what initially seemed chaotic, was ascribed to good and/or evil primordial powers. This was the case in the pagan thought of almost all religions throughout the world (cf. sec. 3.4 above).

Here we see the "seam," the "boundary line," which at the same time is the connection, between "science and faith." The *diversity and coherence* that could be scientifically established and verified begged explanation, and from the beginning the explanation contained a reference to an origin, an *"Archè."* The *Christian* faith consciously answers these questions on the basis of a biblical belief in God and his work of creation. Reformational philosophy sums up this answer in the term "divine creation order." This creation order happens to determine the entire *possibility* and *mode* of existence of temporal reality, summarized in the expression "correlation of law and subjectivity"—a possibility and mode of existence that are also typical for the life of faith.

All this demonstrates at the same time that the first two parts of the question of meaning (origin and destination) cannot be asked without this intermediate element, which emerges from the detached theoretical *reflection about* concretely experienced reality and its mode of existence. From this we conclude that the theoretical question of meaning consists of three distinct yet intrinsically connected questions: those of *the origin, the mode of existence, and the destination of our reality.*

It remains true that philosophy cannot answer these questions. Yet it answers them nonetheless, consciously or unconsciously, on account of a *necessity* implicit in the very nature of the questions. Philosophy cannot *not* answer the questions of origin and destination, not even in the form of a declaration of ignorance, which would indeed be a culpable "ignorance." But its answer is an answer (at times theoretically dressed up) of *faith*—either a biblical answer or a different, unbiblical answer which nevertheless retains its *faith character*.

The Christian interpretation of this philosophical prolegomenal question about the meaning of reality suggests the possibility of a philosophical totality system, a system which in its entirety can be called "cosmology," to use a traditional but useful term. Like the cosmos itself, cosmology is centered on man, man in his actual totality. I am particularly referring here to the transcendent fullness of being human, to man's participation in Christ, "in whom" the cosmos and mankind were created and in whom, after the fall, a part of mankind was also re-created.

In the anthropological focus on human practice this anthropocentric cosmology allows us to establish two main *determinants* of human life and the concrete actions it incorporates: (a) the religious determinant, (b) the determinant of the normative temporal structures of the body. I will comment briefly on both.

13.3 THE DETERMINANTS OF HUMAN PRACTICE

13.3.1 THE RELIGIOUS DETERMINANT

The most profound determinant of human action is the *religious determinant*. By religion we mean the heart's focused *concentration*—in principle total and all-comprehensive—on the true service of God or on something idolatrous. In short: religion is the relation to God, factual and at the same time normative.

The identification of faith and religion in everyday usage may suggest that there are people who are non-religious, who have no "relation" to God. But God's self-revelation in creation and redemption contradicts all denial of the *normative fact* that God exists, that He created us, and that He lays claim to our lives for His service, to His glory, and in that to our salvation as well. This is a factual "relation," regardless of a person's subjective stance with respect to it.

Despite this total and all-embracing religious relation, a human heart may be divided and thus inherently doubtful, uncertain, inconsistent, sometimes fearful or rebellious, and the like. Hence my use above of the phrase "in principle." In principle our temporal practice of life draws its subjective certainty, its orientation and lifestyle, from the religious situation of our heart, or to put it philosophically: from our "supra-temporal" center, our *transcendent motivation. From* there flow "the springs of life," and *in* there our entire life is concentrated in an orientation to God—or to what is substituted for Him as an idol, which then in fact begins to *function* in one's life "as God," as the "ultimate meaning" of life, as "ultimate reality," or whatever expression one chooses.

Viewed from the law-side, religion can be summed up in the double commandment of love as formulated by Christ with reference to the Old Testament. But in the Bible this is not, as in philosophy, a philosophically summarizing, structural concept, but a practical guide to life which in just a few words indicates the direction that God wants to see in our lives.

13.3.2 THE DETERMINANT OF THE CORPOREAL STRUCTURES IN TIME

If praxeology is concerned with the structures of human practice, and in particular of course with those of human *action*, it is natural that the main focus of this chapter is on a further analysis of the structure of human actions and human acts. But we already saw in the basic anthropological theory (sec. 11.3) that the act structure in human life is not something separate and self-contained, but is embedded in other function complexes: those referred to in anthropology as the physically, biologically and psychically qualified substructures of our temporal mode of existence.

In the previous section I spoke of the "transcendent" motivation. Here I want to emphasize that all other, *temporal,* motivations can be summed up as the "transcendental" determinants of a corporeal kind. I have in mind the structural determinants that *make this reality possible,* including its transcendence-oriented concentration tendency (being created "unto God"). In this broad sense the act structure, too, belongs to our entire *temporal* mode of existence, our "corporeality." Granted, philosophical abstraction may temporarily disregard the (temporally) transcendent center of life, the heart, but that which is abstracted should not be forgotten, on penalty of a horizontalization of our outlook on concrete life.

In the same way the interwovenness of the act structure with the other, "underlying" corporeal structures is so intense that this has led to all kinds of theoretical "isms," in which human action is scientifically explained on the basis of empirically analyzable "causes." Thus in praxeology ("ethics") we encounter physicalism, biologism, psychologism, historicism, symbolism, socialism, economism, an absolutization of politics, and so forth. All these "isms" have observed something very real in reality, but through a narrowing of vision and a desire for reduction they lapse into an absolutization of that aspect of reality that has "seized" their attention.

13.3.2.1 DETERMINANTS, NOT DETERMINISM

In the heading of sec. 13.3 we deliberately opted for the rather neutral word "determinant." Something can be determined in different ways. One may for instance have a mechanical, causal determinant, an idea that certain natural sciences must work with, even though modern physics recognizes certain limits to this concept of causality so that it is interpreted less absolutely than in the past.

Certainly when it comes to human life one must be careful not to lapse into an absolutization of this type of causality. Think of miracles, which exceed the limits of normally operative causality by having natural facts encapsulated in human or divine action. Natural laws are not rigid and closed off; they can be opened up and deepened.

The causality in question, however, is practically always in force, since the physical substructure is encapsulated in our human existence. We are therefore justified in this case to speak of a *compelling determinant*. Thus every human being intuitively and naturally takes the determinant of gravity into account in most of their actions. The term "determinism," however, would be too strong when related to human action. Think for instance of Jesus walking on water, and in general of biblical and extra-biblical miracles (also today). The opening up of the physical by its functioning in later aspects, in particular by faith, may in fact lead to remarkable results.

From these generally *compelling* determinants we can distinguish weaker determinants in the organic and psychical substructures. These can be called *conditioning and/or predisposing* determinants. Thus someone may be seriously hindered by a physical handicap yet often be able to compensate this determinant by overdeveloping other organs.

These three types of determinant—compelling, conditioning and predisposing—can therefore be seen as a series of determinants in individual behavior which represent a sharply declining measure of "causal" determination, if indeed we can still speak of causality here. To this series we need to add *interpersonal* determinants inherent in family, social milieu, culture and social or political situations.

These compelling, conditioning and predisposing determinants are not exclusively connected with the physical, organic and psychic substructures respectively. All three occur in all three substructures, but to a different degree. Let us look at a few more examples.

13.3.2.2 COMPELLING DETERMINANTS

If our body suffers from a severe lack of water, all kinds of chemical processes will start to dysfunction, which also has organic and psychical consequences. If the process of dehydration is not stopped, our entire temporal mode of existence will be destroyed. That is why this corporeal substructure *compels* us to carry out actions that will provide us with sufficient liquid, in other words, that will compel us to eat and drink healthily, and in certain cases, as on a desert journey, to take additional measures.

13.3.2.3 CONDITIONING AND PREDISPOSING DETERMINANTS

The same can be said about the biotically qualified substructure. It too compels us in all kinds of ways to take very specific actions, in particular actions that preserve and foster our bodily mode of existence. Nor is that all. Precisely because our *human* organs are encapsulated in the whole of our typically *human* mode of existence, our organs *predispose* us to actions which form part of our typically *human* activity. Often our eating habits are not just culturally but also individually determined, so that we control and sometimes change what we eat and drink. Often we also correct our usual diet with medicines or with abstinence.

Unlike the vast majority of animal species, we use *instruments* because we are unable to realize our intentions sufficiently with our natural organs. Sometimes we can even compensate for a physical handicap by using instruments (eyeglasses for instance), but also by overdeveloping other organs (for example, making a painting with the brush held between the toes). Our organic and psychical sub-structures compel or at less predispose us to a certain *typically human* way of life, both in our physical actions and in many technical and other cultural activities.

The same goes for all kinds of sensitivities, emotions, drives, and perhaps also instincts. It also applies to personality character, habits, customs, social structures, social milieu, and so on. From the organically and psychically qualified founding structures our actions are determined partly in a *compelling, conditioning* or *predisposing* way.

13.3.2.4 NORMATIVE DETERMINANTS

Finally, there is the act structure. As such this substructure of our temporal-corporeal mode of existence, as we tried to explain, has *no qualifying function*. In the nature of the case, concrete human acts and actions can have very different qualifications, but not the act *structure*.

The act structure is that structure in which our actions are determined by *norms*. Obviously this is the main substructure of human action. As such the act structure is the leading and most typically human substructure within the total *intertwined and encapsulated nexus* of the four structures that make up our temporal mode of being.

Ultimately this normative determinant also *guides* those other, more compelling, conditioning and predisposing determinants and the human activities that flow from them. Man also bears a typically human *responsibility* to ensure that he is in good condition, organically and psychically. Not every disturbance in these substructures relieves a person of accountability. We human beings have the ability and the calling to *control* and *guide* our lives to a large extent, not just in accordance with so-called autonomous laws of nature (including psychical laws), but *first of all* in accordance with *normative* considerations, albeit with restrictions arising from the non-normative determinants that come with them. But this question of norms is rather complicated, so more on this in the next section.

13.4 THE EXECUTION OF ACTS AND ACTIONS

13.4.1 THE DISTINCTION BETWEEN ACTS AND ACTIONS

We distinguish acts from actions. Acts are internal and intentional: a person purposefully and intentionally *appropriates* something in reality or in the world of his imagination; that is to say, he relates that something to his I-ness, his selfhood. He usually does this in order to express his internal act into an external activity, an *action*. So determination by norms relates not only to the outward expression of human activity, but also to what precedes it inwardly.

The Christian view of human behavior should therefore never

confine itself to external actions.[114] Strictly speaking, purely external actions do not exist, or they exist only in an idea, as a (practical or theoretical) abstraction. In reality, external actions are actions of the whole person, flowing from his heart and taking shape in time both internally and externally in a vast interlacement of all kinds of determinative and normative structures, which also determine the specific *nature* of an act or action.

Hence great caution should be exercised when judging someone's actions. Usually we see only the outside and the surface. To a certain extent we may draw our conclusions from that, also about intentions or other motives, but in the end we cannot with certainty pass judgment on someone's religious stance in the heart of his existence.

13.4.2 Norms are primarily principles

In all normative aspects—hence in the top nine in our schematic series—it is *norms* that determine the nature and content of our actions. Thus they are distinct from so-called *natural laws*, which are not "norming," suggesting some proper action, but which are compelling, predisposing or stimulating. Norms are that too, but they are more. *They appeal to human freedom of action.*

The curious thing here is that norms are not usually given to us in the complete form of positively formulated precepts, with some explicit exceptions or restrictions as the case may be. Norms, as "givens," are given to us in beginnings, starting-points, principles. Love, thought, justice, social intercourse, beauty, thrift, faith, language, formative power: these are just nine words denoting the *nucleus* of an enormous *complex* of normativity. They are "principles" that merely indicate a *beginning*, which requires *follow-up*.

13.4.3 Principles are followed by further "positivization"

In legal language we call this follow-up the *process of positivization*. For instance, the principle of traffic safety must be *positivized* in spec-

---

114. Cf. Heidelberg Catechism, Lord's Day 33, Question 91: "What do we do that is good? Answer: Only that which *arises out of true faith*, conforms to God's law, and *is done for his glory* . . ." Again, Lord's Day 40, Question 105: "What is God's will for us in the sixth commandment? Answer: I am not to belittle, insult, hate, or kill my neighbor—*not by my thoughts*, my words, my look or gesture, and certainly not by actual deeds . . ." (emph. added).

ifications of general rules and secondary regulations, in short the complete traffic code. This may differ per country, for instance the general rule of driving on the right or the left.

Thus for the domain of our faith life we have *the Bible* as normative principle. And what we find in the Bible can be seen as a human positivization, guided by God's Spirit, of what was normatively revealed ("inspired") to the writers of the Bible. The various *church confessions* particularize and give positive form to all sorts of (of course by no means to all) biblical or extra-biblical principles for our faith life and our church life. *Sermons* follow through on these and apply them, usually in a very practical sense. We could again say: sermons "positivize" the norms.

The normative principle of beauty, too, is worked out in a great many ways. In painting, for instance, there are basic requirements (principles) for the use of brush and paint, and fundamental rules of composition. Music and sculpture are governed by still other principles. All such fundamental rules come under the subject areas of aesthetics, the theory of art. Thus every professional activity has its own norms and rules of action. However, the fundamental horizontalization of "natural" life has separated "good and evil" from this life and from God himself and recognizes only a very small part of it as a field of inquiry for "ethics."

To mention just a few other examples, very briefly: grammar and the theory of style and syntax are concerned with positivizations of the *lingual principle*; economics studies the laws and norms required by the *principle of thrift*; logic has basic rules and logical laws which elaborate on the principle of *correctly distinguishing* (analysis). The government's public legislation, particularly the constitution, gives positive form to the principle of *public* justice, just as the goals or objectives of private associations often function as the guiding principle, which is then further positivized in statutes and by-laws. The principle of social intercourse calls for particularization in the positive form of rules of etiquette, codes of behavior, ceremony, customs and traditions, all of which are culturally, regionally or ethnically co-determined. The principle of love calls for typical elaboration in rules, customs and usages for marital love, and still other positivizations (concrete forms) for parental love, filial love, love of the brothers and sisters in the faith community, friendship, love of country, and so on.

All these examples involve positivization in the form of more or less concrete, positive rules, codes of behavior, customs, traditions, regulations, precepts, programs, confessional standards, and the like. Yet the (verbal) interpretation and formulation of the principle is no more than an intermediate phase. *The end-point of this process of positivization is concrete action itself.*

In this way man with his concrete life gives positive form to his *central answer* to the *principles* of the divine law-order for our existence. The entire normativity or complex of norms for the many-sided practice of life in the many different spheres of life can be seen *in its principles* as God's will and appeal addressed to man(kind). The normativity of temporal life can therefore also be called the *answer structure.* Concrete human life is the answer that proceeds from the *heart* in its religious choice for or against God, but which structurally "passes through" all the complex structures of human action.

13.5 Positivization as an opening or disclosing process

13.5.1 Positivization as responsibility

The life of man, singly and collectively, is a process of positivizing the principles of God's law of life for man and cosmos. In this cosmic law-order God has also set the principle of historical formative control, by virtue of which mankind is called to *give form* to life and thus to positivize normativity. In order to form the normative guidelines for concrete patterns of behavior or actions, man(kind) must fill in the normative principles as if they were dotted lines and chalk marks.

Humanism of course also recognizes this aspect of human life, but it absolutizes it. Man certainly can and should freely give form and shape to life, but he must do so *response*-ably, following *all* the principles of the *divine law-order*, thus *not autonomously*. He must not willfully exclude certain aspects of normativity, such as the aspect of faith, or divine revelation, or the moral aspect, the economic aspect, the logical aspect, and so on.

13.5.2 Positivization as opening or closing

In the structure of every modality in reality we distinguished a nucleus and two kinds of analogies: anticipatory moments that point ahead in the direction of "later" aspects, and retrocipatory moments that point back to "earlier," foundational aspects. When those anticipatory moments in a modal aspect are influenced by a following, "later" aspect, we talk about opening or disclosure.

To mention just a few examples for now: a small child that cannot yet speak does have feeling but does not yet have a specifically developed feeling for language, or a sense of justice, or a sense of beauty, or even a sense of morality. Only as the child develops further does its emotional life begin to differentiate, so that these specific types of feeling can unfold and blossom.

Technical instruments can be opened up by the aesthetic aspect into beautiful, even artistic objects, such as vases, clocks, candlesticks, a dinner service, and similar things.

Another example: a mature faith may deepen one's love in marriage and family. This is the case even if that faith is not the Christian faith but instead a belief in "humanity" as the highest value (in other words, human life conceived apart from God), or a belief in one's own country and people as the highest value. Such beliefs can imprint and intensify this love. The same holds for socializing within the home: it can be deepened by love so that the family's interaction becomes something other than cool correctness in social relations.

Another topical example: all people of all times are able to think, but it takes many centuries before the concrete subtype of *theoretical* thought unfolds, develops, crystallizes. Something similar applies to children's ability to think, so that they need differentiated schooling in which instruction keeps pace with their intellectual development.

In principle, life in apostasy from God is life-disrupting, confusing and even destructive; but this is not an automatism. A well-known term here is "common grace," which refers to God's general goodness for all life and all creatures, even when they develop along spiritual lines of apostasy from God. Mindful of this, we can have appreciation for a cultural development from "primitive" to "open" cultures, and likewise for all kinds of unfolding processes within these cultures (social progress, scientific expansion, economic development, and so on). This too can be called an opening up or disclosure, so long as we bear in mind that *development* is not the only possibility: *closure* can also take place—a silting up or a fossilizing of creational potentials that cannot come into their own as a result, for instance, of living in cultural isolation or needlessly clinging to traditions.

In principle, therefore, the process of positivization—the concrete effectuation of life—may exhibit two religious tendencies, which may also exhibit themselves in two different cultural tendencies. The two occur together and mingle together. Cultural development is not necessarily a religious deepening in service to God, and conversely, true faith is not automatically cultural development. A few more remarks about both.

13.5.3 The unfolding of life in two directions

In principle the central-religious orientation of the human heart to the service of God as our Creator and Redeemer involves a renewal and unfolding of life in which God's original creative will is subjectively realized in human life and society. The power of the devil, the effect of sin and the disruption of all creation (in and outside of man) is vast, and we are facing it more and more in this life; but in Christ these powers are overcome and no longer have the last word. The unfolding of life will make manifest that creation is a storehouse of riches present in man himself and in all the rest of created reality. What is stored within will come out, in part at least.

Yet this entire opening-up process may also be inspired by a spirit of apostasy. In our present-day culture this spiritual orientation is in fact dominant. It is, in biblical terms, the great battle of the kingdom of darkness against the kingdom of light. Only the second coming of Christ will reveal that He has already won that battle. But even though this spiritual orientation of world history is idolatrous, the *richness of creation* is being revealed bit by bit in spite of it. God does not abandon what He began with creation. Thankfully, the dynamics of development is a dynamics of dis-closure—though in a strongly hampered, internally divided and *imperfect* realization of the normativity for created reality. The next section deals at greater length with this opening up of culture.

13.5.4 Rigidity and dynamism

The positivization process successively liberates, as it were, the anticipatory moments of all the aspects of life by releasing them from being rigidly bound to their founding moments. They are opened up, disclosed. Justice, for instance, with its balance of crime and punishment, is opened up by neighborly love into *fairness,* which is a juridical anticipation of the moral. That is why we often call a strict adherence to the words of the law "formalism" or "rigorism" if the element of fairness is neglected.

This example can be further illustrated from Scripture. In a primitive system of law a person is accountable for the consequences of his action, regardless of the motives behind the action. Moreover, he is not seen in isolation from his family, so that there is a collective accountability. In ancient Roman law the *pater familias,* the head of the family, was accountable for the crimes of members of his family. Roman law also applied the principle of *jus talionis,* the law demanding that a certain crime be paid "in kind"—an eye for an eye, a tooth for a tooth. This was indeed a primitive awareness of a just balance between crime and punishment. Compare also Lev. 24:17–21, where the inner *disposition* of the offender is ignored.

We also find this to a limited extent in the Mosaic law on cities of refuge. Someone who accidentally (that is, unintentionally) killed somebody could flee to a city of refuge, to avoid revenge according to the *talio* principle. But if he walked outside the city of refuge, he was again outlawed and could be killed (Num. 35:9–28).

In a modern constitutional state such a law would be totally unacceptable, utterly "inhuman." And initially the second commandment recognized something like collective responsibility (which was the subject of much debate after World War II in connection with the holocaust): God will visit the iniquity of the fathers upon the children to the third and fourth generation of those who hate him. But later, in Ezekiel 18:20, the position has already changed: "The soul that sins shall die. The son shall not suffer for the iniquity of the father." Compared with the second commandment we see here *historical progress* in the proclamation of God's will, though this does not imply a complete individualization or a denial of all collective guilt.

Not until the sense of justice in a culture is deepened by the moral love aspect—in other words, not until the juridical anticipation of the moral aspect is opened up—is there room for a refined and more balanced administration of justice. Then the internal *disposition* of an offender (or his social milieu) comes into play. Manslaughter is then not necessarily "murder," just as present-day law distinguishes between involuntary manslaughter, voluntary manslaughter, and murder in the third, second or first degree.

The sixth commandment prohibits "murder," as the Heidelberg Catechism confesses and teaches so well in Lord's Day 40.[115] The sixth commandment is not a legal prohibition, but a moral prohibition and commandment. The simplistic slogan "abortion is murder" is therefore to be rejected as a formalistic superficiality. Abortion *can* be murder, but it is not always so.[116] The same can be said about euthanasia.[117] In anthropological terms we can put it like this: external actions should not be divorced from their internal depth layers of dispositions and ethos. That would be a primitive externalization and lead to a juridification and rationalization of morality. That is the opposite of disclosure: an *ossification* of both law and morality in the form of logical definitions, formal application of laws, and frozen traditions.

---

115. See previous note.

116. Cf. my article "Antropologie en reageerbuisbevruchting" [Anthropology and in vitro fertilization], *Radix* 11 (1986): 24–53.

117. Cf. my articles "Christelijke euthanasia" [Christian euthanasia], *Opbouw* 30 (2 and 16 May 1986).

Chapter Fourteen–
Logic and Epistemology

CHAPTER FOURTEEN
LOGIC AND EPISTEMOLOGY

14.1 LOGIC
14.1.1 NO NEUTRAL LOGIC

One of the normative aspects typical of *all* temporal reality, and so not just of human beings, is the logical-analytical aspect. The laws for human logical thinking about things and about what transpires in human life are traced and formulated in the science known as "logic." The content of logic is formed by a whole series of topics. I merely mention: the act of distinguishing; the theory of concepts, judgments, argumentation, intuitions, and syllogisms; the theory of probability; and many more topics. Most are not directly relevant to theology.

Through the centuries, particularly in modern times, logic has expanded to such an extent that it hardly has room anymore for the logic of Aristotle, the "father of logic." Almost all philosophical schools develop their own logic. The hoary idea that logic is a technical, purely instrumental, religiously neutral science has long been superseded, though the title of Vollenhoven's book of 1932, *The Necessity of a Christian Logic*, still caused hilarity at the time.[118] Today, however, it is broadly held that every system of logic uses pre-theoretical or philosophical starting-points and that there are scores of variants of the science of logic.[119]

---

118. D. H. Th. Vollenhoven, *De noodzakelijkheid eener Christelijke Logica* (Amsterdam: H. J. Paris, 1932). [*Editor:* See also Vollenhoven's introduction to the theory of knowledge in *Isagôgè Philosophiae: Introduction to Philosophy* (Sioux Center, IA: Dordt College Press, 2005), pp. 108–38.]

119. To gain an impression of this confusing situation, which became increasingly complicated in the course of centuries, one may read the 75 pages (150 columns) in the great four-volume *Enzyklopädie Philosophie und Wissenschaftstheorie*, ed. by Jürgen Mittelstrass, 4 vols. (Mannheim, 1980–1996), 2:626–99, or also the 128 columns of the *Historisches Wörterbuch der Philosophie*, vol. 5, cols. 355–482.

To illustrate, one striking feature of the current situation is the confusion or even identification of the analytical with the lingual aspect, something that Vollenhoven already warned against with strong arguments in his book of 1932. In Antiquity it was already well known that if word and concept were the same there could hardly be any question of international conceptualization in science.

For the limited aims of this introduction to Dooyeweerd's Reformational philosophy it seems enough to mention just one example of the themes discussed in logic. Let us take the theory of concepts and conceptualization, since it is directly relevant to theology. In theology we constantly encounter what are referred to in linguistics as "metaphors." This concept is also needed in epistemology and logic, in connection with the limits of concepts and conceptualization. Precisely theology has a great deal to do with the idea of conceptual limits in the knowledge of what transcends these limits. For instance, can we have a concept of God, or of God's activity, or of God's dwelling-place, and so on? Can we have a concept of angels and demons and of their "habitations"? If so, what are the limits of such concepts? And if not, does theology then not necessarily become "negative theology," at times tailing off into mysticism?

Logic, however, like any other discipline, cannot function by itself but only in the larger context of philosophical theories about man and cosmos—in other words, in the context of anthropology and cosmology. Hence it cannot dispense with philosophy, nor with the special philosophy of logic, namely epistemology. Further on we will distinguish in logic between *concepts and ideas*, a distinction of fundamental importance to theology.

14.1.2 A CONCEPT OF GOD? "ANTHROPOMORPHISMS"

Most of what we read about God in Scripture and what we confess about Him in the Christian creeds is formulated in terms of *ideas*, or as we also say: in parables, images, metaphors. When we talk about God as *father*, or about His *eyes* or *hands*, His *all-seeing* power and *omnipresence*, we are using words that derive from human life and cannot be applied in a creaturely sense to God. The same goes for an image in which something from animal life is used to denote an activity of God, like the spreading of His wings.

The reality of God transcends our human, creaturely concepts. That is the reason why these concepts are just not "adequate" or "exact." They refer to creaturely situations, to a very precise representation of some or other knowable fact in created reality. Human concepts about God therefore cannot be described as "exact" or "adequate," terms that derive from the "exact sciences."

Nevertheless, such human thoughts and words about God can be altogether *true and reliable*. They *refer* to Him who is not a creature himself. The knowledge of God is therefore not confined in a creaturely sense to the structure of a concept. Our artificially formed concepts like omnipresence and omniscience should not, *as concepts*, be taken "literally," or at least should not be confined to their creaturely structure or meaning. In short, they cannot be "defined." They merely *point to* what is incomprehensible and inexpressible within out creaturely horizon: they point *to God*. These terms do not point to God "exactly," but they do evoke an "idea" of what is referred to. Not a "vague idea," but precisely a *concept deepened* into an "idea," by which the conceptual is transcended and knowledge is gained of "what eye has not seen and ear has not heard."

14.1.3 CONCEPT AND IDEA
The Bible itself is often far from "exact," as for instance in Genesis 11. We read there that *God* (whom we confess to be omnipresent, all-knowing and all-seeing) *came down* to look at the building of the tower of Babel, whereupon He sees (discovers) certain things and decides to go down again. If the above terms—omnipresence, omniscience, all-seeing power, decides to come down—exactly described what we mean by these terms of our own making, all of Genesis 11 and many other biblical passages that talk about God in the same style would be incomprehensible or contradictory, or reporting perfectly pointless actions by God.

In our Christian exegetical tradition we therefore say that God talks about himself, and the biblical authors talk about God, in an "anthropomorphic" way. Rightly so, as long as we do not say of it that it is "only figurative." Nor should we associate it with theoretical exactness in a physical, psychological, historical, jurisprudential or ethical sense. Biblical God-talk is only true in the sense of *religious* truth.

We are right, I think, to speak in theology about the anthropomorphisms of God, but in doing so we are in danger of doing insufficient justice to the described reality of God. The "figurative" or "anthropomorphic" is then considered a mere circumlocution, an indirect and less exact mode of expression, which can perhaps be better translated or explicated by means of a more direct, a more non-metaphorical, or idea-knowledge, but theoretically deepened and therefore (once again) *conceptual* theological formulation. In that way we could presumably "grasp" the object more clearly, less "vaguely."

But this leads to the next problem: when *should* we take a certain expression literally and when not? For instance, not when the Bible talks about God's repentance? Yes when it talks about God's patience? Not when Scripture talks about God's vengeance, yes when it talks about God's forgiveness? And may we not talk about God's inconsistency when we compare, say, verses 7 and 8 in Genesis 6? Verse 7 says: "I will blot out man whom I have created from the face of the earth . . . both man and beast . . . for I am sorry that I have made them." Verse 8 reads: "But Noah found favor in the eyes of the Lord."

This is where we need the concept of "idea," which in logic is not simply a "concept" but what is called a *"boundary concept,"* a concept that cannot grasp or comprehend what the concept is intended to "grasp." It goes beyond its boundaries. We therefore talk about *faith* knowledge as being *concept-transcending* knowledge. It relates directly to God and to his divine actions. That is what distinguishes faith knowledge from other, equally distinctive types of knowledge, including theological knowledge, which is a subtype of "scientific" knowledge.

14.1.4 LOGICISM AND ANTHROPOMORPHISMS

This also bars the way to a logicistic use of biblical words, as if they were *concepts* from which we might freely and effectively draw logical conclusions about what is not said directly. For instance, it would be *blasphemous* to conclude from the truth that God is the Father of His son Jesus Christ and from the concept of father that there is a blood relationship between God the Father and God the Son. Or to ask, in line with pagan myths: Who is the divine "mother" of God's son? Or to conclude from the concept of omnipresence that praying for God's nearness is pointless. Or to say that God *cannot* "forsake" anyone because He is *omni*present. Or to conclude logically from the Bible's references to God's hands and eyes that God must also have eyebrows and twice five fingers with nails.

Logicism, which occurs quite often also in traditional orthodox theology, will stop at nothing. For instance, shortly after the great Reformation a Reformed theologian (Beza) observed that what can be logically inferred from Scripture has the same authority as Scripture itself—a view that was already found in the Middle Ages.

Another example of this is the formulation of the so-called *extra calvinisticum* in the Heidelberg Catechism, Lord's Day 18, Q & A 48.[120] In his edition of "The Three Forms of Unity"[121] Abraham Kuyper, on his own authority, inserted the words "cannot be contained by anything" because he felt that the original text, which simply has the word "illimitable," could no longer in his time express with that one word what it was intended to express. In my view, this was an unfortunate intervention. And it would be even better, I believe, if Question 48 itself were struck from the Catechism. The question is purely logicistic as well as theoretically disputable. Moreover, it is not relevant for understanding what Scripture teaches about Christ.

In calling this whole way of speaking "anthropomorphic" we are justified only insofar as we use it to confess our *faith* that God is *different* from us and that our *faith* accepts that nonetheless we can be assured that we know God as He is. Everything that is said about God in anthropomorphic words applies to Him inexplicably in a *divine* way.

14.1.5 LOGIC AND EPISTEMOLOGY

Logic is a *special science*. It focuses its analysis on what is qualified by the logical-analytical aspect of reality. That is to say, logic focuses on the relevant human subjective activities, namely on the logical object-side of the rest of reality as well as on the law-side of reality. *Epistemology* is then the *philosophy* of logic-as-a-special-science.

The *philosophy of logic* analyzes, according to law-side and subject-side, the differences and the ties between the logical aspect and the other aspects, as well as the logical subject functions and object

---

120. *Question:* If Christ's human nature is not present wherever His divinity is, are not then His two natures separated from one another? *Answer:* Not at all; for since divinity is illimitable and omnipresent, it is evident that Christ's divinity is beyond the bounds of the human nature it has assumed, yet nonetheless is in this human nature and remains personally united to it.

121. *De Drie Formulieren van Eenigheid, voor kerkelijk gebruik uitgegeven door Dr. A. Kuyper* (Amsterdam, 1883; many editions and reprints), containing the Belgic Confession (1561), the Heidelberg Catechism (1563), and the Canons of Dordt (1618/19). (*Editor*)

functions within these, all within the wider context of cosmology. That wider context includes anthropology, since knowledge, as a product of the activity of "knowledge acquisition," is a human possession. Knowledge is a concrete phenomenon, an "entity" within the total network of aspects and cosmic structures, including those of man. Accordingly, epistemology or the theory of this concrete phenomenon called "knowledge" involves not just the analytical aspect but the structural *totality* of the knowledge phenomenon, and it is therefore of a *philosophical nature*.

The phenomenon of knowledge is also called "truth" if the knowledge is sound. Otherwise it is an error, a lie, or something similar. Knowledge, as the possession or expression of truth, is therefore concrete; it consists of *people*'s concrete thoughts or statements. Knowledge consists of thoughts or statements that "agree" with the things one is thinking or talking about. The logical *aspect* of these things is the *qualifying and leading aspect*, as it is of other cognitive activities, like perceiving, distinguishing, formulating, memorizing, and so on.

At the same time we need to add and clarify something. *Knowledge does not exist in and by itself*, and it always consists of more than just logical-analytical understanding. Concrete knowledge is always knowledge *by someone* and knowledge *about something*, and that determines what the *qualification* of this knowledge as a concrete entity will be. Thus we have legal knowledge, aesthetic knowledge, faith knowledge, moral knowledge, and so on (see also sec. 14.2.5 below: the structure of the knowledge process.) Knowledge is therefore not simply an entity, but a sub-identity, which is encapsulated in some or other type of *concrete* knowledge. This encapsulation is also called "enkapsis."

Knowledge (or truth) always stands in yet another relation as well. It is always relational in a double sense: in relation to the human person who possesses this knowledge, and in relation to something that it is knowledge *about*. Cosmologically speaking it can be formulated even more broadly: all the relationality of concrete knowledge also stands in the "transcendental" *fundamental relations of law/subject and subject/object, as well as in the fundamental relation between its supra-temporal fullness and its temporal manifestations*.

In all great philosophy throughout the centuries the problem of knowledge or "the question of truth" has rightly been an important theme, and this is also true of Reformational philosophy.

14.1.6 THE TRANSCENDENT FULLNESS AND UNITY OF KNOWLEDGE OR TRUTH

In my opening chapter I referred to philosophy as being, among other things, an orientation to the unity and fullness of existing creaturely reality. This is also the perspective of philosophy when it turns to knowledge and truth—if only by virtue of the fact that knowledge and truth are products of a "fully human" activity. I choose this wording advisedly, because casual everyday language far too often personifies and substantializes "thought" in contrast to other activities or "capacities," so that its full *humanity* remains hidden. Yet it is not "thought" that thinks, but *man*—a human being, with everything that he or she is and has.

This truism plays a big role also in theology. Partly for this reason it is important to recognize that philosophical theories of knowledge and science are not neutral affairs, as if "thought" with its concepts and results is but a neutral, technical *"instrument"* or *"conceptual apparatus"* that can only be known empirically; as if "thought" is comparable to a hammer or a pair of pliers that one can borrow from his neighbor. Reformational epistemology will therefore have to admit in all frankness that it wants to approach knowledge, and so the problem of truth, *in its totality*. Hence the *totality of its view of man and reality* will have to come first (at least in a systematic discussion; sometimes a dialogue situation may require a different order.)

In the light of the biblical ground-motive of the creation of *all* things *in* Christ, we *confess* Christ as the fullness of all creaturely reality, its totality and unity, and its origin. This also comprehends the full truth about reality. Christ could therefore say: I AM the truth.

Christ's statement should be taken literally and not be explained away to mean that everything that Christ said was nothing but the truth in the sense of being "correct." His word "I AM the truth" (John 14:6) is a statement that must be incomprehensible to a rationalist who restricts the idea of truth to logical "agreement between thought and being," between the event and the story about the event—just as incomprehensible as the biblical expressions that talk about *"doing"* the truth or *walking* "in the truth." Truth is more, indeed much more, than a purely logical affair, though of course logical activity is fully involved in it. Historical truth is therefore *more* than that something "really happened." Scripture says in Col. 1:17 that "all things" have their *existence* "in Christ." That is saying more than just that all things were historical realities at one time. See also Heb. 1:3.

Dooyeweerd writes in this connection that the statement "twice two makes four" is patently untrue if it separates this state of affairs from God's order of creation.[122] He speaks here of the "perspective structure of truth,"[123] by which is meant that the truth, like the reality to which it refers, regardless of all the different types and levels, is an inner unity. It is a unity which, transcending all its temporal types, levels, forms and limitations, has its supra-temporal *fullness or concentration* in Christ. It is a fundamental (normative) intention or tenor in all creatures, just as Scripture says that all things were created *"unto God"* (Rom. 11:36; 1 Cor. 8:6) or *"for Him"* (Heb. 2:10).

"All relative truths within our temporal horizon are only true in the fullness of Truth, which was revealed by God in Christ."[124] Or to put it in the simple language of faith: all truth is only really truth if it is spoken by someone who partakes of Christ (because He *is* the fullness of truth) and who does not separate the reality to which the statement refers from "the alpha" of creation (Rev. 3:14) and the order of creation.

For the *Christian* faith, this *full* truth is the content of the "religious ground-motive" of creation and redemption in Christ, as the driving force, the author and motor in all movements of life and thought in the direction of the Truth.

Additionally, the religious worldview presuppositions of the philosophical view of reality include certain ideas about the distinctive nature of the various creatures (among which the idea that faith and science are each "after their kind"—Genesis 1). Where necessary, these ideas will come up for discussion in what follows, but at this juncture we would like to set out in systematic fashion some of the main features of epistemology, and on that basis look in the next chapter at some of the main lines in the philosophy of science.

---

122. H. Dooyeweerd, *A New Critique of Theoretical Thought*, 2:572: "Even the judgment: 2 × 2 = 4 becomes an untruth if the law-conformable state of affairs expressed in it is detached from the temporal world-order and from the sovereignty of God as the Creator."

123. Ibid., 2:577.

124. Ibid., 1:116.

14.2 EPISTEMOLOGY

14.2.1 THE LOGICAL-ANALYTICAL ASPECT

We already said that epistemology is the philosophy of logic-as-a-special-science. Like all special sciences, logic relates to everything that is qualified by a certain aspect, in this case the "logical-analytical" aspect.

This double term "logical-analytical" is not superfluous, because analyzing in the sense of distinguishing occurs not only in human beings but also in animals. "The ox knows its owner and the ass its master's crib . . ." Animals distinguish a great deal in their immediate living environment, but they probably do not have any *self-knowledge*. They do not, like humans, stand above the multiplicity of their temporal activities in the unity of a "self-consciousness" so that they could mentally distinguish and dissociate themselves from these activities by a process of "objectification." Animals do not distinguish these activities from themselves but probably experience them unconsciously, completely interwoven as they are with their instinctive mode of functioning, usually in a rigid dependence on their habitat and hereditary patterns of behavior. Their distinguishing is identifying, but not *logically* analyzing, which in human beings is an activity experienced as normatively determined by the law for this activity, namely: Take care, *distinguish well*, otherwise you will make a mistake. More on this in sec. 14.2.3 below.

14.2.2 THE LOGICAL-ANALYTICAL ACTIVITY

In discussing the act structure of human activity we talked about four depth dimensions (acts, dispositions, ethos and the I). We need these distinctions also in analyzing human activities in the process of knowledge.

As a simple start we can state that knowledge is the result of the process of knowing, the acquisition of knowledge, "coming to know," thus a concrete human activity. We might speak of *"knowledge"* as a *result of the process of knowing, dispositionally recorded in our memory*. This result can be preserved in the memory or retrieved in commemoration.[125]

---

125. This image should not mislead us into thinking that the activity of knowing, "coming to know," can be compared to the picking up of an object. Truth can just be "picked up" in popular speech, never in science. The common image of "sources" of knowledge, on which we can simply "draw," may therefore suggest a wrong idea.

For each of the activities in the process of knowledge acquisition (distinguishing, perceiving, conceptualizing, interpreting, formulating, remembering, memorizing, etc.) the logical-analytical aspect is the *qualifying* aspect. This also means that all other aspects of reality are present and function in it, but that in all this many-sided functioning the analytical aspect is the *leading* and *qualifying* one.

The entity "human knowledge" can be roughly represented as in Figure 7 in the Appendix. However, this logical-analytical functioning, though *qualifying* for the activity as such, is not always *dominant* or *sufficiently* dominant. Our process of knowledge acquisition remains knowledge acquisition, but can become seriously disrupted or clouded by, for instance, our functioning in the sensitive, emotional aspect, or in the social aspect, and so forth. Besides becoming disrupted or clouded, this process can also be stimulated, purified or opened up as a result of our functioning in all supra-analytical aspects, thus in the faith aspect, the moral aspect, and so on.

14.2.3 Law and subjectivity

As is the case with all concrete "things," theory of knowledge must distinguish between law-side and subject-side of the analytical activity, and on the subject-side between subject and object. On the law-side of the knowledge process "the laws of logic" apply, or more precisely: the laws *of* God *for* human logical distinguishing, laws which the science of logic seeks to formulate. So logic with its various principles is a special science, one that we need not deal with any further in this introduction after what we have already covered in this chapter.

Usually all adult people with "common sense" have an *intuitive awareness* of what the principles of creation require for logical functioning. They do not need a study in formal logic for that. Illogical reasoning is anti-normative, "against the rules," an expression of human weakness or evidence of deficiencies in the very functioning of "common sense." Through the disruption of human life by sin our existence (co-determined as it is by traditions and the contemporary fashionable mindset) is often impaired by all kinds of erroneous

---

Once again: knowledge is not a thing that exists in and by itself and it cannot be acquired apart from man. It is the result of a norm-bound *activity* in the relation between the complete human being and his objects of knowledge; it is knowledge *of* (someone) and knowledge *about* (something). See also below, sec. 15.2.4.

illogical thoughts and arguments. This can only be remedied to a very limited extent by exercises in logic.

Yet logic is sometimes crucial to the practice of science. It is therefore vital that the science of logical functioning complies with its own norms, in other words, that a sound logic is developed, in strict compliance with the laws of scientific practice. Those laws, too, are logical-analytical laws, but geared specifically to the characteristic type of *scientific* practice, as distinct from *practical* logical thought.

It is a small example of a secularized view of reality when the "laws of logic" are regarded as purely human "conventions" or "rules" without any connection to God, no different than if we were to say that "we" (but who, actually?) happened to have agreed that twice two makes four. In the Christian worldview God is not excluded from anything, and particularly in the law-side of reality God is always actively present with his will—his will to create and sustain, sometimes also his will to restore, renew and consummate.

Note in this connection that it is therefore folly to claim that "everything" that God demands of us is comprised in the Ten Commandments or can be found in the Bible. The idea that the norms of action and Christian ethics should be based exclusively on Scripture is not just an unrealistic but also an unbiblical idea, because Scripture itself refers us to the creation and the normative "kinds" found in it. See, for example, Isaiah 28:26.

The erroneous idea just mentioned can only be entertained on the basis of a fundamental separation (and perhaps a theoretical bridging afterwards) of the two "realms" or "areas" of nature and grace (*general, profane* reality plus *special, supernatural* Christianity). Such an idea testifies to a fundamentally secular view: existing reality is no longer seen as in correlation with God's laws of creation, placed under them as its precondition. In principle this view introduces a deistic *separation* between God and creature, between law and reality, instead of just a practical *distinction* in the *correlative relation* between the two. The law-side, the normative precondition and distinctiveness of reality, has then been separated from "the neutral brute fact."

14.2.4 THE SUBJECT-OBJECT RELATION

It is important to recall as well the discussion of the subject-object relation in chapter 6. In that chapter we encountered something of the *connection* that exists between man and his "surrounding world," and also of the connection between the various aspects of existence. In the logical-analytical activity an *interlacement* takes place between the logical subject (man in his analytical distinguishing and identifying) and the logical objects on which this human subjective logical activity focuses and with which it becomes entwined in the process of (sound or erroneous) knowledge acquisition. This "interlacement" is more than and different from an "agreement" (an *"adaequatio"*) between two supposedly separate, substantialized entities ("thought" and "being"). The subject-object relation is an integral fabric within the whole of human activity and its environment.

What people call objective reality is always interwoven with man, and even as it has the potential of being experienced, it cannot actually be experienced without the activities of experiencing man in his perceiving, analyzing, interpreting, identifying, naming, and so forth. This functioning of "objective reality," of reality's *"potential for being experienced,"* is what we define as reality's *object functions*— potential but real properties of reality and not therefore fantasized constructions mentally added by us. These object functions exist only in relation to human subject functions, and vice versa.[126]

So there is no objective reality *apart* from man, and in the contact between man and his "surrounding world" man is always *active* in *all kinds of ways.* The human mind (including sensory perception) cannot be compared to a camera through which reality impresses itself mechanically and automatically on a passive film. Rather it can be compared to a painting or a poetical description.

14.2.5 THE STRUCTURE OF THE KNOWLEDGE PROCESS

In the concrete process of knowledge and in its result we can therefore distinguish many other aspects than the logical-analytical aspect (see Figures 1 and 9). The subjective logical-analytical activity is interwoven with many differently qualified acts and actions. In epistemology, as the special philosophy of logic, we could make an extensive analysis of this, but for our purposes (in an "introduction," after all) it need only be discussed to a very limited extent.

---

126. In so-called theological epistemology I had to address this point again in connection with the question in what sense God can or cannot be the "object" of knowledge or of scientific theology; cf. my *Vakfilosofie van de geloofswetenschap* [Philosophy of the science of faith] (2004), pp. 95–97.

We confine ourselves to the *result* of the knowledge process that takes place in human thought, thus to "knowledge." *Strictly speaking* (which is not always necessary in everyday practical usage) knowledge is the same as truth, otherwise we do not speak of knowledge but of ignorance or error—of incorrect "knowledge," the result of a failure to analyze soundly, observe or reflect properly, or of the uncritical adoption of an incorrect view.

In the light of our entire philosophical systematics we can say of concrete knowledge or truth that *all* modal aspects can be distinguished in it, as in all other entities. But we should stress that knowledge or a truth can also be *qualified* in other ways than just by the logical-analytical. We confine ourselves now to this subject.

The concrete logically-analytically qualified *act of knowing* (or *knowledge) is always encapsulated as a "substructure" in a differently qualified activity*, for instance in celebrating Holy Communion, in sculpting, in paying a birthday visit, in painting a window sill, signing an employment contract, eating bread, and so on. In all these cases of concrete activities the *qualifying* aspect of this "enkaptic interlacement *whole*" is different from the logical-analytical aspect.[127] See Figure 9.

Thus thought or knowledge that is *encapsulated* in for instance an economic, moral, aesthetic or religious act cannot be otherwise qualified than by these *concrete acts*, each "after its kind" with its own qualifying aspect. The encapsulated knowledge has its own logically qualified entity structure, but *as a substructure* it is *encapsulated* in another entity, and acquires from that entity its new typical, distinctive nature (for example, as juridical knowledge, faith knowledge, economic knowledge, and so on), as will be set out more fully in sec. 14.2.6.

The situation is somewhat different for a typically scientific *thought-act*, or the result of that act: a formulated *scientific proposition*. Those acts are in fact also logically *qualified*, even should they contain errors.[128] But there are two principal kinds of typically logical entities that require our special attention: the *practical and the theoretical* types of

---

127. "Enkaptic interlacement whole" was the technical term for an entitary totality in which several entities are encapsulated; cf. sec. 7.3.12 and 7.3.13.

128. To be logically qualified means to be of a logical nature. The illogical can only exist by virtue of typically logical norms to which it is subject and with which it ought to be in agreement—just as an expression of lovelessness, no matter how immoral, can be designated as immoral or loveless precisely because it is of a moral nature. Untruth exists only by virtue of the law-of-truth which can be sinned against.

thought and truth. We will discuss the difference and the connection between the two in the next chapter, but we must briefly anticipate the main point about the distinction already here.

14.2.6 TYPES OF KNOWLEDGE OR TRUTH

Depending on the way a logical act of knowing (or its result) is woven as a *substructure* into a non-*logically* qualified act of knowledge, we are talking each time about a different type of practical knowledge. In the "enkaptic interlacement" of logical knowledge in another concrete act or action, the functioning of this knowledge *part* acquires its qualification from the leading function of the *whole*.

Thus in theology we talk explicitly about faith *knowledge* when we are not referring to the concrete whole of the faith act itself but only to the knowledge component in it, hence to a substructure of concrete *believing*. Believing does *imply* knowledge, both from a modal and an entitary point of view, but it is itself not typically logical in nature, not logically *qualified*. Believing is not the same as knowing, nor the same as knowing-plus-feeling, or knowing-plus-love, or knowing plus something else: it is an integral unity with a *distinctive nature of its own*. That is to say: it cannot be reduced to anything else, nor to a sum of other functions or of other encapsulated substructures. In the nature of the case, it is an integral unity with many "modal aspects" to it, but also with a variety of *substructures in it*.

The same holds for many other kinds of knowledge. The knowledge that is interwoven in loving, as a "component part"—as an analytically qualified *substructure* in love—is ultimately moral in nature, not typically logical, nor typically juridical, and so on. The love in which for instance a spouse "knows" his or her partner is totally different from psychological (scientific) knowledge about him or her.

To name another example: knowledge of art, as an analytical substructure, is (typically) logical knowledge, yet it too is not simply *typically* logical in nature without further qualification: ultimately it is typically *aesthetic* in nature, on account of its encapsulation in a *unity*, in a *whole* that must be called typically aesthetic functioning. An aesthetic truth is therefore not always the same as, or necessarily connected with, a typically scientific truth from (the science of) *aesthetics*. The truth of a work of art—for instance, a novel or a painting—is not a theoretical truth but a practical truth which is intuitively known and recognized, and which is of an aesthetic nature.

Similarly, *religious* truth is not typically scientific truth; that is to say, it is not a theological truth, nor a historical truth. Religious truth is of a different nature; it is qualified by the human being who listens directly or implicitly *in faith* to God himself, a human being who *a priori* affirms God's Word, trusts in it and grounds his deepest certainty in it. Religious truth lacks the typically theoretical structure of scientific truth as formulated in (the science of) theology. It is *different!* It is different *in nature.* Also, religious truth is a creaturely product of human cognitive activities in the process of knowledge acquisition and is therefore subject to the familiar expression of Genesis 1: "created after its (own) kind." This is what we mean when we say and hear so often (but not nearly often enough) that faith is different from scientific theology, be it academic or popular.

14.2.7 HOW THEOLOGY AND FAITH CAN INFLUENCE EACH OTHER

Yet it is still possible, also here, that in the course of time a scientific (theological) truth is taken up—encapsulated—in the concrete life of faith. This happened, for instance, with the pre-Reformation theory of transubstantiation. Our faith then partly becomes a faith in theology instead of in God and his Word. Hence an incorrect or bad theology, owing in part to the factual power of theology in the churches, can even harm our faith life.

Many other examples could be mentioned. If a certain theological view is popularized through preaching and broadly accepted by a church, theology has taken control of faith on that point, instead of the other way round. To put it more pointedly: the firm *belief* in a certain theological view has then won out over the belief in God's revelation. In other words: here we no longer find a "tension" between "faith and science" but a *contradiction and synthesis within faith itself*: belief in God's revelation and belief in human theories.

And conversely: theology can stray as a result of inadequate religious surrender to God as He addresses us through the Bible. One of the finest functions or purposes of theology is realized when *faith knowledge*, as a component part of existential believing, is corrected and deepened by *good* theology. This cannot always be equated with a deepening or strengthening of *faith*, but it is a deepening of *knowledge*, an improvement of faith knowledge, which is of course very important in itself, precisely because faith knowledge is a founding element in concrete believing, is encapsulated in it as a founding substructure.

Besides faith knowledge as a "component" of faith, there is also linguistic knowledge, economic insight, the knowledge of love, a sense of justice, social intuition and aesthetic knowledge. All these terms from everyday language refer to the knowledge *element* present *in* loving, *in* the exercise of justice, *in* art appreciation, *in* speech, and so on. These are all normatively qualified *types of knowledge*, which are encapsulated in the complete entity structure of concrete human expressions of life. Intuitively and rightly, these activities are not judged to be exhausted by logical-analytical activity (*intellectualism*) or by some sort of popularization of science (*scientism*), even though all such activities can play a role in specific cases.

14.2.8 DIFFERENT TYPES OF HISTORICAL KNOWLEDGE

In the present context it is useful to add the example of knowledge about what happened in the past and was passed down in the biblical narratives. This is particularly relevant to theological hermeneutics.

Historical facts are known to us (often very partially) through tradition, but this tradition is usually not (or not just) the result of scientific research, though that is of course possible too. The past comes down to us first of all in the form of orally transmitted "stories," recorded "histories," testimonies in stone, in images or in writing. So this is already the second meaning that the word history can have: first the events themselves, second the oral or written accounts of them—the telling or writing of history (in a non-scientific sense). A third meaning of the word history refers to the product of historical scholarship (often ambiguously called "historiography"): history as a science, the result of a methodical study of the sources, including their analysis and the reasons for their selection, interpretation and narrative composition.

It is therefore too simple and often very confusing when history is only taken to mean "the hard facts." In our engagement with the past, and thus in our knowledge or truth about the past, we are always dealing with more than the facts that actually happened in the past; that is, we are always dealing with two different types of interpretations: (1) the ordinary oral or written accounts of them in the *tradition*, (2) the scientific type of knowledge as the product of historical scholarship. Finally, there is again the process of recording, adopting and transmitting the tradition by those who have become acquainted with this tradition (including the variations within it) or with this scientific scholarship (including the varying interpretations of it).

All these different types of interpretation have their own type of reliability, correctness and function. They also have their own "hermeneutics" in the sense of theory about the correct observation, representation and interpretation of the facts and their transmission. Think of the frequent shades of emphasis and conflicting testimonies about the same event during court trials, or the endless disagreements in the interpretation of many historical facts, also among professional historians. It has been said that every generation of historians writes its own books about the same past. Think also of the many unsolved puzzles in the exegesis of all kinds of Bible texts.

14.2.9 HISTORY OR HISTORICAL SCIENCE IN THE BIBLE?

Think also of the differences between the Gospel writers who often describe the same event with all kinds of minor or major differences, or of the differences or "irregularities" (a euphemism!) between the books of Samuel, Kings and Chronicles. It would be wrong to regard these *"stories"* as exact scientific accounts of the facts, and then to begin talking, like higher critics, about "contradictions in the Bible," or to engage, like fundamentalists, in "harmonizing" these accounts. This last effort is inspired by a *rationalistic* (scientistic) *conception* of divine inspiration which dictates that the biblical narratives cannot or *should* not, from the point of view of scientific history, be in conflict with each other. As if Scripture uses a scientific concept of the truth instead of a practical *religious* idea of the truth, in direct orientation to the *fullness* of the truth which is "in Christ": "*I am* the truth"!

In short: in the knowledge of Scripture, too, faith and theology, religious truth and scientific theological truth can certainly be *distinguished* (which is not the same as *separated*). These "truths" are not identical; they are of a different nature. The content of faith, the truth of faith is the result of believing with all our heart, believing God's revelation, believing in the truth of God's revelation concerning himself and his works.

Scientific-theoretical research is a different approach to Holy Scripture, an approach that is limited, and must be willing to be limited, to the *theoretically abstracted* "human character," the "servant status" of the biblical text, which is a collection of certain transmitted human texts canonized by the church in the nineties of the fourth century.

Both faith and theology are oriented in different ways to the reliable (creditable, *belief*-worthy) *testimony* of the biblical authors regarding *God's* words and works. Those words and works are *not as such* accessible to scholarly investigation or susceptible to theoretic proof or scientific evidence. *God's* words and works cannot *as such* be "seen" (Heb. 11:3). *Faith* alone, with its heartfelt prior surrender and devotion to God, is the evidence of God's words and works (Heb. 11:1), not the detached study of academic theology and its scholarly results. The many biblical calls to contemplate God's works presuppose a *religiously* qualified contemplation, not a purely sensorily qualified observation—faith, not sight.

It is better not to call theology simply a "support" for faith, since that would suggest that the power of scientific argumentation is stronger than the power that the assurance of *faith* (with its devout simplicity) possesses. At most theology can at times support and clarify faith *knowledge* (as a substructure within faith), not concrete faith itself. That is also why we are justified in having some reservations about the tradition of "apologetics." We still read grateful and even triumphant press releases when some scientist and Nobel Prize winner declares openly that there must be a superintelligent Origin or Force behind the universe. But this will never lead anybody to the certainty of *biblical faith*. Certainty of faith is something *different* and stronger than mathematical or other scientific certainty.

14.2.10 TWO PRINCIPAL TYPES OF KNOWLEDGE OR TRUTH

In Figure 9 we have sketched different types of knowledge, depending on the *qualifying function* of the whole in which the knowledge functions as a substructure. In our Western culture one of these types has come strongly to the fore, the type that is qualified by the logical-analytical function itself, and specifically the *theoretical* subtype. This type of knowledge and knowledge acquisition is *"typical"* of the scientific attitude of thought which determines the character of its activities and its results.

However pervasive this type of thought is in our culture, it remains a type of thought and knowledge that can only be acquired and handled by a very limited number of people. The vast majority of people are not capable of this, nor need they be. Nonetheless, the public at large, and especially the "intelligentsia," puts a great deal of trust in "science" for many areas of life, a trust that often takes on the features of idolatry. "Studies show" is the assertion that is supposed to trump all doubts. Reformational philosophy calls us back from this typically Western idolatry of the sciences, *including the science of theology.*

That brings us to the controversial issue of how we can correctly characterize the difference between practical and scientific knowledge, between practical and theoretical thinking and knowing, for instance between faith knowledge and theology, between knowledge from business experience and knowledge of economic theory, and so on. The proper encyclopedic place of this inquiry is *philosophy of science,* of which we will now sketch a few broad outlines in our last chapter.

Chapter Fifteen – Philosophy of Science

CHAPTER FIFTEEN
PHILOSOPHY OF SCIENCE

15.1 DIFFERENCES BETWEEN PRACTICAL AND THEORETICAL KNOWLEDGE

15.1.1 INSIGHT INTO THE DIFFERENCE BETWEEN THE TWO TYPES

For about as long as science has been around people have been aware that there is a difference between scientific knowledge and everyday practical knowledge.[129] The ancient Greeks soon came up with two different words to represent them: *doxa* and *epistèmè*, opinion and (real) knowledge. These words would later be associated with, respectively, the unstable and fickle "appearance" of things on the one hand, and permanent or timeless "being" on the other. The words were later linked with mere "sensory perception" and rational formation of knowledge or reason-able thinking. These expressions themselves show a clear tendency towards privileging rational knowledge over the results of knowledge gained through, for instance, the senses.

The relation was usually taken to be that the one kind of knowledge was deceptive or at least uncertain, while the other came with certainty, permanence and real truth. The difference was also expressed in terms of more or less precise, more or less reliable knowledge. This contrast in appreciation has remained dominant in our culture, although there have always been modish fluctuations in connection with rival rationalist and irrationalist currents in worldview thinking and in philosophic thought.

The awareness of two kinds of knowledge emerged in a period when an important change in the history of Western culture took place: the opening up of Greek culture through, among other things, the rise of scientific thought. We pointed out in sec. 11.2.4.1 that this cultural change was far from religiously neutral, for in its

---

129. This chapter, too, claims to be no more than a "first introduction" and is therefore confined to some of the main problems in philosophy of science.

initial period science partly served as a "reason-able alternative" to a religious tradition which in origin was strongly tied to external cultic rituals but had increasingly come under attack by a process of secularization within paganism. Increasingly, external rituals were able to survive without the oppressive traditional beliefs about mythical deities. The traditional knowledge about the gods and their activities did continue to be believed for centuries but was more and more characterized by un-belief. It became purely "outward knowledge," that is, unbelieving knowledge.

This development tilted Western culture towards an alternative religious trust in human—specifically scientific—reason; and opposite or alongside this idol stood an independent, demythologized, "disenchanted" natural reality from which anything divine or miraculous had been mentally erased. Modern thinking would begin to refer to this reality as simply "empirical reality," composed of "neutral, hard facts," divorced from "the divine."

In general we present-day Christians cannot get away from this demythologized (and thus unconsciously secularized) modern thinking about reality. One of the most regrettable consequences is that public opinion has introduced a separation between words and deeds, and Christians have introduced a separation between God's Word and God's revelation in his works. As a result, many of us continue to experience a gap between believing and thinking— between believing in God's Word and thinking about scientific facts. This has also given rise to the interminable, wrongly framed and therefore insoluble problem of the relation between faith and science, a problem to which Christian academics have devoted countless conferences and voluminous papers for nearly a century.

In general we are unable to realize that this approach to the problem is scientifically askew, because we "believe" (dogmatically) that there is an independent reality (of "hard facts") and that real science regarding these facts does not contain a founding belief. This irresolvable "tension" is fundamentally a tension *in our faith*, namely the internally contradictory combination of Christian faith with a humanist faith in science. To see this more sharply we need a different view of the facts of total reality itself (including science), namely a radically Christian view of reality in the light of the biblical belief in creation.

In this connection let me touch on something tangential to our concerns here: the widespread custom, not least in orthodox Protestant circles, of equating (real) science with the natural sciences and technology, the so-called exact sciences—as if the humanities and the social sciences are not really scientific because they lack "mathematical certainty"! But we can let this perennial issue in the general theory of science rest for now.

15.1.2 ENDURING AWARENESS OF THE DIFFERENCE

Scientific thought as sketched above developed lofty pretensions and an air of superiority over practical thought (whether or not dependent on myths), thought that could only produce "opinions." However, it left the practical life of most or at least many people unchanged and unconverted to the glorification of science. This has remained so.

We see this in our time, for instance, in a renewed appreciation of "practical experience" over academic theories. Many employment advertisement nowadays stress the need not only for a diploma but for some years of practical experience. The new emphasis is also found among the broad mass of people who are aware that this or that account may be a "fine theory" but that it fails to do justice to everyday experience. It is also found in many congregations where people have little taste for "dogmatic" sermons and ministers switch to practical, pastoral messages, addressed not just to the intellect but above all to people's "experience of God," to the "heart" and the problems of everyday life—ministering to the listeners more than administering the Word.

This awareness of the distinctive nature and value of practical thought alongside or opposite theoretical thought has always existed, even in the first phase of science. A story often recounted in this context is that of the Thracian slave girl who laughed when she saw how Thales, the first philosopher-astronomer, was gazing at the stars with his nose in the air and philosophizing about the cosmos, but failed to see the ditch with water in front of his feet, tripped and fell into it. According to some later legends, this is perhaps why he claimed that all things consist of water.

Our "postmodern" era has seen the addition of a strongly reactionary element. After a period in which the adoration of "reason" dominated the public mentality and rationalism prevailed in science and worldview, irrationalism is gaining ground all the time.[130] That is one reason why I address this subject repeatedly in my book *Vakfilosofie van de geloofswetenschap*, where I critique the traditional search for a "balance" between intellectual and experience-oriented preaching, between "head and heart"—we may also say, between "scholasticism and mysticism," between theology and experiencing God, between "purely intellectual knowledge" and "experiential piety."[131]

15.1.3 HOW PHILOSOPHY OF SCIENCE INTERPRETS THE DIFFERENCE

It is one thing to be aware of the difference between scientific and non-scientific knowledge, another to have a scientific or epistemological analysis and interpretation of it. Most people, living as they do outside the sphere of intimate acquaintance with the complex problems of epistemology and philosophy of science, apply the difference in practical life but usually interpret or understand it within the confines of their (still important!) pre-scientific experiential knowledge. It is fortunate that pre-scientific knowledge is able to recognize the difference in practice, but of course it lacks any scientific, structural understanding of it.

In pre-theoretical experience, accordingly, the interpretation and characterization of the difference remains tied to the intellectual criteria of correct, reliable, precise, exact—tied, in other words, to what the Greeks meant by the distinction of mere opinion (*doxa*) versus true knowledge (*epistèmè*). This has been a temptation for the "intelligentsia" to adopt a domineering and elitist attitude, and for the "masses" to develop an inferiority complex in the face of "science."

Due to the powerful influence exercised by the worldview of both ancient and modern humanism, our everyday experience itself has been corrupted by these traditions, and it has long been commonplace to concur with the standard disqualification of experiential knowledge as opposed to scientific knowledge. Only in recent decades have we again seen a greater appreciation of "experiential knowledge," not only in job advertisements but also in philosophical theories about

---

130. Remember as well Vollenhoven's frequent caution that irrationalism always retains an element of rationalism as its background.

131. A. Troost, *Vakfilosofie van de geloofswetenschap* [Philosophy of the science of faith], passim. See also above, sec. 4.12.

knowledge and science. This trend is also related to more than a hundred and fifty years of various irrationalist reactions to old-fashioned rationalism, such as vitalism, existentialism, personalism and emotional moralism. (Not that these are acceptable alternatives for us.)

At the same time there is also scant agreement in the community of scientific philsophers on the *interpretation* of the generally recognized difference between practical and scientific knowledge. This is due to the fact that philosophical theories of knowledge and science are not, as was long believed, neutral or isolated products of autonomous "thought." Every theory of knowledge and science employs general philosophical or "ontological" concepts and ideas, patterns of thought that largely frame the problems in the theory in question and determine the evaluation of the facts under discussion. There are in fact many theories of knowledge and science. Yet this general philosophical framework that necessarily encases any theory is not religiously neutral either, as we discussed in chapter 2 on the "prolegomena."

15.1.4 IS THERE A THIRD KIND OF KNOWLEDGE?

Meanwhile, in the various special sciences there are many experts who do not attach much importance to the difference between the two types of knowledge. And of course it is tempting for scientists to simply adapt their appreciation of this difference to the abovementioned custom in our culture, the more so since it upholds the public status (and power) of the educated intellectual. The difference between the two types of knowledge is preferably interpreted as a difference on a continuum that starts with primitive, sensory, deficient knowledge and gradually shades off into the more genuine and reliable knowledge of the scientific specialist.

In the last fifty years various schools in philosophy of science have increasingly questioned this traditional attitude. Begun in Antiquity, the tradition pushed ahead during the secularized Renaissance (the rebirth of Antiquity) and was popularized by the Enlightenment. The last hundred years, however, have seen a growing awareness of the distinctiveness and irreplaceable value of typical non-scientific knowledge.

This is particularly true for the science of religion, with its affinity to ethnology and also to the brand of theology that sympathizes with the latter. Indeed, more and more voices today are talking about the need for a *remythologizing* of our conception of religious knowledge. The demythologizing program of Bultmann is no longer the prevailing fashion in theology as it was three decades ago. No doubt this has to do with the irrationalist climate in all kinds of cultural and academic circles and not just in "far-out alternative" groups. Partly in connection with the openness to Eastern religions and philosophies, there is also a revival of "religion," or at least religion is no longer dismissed out of hand as laughable. "Religion is back," the media in our New Age proclaim.

The current trend also calls for a deprofessionalization of various professions and professional language. We can refer here to Albert Schweitzer, who pointed out as early as the 1920s that between pre-theoretical and theoretical thought we need to distinguish a third type of thinking and knowing, which he proposed to call "reflection."[132] Schweitzer believed that this was the hallmark of thinking and knowing in ethics and aesthetics. Philosophy too was to give up the illusion that it was true science; it too consisted of "reflections," a distinct type of knowing. Schweitzer failed to gain much support for this view, however, so we will leave it aside for now.[133]

Nowadays people like to use terms like *reflection, meditation, contemplation,* in order to avoid having to give a consistent account of the difference between theoretical and non-theoretical thought, between worldview and scientific philosophy. They resort to those other terms because they cannot theoretically account for the structural difference in kind. Where Schweitzer at least distinguished three different types of thought and knowledge, they often prefer to fall back on the easy and vague idea of a *continuum* in the "gradual" transition between inferior and superior knowledge.[134] "Knowledge" as such, like "thought," is for many an undivided, fundamentally uniform concept that denotes a general human phenomenon, if with differences in *quality.*

Regarding this continuum of a gradual transition, one can ask:

---

132. A. Schweitzer, *Civilization and Ethics* (London, 1923), chap. iii.

133. Something of it can be spotted in the later philosophy of Georg Picht, who is keenly aware of other truths besides the rational.

134. Thus, for example, along with many others, John M. Frame and Leonard J. Coppes, *The Amsterdam Philosophy: A Preliminary Critique* (Nutley, NJ: Presbyterian & Reformed, 1972), quoted with obvious approval by Jochem Douma, *Another Look at Dooyeweerd: Some Critical Notes Regarding the Philosophy of the Cosmonomic Idea* (Winnipeg: Premier, 1981), pp. 68, 74.

transition from what to what? "Transition" already implies difference. Are we talking about a transition from something that differs in nature or structure, or only about a difference in greater or lesser degrees of precision, completeness, reliability, "purity" within the single phenomenon called "knowledge," which cannot be further differentiated as to kinds? But in that case we are back to square one—to the Western idol of faith in science, where science is a *better* kind of knowledge.

We will now discuss the various features of the two types of knowledge, practical and theoretical, which are generally recognized but differently appreciated and also differently analyzed and characterized.[135] But first a terminological remark.

15.1.5 TERMINOLOGY
Current theory of knowledge and philosophy of science uses a wide variety of terms, each of which has its pros and cons. Especially now that the connection between language and thought is being studied so extensively, authors discuss the difference between "ordinary language," "everyday usage" or "common parlance" as opposed to scientific "jargon," the theoretical knowledge that is formulated in "specialist terms" and in a "technical language" which sometimes can be understood by only a few outside the profession.

As in language, so in discussions about cognition, notice is taken of the difference between "everyday practical or pre-theoretical knowledge" and scientific knowledge or truth. The former is often called pre-scientific knowledge. However correct this term is, it is liable to suggest that this *"pre"*-scientific knowledge no longer plays a role in science, that it has served its purpose and been laid aside, replaced by "better" knowledge. Partly for this reason Dooyeweerd frequently chose to speak of the "knowledge of naive experience," but here too there is the risk of the word "naive" suggesting the same faulty (and also somewhat discriminatory) notions.

---

135. In recent decades some present-day Roman Catholic *Fundamentaltheologie* displays a marked trend toward a more or less strong differentiation in the concepts of knowledge, truth and rationality and particularly in what is seen (I believe rightly) as the principal distinction, that between scientific knowledge and practical knowledge in the sense of life wisdom. For a survey of these movements and conceptions, see the dissertation by Martin Hailer, *Theologie als Weisheit. Sapientiale Konzeptionen in der Fundamentaltheologie* (Heidelberg, 1997).

Nevertheless we still have several useful terms at our disposal. Besides naive or pre-theoretical we also read of everyday, practical, concrete, experiential, or existential, spontaneous, ordinary knowledge, as opposed to scientific, abstract, theoretical, exact, universally valid, detached, impassive knowledge. All these terms have their pros and cons, depending very much on the worldviewish or scientific context in which they are used. Personally I would not commit myself to any one pair of terms, although I do have a slight preference for *practical* versus *theoretical*. All the other terms I therefore take to be roughly akin to, or synonymous with, one of these two.

The only drawback I see in the distinction of "practical" and "theoretical" is that it sometimes carries with it the notion, fashionable today, that the practice of science, including theory formation, is not a deadly serious sector *in the full practice of life*.[136] Reformational philosophy therefore argues for a *Christian practice* of science, both in philosophy and in all the special sciences, if for no other reason than that the practice of science, too, belongs to the practice of life. Theoretical truth, too, is truth, and should positively participate in the fullness of truth, in Christ who IS the truth. In the world of science this can only be realized by way of recognizing the *philosophical basis* of all special sciences and no longer by combining supposedly neutral science with Christian theology.

15.2 STRUCTURAL FEATURES OF PRACTICAL KNOWLEDGE

15.2.1 SYSTASIS

In our cosmology we learned to distinguish the abstract modal aspects present in the concrete entities of reality. These modalities form the gateway to a correct theoretical analysis of any part of reality because they allow us to recognize the ultimately irreducible quality or nature of the phenomena. They can be called scientific ground-categories, basic concepts or core ideas. We will now apply the method of modal analysis to the concrete phenomenon of human knowledge

---

136. All science, with its primary goal of searching for theoretical truth in a certain field, also wants to be useful for everyday practice. The same is true of the science of philosophy. However, the practice at which *philosophy* is directed is the practice of the sciences, in particular the special sciences. They too belong to the *practice of life*; they even represent a highly important sector in our culture!

as it functions both in everybody's daily practice of life and in the scientific work of a small percentage of people. (What follows next can be read as a continuation of sec. 14.2.4.)

One of the main features of the structure of reality, and so also of the practical activities of thought and their yield in "knowledge" or knowing, lies in the factual coherence or interlacement of these modal aspects, particularly in the subject-object relation, that we will examine below.

Practical knowing is integrally interwoven into the experience of life itself. Everything we do as adult human beings contains an element of logically distinguishing between (entitary) this or that, and also between (modal) thus or so. This "element" is not separate or self-existent but is intertwined, rather, with the very language in which we formulate our understanding; it is also intertwined with our action itself. We are not talking here about scientific knowledge but simply about "using our intelligence" in whatever we do.

This feature of *concrete, integral intertwinement with life itself and all its aspects* distinguishes practical thought and knowledge from theoretical thought and knowledge.[137]

In epistemology this can be designated by terms like "systasis," "enstatic" or the "knowing experience."

The technical term "systasis" means: not standing by itself but standing together, not self-sustaining or self-existent, separate or isolated. "Enstatic" means: standing in, not standing opposite like an artificially constructed theoretical "Gegenstand" (object). The latter is mainly characterized by being the product of abstracting (drawing out) a certain aspect and (temporarily) isolating it. More on this in the next section. But first we need to say something yet about practical wisdom.

15.2.2 EXPERIENTIAL KNOWLEDGE AND WISDOM

Whenever practical knowledge, as experienced in everyday life by ourselves and others, relates to concrete distinctive activities—like blacktopping a road, running a household, being introduced to someone we do not know, drinking a cup of tea, and so on—, we call the knowledge so expressed or acquired "experiential knowledge." Intuitively we realize at once that this is a different kind of knowledge than scientific, theoretical knowledge.

In addition, the whole of our practical life often involves *wisdom*.

---

137. Cf. Appendix, Figures 7, 8 and 9.

Our life is full of questions and problems big and small, and there is no course we could enrol in to learn *how to* solve the thousand-and-one major or minor questions that everyday life confronts us with in carrying out our work, raising our children, spending our leisure time, or simply choosing the right food or clothes. Government laws, administrative rules, group customs and traditions, church pronouncements, ethical norms and the like can usually do no more than indicate a very broad *framework* within which life ought to be lived, without making it clear in advance what exactly should be done or not done, said or not said in many unforeseen situations. Usually they do little more than indicate a general *direction*.

The common saying, sincerely meant, that God's Word is a light on our path that shows us the way "in all things" should therefore not be taken formally-rationalistically, in a biblicistic and legalistic sense, as if all our concrete actions in life are normatively indicated by Scripture and Scripture alone. That would be at odds with Scripture itself, which is not a collection of precepts but primarily points to a personal relationship with God ("the fear of the Lord") as "the beginning," the principle, the source and direction of wisdom, and which sometimes also looks positively on the wisdom of heathen peoples or persons, even though such wisdom stems from a different religious source.

Wisdom as a rule is an *intuitive insight* into the normative structures of our life which steer and guide our actions. Even when a farmer prepares his fields prudently, Scripture says, "his God teaches him" (Isa. 28:26). How does this teaching take place? Via the (nontheoretical!) knowability of the laws of existence that God imposes on creation, including (agri)cultural procedures, thus determining their "distinctive nature"—laws of existence in which God's will remains actively present and which man comes to know, partly for this reason, through "experience" and "common sense" (we don't always want to say that man learns them by being "challenged").

15.2.3 The logical subject-object relation

In chapter 6 ("subjects and objects") and in sec. 4.2 we already talked about the intricate interwovenness of the modal aspects which we had theoretically distinguished in cosmology. One of these forms of interwovenness (besides that of analogies) was the modal subject-object relation. We will confine our discussion of this relation to the relation in which the acting subject is man, though the relations between things, plants or animals contain subject-object relations as well.

Modal interwovenness implicitly indicates that the relation between concrete identities is present already on a modal level. That is the cosmological foundation for—the "gateway" to (Daniel Strauss)—a closer analysis of concrete subject-object relations between, say, humans and things. The latter relations are actual, for instance, when a human activity is focused on an object or an event. This may be the case in sensory perception, sensitive enjoyment, lifting a suitcase, aesthetic admiration, owning a thing, running a business, believing Scripture, thus in all activities that we call human "distinguishing" or "knowing."

In these activities the "objects" no longer have a *latent* (i.e., potential) but rather an *opened*, realized "object function" that relates to human actual subject functions, and vice versa. This interrelation or interlacement, owing to which a subject is not possible without objects and objects cannot exist without relating to subjects, is characteristic of all created reality. It is a facet of the general cosmic interwovenness of all individual creatures.

This also applies to the logical-analytical cognitive relation between subject and object. This insight alone can break down the traditional substantialization of subject and object. The modal structural subject-object relation is the potential possibility of every concrete realization of these relations. If things, for example, did not have objective visibility in themselves—if they were never an object in a possible concrete subject-object relation—we would not be able to see them. The same goes for their nameability (lingual object), their hardness or softness (sensory object), their audibility, their knowability, and so forth. Nearly all terms that end in "-ability" point to this objectivity, to these potential object functions.

So these object functions are not just attributed properties; they are these objective properties themselves. They make up the "object-side" which is proper to all entities, which forms "part" of them and without which these entities do not exist.[138] This reality or "property"

---

138. In everyday language we often call things themselves "objects." Our

is also present in the cognitive relation between cognitive subject and cognitive object (cf. Figure 7). We call this the subject-object relation that is characteristic of practical knowledge, as distinct from the more detached artificial, theoretical knowledge arising from the scientific approach to a given cognitive object and the analysis thereof. As we already said, that scientific knowledge is a separate (sub)type of knowledge, which we will discuss in 15.3.

Our logical-analytical thinking and knowing is woven into practical knowledge and wisdom, or to put it philosophically: it is systatically given, enstatically present—Dooyeweerd would say: "enkaptically interlaced." Nobody can call *this* particular wisdom and knowledge "scientific." So in reality this knowledge is not a concrete fact in itself, it is not "separately obtainable," but it is only concrete when encapsulated in a certain concrete activity which itself is otherwise than logically qualified. From there the knowledge gets its *content*.

For theology it is important to bear in mind here that God is not (scientifically speaking) an "object" of our knowledge. Objects are always *creatures*; they constitute a *side* to entities (the "object-side"), endowed with a creaturely structure and interwoven with creaturely subject-functions. "Object" is not just a "name" or a technical term that we have devised and attributed to something; that would be nominalism. This whole topic will have to be dealt with at greater length in the whole complex problem of faith/revelation/theology, thus in the epistemology to be worked out in the context of the philosophy of theology (so not in theology itself, whose field of analysis is altogether different from the analysis of itself as a science).

15.2.4 So-called "sources of knowledge"

The term "source of knowledge" is well-established in our language, also in theology. It is obviously meant to indicate where we "draw" our knowledge from or by what means we can "pick up" the desired knowledge. Thus theologians readily talk about Scripture as our source of knowledge for faith and theology, or about "nature and Scripture" as the source of our knowledge about God. For someone who understands this correctly in the style of faith, the expression,

---

philosophy talks about "objects" not with a view to things themselves, but to a "side" of them, alongside the subject-side. Both "sides" function in an objective or subjective way in all aspects.

though not ideal, is useful. It would not be useful, however, in theology proper, which as a science must make finer distinctions.

For someone not familiar with epistemology the word "source" may wrongly suggest that knowledge and truth are lying "out there somewhere" and that we only need to "pick them up." People may assume, for instance, that the truth about God lies ready for us, if not so much in nature then clearly in Scripture: we merely need to "draw" it from there as from a source.

Strictly speaking, this is an objectivist view which may lead to all kinds of misunderstandings. It is therefore good to realize what the structure, the "architecture" of knowledge or truth looks like. As far as I know, Vollenhoven was the first to point this out, briefly but sharply, when he said: knowledge is the result of "coming to know" and not of drawing ready knowledge from a "source of knowledge." Because of Vollenhoven's notorious succinctness (his "breviloquence"), it is easy to read past this and miss its far-reaching and antithetical force. From a different perspective Henk Geertsema has rightly warned that, in order to characterize "knowledge" we should not be too quick to use the ancient metaphor of "seeing," common since Plato in particular.[139]

Indeed, seeing, but also hearing (as Geertsema proposes) and especially "drawing from a source" are all figures of speech which may have some value as popularizing metaphors but which are unable to give a correct theoretical analysis of the phenomenon of knowledge and knowledge acquisition. Such an analysis requires a conscious cosmological and anthropological totality view as the framework for a theory of the *structure* of human knowledge and its formation.

Following in Vollenhoven's footsteps, I would like to emphasize that knowledge is the result of "coming to know," in other words: of a production process, the cognitive process, the process of knowledge acquisition, of "getting to know." This means that we are primarily dealing with a human activity, regardless whether or not, or to what degree, it is in keeping with the norms obtaining for those activities. The cognitive process yields a result that is "objectified" in concepts and words and is somehow, somewhere, within or without the

---

139. H. G. Geertsema, *Het menselijk karakter van ons kennen* (Amsterdam, 1992), pp. 40–68, at 60. *Editor:* See also idem, "Knowing Within the Context of Creation," *Faith and Philosophy* 25 (2008): 237–60.

functioning subject, "stored" in a book or "deposited" in someone's memory, from where it can later be "retrieved" or "recalled."

Accordingly, we are first of all dealing with subjective *activities* in the cognitive process: with perceiving with eyes and ears or organs of touch; with thinking, pondering, distinguishing; and with possible subactivities such as identifying, formulating; and so on. Next, we are dealing with the somehow permanent *result* of these activities: knowledge or error, or a mixture of both. This last depends on whether or not, and in what measure or respect, the subjective activity in the cognitive process has been carried out in accordance with the norms obtaining for this cognitive activity. The image of "sources of knowledge" in which knowledge, free of any ties, external to us and independently, is objectively "ready to hand" and need only be "drawn" or "picked up"—that image paints a very distorted picture of what knowledge or truth is all about and how it is to be acquired. What is at stake here is a different view of reality, a view, by the way, that is of eminent importance for all kinds of key topics in theology.

15.3 SCIENTIFIC OR THEORETICAL THINKING AND KNOWING

15.3.1 THE THEORETICAL COGNITIVE RELATION ("GEGENSTAND-RELATION")

Whereas the *practical* forms of everyday knowledge are "systatically" or "enstatically" interwoven with the reality of concrete human life itself and encapsulated in non-logically qualified activities, the main characteristic of *theoretical* knowledge is that it is non-systatic, non-enstatic; in other words, it is detached, critically contemplative, and it abstracts one or more particular aspects.

In theoretical knowledge the object of knowledge is not a "given"; it is *made*, artificially. It is made by a human activity that *abstracts* from the full reality of life. And there is more to be said. The result—scientific knowledge—can exist "objectively" by itself as knowledge, thus without being encapsulated in something else. It is an independent entitary reality, logically-analytically qualified, characterized as theoretical and potentially substantialized and objectified in the form of a text in a book or article.

We are indeed dealing with abstraction here. However, there are different kinds of abstraction and the kind in question here is *modal abstraction.* When we are dealing with *concrete "givens"* (!) from full reality one of the possibilities is that we are momentarily having a "restriction of attention" (Vollenhoven). This too is a kind of abstraction from full reality, but it is not yet an abstraction of modal aspects or viewpoints—in other words, it does not follow that it is a kind of theoretical or scientific abstraction. Thoughtful attention involves "abstraction," but that does not necessarily make it scientific thought.

Scientific, modal abstraction means for a given discipline that a concrete field of inquiry, a concrete thing, a concrete event, a concrete mode of human action, is looked at and studied *from the viewpoint of one of its modal aspects,* and primarily *of the qualifying aspect.*

A biologist looks at a pine forest primarily from a different viewpoint than, say, a hunter, an artist, a regional planner or a project developer. So do an economist or a lawyer. Each of these experts sees the same forest from a distinctive point of view and can say things about it that others had not noticed or do not even understand. In the language of philosophy of science: *they abstract a certain (modal) aspect* of the forest and form their primary judgment about it from the viewpoint of that one (modal) aspect. The fact that they secondarily must also take other aspects into account is no more than prudent, for those other aspects also exist. Only, they do not *qualify* the specific expertise each time. Thus in principle every special science can occupy itself with all manner of things, but the particular nature of that science implies a kind of abstraction of a *particular* modal aspect which is of central and primary interest to that science. Thus, on the basis of his Christian worldview, a Christian theologian can consider everything in reality (be it sports, the economy, art, the family, and so on) *from the viewpoint of faith.*

(We should note here that this scientific cognitive relation in Reformational philosophy of science is referred to by Dooyeweerd as the "Gegenstand-relation." The term, and what it stands for, is much debated, but for our purposes I think it is not important enough and too specialized to discuss more fully in an introduction such as this.[140])

It would seem advisable at this juncture to take a moment and shield the principal feature of theoretical knowledge from some popular misunderstandings regarding the nature of science. But first a brief remark on the term "aspect."

---

140. I spend some more time on it in my book *Vakfilosofie van de geloofswetenschap.*

15.3.2 THE TERM "ASPECT"

Above we sometimes added "modal" (in parentheses) to the term "aspect," because in everyday language the word "aspect" is not used in a strictly philosophical sense. It usually refers to no more than a part or a subordinate component and so remains tied to concrete entities. In the context of Reformational philosophy "aspect" is something different: the word does not designate a concrete part or component but an abstract *mode of being*. Not this or that, not this or that part, but this way or that way, thus or so, a quality (cf. sec. 5.2 and 5.3). This meaning of "aspect" relates to the way we talk practically about a certain viewpoint from which something is looked at ("aspect," from *ad-spicere*, to look at something).

15.3.3 METHODICAL AND SYSTEMATIC ARE NOT UNIQUE TO SCIENCE

A popular opinion about the difference between theoretical and non-theoretical knowledge is that the former is methodical and the latter is not. It is curious that this view still occurs in the specialist literature. Everybody knows that methodical work and thought is by no means confined to scientific activities. The popular view obviously is not using the word method in a scientifically well-considered way.

For what is a method? It is an established pattern in the work to be carried out, with a fixed order (a *"hodos"*) of first this and then that. Such orderliness is certainly and necessarily present in scientific work, but no less in everyday actions in much of our practical lives. A window cleaner works just as methodically as a kindergarten teacher in her schoolwork, or as a bricklayer, a house painter, a garbage collector, a housewife, a storekeeper, and so on. Someone who is not methodical in their actions will often in equal measure become chaotic, slipshod, vague, disorderly or capricious. So here, too, we need to talk about two kinds of method: a practical method in our practical lives, and a scientific method in our scientific work (an example of the latter is to always start by distinguishing law-side and subject-side as well as aspects and entities).

We can say roughly the same about what is sometimes called another defining feature of scientific work, namely its systematic quality. Practical human activities are by no means always unsystematic; and conversely, not every scientific discipline strives to work systematically or aims for systematic results. Often that is even disqualified as "scholastic" and "rigidifying" for thought. That is certainly true in the case of a faulty systematics, or a faulty use of systematics; but a sound systematics is usually even heuristically helpful, leading to new discoveries.

In our reactionary, irrationalist times, pervaded by a pragmatic, moralistic ethos, many semi-intellectuals systematically (!) devalue scientific systematics. For philosophy this often means that scientific philosophy is traded in for practical meditations that have a one-sidedly pragmatic focus, serving life outside the world of science in a bid to be "socially relevant" or to advance one's career, gain prestige and make a good living. However vital this worldview approach and practical attitude may be for science, it is not itself science.

Summing up, we can therefore state that "systematic" no more than "methodical" is a clear criterion for distinguishing and characterizing scientific and non-scientific thought and knowledge.

15.3.4 "ISMS" IN SCIENCE

A significant number of the special sciences can be easily recognized as sciences that are focused on a part of reality that is qualified by a particular modal aspect. We can think here of theology, economics, psychology, linguistics, legal science, ethics, logic, sociology, technology, physics, arithmetic and geometry, chemistry, and perhaps even more.

Through the centuries almost every one of these special sciences has had practitioners who for a longer or shorter period claimed to be spokesmen of the most important or all-controlling science, or at least of the necessary foundation for all the other special sciences. All reality, or an important part of it, is then reduced to a form or a resultant of the physical (physicalism), or of "life" (biologism), the psychical (psychologism), language (lingualism), history (historicism), or the logical-analytical (logicism), and what have you. In our time this sort of claim is often made by the linguistic and textual sciences.

All these reductions have a semblance of truth to them, in fact even more than that. By virtue of the "sphere-universality" discussed in sec. 5.11, we can indeed notice everywhere in reality something of every cosmic aspect, so that when a researcher is fascinated by a certain aspect he is tempted to (rightly) discover it everywhere, but (not rightly) to overestimate it and trace and reduce all the rest (in whole or in part) to this one aspect. This leads to the "isms" in science that we talked about earlier.

The phenomenon of the universality of every aspect also leads to an increasing number of specialties within every discipline or university department. As a result, there has been a tendency among administrators to take all kinds of faculties and subfaculties and replace them with teams of "socially relevant" specialists.

15.3.5 Intellectualism and scientism

Another set of "isms" is intellectualism and scientism, sometimes lumped together as "rationalism" or as a "cerebral attitude to life." Intellectualism usually finds knowledge (theoretical but also practical knowledge) more important than all other functions in life—just as others see the economic, the sexual, the moral, and so on, as the most important facet of life. This can easily lead to the suppression of "values" like love, art, faith and sociality.

That said, intellectualism does have a basis in reality. In human life, logical distinguishing serves a kind of foundational function. This explains the founding place or foundational position of the logical-analytical aspect in the series of modalities that involve typically human activities.

In scientism, which is a particular form of intellectualism, scientific knowledge is honored as the ideal type of knowledge and seen as the most important factor in our culture.

Applied to the relation of faith and theology, scientism has the effect that *faith knowledge* (which unquestionably is "enkaptically interlaced" with all typical religious activity and constitutes an indispensable part of concrete faith) is thought to be more important than the full concrete experience of faith itself. One can point to periods and movements in church history where this brand of intellectualism predominated in much dogmatics and also in much preaching. The personal, existential bond of faith with Christ was seen as merely "subjective."

Our time is experiencing a strong reaction to this, following in the footsteps of what the history of the church has always witnessed as reactions against the rationalization of faith: asceticism, monasticism, mysticism, "pietism" or "Further Reformation," present-day "spirituality," and the like. All these are understandable but deficient alternatives to intellectualism and dogmatism. Why not simply "faith"?

Intellectualism can even be trumped by *theologism*. This happens when theological knowledge can no longer be distinguished from faith knowledge and is therefore felt to be of a better or higher quality than ordinary faith knowledge. From this perspective, theology is a "supernatural" and superior faith and the theologian is a better believer than one who is thought merely to adhere to the faith of "ordinary people." In church life this can have disastrous effects and can lead, via a centralist or hierarchical form of church organization, to the domination of the congregation by theological "experts," camouflaged by the biblically inspired notions of "properly ordained" leadership and "pastoral care" in the face of erroneous winds of doctrine. As long as these experts do not make statements that go against "Scripture and the confessions," theologism often goes unrecognized within the atmosphere of the church. If it transpires that theological tension or incompatibility with the (theologically interpreted) confessional standards is at the center of the debate, our lamentable tradition has shown that the theology of the majority of theologians will win the day.

Also typical of the questionable nature of prevailing Christian usage is that theology is sometimes called "Holy Divinity." In reality, a good theologian is no more than a professional Bible scholar, one whose work is no more "holy" than that of a chemist or an economist. In every discipline we are dealing with the works of God. The nature/grace scheme of scholasticism has never been completely eradicated from Protestantism, certainly not in how theology and science in general are regarded. Most arguments about the "tension" (!) between faith and science are pervaded by this dualism. It shows up in various formulations: faith and reason, faith and science, revelation and science, sacred and profane, religious and secular, church and world, and so on and so forth. The underlying view of reality usually lacks a perspectival orientation to reality's transcendent center, its supra-temporal unity and concentration.

15.3.6 GENERAL ENCYCLOPEDIA OF SCIENCE

Another subject in philosophy of science is the general encyclopedia or classification of the branches of science. As part of its content, "encyclopedia" provides a survey of the current state of affairs with regard to the ongoing differentiation of the sciences, including an inventory of distinctive types of scientific practice.

A well-known division in this regard is that between the natural and the social or human sciences. The former group is classified as belonging to the "hard" and the latter to the "soft" sector in science. Along the same lines but going somewhat further, some wish to recognize only the "hard" natural sciences as "real" science. The criterion in this kind of discussion has often first been supplied by and adopted from the traditional empirical natural sciences, which work with "material" that is observable and verifiable, repeatable, supposedly "objective" and recognized as "universally valid." Only then, presumably, can one talk about real science.[141] We will leave the subject aside in this "first introduction," but counter only that *the principal criterion for science* does not lie in the repeatability and verifiability of research, nor in the consensus of experts on its results, but in thought that operates from a *modal-abstracting, aspect-opposing* and detached, critical *attitude,* as distinct from the empathetic systatic thought that is woven into the everyday universal experience of reality, the "knowing experience."

Meanwhile the process of differentiation mentioned above continues almost unabated. We are seeing the arrival of more and more specializations in virtually every discipline. The introduction of all these new subject areas, however, can often be justly criticized when no account is given of the question whether we are dealing with a genuine scientific specialty or simply with a differentiation in a certain practical disciplinary skill, as one can also find among carpenters, attorneys or tax inspectors.

Often the reason for this unchecked proliferation lies in the absence of any orientation to the various cosmic aspects and their inter-wovenness through retrocipations and anticipations. Usually, for the sake of "social relevance," scientists orient themselves much more to certain *sectors* of concrete reality. But these sectors then need to be studied in an "interdisciplinary" way, because the reality of modal diversity, which simply cries out for a corresponding diversity of disciplines, cannot be ignored in the serious practice of science.

In the drawings of Figures 8 and 10 I have obviously confined myself

---

141. It is curious that this limited view of "real science" as chiefly "natural science" is still found in general usage and in a large part of the popular press. I merely mention the "science" column in our country's Christian dailies; but the usage is quite general.

to the main division of sciences, oriented to the modal aspects. The prevailing but perhaps oversimplified view is that Western science began with philosophy, and that various special sciences gradually, particularly in the modern era, separated from it and (supposedly) became independent, *without containing any philosophy*. This diversity soon gave rise to the simple division into the natural sciences and the social or human sciences. This scheme then wrongly became the basis for the distinction of just two kinds of methodology, instead of an investigation into the heuristic value of the hypothesis of Reformational philosophy that each science has to develop its own *aspectually determined* method.

15.3.7 MODAL ABSTRACTION IN SCIENCE AND THE CHARACTER OF PHILOSOPHY

In this connection I should add that this modally-abstracting character of science must not be seen as in conflict with the character of (scientific) philosophy, which is directed at coherence and totality. Philosophy's orientation to the totality exists only on the basis of first modally distinguishing aspectual diversity and the modal qualification of entities.

Moreover, philosophy's orientation to the totality is different from that of the religiously qualified worldview that makes philosophy possible to begin with. It is therefore precisely this philosophical modal analysis of the cosmos which, in line with tradition since the birth of philosophy, gives rise to the philosophical question about the totality and unity-in-diversity, even though philosophy cannot by itself provide a true answer to this question.

Orientation to the totality is already implicit in the created dynamics of all thought and all reality. For "all things" (*ta panta*) were created "unto God" (Rom. 11:36); this is characteristic of all things. These "ta panta" include theoretical thought, regardless of whether it seeks this totality in the right or the wrong direction. But the direction of the right way "unto God" runs via Christ, who is in fact the root unity of all creation and who also called Himself "the way" and "the truth." For all things were created "by Him," the "firstborn of all creation" (Col. 1:15, 16). He is the unity and the totality of all the riches of creation that come to be revealed in time. As "beginning and end," as alpha and omega, He is the sum of the entire alphabet of reality, comprehending and transcending everything in all history.

15.4 Theory and practice in everyday language

15.4.1 How to handle the distinction between theory and practice

It is quite common in journalism and in the language we speak every day to freely make use of the distinction between theory and practice. Of course, this use is not always "scientifically sound." Nor need it be, fortunately. Any such demand would point to an unconscious desire to submit our lives to the dictatorship of intellectualism or scientism.

In Christian circles the distinction of theory and practice is often used when speaking critically about sermons. People will divide sermons into dogmatic homilies and practical, pastoral or experiential ones. The first type is also called *theoretical*. But, people will add, the important thing is what you do with it in *practice*. What is the use of dogmas or dogmatics for everyday life? They are only valuable when "applied" in daily living.

But if philosophy of science has given us any idea of how the structure of science fits within the structure of practical life (of which it is a part after all), and if we recognize the structure of the theoretical cognitive relation (cf. sec. 15.2.3 and 15.3.1), then we have a criterion for a discriminating use of the word "theory" in a practical and a theoretical or scientific sense.

In everyday language "theory" is by no means always real theory. Often, when we say, "That is just a theory," we simply mean a view that is not catching on, or an opinion or conviction that is difficult to put into action, or a truth that plays no further role in our daily lives. Thus we can use the word theory when talking about the practical uselessness of the belief in creation—when the knowledge that God created everything plays no concrete role in our experience of life. In that case religious truth is a "dogmatic truth," a "theoretical" factoid which we certainly do not want to deny but which cannot help us any further either. Creation is then a historical fact from a remote past which is accepted as true because it is in the Bible but which is not an important or topical subject in the confessions, in preaching, or in the congregation's faith experience. When that is the case the belief in creation is said to be a "theory."[142]

---

142. In recent decades the theological doctrine of creation has tried to improve this by strongly involving environmental issues in the discussion. Well-known in this

As we said: we can live with this; everyday language need not always be scientifically sound. But we will now take a critical step beyond that.

15.4.2 IS DISQUALIFICATION OF "THEORY" SOUND?

For all the flexibility required by practical language, once we know the phenomenon of "theory" in its structure we need to be vigilant. The examples in the previous section are liable to reinforce the wrong habit reflected in the popular saying: "In life it always comes down to practice, not theory." There is a tendency to be in reaction against preachers or periods of church history that emphasized, more strongly than today, correct and detailed *knowledge* of the Scriptures.

But as Christians we ought to say: Theory, that is to say genuine scientific theory—the search for theoretical truth, engagement with it in the university, the lab and the private study—is also part of human practice. It is in fact a distinctive and often separate, sometimes even rather isolated sector of human practice, a sector in which only a very small percentage of humanity is active. Nevertheless, it is a small province or region in the kingdom of God, a field where it is no less necessary to live and work along the normative lines of God's revelation. As such it is no less valuable or important than what is called "practice." Only, it is a different part of practice from that in which most people live and are active. That is why Christian academics should pursue and practice Christian science, by which I do *not* mean: neutral science supplemented and "integrated" with theology, or neutral science practiced by Christian men and women, or neutral science in the context of a Bible study group, or neutral science bathed in prayer and thanksgiving. The issue is what Reformational philosophy calls *the inner reformation* of scientific thought itself, via a different, pre-theoretical view of reality based on biblical faith. In one word: the issue is *Christian* science. The case is no different from what people pursue and practice elsewhere, as in Christian politics, or Christian health care, or an *integrally* Christian way of engaging in work, sports, art, and so on.

---

respect is the creation theology of authors like Jürgen Moltmann, Abraham van de Beek, Christian Link, Leo Scheffczyk, Wolfhart Pannenberg, Alexandre Ganoczy, Oswald Bayer, and others. No doubt this is a well-intentioned and necessary enterprise. However, in my view it is far from sufficient and in method and argumentation often unacceptable, though I readily concur with the practical conclusion that we must treat nature responsibly also in terms of faith.

Starting from a Christian philosophy of science, we must guard against discrediting or devaluing the work of theory building in science. In its own sphere Christian orthodoxy still has to wage a difficult battle against traditional influences of non-Christian cosmologies, anthropologies and theories of science which are also operative and often deliberately sought out in theology. This last occurs thanks to the traditional basis of all theological "scholasticism," which believes that faith and science should be integrated yet is unaware of the non-Christian faith hidden in so-called neutral science. That is why we plead for a renewal of Christian theology on the basis of Reformational philosophy.[143] The pursuit of (theoretical) theology, too, is part of the practice of life, bound by God's ordinances for life, in this case for thought in science. But that project will have to be set out more fully in the special philosophy of theology.

15.4.3 THEORY AND PRACTICE IN THE PURSUIT OF SCIENCE

We have thus indicated the line of approach to be taken as we engage in scientific theology. In all its "subjects" or subdisciplines theology works with headings and divisions of that section of reality on which its research is focused. In doing so it tends to use standard concepts and schemas. Precisely these borrowings always manifest a worldviewish and/or philosophical view of reality.

Let us take an example. A theologian cannot talk scientifically about "faith" without having taken a position with respect to the philosophical/anthropological dilemma that faith is either an entirely distinctive human function called believing, or it is composed of other functions (which are recognized as distinct) so that faith is seen as a sum of, say, intellect plus love, or intellect plus feeling, knowledge plus trust, or similar combinations.[144] The latter choice will give rise to many fundamentally insoluble problems that daily engross a

---

143. Cf. my address of 1990 at the Gereformeerd Seminarie in Amersfoort, entitled "Is er vernieuwing van de gereformeerde theologie mogelijk? Reformatorische wijsbegeerte als onmisbare grondslag" [Is a renewal of Reformed theology possible? Reformational philosophy as indispensable foundation] (avail. by writing to Zeegat 14, 3224 SJ Hellevoetsluis, Neth.).

144. A striking example is Luther's claim on the basis of 1 Thess. 5:23 that man consists of three parts: body, soul and spirit. With the help of this scheme he developed his view of human life in his exegesis of the Magnificat (1520). Cf. *Evangelischer Erwachsenen Katechismus*, 6th ed. (Gütersloh, 2000), pp. 153–55.

host of Christian media. Many believers fret and brood over these problems in their search for a "balance," and many theologians battle against one-sided positions which put too much emphasis on this or that part of faith. Even a great deal of dissension in the church is maintained in this way. A better philosophical view of reality could prevent or remedy many insoluble issues in the traditional dilemmas of theological thought.

For a theology student who aspires to becoming a pastor it is therefore important to know about these philosophical problems. Not that he now needs to bring a different philosophy or a different theology to the congregation—the traditional scientistic ideal of enlightenment—, but he can try to prevent much anxious introspection by avoiding false theories about what faith is, or by exposing them as products of a non-Christian view of reality.

Our approach to the pursuit of theology is therefore that philosophy needs to be applied to the field of theology in the transitional area that still forms part of philosophy but that tries to make philosophical insights fruitful for theology. That was the idea behind the subject that used to be called "encyclopedia" and that is making a big comeback in our time under the name *Fundamentaltheologie*.[145] In Protestantism, too, many theological camps are (finally) coming over to the view that theology is intrinsically tied to philosophical concepts and schemas regarding the structures of reality.

Although this does not make the study of a discipline any easier, it does make it more fruitful. In practice people have therefore long learned that the necessary knowledge of philosophy in every discipline does not benefit most from voluminous books on the history of philosophy with its countless schools and important philosophers. This only creates the foolish suggestion that students can decide for themselves with which philosophy they feel most comfortable. Much better to provide a brief survey of the history of philosophy, combined with the special philosophy geared to the discipline in question.

15.4.4 THEORY AND PRACTICE WITHIN THE TOTAL PRACTICE OF LIFE

Although it is true, therefore, that theorizing itself is a legitimate and

---

145. Incidentally, this "fundamental theology" is fundamental all right, but it is not theology, even though it ought to be taught in a theological faculty or seminary.

useful part of practical life in the sphere of scientific study, this does not say everything about the relation *within* the total practice of life between this totality as a whole and its sector of (theoretical) scientific study.

Nobody today, not even in anti-rationalist circles, will deny the great importance of science in the sense of practical usefulness. What matters for us now is that we do not lapse either into the one-sidedness of scientistic overestimation or into the opposite extreme of irrationalism and "practicism." The correct view, to say it once again, does not lie in a "balance" between one-sided positions but first of all in a practical religious view of the call to live the Christian life in the totality of our existence. That view does not depend on the philosophical view of the totality, though it is surely deepened and stimulated by it, particularly when it is applied in the philosophy of science. Precisely because the entire field of scientific practice is neither more nor less than an important but limited sector of life as a whole, it is crucial to view and live this part of practical life, too, in terms of our worldview and our deepest religious faith.

APPENDIX

Twelve Figures To Accompany The Text

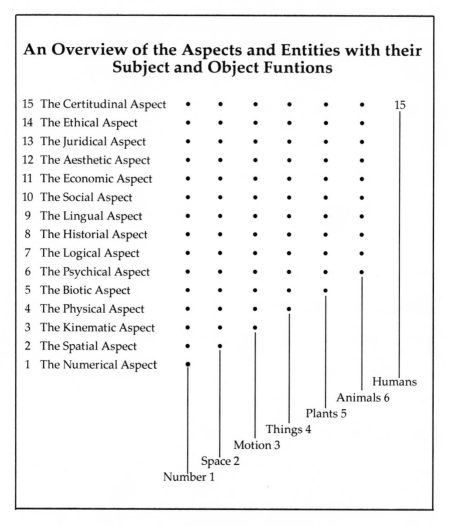

Figure 1

Vertical lines indicate the number of Subject functions,
dotted lines the Object functions.

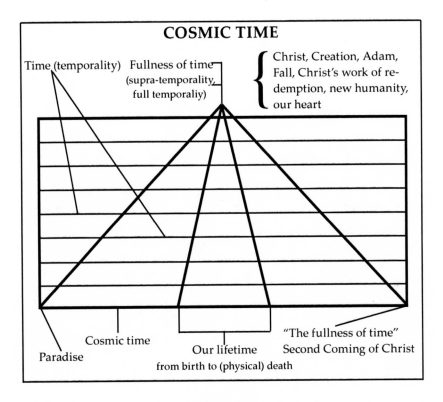

Figure 2

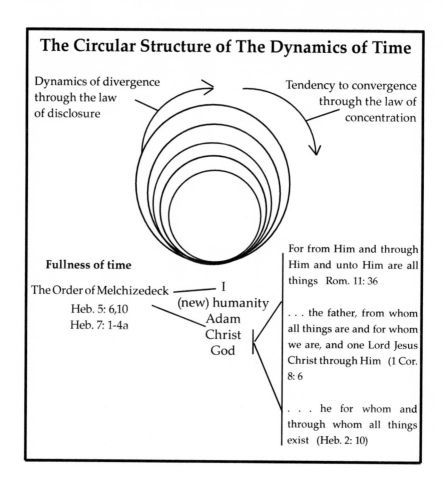

Figure 3

SCHEMATIC REPRESENTATION OF
THE BODY'S STRUCTURE

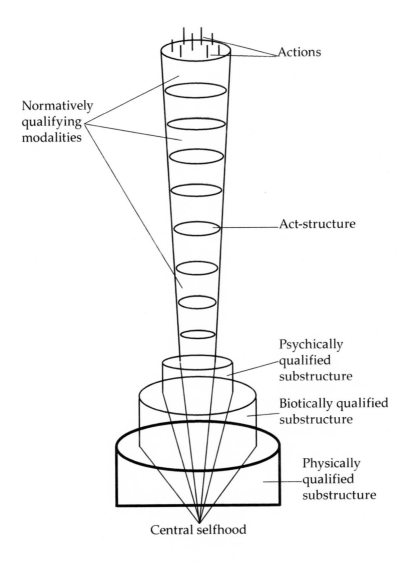

Figure 4

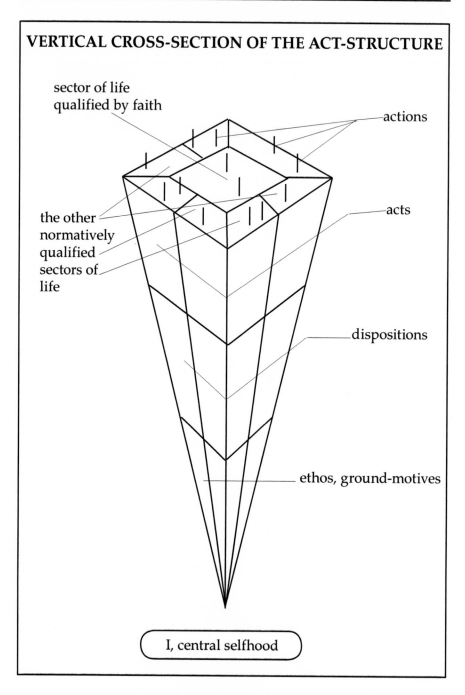

Figure 5

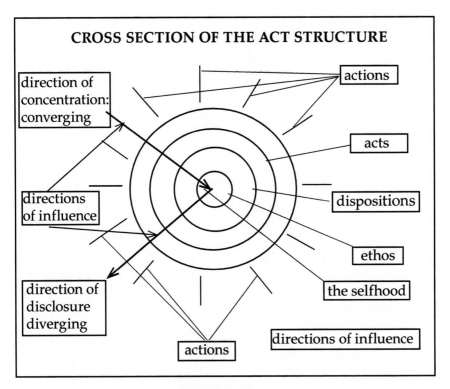

Figure 6

Figure 7

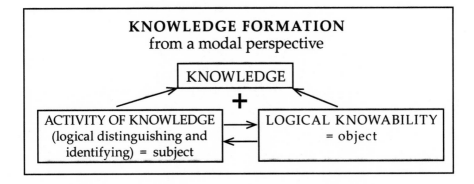

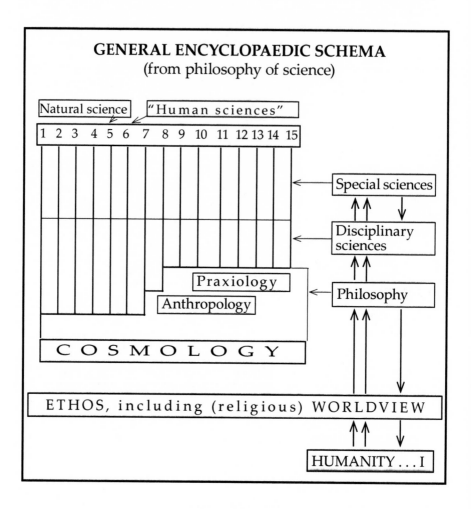

Figure 8

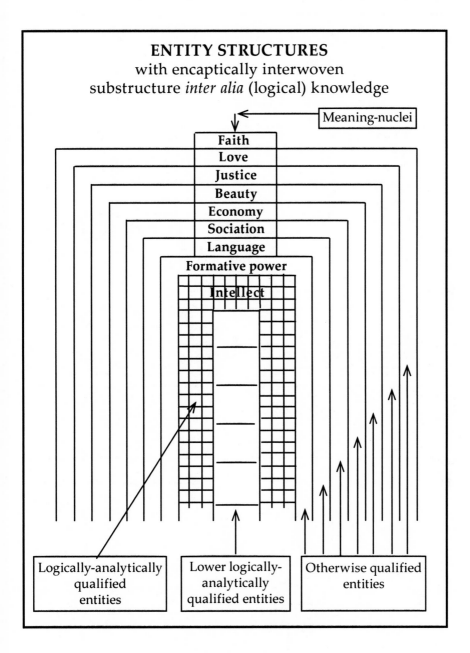

Figure 9

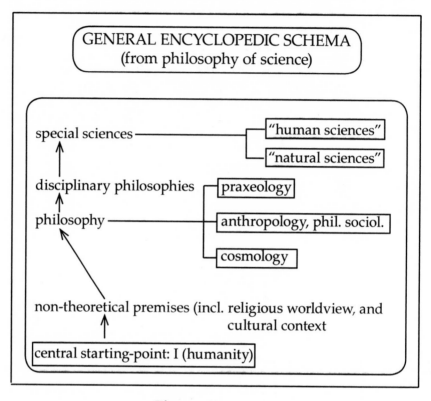

Figure 10

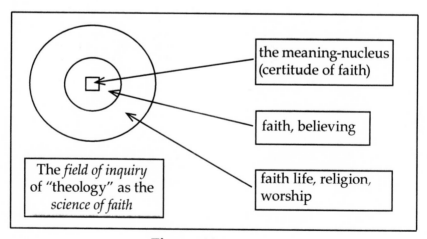

Figure 11

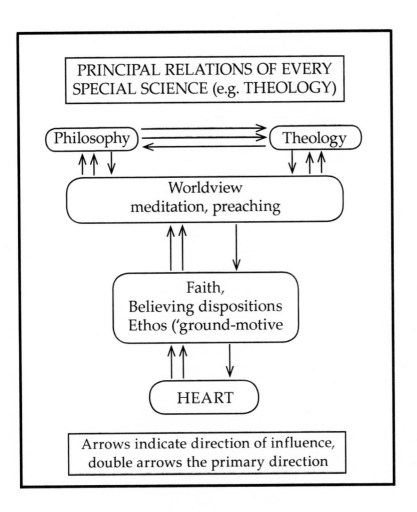

Figure 12

Glossary

[The following glossary of Dooyeweerd's technical terms and neologisms is reproduced and edited by Daniël F. M. Strauss, with the permission of its author, Albert M. Wolters, from C. T. McIntire, ed., *The Legacy of Herman Dooyeweerd: Reflections on Critical Philosophy in the Christian Tradition* (University Press of America, Lanham MD, 1985), 167–171.]

THIS GLOSSARY OF HERMAN DOOYEWEERD'S terms is an adapted version of the one published in L. Kalsbeek, Contours of a Christian Philosophy (Toronto: Wedge, 1975). It does not provide exhaustive technical definitions but gives hints and pointers for a better understanding. Entries marked with an asterisk are those terms which are used by Dooyeweerd in a way which is unusual in English-speaking philosophical contexts and are, therefore, a potential source of misunderstanding. Words or phrases in small caps and beginning with a capital letter refer to other entries in this glossary.

* **ANALOGY** – (see LAW-SPHERE)– Collective name for a RETROCI-PATION or an ANTICIPATION.

* **ANTICIPATION** – An ANALOGY within one MODALITY referring to a later modality. An example is "efficiency," a meaning-moment which is found within the historical modality, but which points forward to the later economic modality. Contrast with RETROCIPATION.

* **ANTINOMY** – Literally "conflict of laws" (from Greek anti, "against," and nomos, "law"). A logical contradiction arising out of a failure to distinguish the different kinds of law valid in different MODALITIES. Since ontic laws do not conflict (Principium Exclusae Antinomiae), an antinomy is always a logical sign of ontological reductionism.

* **ANTITHESIS** – Used by Dooyeweerd (following Abraham Kuyper) in a specifically religious sense to refer to the fundamental spiritual opposition between the kingdom of God and the kingdom of darkness. See Galatians 5:17. Since this is an opposition between regimes, not realms, it runs through every department of human life and culture, including philosophy and the academic enterprise as a whole, and through the heart of every believer as he or she struggles to live a life of undivided allegiance to God.

ASPECT – A synonym for MODALITY.

COSMONOMIC IDEA – Dooyeweerd's own English rendering of the Dutch term wetsidee. Occasionally equivalents are "transcendental ground idea" or "transcendental basic idea." The intention of this new term is to bring to expression that there exists an unbreakable coherence between God's law (nomos) and created reality (cosmos) factually subjected to God's law.

DIALECTIC – In Dooyeweerd's usage: an unresolvable tension, within a system or line of thought, between two logically irreconcilable polar positions. Such a dialectical tension is characteristic of each of the three non-Christian GROUND-MOTIVES which Dooyeweerd sees as having dominated western thought.

* ENKAPSIS (ENKAPTIC) – A neologism borrowed by Dooyeweerd from the Swiss biologist Heidenhain, and derived from the Greek enkaptein, "to swallow up." The term refers to the structural interlacements which can exist between things, plants, animals, and societal structures which have their own internal structural principle and independent qualifying function. As such, enkapsis is to be clearly distinguished from the part-whole relation, in which there is a common internal structure and qualifying function.

FACTUAL SIDE – General designation of whatever is subjected to the LAW-SIDE of creation (see SUBJECT-SIDE).

FOUNDING FUNCTION – The earliest of the two modalities which characterize certain types of structural wholes. The other is called the GUIDING FUNCTION. For example, the founding function of the family is the biotic modality.

* GEGENSTAND – A German word for "object," used by Dooyeweerd as a technical term for a modality when abstracted from the coherence of time and opposed to the analytical function in the theoretical attitude of thought, thereby establishing the Gegenstand-relation. Gegenstand is therefore the technically precise word for the object of SCIENCE, while "object" itself is reserved for the objects of NAIVE EXPERIENCE.

GROUND-MOTIVE – The Dutch term grondmotief, used by Dooyeweerd in the sense of fundamental motivation, driving force. He distinguished four basic ground-motives in the history of Western civilization:

(1) form and matter, which dominated pagan Greek philosophy;

(2) nature and grace, which underlay medieval Christian synthesis thought; (3) nature and freedom, which has shaped the philosophies of modern times; and (4) creation, fall, and redemption, which lies at the root of a radical and integrally scriptural philosophy.

GUIDING FUNCTION – The highest subject-function of a structural whole (e.g. stone, animal, business enterprise, or state). Except in the case of humans, this function is also said to QUALIFY the structural whole. It is called the guiding function because it "guides" or "leads" its earlier functions. For example, the guiding function of a plant is the biotic. The physical function of a plant (as studied, e.g., by biochemistry) is different from physical functioning elsewhere because of its being "guided" by the biotic. Also called "leading function."

* HEART – The concentration point of human existence; the supra-temporal focus of all human temporal functions; the religious root unity of humans. Dooyeweerd says that it was his rediscovery of the biblical idea of the heart as the central religious depth dimension of human multifaceted life which enabled him to wrestle free from neo-Kantianism and phenomenology. The Scriptures speak of this focal point also as "soul," "spirit," and "inner man." Philosophical equivalents are Ego, I, I-ness, and Selfhood. It is the heart in this sense which survives death, and it is by the religious redirection of the heart in regeneration that all human temporal functions are renewed.

* IMMANENCE PHILOSOPHY – A name for all non-Christian philosophy, which tries to find the ground and integration of reality within the created order. Unlike Christianity, which acknowledges a transcendent Creator above all things, immanence philosophy of necessity absolutizes some feature or aspect of creation itself.

* INDIVIDUALITY-STRUCTURE – This term represents arguably one of the most difficult concepts in Dooyeweerd's philosophy. Coined in both Dutch and English by Dooyeweerd himself it has led sometimes to serious misunderstandings amongst scholars. Over the years there have been various attempts to come up with an alternate term, some of which are described below, but in the absence of a consensus it was decided to leave the term the way it is. It is the general name or the characteristic law (order) of concrete things, as given by virtue of creation. Individuality-structures belong to the law-side of reality. Dooyeweerd uses the term individuality-structure to indicate the applicability of a structural order for the existence of individual entities. Thus the structural laws for the state, for marriage, for works of art, for mosquitoes, for sodium chloride, and so forth are called individuality structures. The idea of an individual whole is determined by an individuality-structure which precedes the theoretical analysis of its modal functions. The identity of an individual whole is a relative unity in a multiplicity of functions. (See MODALITY.) Van Riessen prefers to call this law for entities an identity-structure, since as such it guarantees the persistent identity of all entities, *Wijsbegeerte,* [Kampen, 1970], 158). In his work *Alive, An Enquiry into the Origin and Meaning of Life.* Vallecito, California: Ross House Books, 1984, M. Verbrugge introduces his own distinct systematic account concerning the nature of (what he calls) functors, a word first introduced by Hendrik Hart for the dimension of individuality-structures (cf. Hart: *Understanding Our World, Towards an Integral Ontology.* New York, 1984, 445–446). As a substitute for the notion of an individuality structure, Verbrugge advances the term: idionomy (cf. *Alive,* 42, 81ff., 91ff.). Of course this term may also cause misunderstanding if it is taken to mean that each individual creature (subject) has its own unique law. What is intended is that every type of law (nomos) is meant to delimit and determine

unique subjects. In other words, however specified the universality of the law may be, it can never, in its bearing upon unique individual creatures, itself become something uniquely individual. Another way of grasping the meaning of Dooyeweerd's notion of an individuality-structure is, in following an oral suggestion by Roy Clouser (Zeist, August 1986), to call it a type-law (from Greek: *typonomy*). This simply means that all entities of a certain type conform to this law. The following perspective given by M.D. Stafleu elucidates this terminology in a systematic way (*Time and Again, A Systematic Analysis of the Foundations of Physics.* Toronto: Wedge Publishing Foundation, 1980, 6, 11): typical laws (type-laws/typonomies, such as the Coulomb law – applicable only to charged entities and the Pauli principle – applicable only to fermions) are special laws which apply to a limited class of entities only, whereas modal laws hold universally for all possible entities. D.F.M. Strauss ("Inleiding tot die Kosmologie." SACUM, [1980]) introduces the expression entity structures. The term entity comprises both the individuality and the identity of the thing concerned – therefore it accounts for the respective emphases found in Dooyeweerd's notion of individuality-structures and in Van Riessen's notion of identity structures. The following words of Dooyeweerd show that both the individuality and identity of an entity is determined by its individuality-structure: "In general we can establish that the factual temporal duration of a thing as an individual and identical whole is dependent on the preservation of its structure of individuality" (*A New Critique*, vol.3,79).

IRREDUCIBILITY (IRREDUCIBLE) – Incapability of theoretical reduction. This is the negative way of referring to the unique distinctiveness of things and aspects which we find everywhere in creation and which theoretical thought must respect. Insofar as everything has its own peculiar created nature and character, it cannot be understood in terms of categories foreign to itself.

* LAW – The notion of creational law is central to Dooyeweerd's philosophy. Everything in creation is subject to God's law for it, and accordingly law is the boundary between God and creation. Scriptural synonyms for law are "ordinance," "decree," "commandment," "word," and so on. Dooyeweerd stresses that law is not in opposition to, but the condition for true freedom. See also NORM and LAW-SIDE.

LAW-SIDE – The created cosmos, for Dooyeweerd, has two correlative "sides": a law-side and a factual side (initially called: SUBJECT-SIDE). The former is simply the coherence of God's laws or ordinances for creation; the latter is the totality of created reality which is subject to those laws. It is important to note that the law-side always holds universally.

LAW-SPHERE (see MODAL STRUCTURE and MODALITY)– The circle of laws qualified by a unique, irreducible, and indefinable meaning-nucleus is known as a law-sphere. Within every law-sphere temporal reality has a modal function and in this function is subjected (French: *sujet*) to the laws of the modal spheres. Therefore every law-sphere has a law-side and a subject-side that are given only in unbreakable correlation with each other. (See DIAGRAM on p. 347.)

* MEANING – Dooyeweerd uses the word "meaning" in an unusual sense. By it he means the referential, non-self-sufficient character of created reality in that it points beyond itself to God as Origin. Dooyeweerd stresses that reality is meaning in this sense and that, therefore, it does not have meaning. "Meaning" is the Christian alternative to the metaphysical substance of immanence philosophy. "Meaning" becomes almost a synonym for "reality." Note the many compounds formed from it: meaning-nucleus, meaning-side, meaning-moment, meaning-fullness.

* **MEANING-NUCLEUS** – The indefinable core meaning of a MODALITY.

MODALITY (See MODAL STRUCTURE and LAW-SPHERE)– One of the fifteen fundamental ways of being, distinguished by Dooyeweerd. As modes of being, they are sharply distinguished from the concrete things which function within them. Initially Dooyeweerd distinguished fourteen aspects only, but in 1950 he introduced the kinematical aspect of uniform movement between the spatial and the physical aspects. Modalities are also known as "modal functions," "modal aspects," or as "facets" of created reality. (See DIAGRAM on p. 347.)

MODAL STRUCTURE (see MODALITY and LAW-SPHERE)– The peculiar constellation, in any given modality, of its meaning-moments (anticipatory, retrocipatory, nuclear). Contrast INDIVIDUALITY-STRUCTURE.

* **NAIVE EXPERIENCE** – Human experience insofar as it is not "theoretical" in Dooyeweerd's precise sense. "Naive" does not mean unsophisticated. Sometimes called "ordinary" or "everyday" experience. Dooyeweerd takes pains to emphasize that theory is embedded in this everyday experience and must not violate it.

NORM (NORMATIVE) – Postpsychical laws, that is, modal laws for the analytical through pistical law-spheres (see LAW-SPHERE and DIAGRAM on p. 347). These laws are norms because they need to be positivized (see POSITIVIZE) and can be violated, in distinction from the "natural laws" of the preanalytical spheres which are obeyed involuntarily (e.g., in a digestive process).

* **NUCLEAR-MOMENT** – A synonym for MEANING-NUCLEUS and LAW-SPHERE, used to designate the indefinable core meaning of a MODALITY or aspect of created reality.

* **OBJECT** – Something qualified by an object function and thus correlated to a subject function. A work of art, for instance, is qualified by its correlation to the human subjective function of aesthetic appreciation. Similarly, the elements of a sacrament are pistical objects.

OPENING PROCESS – The process by which latent modal anticipations are "opened" or actualized. The modal meaning is then said to be "deepened." It is this process which makes possible the cultural development (differentiation) of society from a primitive ("closed," undifferentiated) stage. For example, by the opening or disclosure of the ethical anticipation in the juridical aspect, the modal meaning of the legal aspect is deepened and society can move from the principle of "an eye for an eye" to the consideration of extenuating circumstances in the administration of justice.

* **PHILOSOPHY** – In Dooyeweerd's precise systematic terminology, philosophy is the encyclopedic science, that is, its proper task is the theoretical investigation of the overall systematic integration of the various scientific disciplines and their fields of inquiry. Dooyeweerd also uses the term in a more inclusive sense, especially when he points out that all philosophy is rooted in a pretheoretical religious commitment and that some philosophical conception, in turn, lies at the root of all scientific scholarship.

POSITIVIZE – A word coined to translate the Dutch word *positiveren*, which means to make positive in the sense of being actually valid in a given time or place. For example, positive law is the legislation which is in force in a given country at a particular time; it is contrasted with the legal principles which lawmakers must positivize as legislation. In a general sense, it refers to the responsible implementation of all normative principles in human life as embodied, for example, in state legislation, economic policy, ethical guidelines, and so on.

QUALIFY – The GUIDING FUNCTION of a thing is said to qualify it in the sense of characterizing it. In this sense a plant is said to be qualified by the biotic and a state by the juridical [aspects].

* **RADICAL** – Dooyeweerd frequently uses this term with an implicit reference to the Greek meaning of radix = root. This usage must not be confused with the political connotation of the term radical in English. In other works Dooyeweerd sometimes paraphrases his use of the term radical with the phrase: penetrating to the root of created reality.

* **RELIGION (RELIGIOUS)** – For Dooyeweerd, religion is not an area or sphere of life but the all-encompassing and direction-giving root of it. It is service of God (or a substitute no-god) in every domain of human endeavor. As such, it is to be sharply distinguished from religious faith, which is but one of the many acts and attitudes of human existence. Religion is an affair of the HEART and so directs all human functions. Dooyeweerd says religion is "the innate impulse of the human selfhood to direct itself toward the true or toward a pretended absolute Origin of all temporal diversity of meaning" (*A New Critique*, vol.1, 57).

* **RETROCIPATION** – A feature in one MODALITY which refers to, is reminiscent of, an earlier one, yet retaining the modal qualification of the aspect in which it is found. The "extension" of a concept, for example, is a kind of logical space: it is a strictly logical affair, and yet it harks back to the spatial modality in its original sense. See ANTICIPATION.

* **SCIENCE** – Two things are noted about Dooyeweerd's use of the term "science." In the first place, as a translation of the Dutch word wetenschap (analogous to the German word Wissenschaft), it embraces all scholarly study – not only the natural sciences but also the social sciences and the humanities, including theology and philosophy. In the second place, science is always, strictly speaking, a matter of modal abstraction, that is, of analytically lifting an aspect out of the temporal coherence in which it is found and examining it in the Gegenstand-relation. But in this investigation it does not focus its theoretical attention upon the modal structure of such an aspect itself; rather, it focuses on the coherence of the actual phenomena which function within that structure. Modal abstraction as such must be distinguished from NAIVE EXPERIENCE. In the first sense, therefore, "science" has a wider application in Dooyeweerd than is usual in English-speaking countries, but in the second sense it has a more restricted, technical meaning.

SPHERE SOVEREIGNTY – A translation of Kuyper's phrase souvereiniteit in eigen kring, by which he meant that the various distinct spheres of human authority (such as family, church, school, and business enterprise) each have their own responsibility and decision-making power which may not be usurped by those in authority in another sphere, for example, the state. Dooyeweerd retains this usage but also extends it to mean the IRREDUCIBILITY of the modal aspects. This is the ontical principle on which the societal principle is based since each of the societal "spheres" mentioned is qualified by a different irreducible modality.

* **SUBJECT** – Used in two senses by Dooyeweerd: (1) "subject" as

distinguished from LAW, (2) "subject" as distinguished from OBJECT. The latter sense is roughly equivalent to common usage; the former is unusual and ambiguous. Since all things are "subject" to LAW, objects are also subjects in the first sense. Dooyeweerd's matured conception, however, does not show this ambiguity. By distinguishing between the law-side and the factual side of creation, both subject and object (sense (2)) are part of the factual side.

SUBJECT-SIDE – The correlate of LAW-SIDE, preferably called the factual side. Another feature of the factual subject-side is that it is only here that individuality is found.

SUBSTRATUM – The aggregate of modalities preceding a given aspect in the modal order. The arithmetic, spatial, kinematic, and physical, for example, together form the substratum for the biotic. They are also the necessary foundation upon which the biotic rests, and without which it cannot exist. See SUPERSTRATUM (and the DIAGRAM on p. 347).

SUPERSTRATUM – The aggregate of modalities following a given aspect in the modal order. For example, the pistical, ethical, juridical and aesthetic together constitute the superstratum of the economic. See SUBSTRATUM.

* SYNTHESIS – The combination, in a single philosophical conception, of characteristic themes from both pagan philosophy and biblical religion. It is this feature of the Christian intellectual tradition, present since patristic times, with which Dooyeweerd wants to make a radical break. Epistemologically seen, the term synthesis is used to designate the way in which a multiplicity of features is integrated within the unity of a concept. The re-union of the logical aspect of the theoretical act of thought with its non-logical "Gegenstand" is called an inter-modal meaning-synthesis.

* TIME – In Dooyeweerd, a general ontological principle of intermodal continuity, with far wider application than our common notion of time, which is equated by him with the physical manifestation of this general cosmic time. It is, therefore, not coordinate with space. All created things, except the human HEART, are in time. At the law-side time expresses itself as time-order and at the factual side (including subject-subject and subject-object relations) as time duration.

TRANSCENDENTAL – A technical term from the philosophy of Kant denoting the a priori structural conditions which make human experience (specifically human knowledge and theoretical thought) possible. As such it is to be sharply distinguished from the term "transcendent." Furthermore, the basic (transcendental) Idea of a philosophy presupposes the transcendent and central sphere of consciousness (the human HEART). This constitutes the second meaning in which Dooyeweerd uses the term transcendental: through its transcendental ground-Idea, philosophy points beyond itself to its ultimate religious foundation transcending the realm of thought.

WETSIDEE – The Dutch original of COSMONOMIC IDEA , literally "law idea." Dooyeweerd's philosophy in known in Holland as the *Wijsbegeerte der Wetsidee* (philosophy of the laws idea). The name derives from the central place of creational LAW in Dooyeweerd's thought.

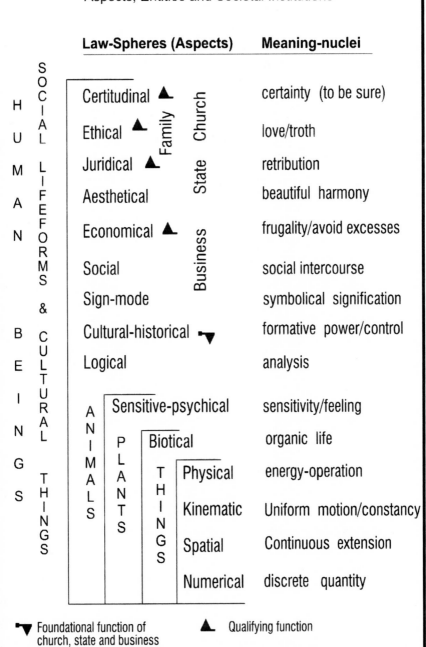

CREATURES SUBJECTED TO CREATIONAL LAWS

Aspects, Entities and Societal Institutions

Law-Spheres (Aspects)	Meaning-nuclei
Certitudinal ▲	certainty (to be sure)
Ethical ▲	love/troth
Juridical ▲	retribution
Aesthetical	beautiful harmony
Economical ▲	frugality/avoid excesses
Social	social intercourse
Sign-mode	symbolical signification
Cultural-historical ▼	formative power/control
Logical	analysis
Sensitive-psychical	sensitivity/feeling
Biotical	organic life
Physical	energy-operation
Kinematic	Uniform motion/constancy
Spatial	Continuous extension
Numerical	discrete quantity

▼ Foundational function of church, state and business   ▲ Qualifying function

347

Index of Scripture Passages

INDEX OF NAMES

Index of Subjects

221n, 327; *see also* original sin
family 53, 104, 106, 117, 193, 229, 273, 275
feminism 228
Fides et Ratio (encyclical) 252n, 256
Fides quadrat intellectum 147
founding aspect or function 106, 118, 293
– of church 233
– of family 229
– of marriage 106, 224
freedom 57, 60, 71, 110, 180, 196, 222, 228, 249, 250, 270
– vs. nature 36, 207-12, 239
Free University xiv
fullness
– in Christ 17, 18, 19, *et passim*
– of time 40, 142, 144, 146-48, 159, 161, 172, 193, 327, 328
full temporal 31, 40-41, 51, 141n, 142-48, 161, 177, 180, 181, 194, 237, 327
fundamentalism 115, 129, 208, 221n, 295
Fundamentaltheologie 7, 305n, 323
Further Reformation, 316; *see also* Reformation, the Second
futures market 156

Gegenstand 92-93, 307, 312-13
gender 106, 224, 225, 229
general revelation: *see* revelation, creational
genotypes 111, 118
ground-motive 13, 33, 60, 186, 200, 202-12, 204n, 239, 330, 335; *see also* dualism
– biblical 205, 209, 285-86
guiding function 107, 108

heart 41-42, 83, 115, 139, 144, 145, 153, 154, 160, 161, 173-79, 186, 190, 193-97, 200, 201, 206, 207, 212, 221n, 222, 265-66, 270-74, 295, 301, 327, 335
heaven, heavenly 6n, 16, 20, 49, 51, 100, 126, 143, 159, 181, 183, 190, 220, 234, 244
Heidelberg Catechism, on
– faith 64, 82
– good works 114
– justification 89
– the natures of Christ 283
– providence 56n
– the sixth commandment 114, 276
Higher Criticism 46, 221n, 295
historical aspect 77, 107, 131, 155, 233
historical law 243
historical relativism, historicism 229-30, 241, 267, 315
historical relativity 104
Historie vs. Geschichte 147-48, 221n
history (event) 90, 128, 129, 131, 147, 162, 184, 194, 221n, 242, 274, 294, 319
– periods in 49, 126-31, 154-55, 211, 256
– primordial 129
– personal 175, 186
– salvation 143
– and Christ 18, 319
history (science) 53, 115, 127-28, 147, 221n, 294-96
holism 43
holocaust 275
Holy Spirit 190, 205, 212
homosexual "marriage" 225
horizontalism 37, 40n, 43, 52, 57, 59, 60, 142, 171, 179, 193,

– religious 304
– scientific 252, 247, 292-316
– self- 161, 223n, 287
– theoretical 41, 84, 296,
    305-06, 310-16
– acquisition of 53, 284,
    287-92, 311
– sources of 287n, 310-12
– theory of 279-324
– types of 292-97
– acc. to Geertsema 311
– acc. to Vollenhoven, 311
– and truth 41, 284-85, 291
    See also faith knowledge

language 64, 72, 73, 77, 78-83,
    114, 155, 305, 307, 333
– biblical 78, 105
– Dooyeweerdian 39, 73, 76,
    80, 177, 237n
– everyday (ordinary, spoken)
    55, 76, 80, 84, 89, 100, 101, 190,
    197, 217, 230, 235, 239, 251, 285,
    294, 305, 309n, 314, 320-21
– legal 270
– non-scientific 55, 181
– philosophical 15, 190, 313
– poetic 105, 108, 203, 290
– religious (faith) 143, 161, 219,
    286
– scientific 76, 89, 114, 251n
– technical 105, 241, 305
– theological 105
language games 14, 71, 83, 203
law-order 55-57, 84-86, 118, 125n,
    145, 186, 242, 272
law-side 35, 56-63, 74, 75, 85, 86,
    89-110, 113, 266, 289
– as the correlate of subject-side
    56, 60-62, 117, 145-48, 184, 283,
    288, 314

law-spheres 15, 73-75, 76, 78, 170;
    see also modalities
liturgical, liturgy 182, 234, 236
logic, logical 5, 12, 26, 51n, 65, 67n,
    77, 82, 95, 102, 154, 162, 202,
    271, 275n, 279-81, 291-307, 310,
    316, 326, 331, 333
– laws (norms, principles) of 74,
    271, 279, 288-89
– limits of 17, 30, 31, 50, 71, 124,
    137, 138, 149, 160, 161, 175, 210,
    239, 262, 263, 276, 285
– as a formal tool xv, 279
– as a special science 279-88,
    308-10, 315
– and faith 108
– and philosophy 202, 238
– and scholasticism 208
– and time 154
logical-analytical 4, 78, 170, 284,
    287-91, 294, 296, 309, 310, 312,
    316
logicism 81, 83, 282-83, 315
love 62, 63, 65, 66, 72, 77, 79, 81,
    104, 106, 108, 114, 208, 266, 333
– familial 104, 229, 254
– filial 79
– marital 79, 104-08, 158, 224-28,
    232, 292
– romantic 228
– of God 64, 186, 195-96, 261
– of neighbor 78, 104, 186, 222,
    225, 261, 275
– disclosure of 114, 275
– types of 104, 225, 229, 271
– and faith 273
– and time 159
Lutheran theology 194n, 259

man 42, *et passim*
– as image of God 42, 45, 184-86
    196

wijsbegeerte der wetsidee 2n, 74
wisdom 7-12, 28, 33, 41, 201, 242,
    251, 254, 255, 305n, 307-10
world-order 54, 91, 286n; *see also*
    creation order

worldview 3, 4, 12, 122, 123, 165,
    201-02, 262
– closed 184, 186
– and mythology 26
– and philosophy 32-33, 121,
    251-52, 263n, 319
worship 221, 233, 234, 236, 251,
    257, 334

CPSIA information can be obtained at www.ICGtesting.com
Printed in the USA
LVOW06s1547170116

471048LV00002B/610/P